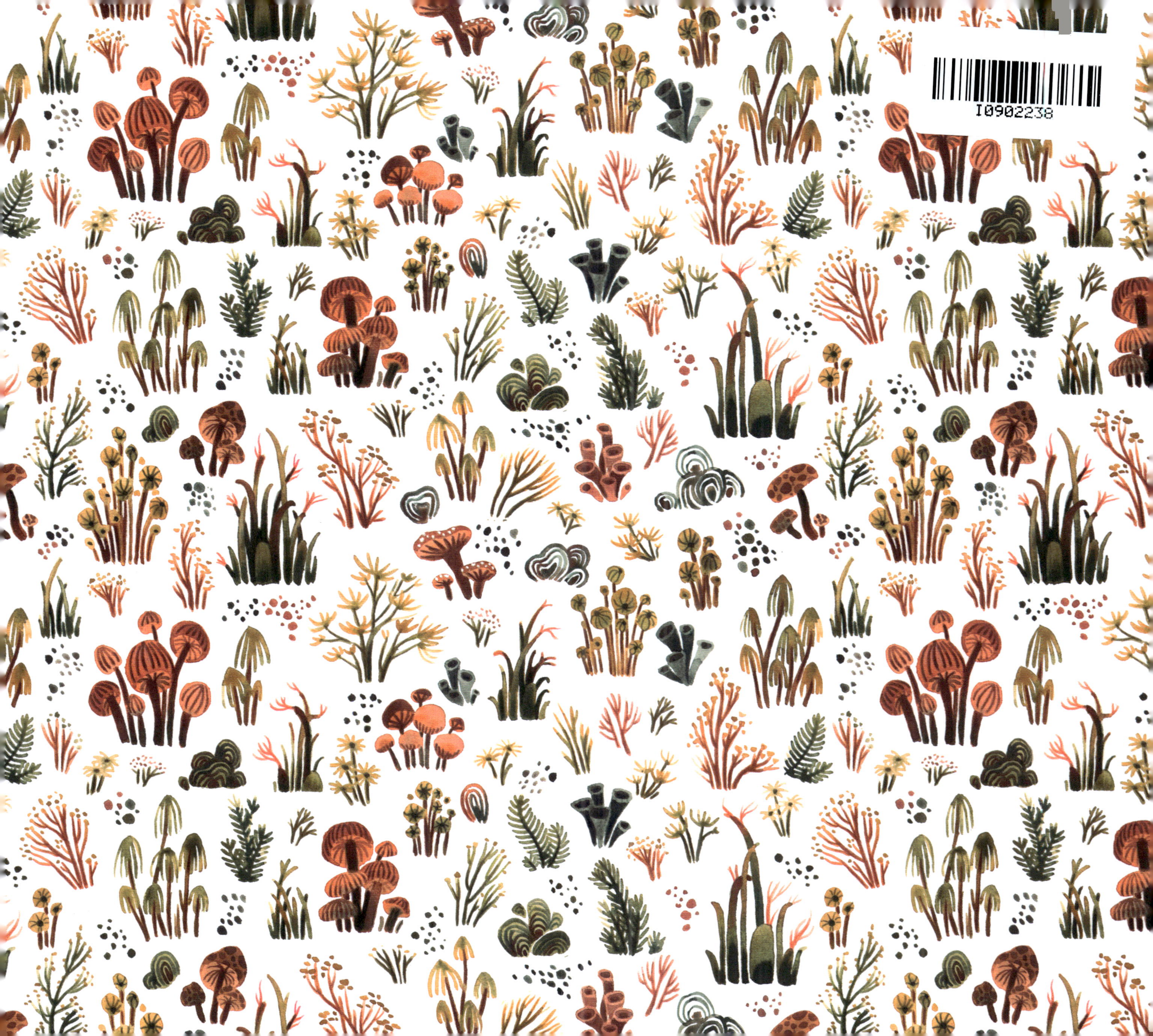

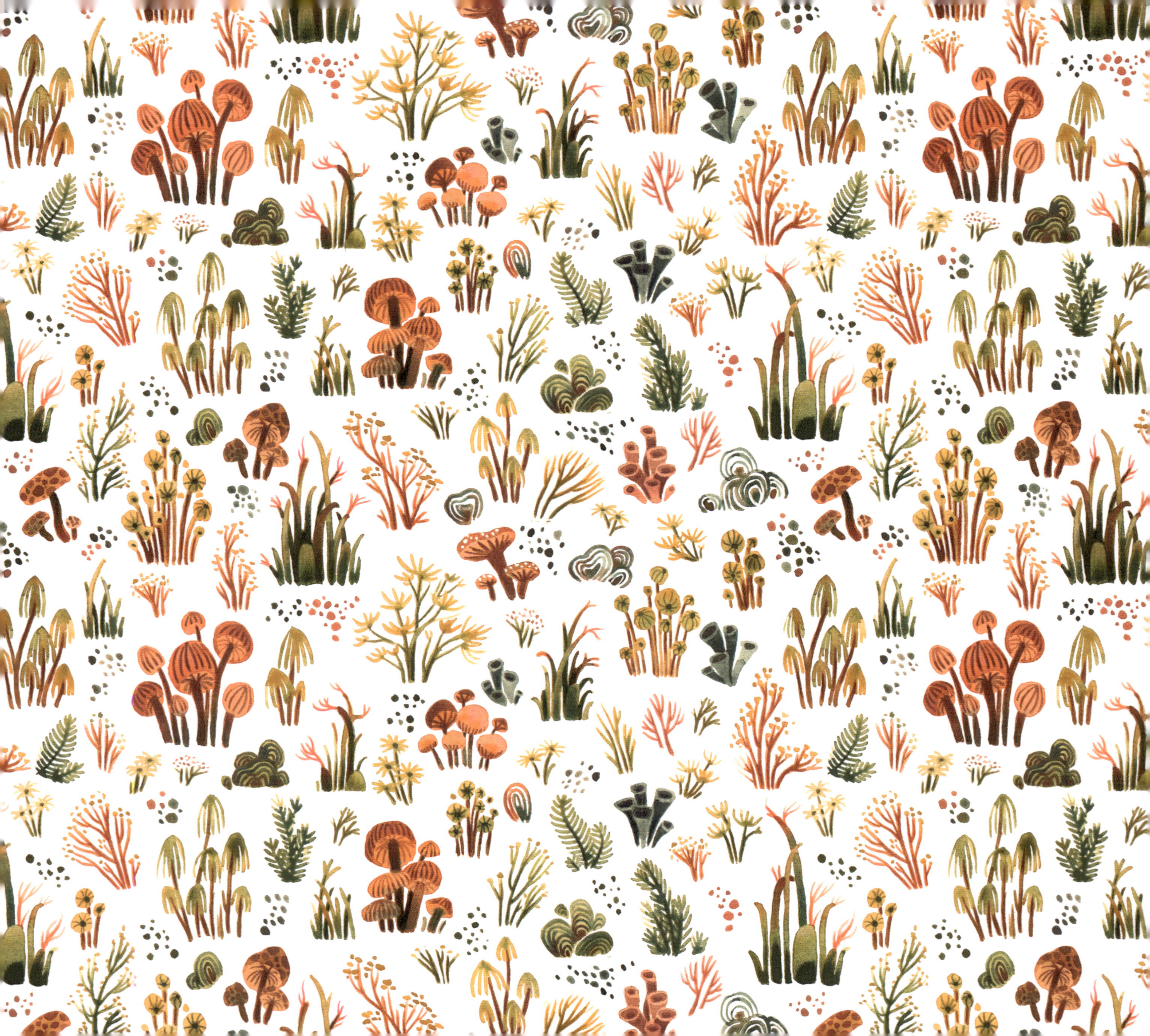

HIDEAWAYS

More Art from Iraville

3dtotalPublishing

3dtotal Publishing

Correspondence: publishing@3dtotal.com | Website: store.3dtotal.com

First published in the United Kingdom, 2023, by 3dtotal Publishing.

Address: 3dtotal.com Ltd, 29 Foregate Street, Worcester WR1 1DS, United Kingdom.

Hard cover ISBN: 978-1-912843-77-0

Printed and bound in China by C&C Offset Printing Co., Ltd

Visit store.3dtotal.com for a complete list of available book titles.

Managing Director: Tom Greenway
Studio Manager: Simon Morse
Lead Designer: Joseph Cartwright
Lead Editor: Samantha Rigby
Editorial Project Manager: Rhiannon Joseph

Contents

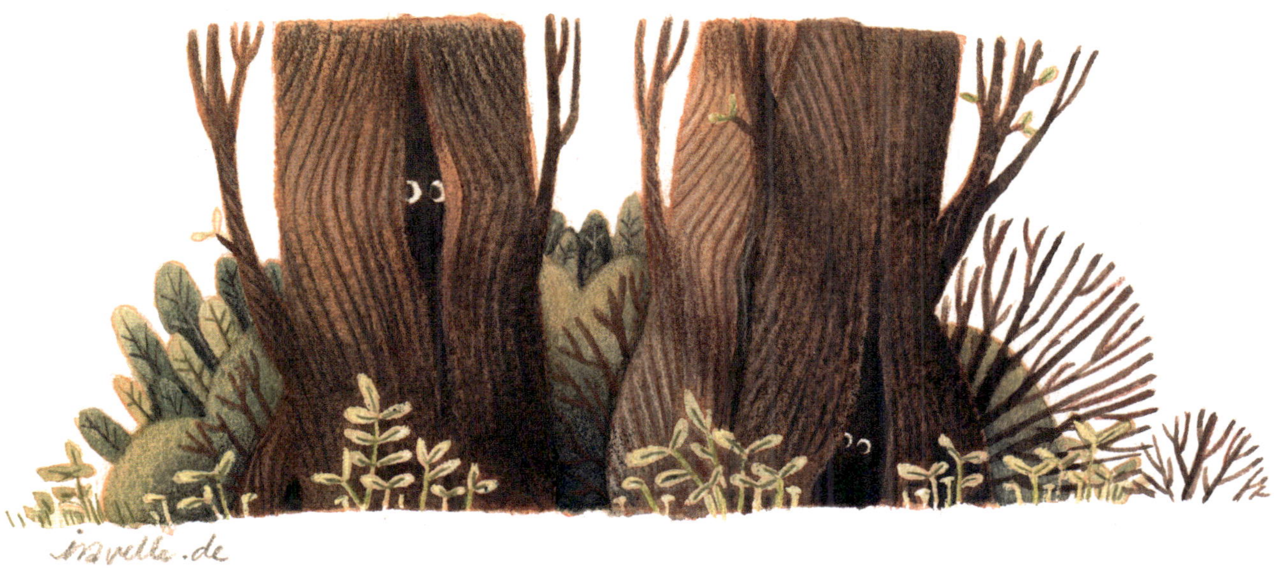

Introduction

This book would not have happened without its predecessor, *Cozy Days: The Art of Iraville*. If you are among those who own a copy, I would like to take this opportunity to express my undying gratitude to you. You helped to make *Cozy Days* a success for me, and as an incorrigible pessimist, it was more wonderful than I could have remotely imagined.

Since I could not have even dreamed that my first book would be successful enough to make a sequel, I had packed it as full as possible with my collected illustrations and insights without compromising my beloved 'white space'.

This second volume gives me the opportunity to show some series that I have been able to complete over the past five years, as well as artwork not shown in the first book. However, the majority of the contents within is new work, and among these pieces are some of my personal favourites and never-before-seen works.

The positive feedback for my first book (and the fact I like it very much myself) strengthened my decision to make this second addition a kind of sequel – a close relative to *Cozy Days*. As before, I have only included freely created works because those are my favourite. I can completely unfold without having to compromise.

You will get a 'behind-the-scenes' look into my painting process and discover helpful insights and interesting anecdotes about individual works. Most importantly, you will find multiple galleries showcasing images that were (almost all) created on paper. They look much better in a book than on a screen, which is why paper is far superior in that respect.

Thank you for your continued interest in my work!

I hope you will have at least as much fun looking at my pictures as I had painting them.

Love, Ira

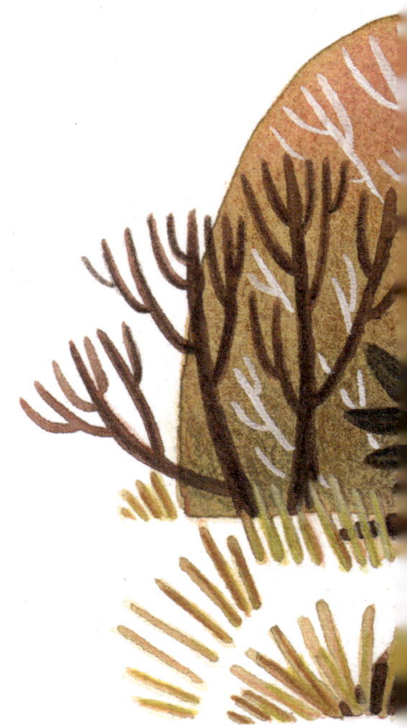

Left:
This poor woodpecker must find a new home because his tree was cut down. That is what I had told my followers on Instagram when I posted that image for the well-known challenge, 'Draw this in your style'. The incoming interpretations from other artists were incredibly diverse and exciting. Some people came up with the beautiful idea of drawing the woodpecker in its new home, which was a cosy tree hole. I was very grateful for the happy ending!

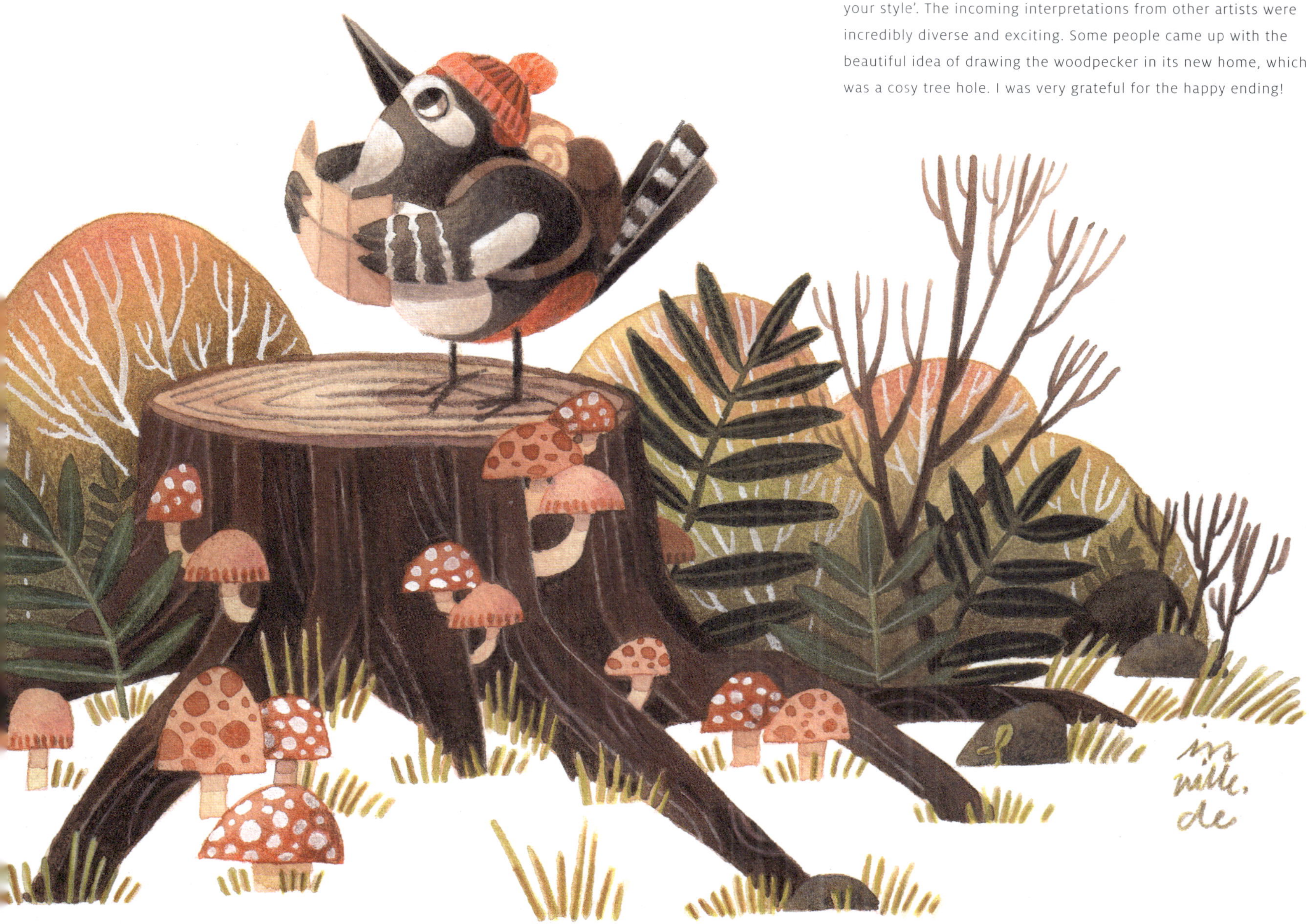

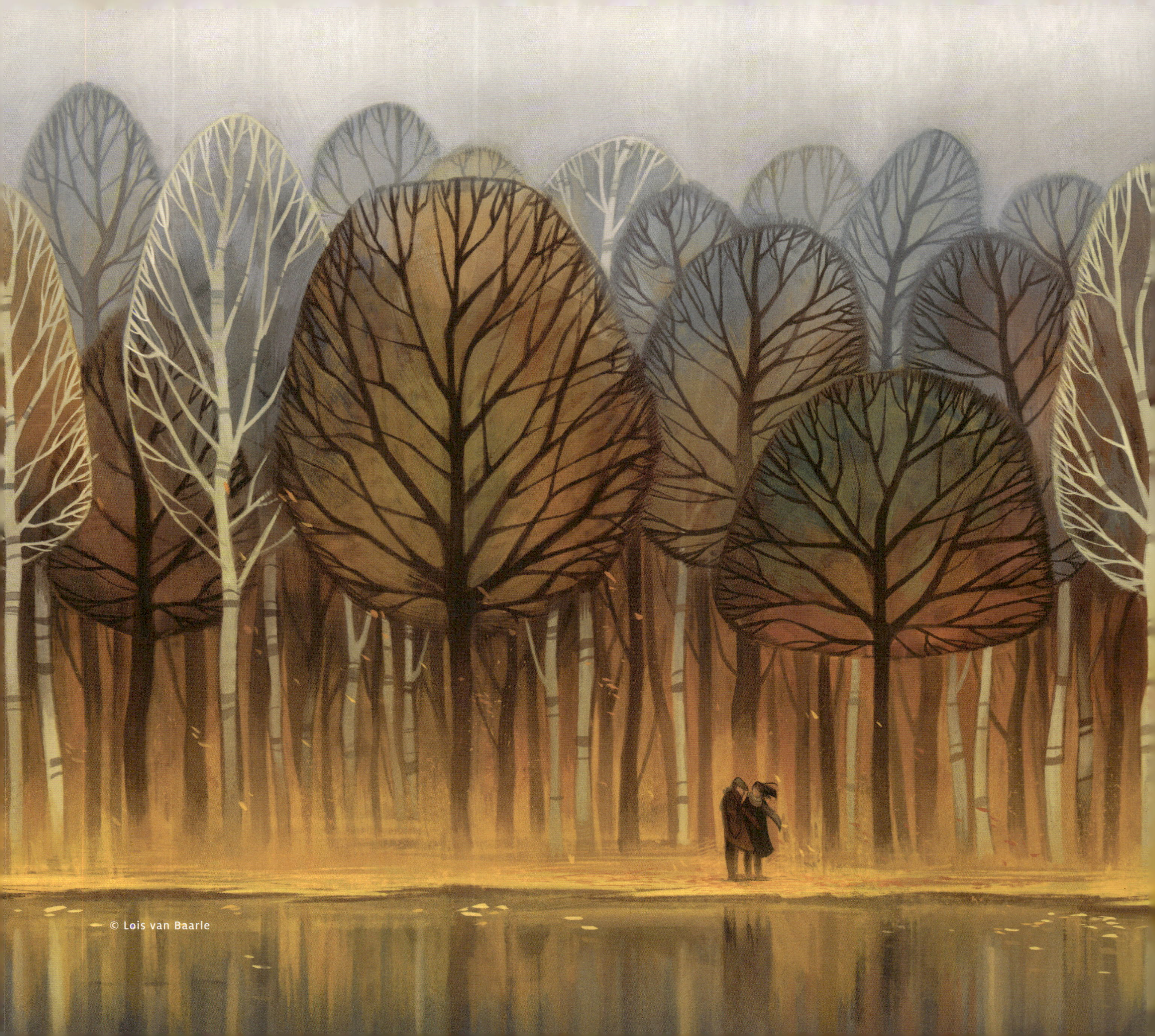
© Lois van Baarle

Foreword

I first discovered Iraville's work the way that many do: through social media. I stumbled upon one of her paintings and instantly found myself scrolling through her feed, consuming each and every post, wanting to see it all. I could spend hours looking at her art, taking in each piece and feeling immersed in the charm of her paintings. Her work is soothing, calming, and endlessly fascinating. It is instantly appealing at first glance, but her work is not just about that one drawing that you like the most. It's about the way they all combine together to form pleasant variations of similar themes, like a beautiful pattern, or a lovely row of trees, each one similar but unique in its own way.

I've always been drawn to autumnal, cosy themes. Autumn has a strong effect on my mood: the cosiness brought on by the crisp air and dark days, the beauty of the orange leaves, and the emotions that a year slowly winding to its end brings. Iraville's art captures these emotions effortlessly. Around the time I discovered her art, I was grappling with a forest-themed painting that just wasn't working out. The mood was too dark and flat. Inspired by Iraville's warm and appealing visual style, I reworked the painting with more focus on simple shapes and a stylized approach to drawing branches and trunks. Suddenly the painting was working! Her work is a big inspiration to me, and is always in the back of my mind as a key example of how to pull off charm, warmth, and appeal when conveying nature.

Iraville's art is instantly likeable at first glance, but the layers and complexity truly hold my attention. The way she builds up detail in her art is so clever. Her use of negative space is just as much a part of her paintings as the details and shapes that fill up the page. Elements of the painting are layered in a way that makes you want to explore what is beyond them. What kind of small, winding streets exist behind those buildings? What kind of dark meandering paths stretch between those trees and shrubs? Her art is a form of world building, where she establishes a visual aesthetic that invites you to explore and engage with the universe she creates, giving you the feeling that it's endless.

Her latest work shows a further expansion of this universe. We not only see her trademark charming landscapes, but also characters, animals, a touch of fantasy, and images that convey emotions and personal struggles. We learn more about the places, people, and creatures that exist in Iraville's artistic world. Next to that, these pages offer a deeper look into her process and ideas behind her work. Readers of this book will love the opportunity to discover the deeper layers, hidden paths, and twisting roads through the world she has created with her art. Flipping through these pages, you will undoubtedly feel what I felt when I first discovered her work: a comforting and soothing escape from real life that only becomes more beautiful the longer you look at it.

– Lois van Baarle, *Loish*

Hideaways

I HAVE LOVED HIDEAWAYS EVER SINCE I WAS A LITTLE GIRL.

Back then, I was quite talented in building retreats. One of my best constructions was located in the garden among three birch trees – I would stretch blankets over their branches and use colourful sleeping bags as walls. Another one of my favourites was located inside our family home, where I would fashion hiding places from chairs, skillfully wedging them against each other until they resembled an impregnable fortress. My red children's high seat would be placed in the middle so that I could spot any potential attacker, as far as the eye could see.

However, among my many innovative designs, the best of all was located in my bedroom. Under the sloping roof, behind a door too small for hobbits, there was a hollow space that was the perfect fit for a little curious girl. In the yellow insulation wool, I pinned animal posters that I had cut out of magazines, and under the friendly eyes of parrots, penguins, and iguanas, I would read my favourite books or draw while listening to kid's cassettes. It was both my secret realm and my sanctuary; I went there when I had arguments with my parents, or if I needed time away from my annoying younger brother. To ensure I was not disturbed by anyone, I took the precaution of building my own version of the Berlin Wall in front of the small door, which was made with tried and tested equipment: more chairs and blankets. I was the only person who knew there was a secret passage behind the wall, and to me, it was freedom.

At around eleven years old, when I had outgrown the hollow space, I upgraded my accommodation to a tent in the garden. There, I would spend my nights with a cassette player and supplies that came in the form of sweets and comic books – normally *Asterix*, *Tintin*, and Disney. My favourite stories were of Uncle Scrooge McDuck because there was always a treasure hunt involved. As I turned page after page, following Huey, Dewey, and Louie into secret tunnels under the glow of a flashlight, I imagined that a barking dog was actually a howling wolf, or the owlet chirping above me was a fully grown bird of prey. Nothing could harm me in my tent, my secret adventurer's lair.

The only real thing I feared was accidentally damaging the Enid Blyton books I borrowed from my (not at all annoying) older brother. The characters Daisy, Larry, Fatty, Pip, Bets, and Buster the Scottie dog became my role models. They also lived in a small, tranquil village like me, and so I thought, 'If there are so many cases to be solved there, there have to be one or two adventures near me!' My friends and I established our own little detective gang and soon we had all the supplies we needed: detective badges, a homemade periscope, notebooks, and even a fingerprint kit. Though our notebooks quickly filled with all the licence-plate numbers in the area, we solved zero cases.

Right:
Me, in one of my impenetrable umbrella fortresses

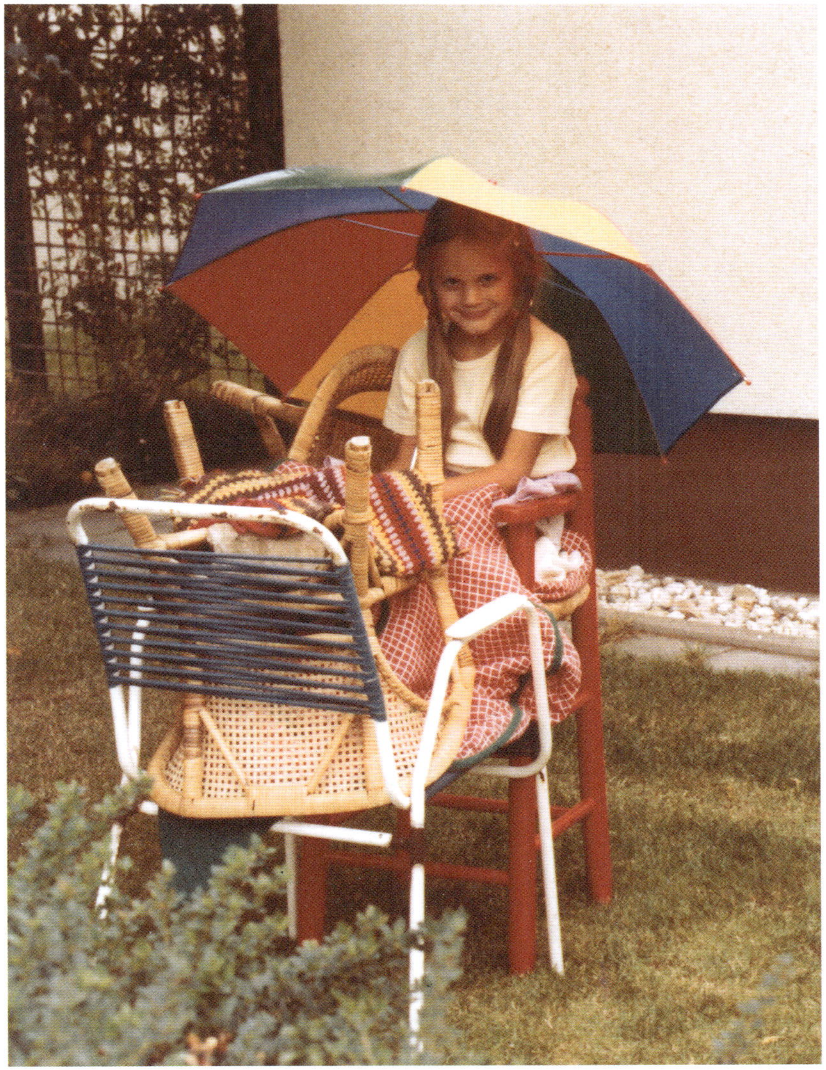

'My home and workspace literally became my hideaway – a place where I could protect myself without altering my life too drastically'

MY NEW HIDEAWAY

Much has changed since those days, and many years have passed. I moved out of my parents' house, studied design, and earned my diploma. After that, I relocated to Munich in the south of Germany; a few years later, I rediscovered my old passion for drawing and painting, which I explained in my first book *Cozy Days*. Now I live for it, and from it too.

Despite all these changes, much has remained the same: my curiosity, imagination, fondness for art, books, and comics, and also my love for little hideaway retreats. My studio is one such place. I prefer to work at night when everything is quiet. When I am busy drawing (while listening to crime audiobooks, most likely), time seems to stand still, and I might as well be sitting in my old hollow-space hideaway like I did as a child.

Of course, I have changed, and positive change is always good. But at my core, I am still the same, and I like to think that most people probably feel that way too. What changes above everything else is the world around us, which is slipping from one crisis to the next. At the beginning of the pandemic in 2020, almost everyone wanted to hide from the virus. Fortunately (and I know I was extremely privileged in this regard), that was easy for me, seeing as my studio is in my apartment. My home and workspace literally became my hideaway – a place where I could protect myself without altering my life too drastically.

IMAGINARY JOURNEYS

While taking safety precautions against the virus, a great insecurity befell me: art block. The inability to create new things felt alien to me, and I wasn't able to finish pieces either. Luckily, I found a remedy quite quickly. I put the watercolours aside and sought out some much needed 'fresh air'.

While others were discovering their love of bread baking, I held creative stagnation at bay by experimenting with new painting techniques. Since we were not able to travel around Europe (which has always been a big source of inspiration for me), I set out on a journey to explore new creative horizons. This detour allowed me to find the way back home to my beloved watercolours. Now, I get to swing back and forth between different techniques, and sometimes I even paint the same motif twice.

I firmly believe that it is good to leave the beaten track now and again. This applies to life as well as art.

My art excursions into previously uncharted terrain can be found in the *Experiments* chapter.

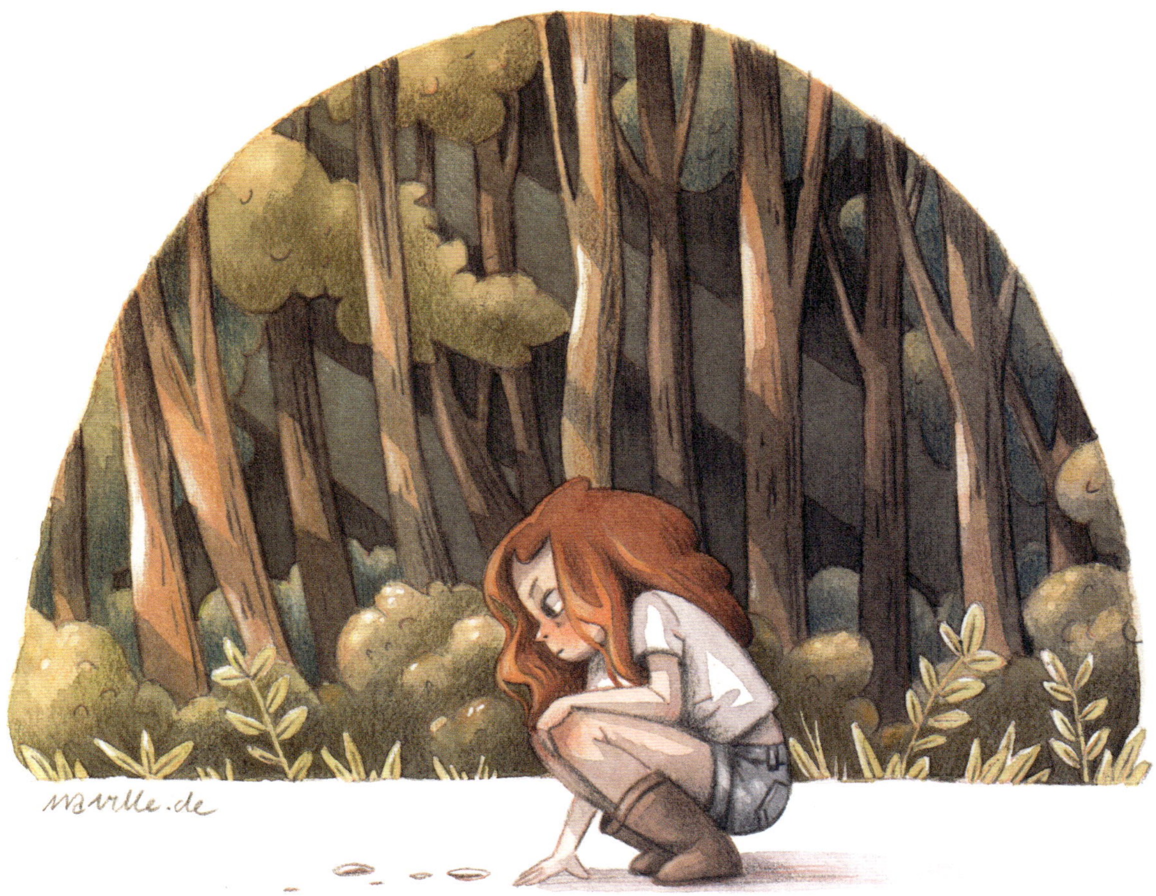

ESCAPE INTO ART

My motifs also reflect my recent developments. While Europe was still in the midst of the aforementioned crisis, someone came up with the idiotic idea of starting a new war. Normal humans like you and me might struggle to understand why and how this could have happened, but it seems to stem from hubris and a disturbed sense of self-esteem. Unfortunately, Germany knows this well from its own history. The world would be a much better place if such people were not allowed into power. People should build and create things, not destroy them.

My way of dealing with the horrors of the world is to paint the beauty in it. My weapons against the idiots are brushes, pens, and paper. However, I am not a caricaturist who can take revenge on them this way.

Instead, I escape by painting places of refuge: villages, or cosy scenes and places, where I would be happy to live. I also paint things I like that are rare in my big city, such as animals, trees, and other various plants. To some, that may seem naive, but for me, it is vitally important because I believe the result is secondary to the journey it takes getting there. It is incredibly relaxing to sit in front of the drawing table and capture beautiful things on paper. That is one of the reasons why my favourite technique is watercolour – it takes longer. I love applying layer after layer, watching how the paint behaves on the paper, and how the image gradually emerges. I often get asked whether I find it frustrating to sit on a subject for so long, and I always reply with the same answer: 'I do not paint to finish quickly. I paint because I enjoy the process itself, every moment of it.'

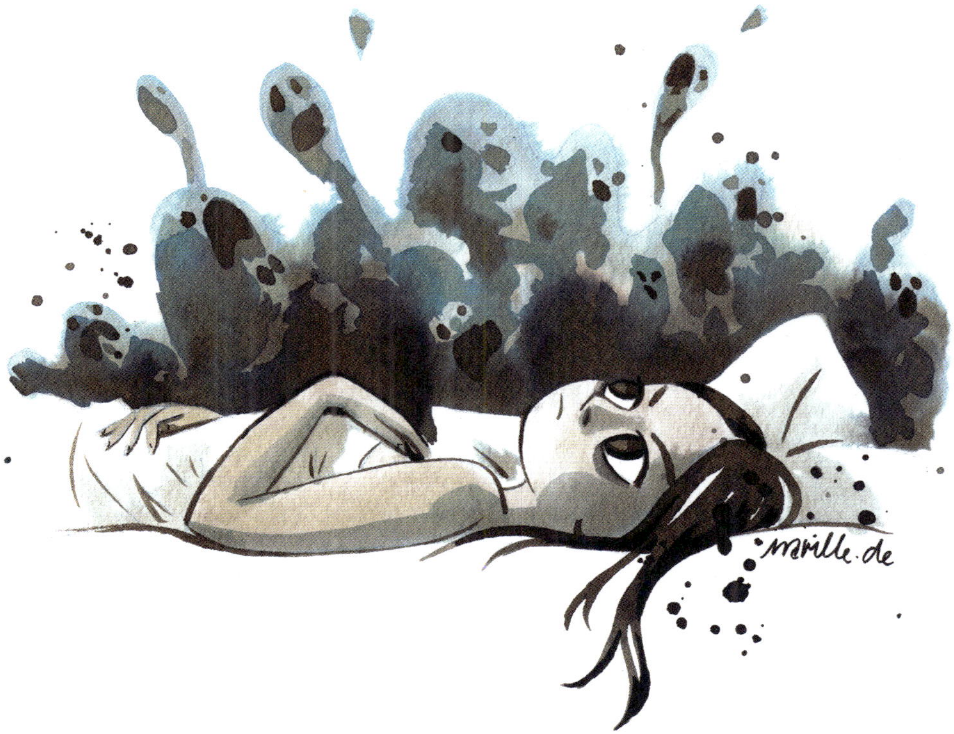

THE PATH IS THE GOAL. I AM CONVINCED OF THAT.

I do not believe in making plans. After all, John Lennon sang, 'Life is what happens to you while you're busy making other plans'.

In fact, even my artist's name was not planned. It spontaneously came to me years ago for a completely different purpose. In university, I had a project where I had to design and program my own portfolio page. My page (which later became my first homepage) displayed a small, illustrated place consisting of a few tiny, crooked houses that stood in front of the menu options. If you clicked on a house, the respective door opened, a beam of light illuminated the darkened street, and the content appeared. I called the place 'Iraville'.

Now here we are, years later, looking at a small world that name helped to create. I hope you will have fun exploring it.

Left:
Traces, watercolour and coloured pencil, 2015

Above:
Insomnia, ink, 2015

GALLERY

Landscapes

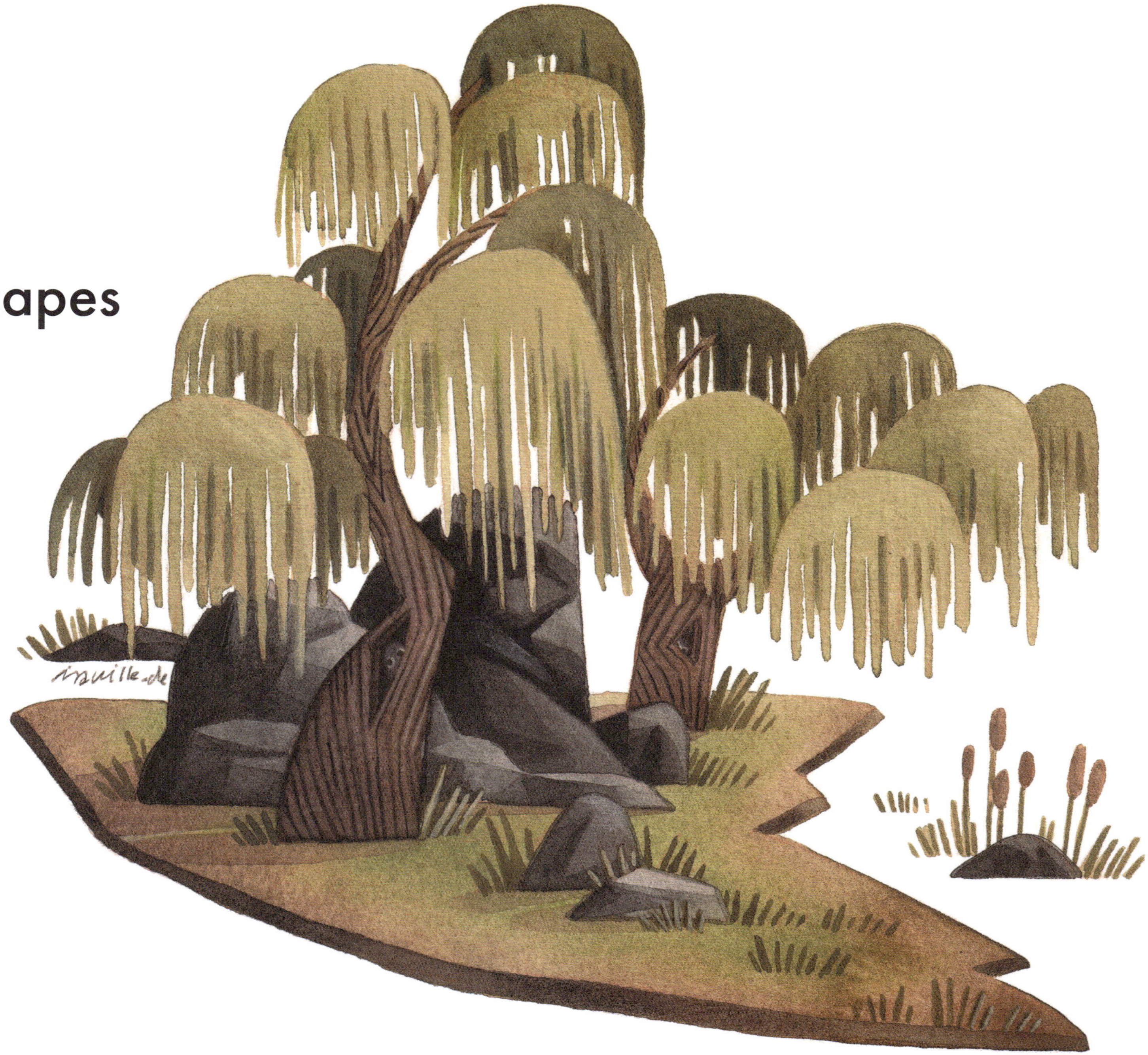

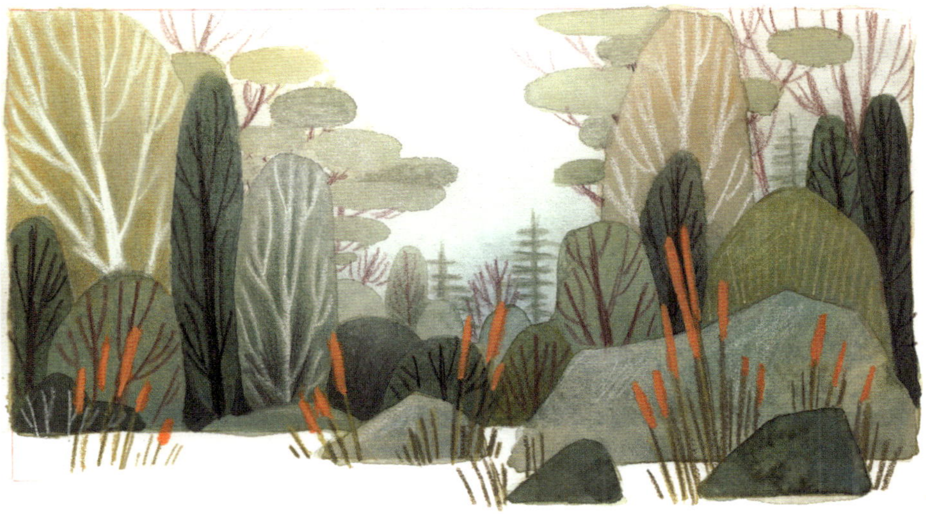

Opposite page:
Willows, watercolour and coloured pencil, 2022

Left:
Foggy Forest Sketch, watercolour, coloured pencil, soft pastel, gouache, 2020

Below:
Foggy Forest, watercolour, coloured pencil, soft pastel, 2020

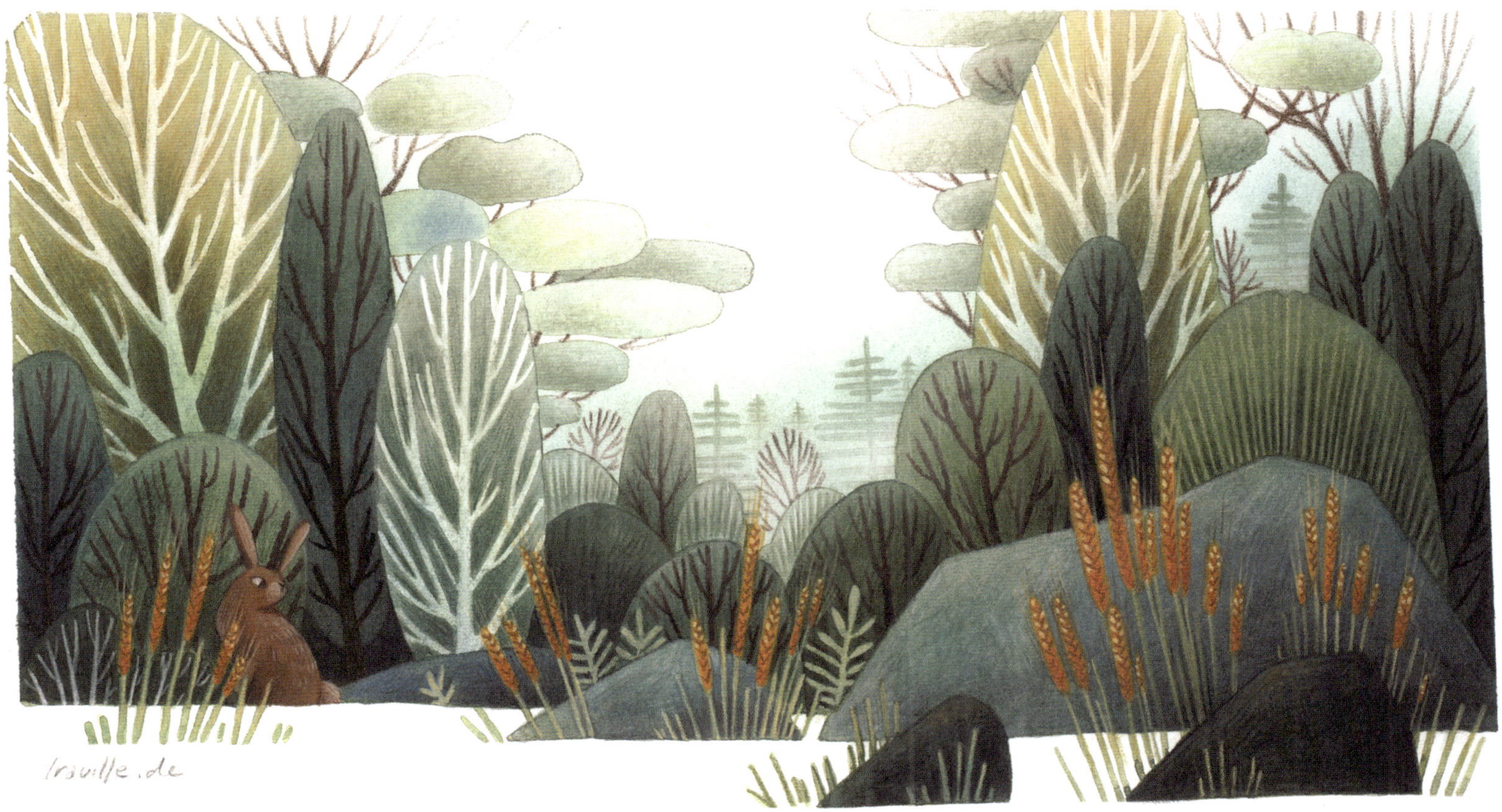

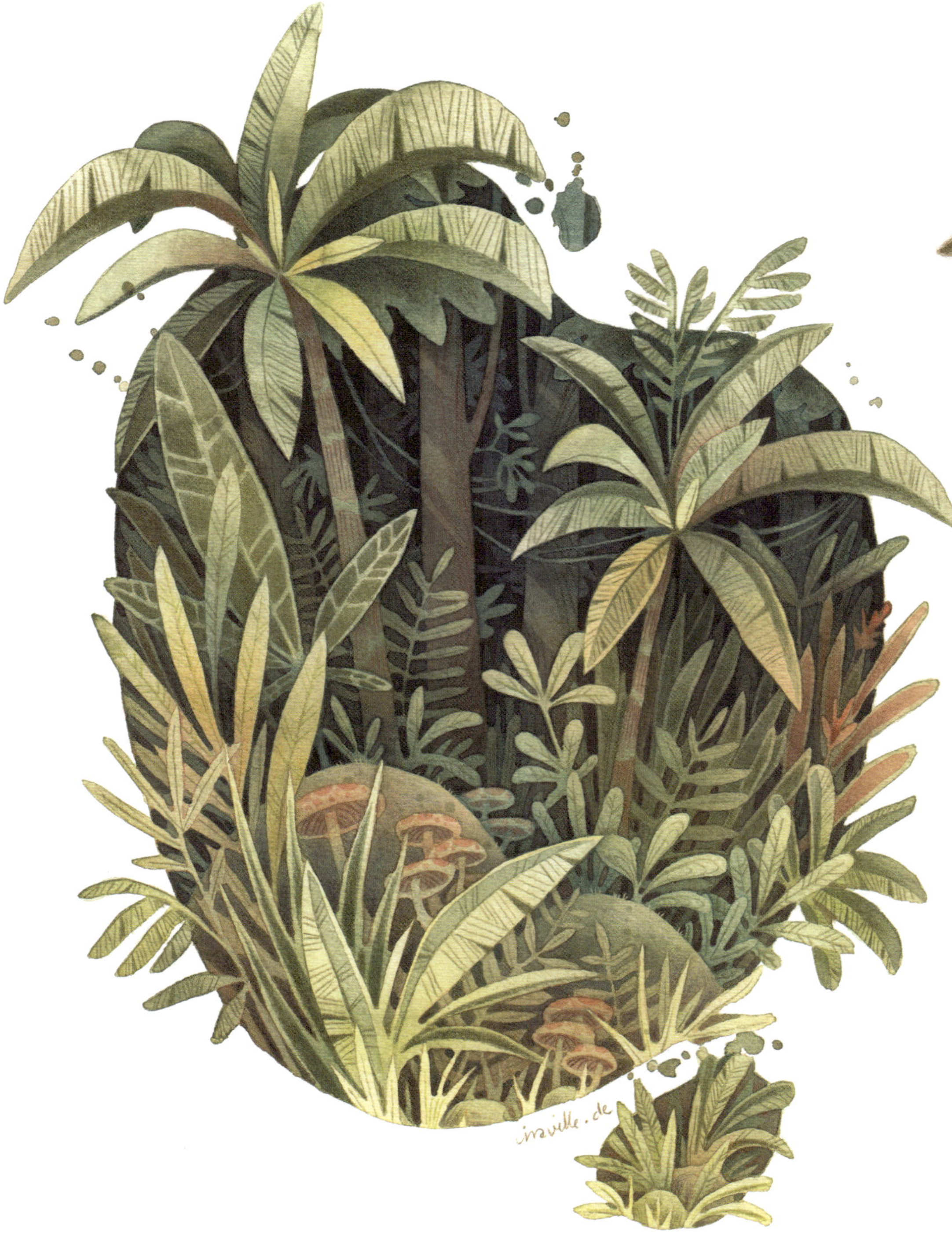

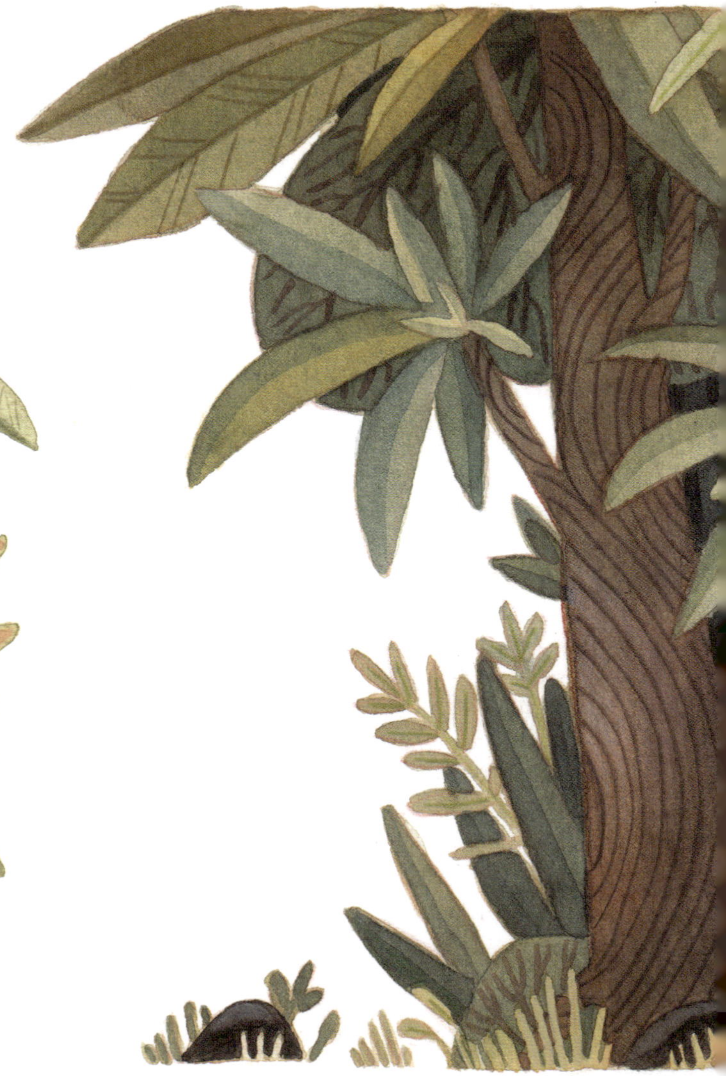

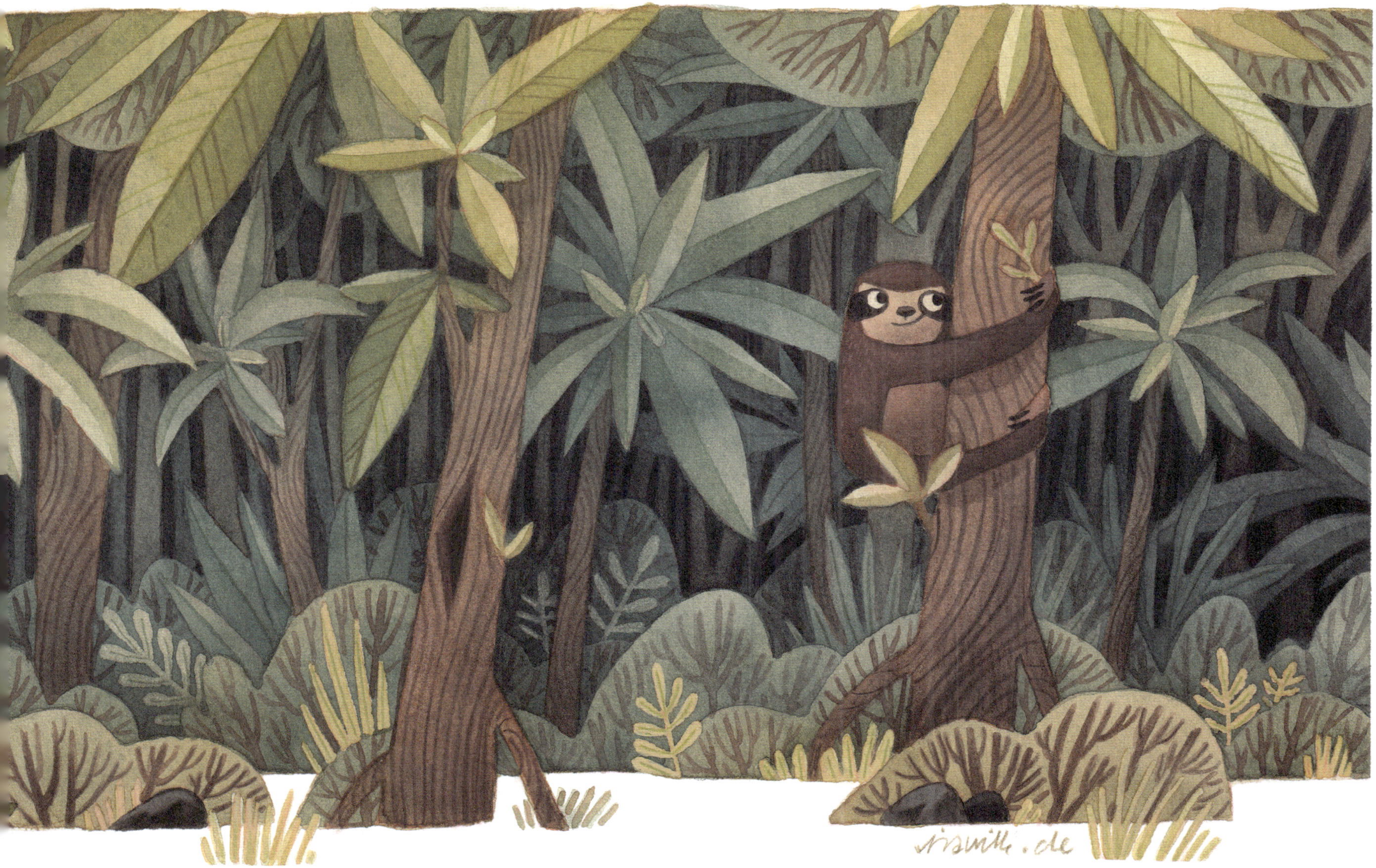

Left:

Earthdraw, watercolour and coloured pencil, 2019

Above:

Sloth, watercolour and coloured pencil, 2022

Right:
Hills in Autumn Sketch, watercolour and coloured pencil, 2016

Below:
Park with Blossom Trees, watercolour and coloured pencil, 2019

Opposite page (above):
Irish Landscape, watercolour, soft pastel, coloured pencil, 2022

Opposite page (below):
Autumn Trees, watercolour and coloured pencil, 2021

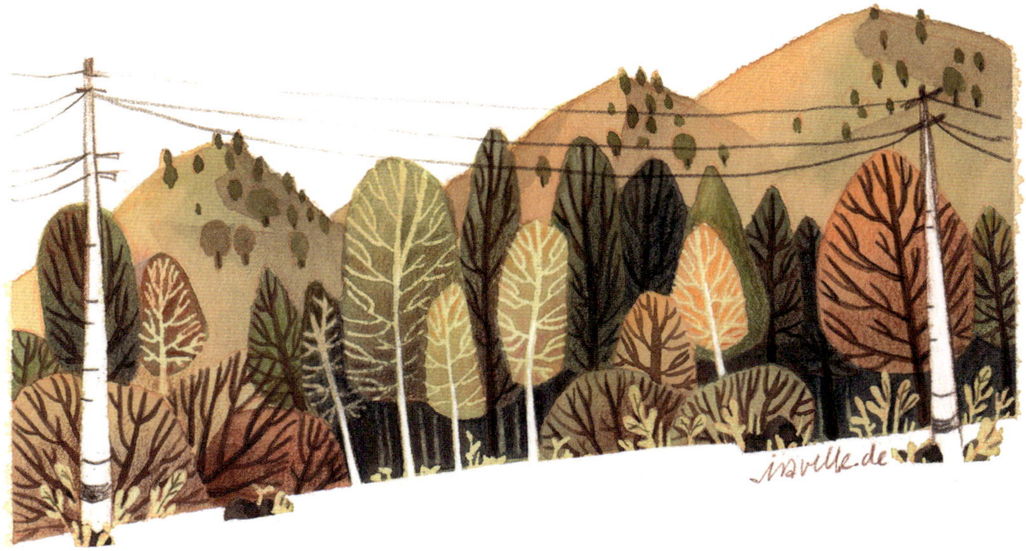

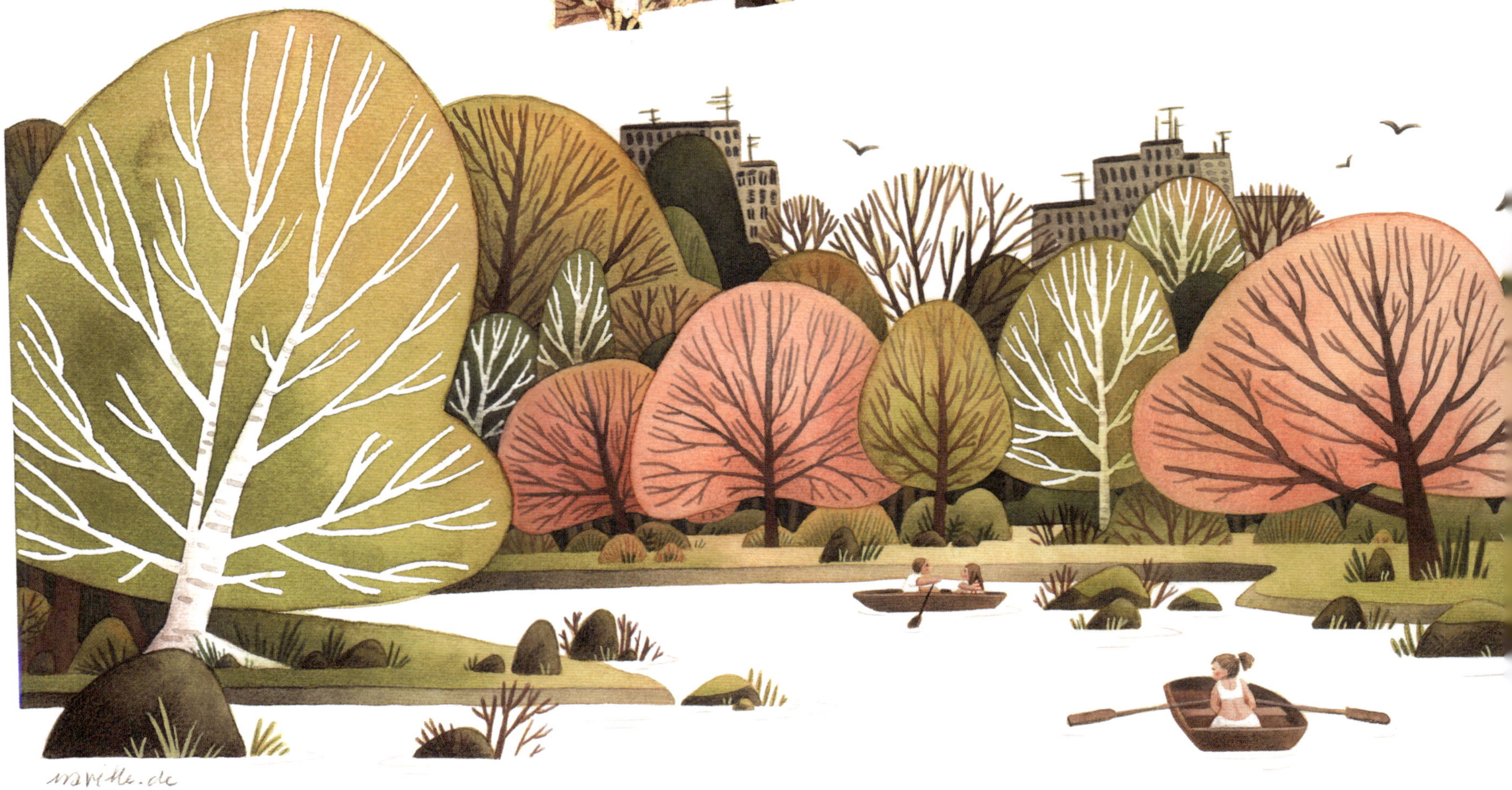

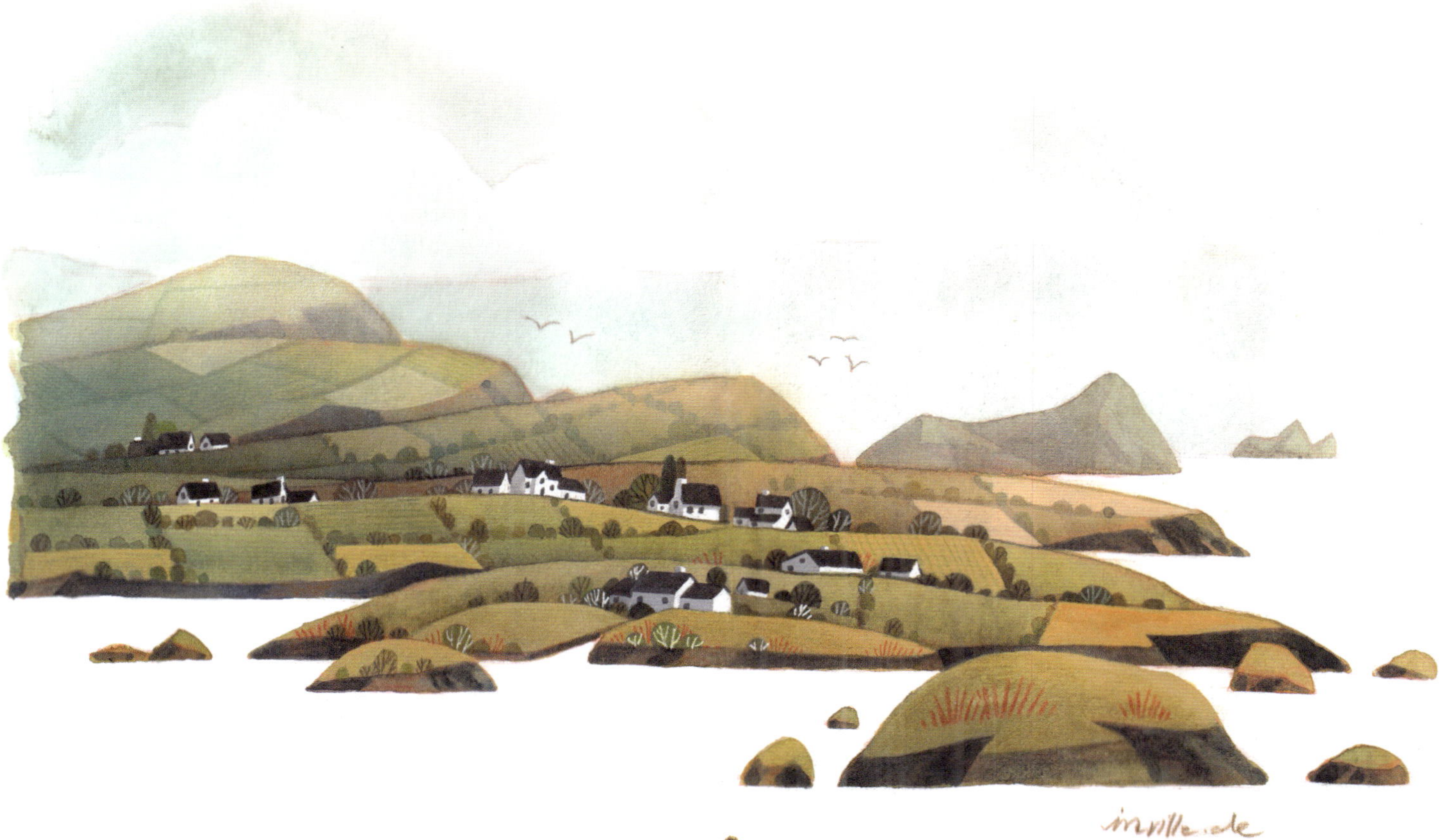

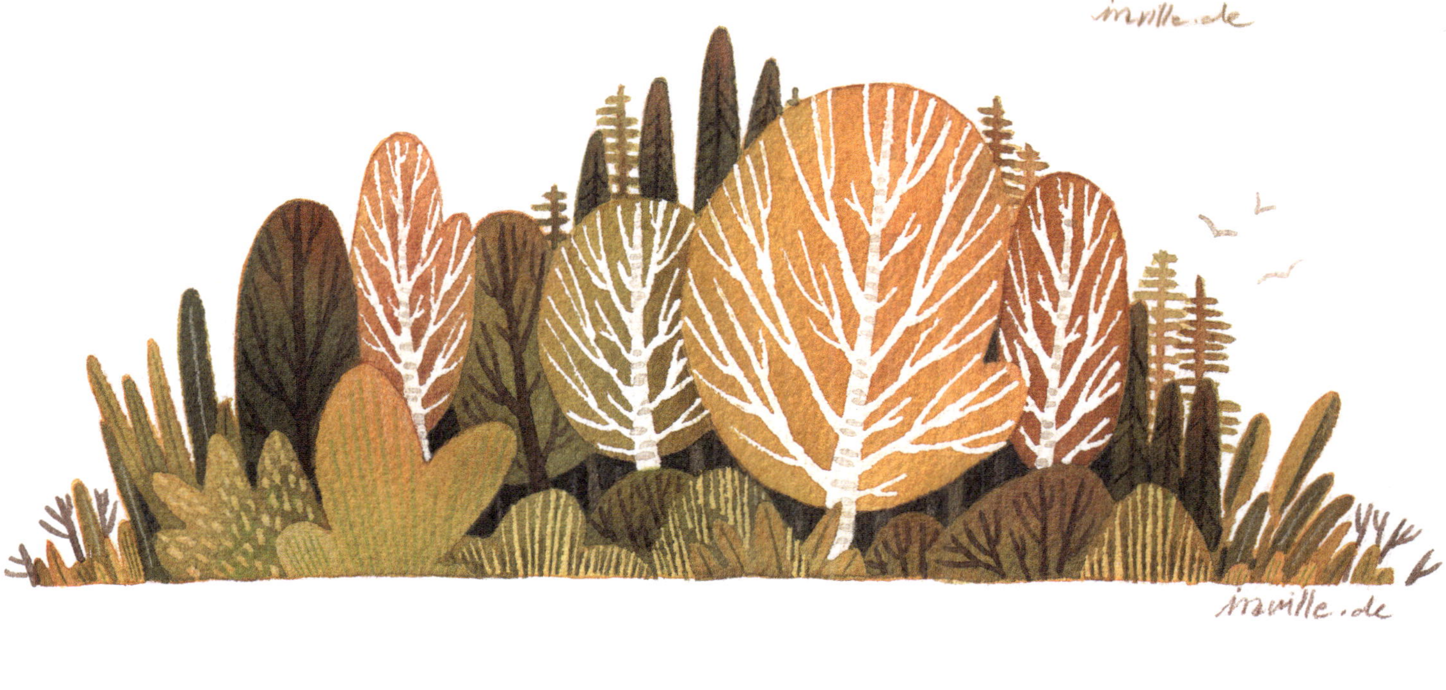

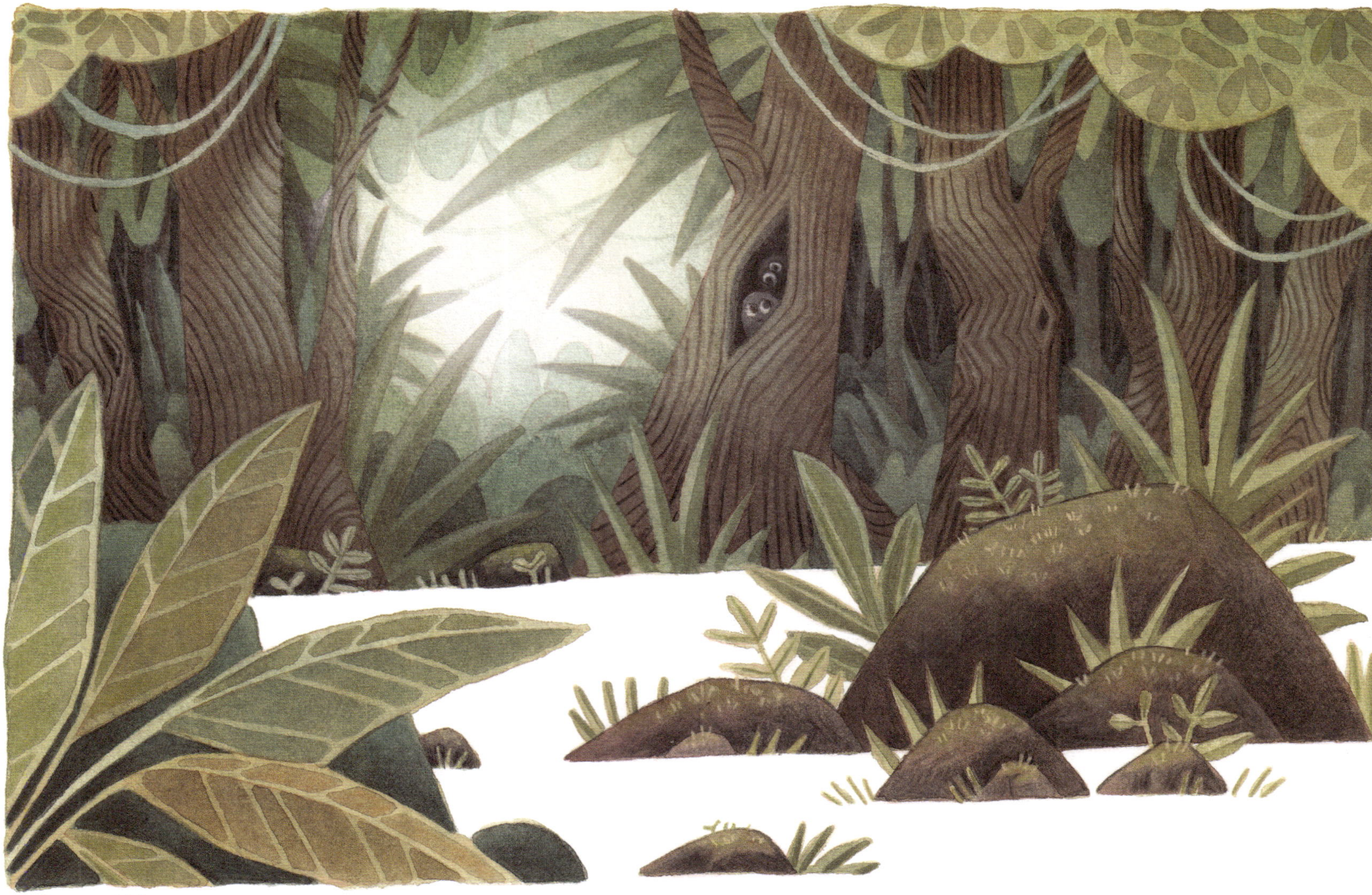

isaville.de

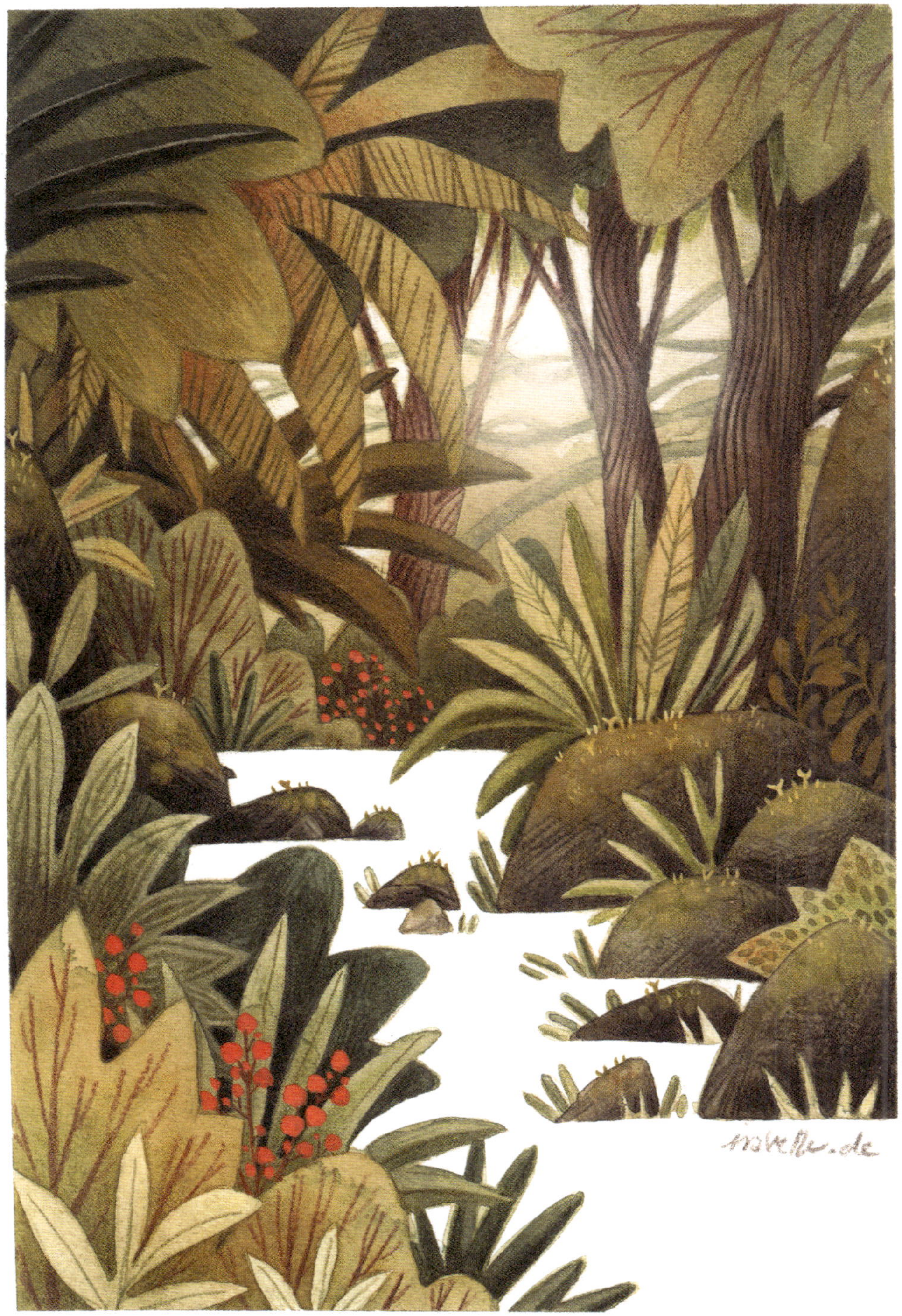

Opposite page:
Jungle 2, watercolour,
coloured pencil, pastel, 2019

Left:
Jungle 1, watercolour, coloured
pencil, gouache, pastel, 2019

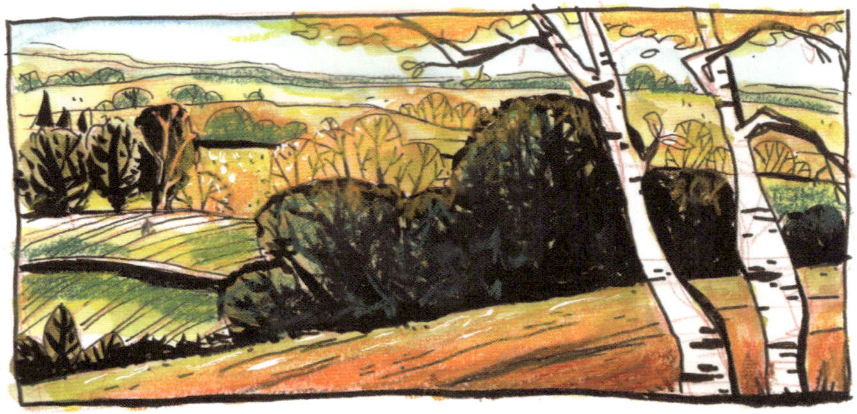

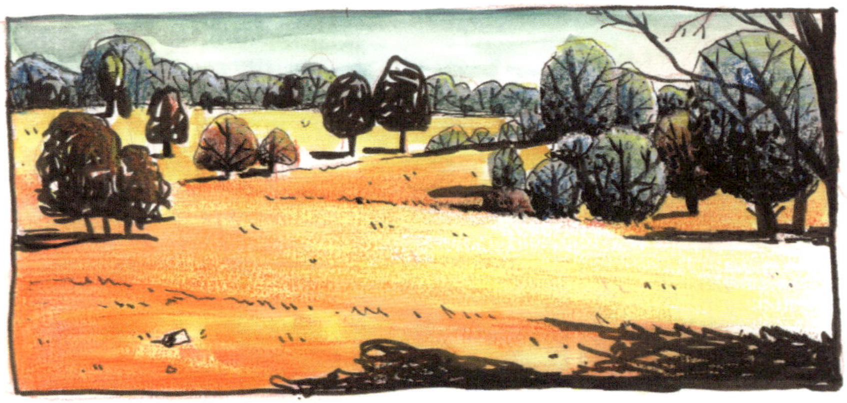

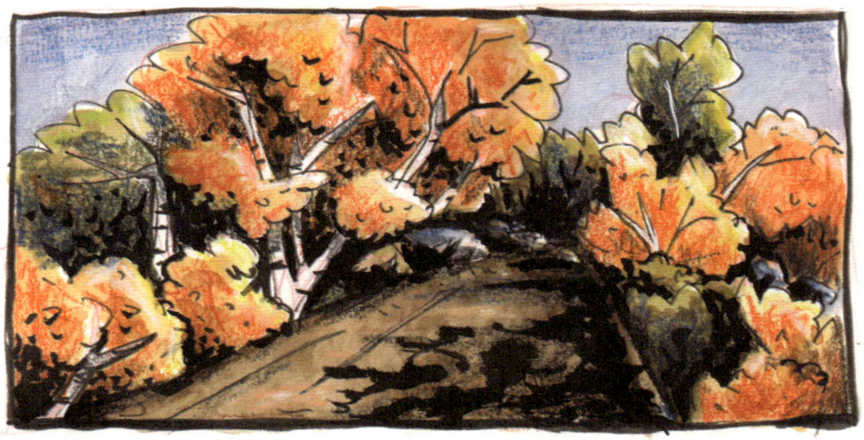

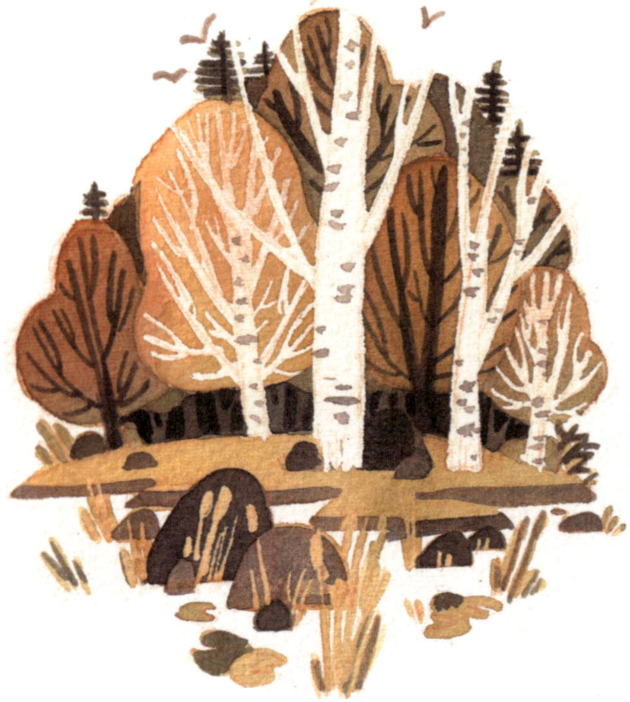

Left × 3:
Landscape Sketches, watercolour, wax pastel, ink, 2014

Above:
Birchtree Island Sketch, watercolour and coloured pencil, 2018

Right:
Birchtree Island, watercolour and coloured pencil, 2018

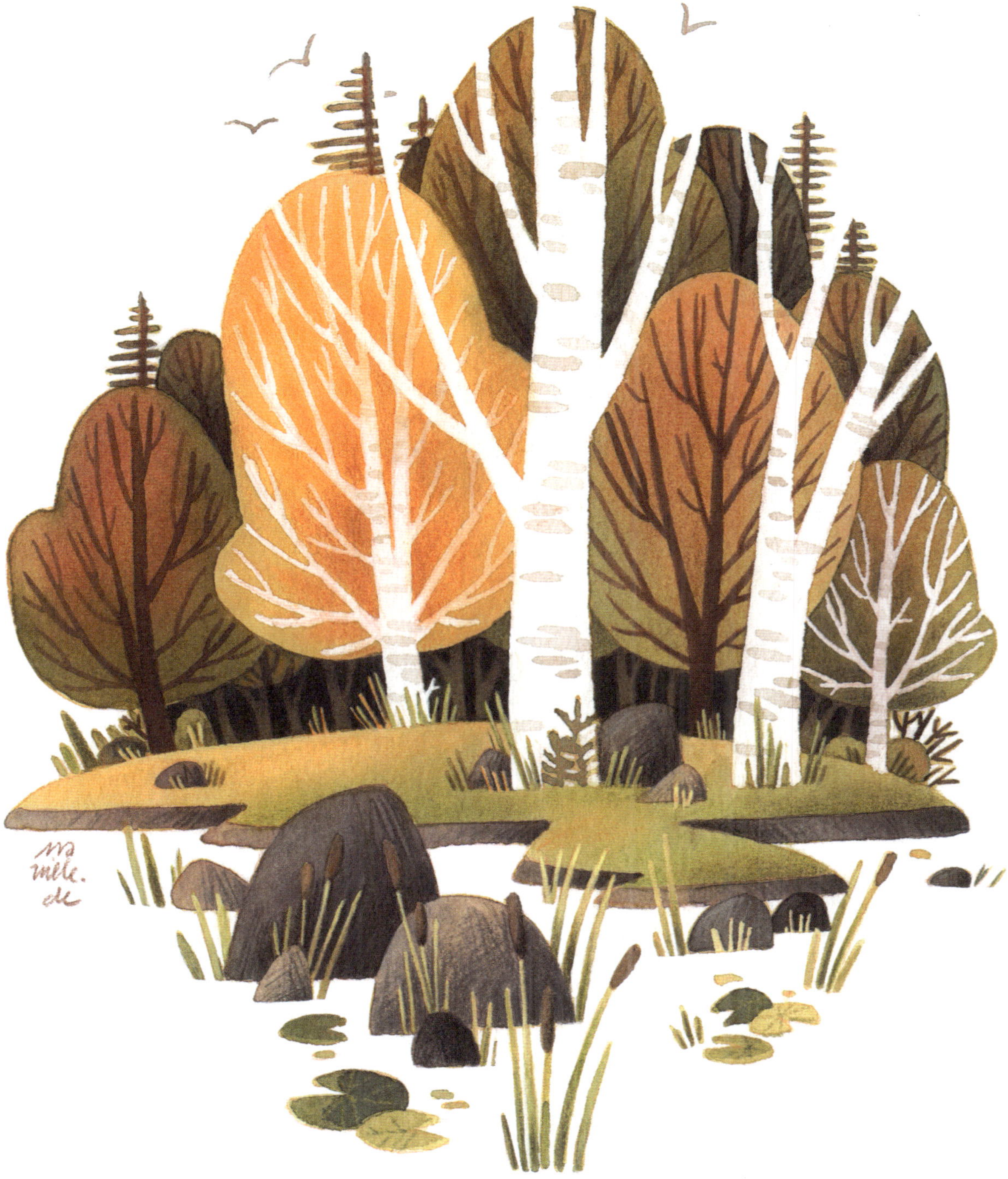

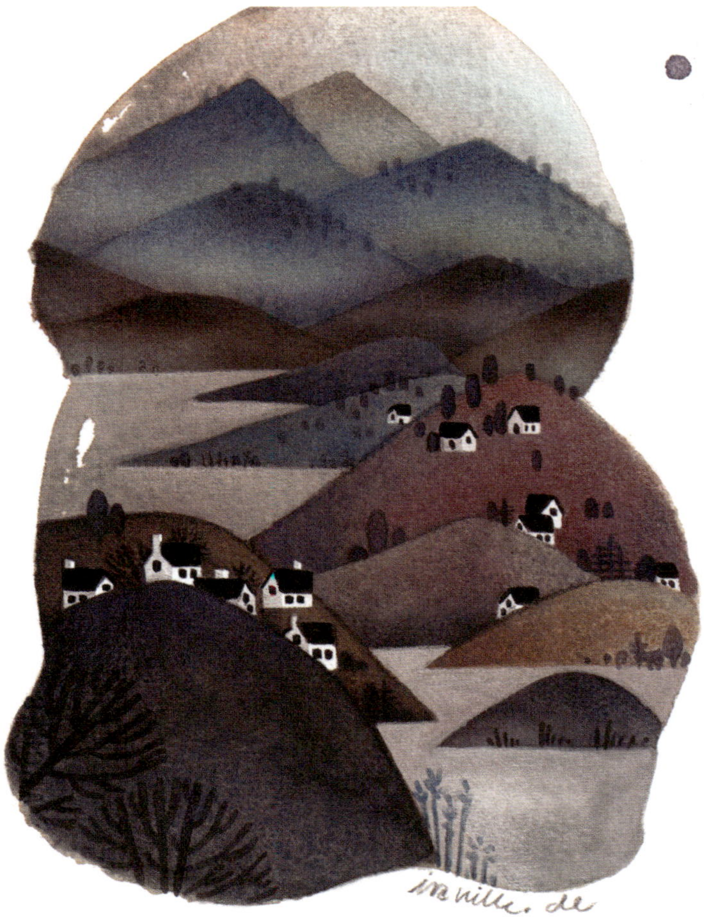

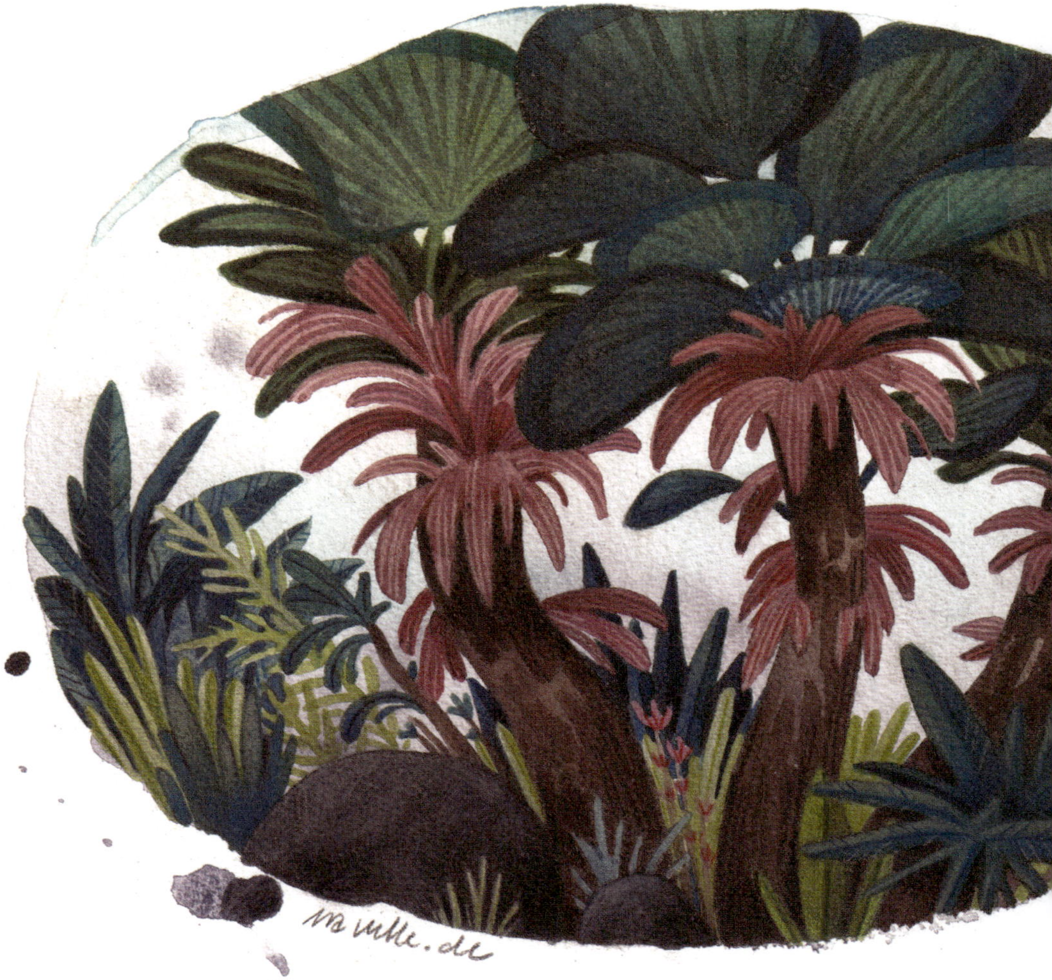

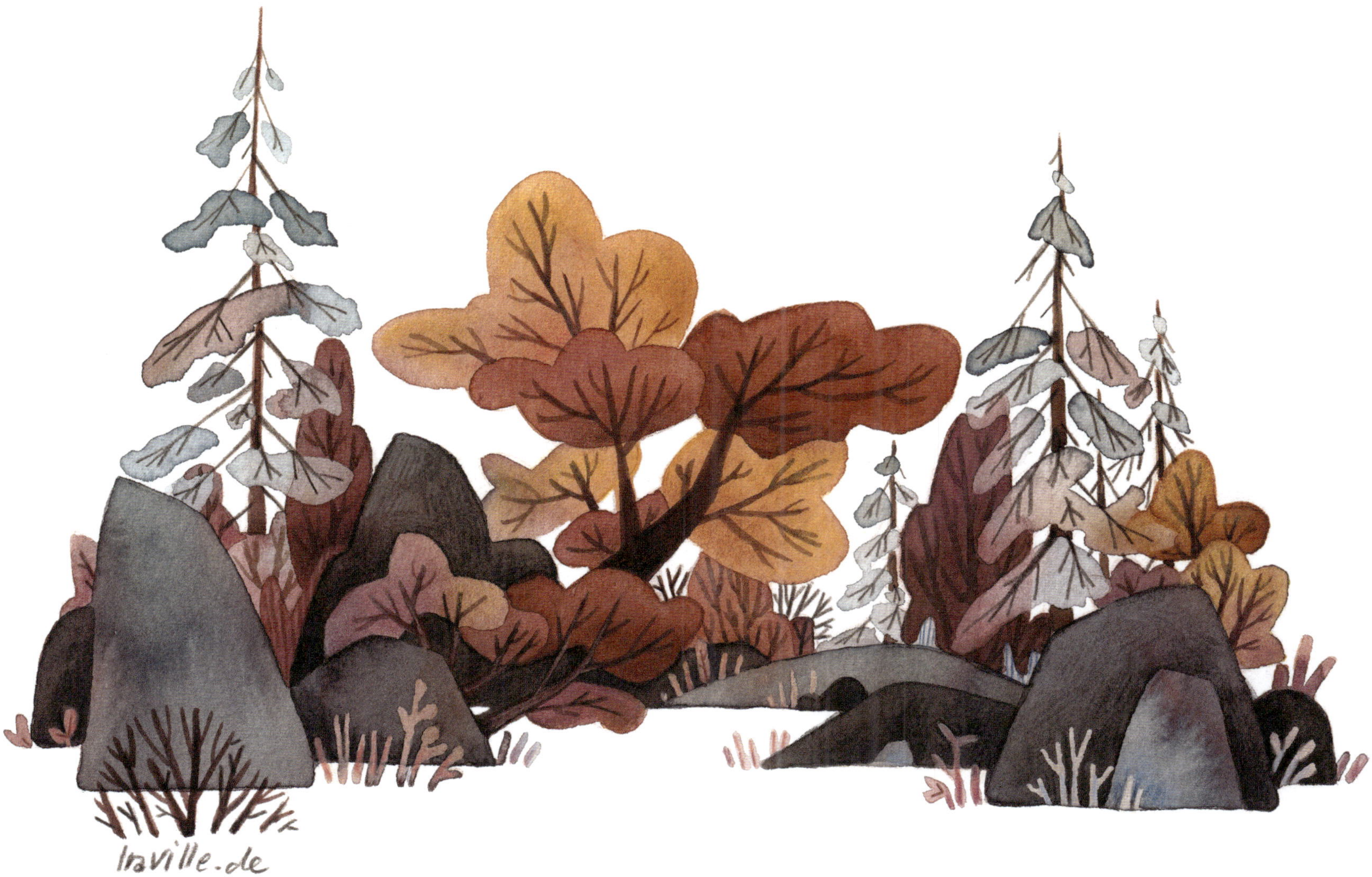

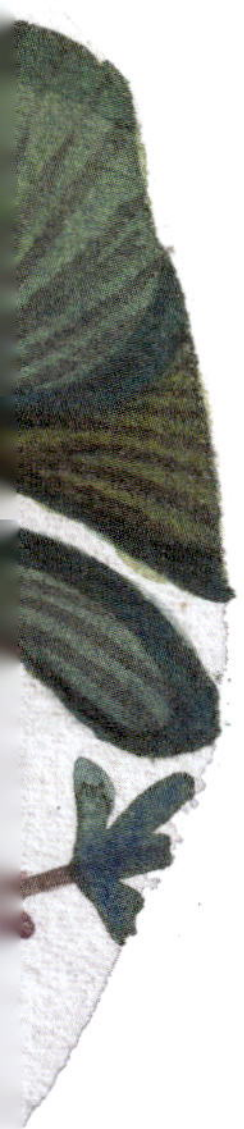

Far Left:
Blue Mountains,
watercolour, pastel,
gouache, 2020

Left:
Imaginary Plants,
watercolour and
coloured pencil, 2021

Above:
Violet Forest,
watercolour and
coloured pencil, 2021

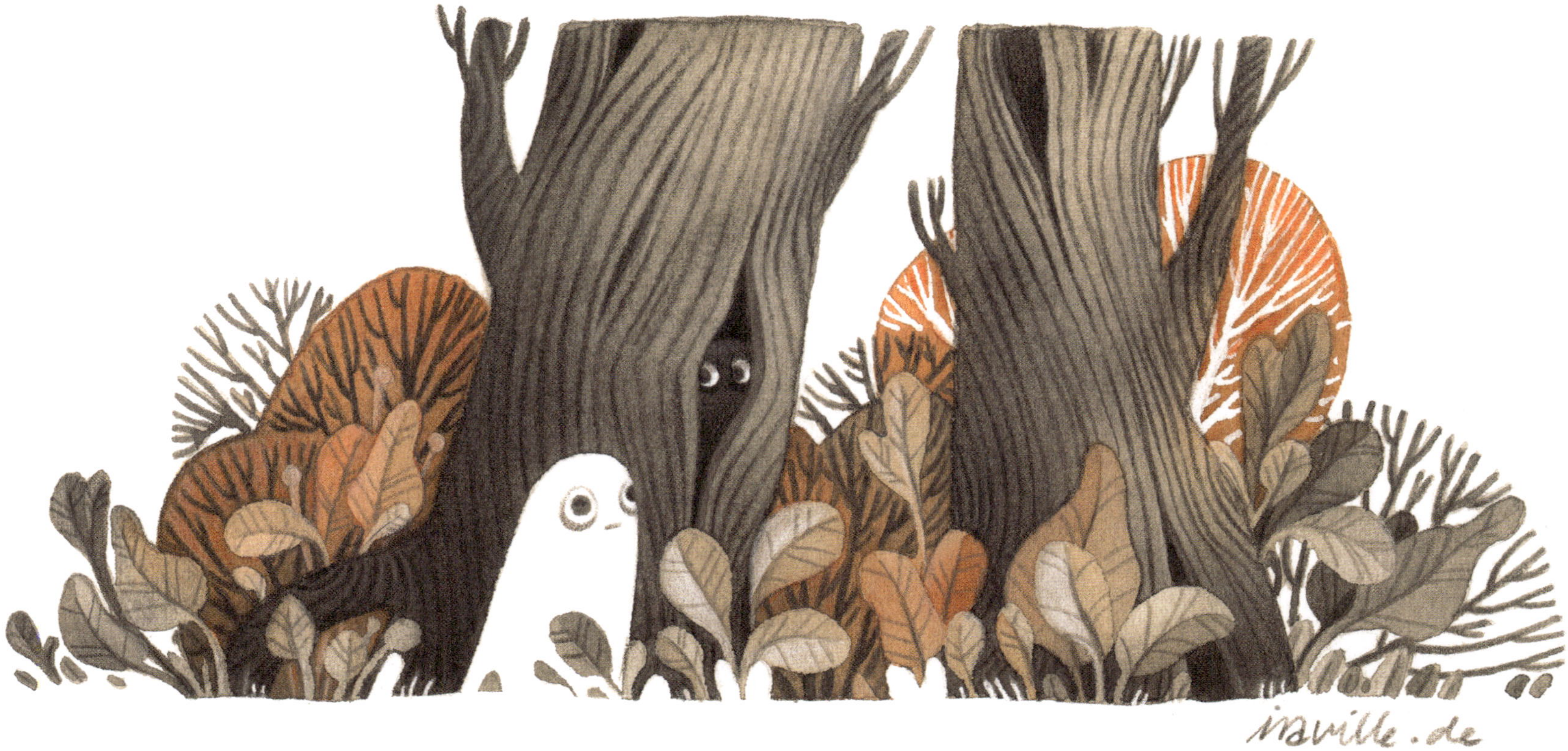
isaville.de

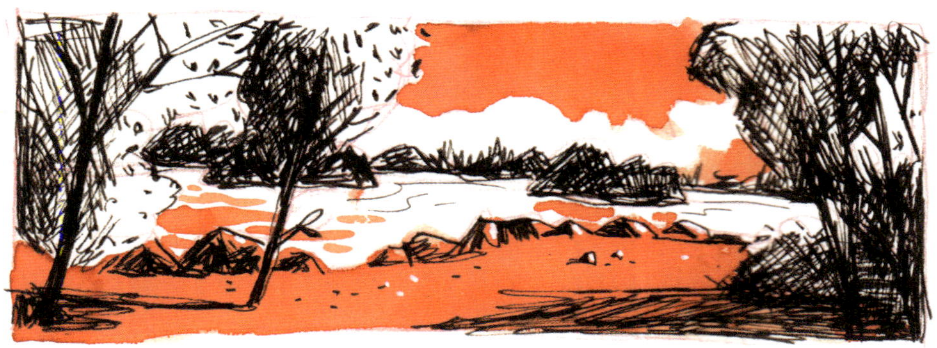

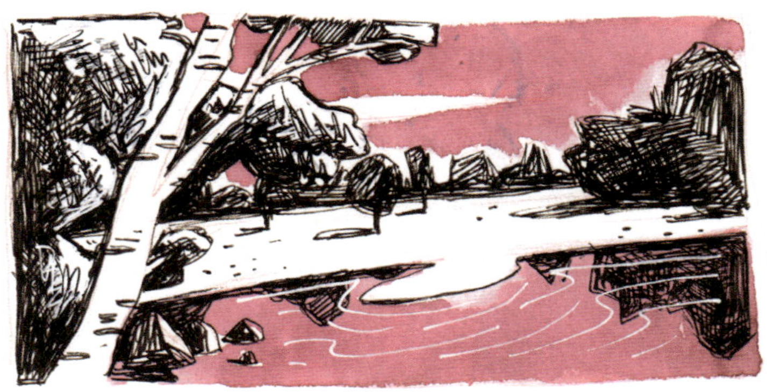

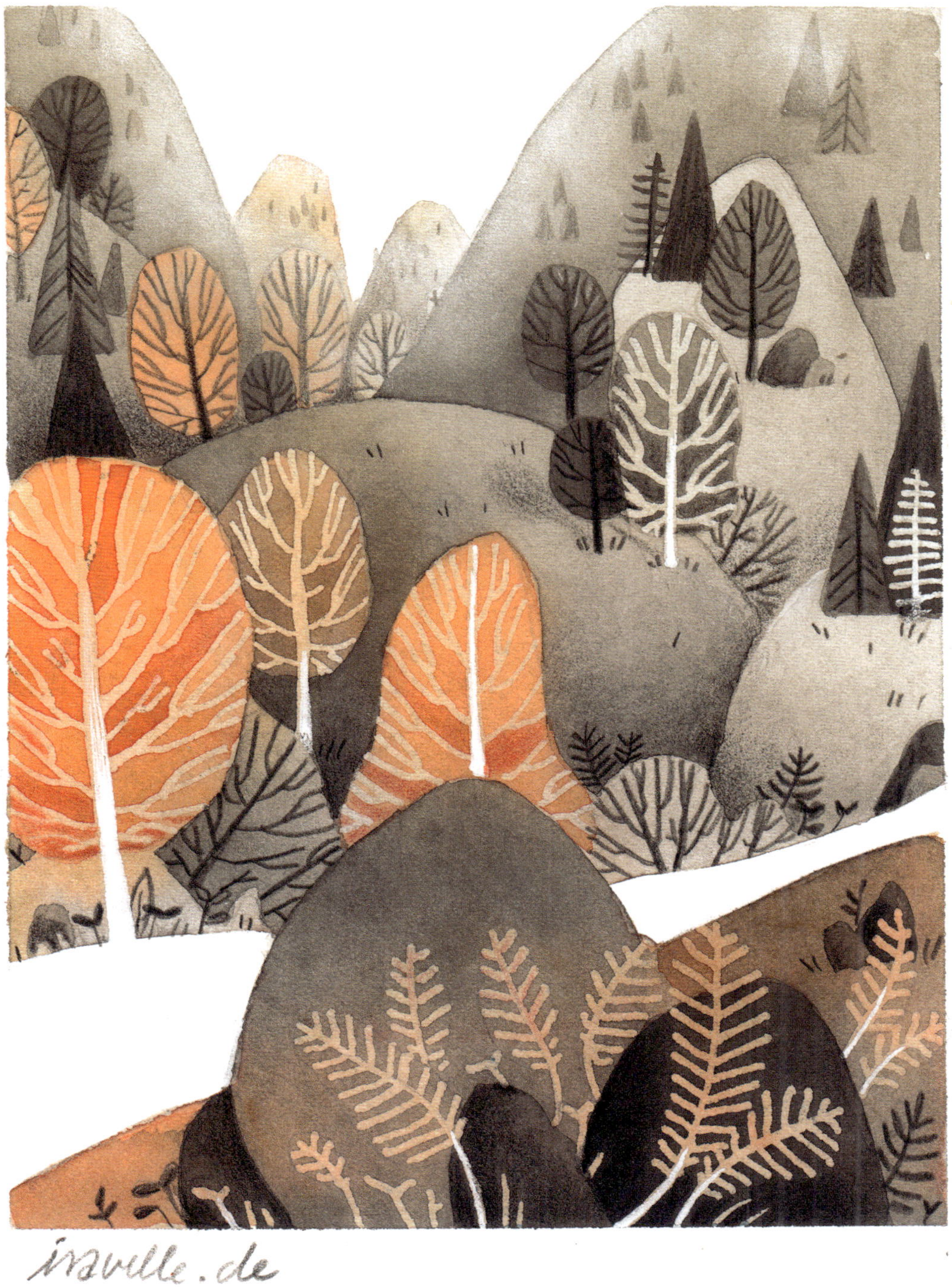

Opposite page (above):
Little Ghost, watercolour and coloured pencil, 2020

Opposite page (below) × 2:
Landscape Ink Sketches, ink, 2014

Left:
Limited Palette Landscape, graphite, watercolour, coloured pencil, 2016

Below:
Greenhouse in Between Autumn Trees, watercolour and coloured pencil, 2019

Opposite page:
Mini Landscapes, watercolour and coloured pencil, 2018

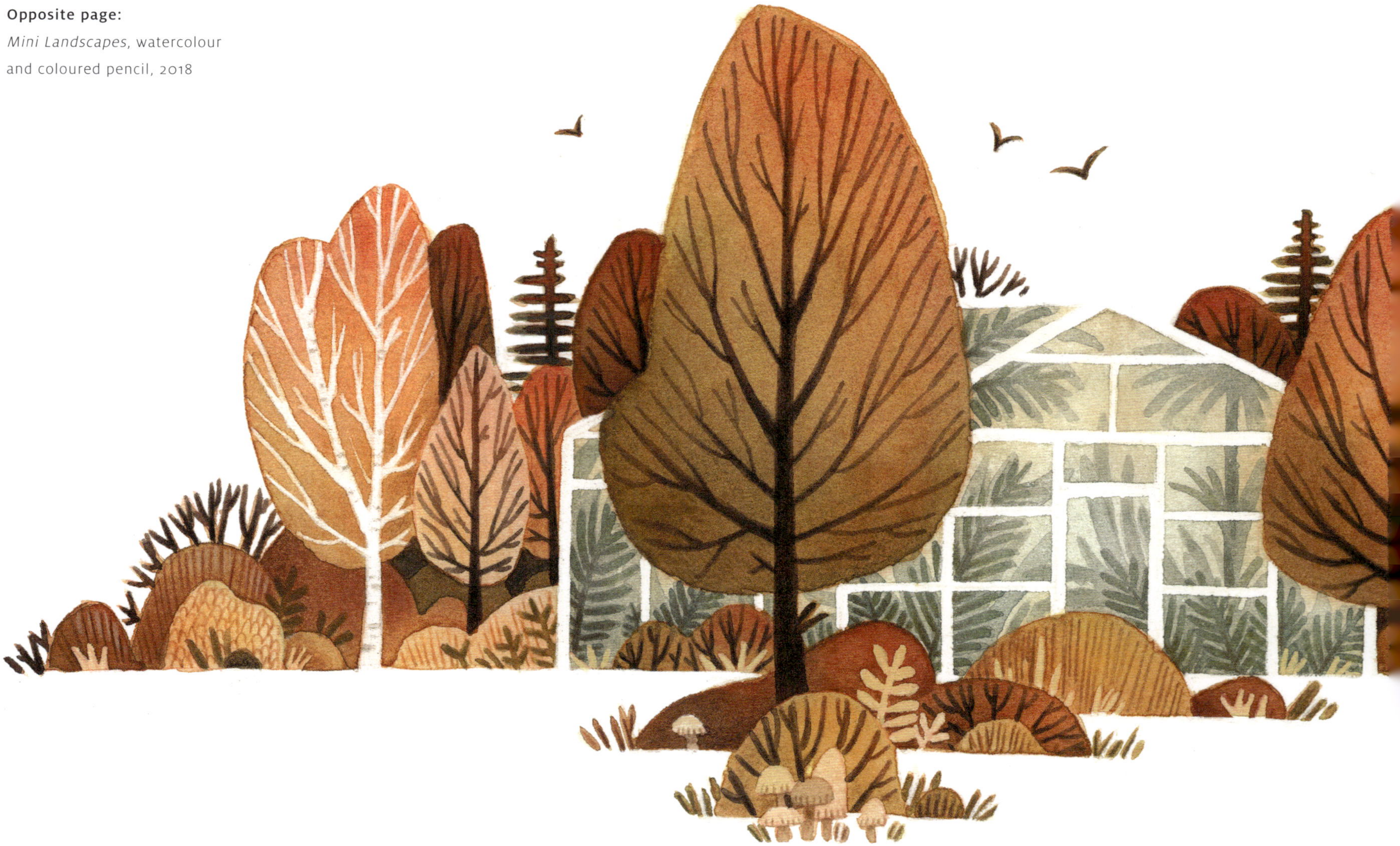

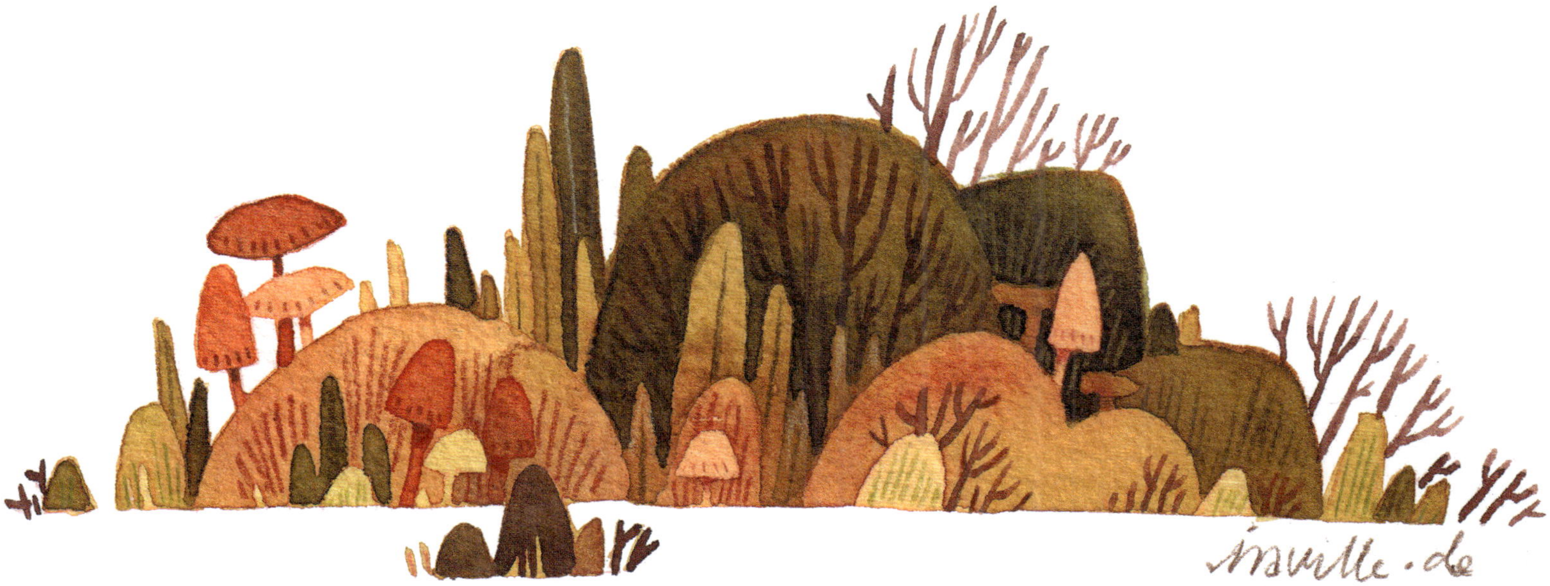
isaville.de

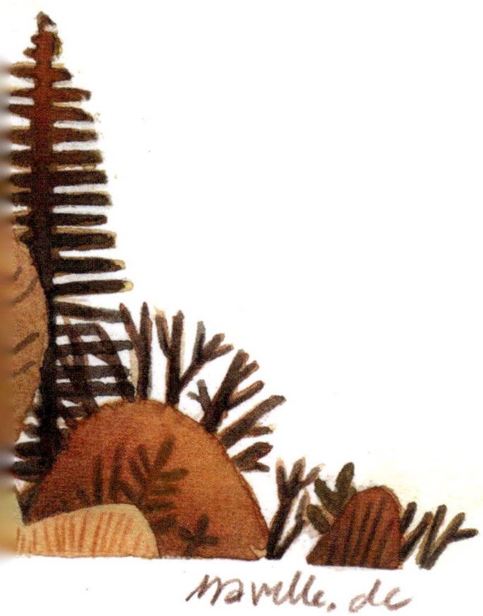
isaville.de

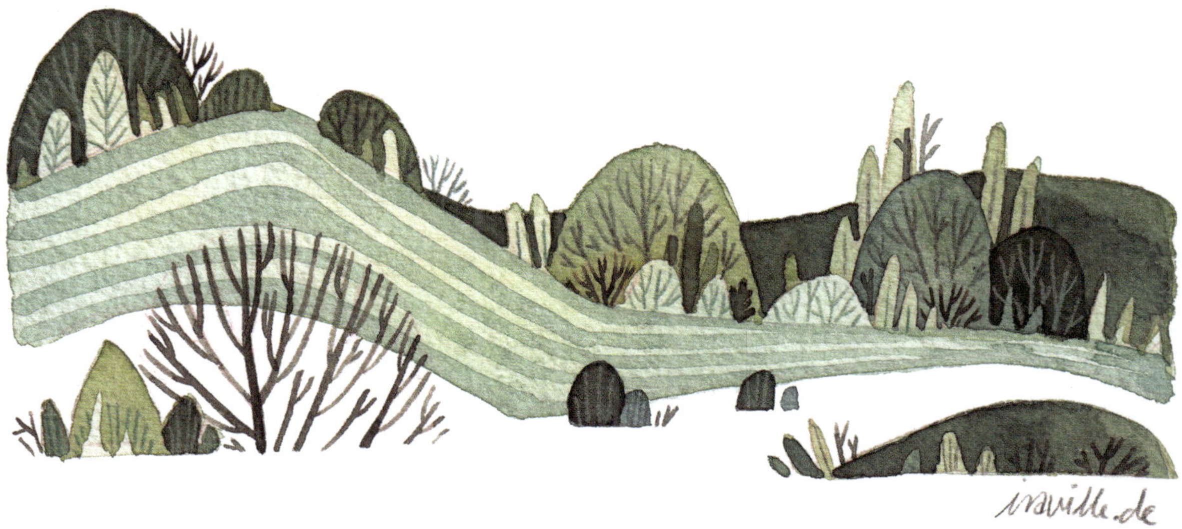
isaville.de

Left:

Summer Thicket, watercolour and coloured pencil, 2022

Below:

Camping Dog, watercolour, coloured pencil, soft pastel, 2019

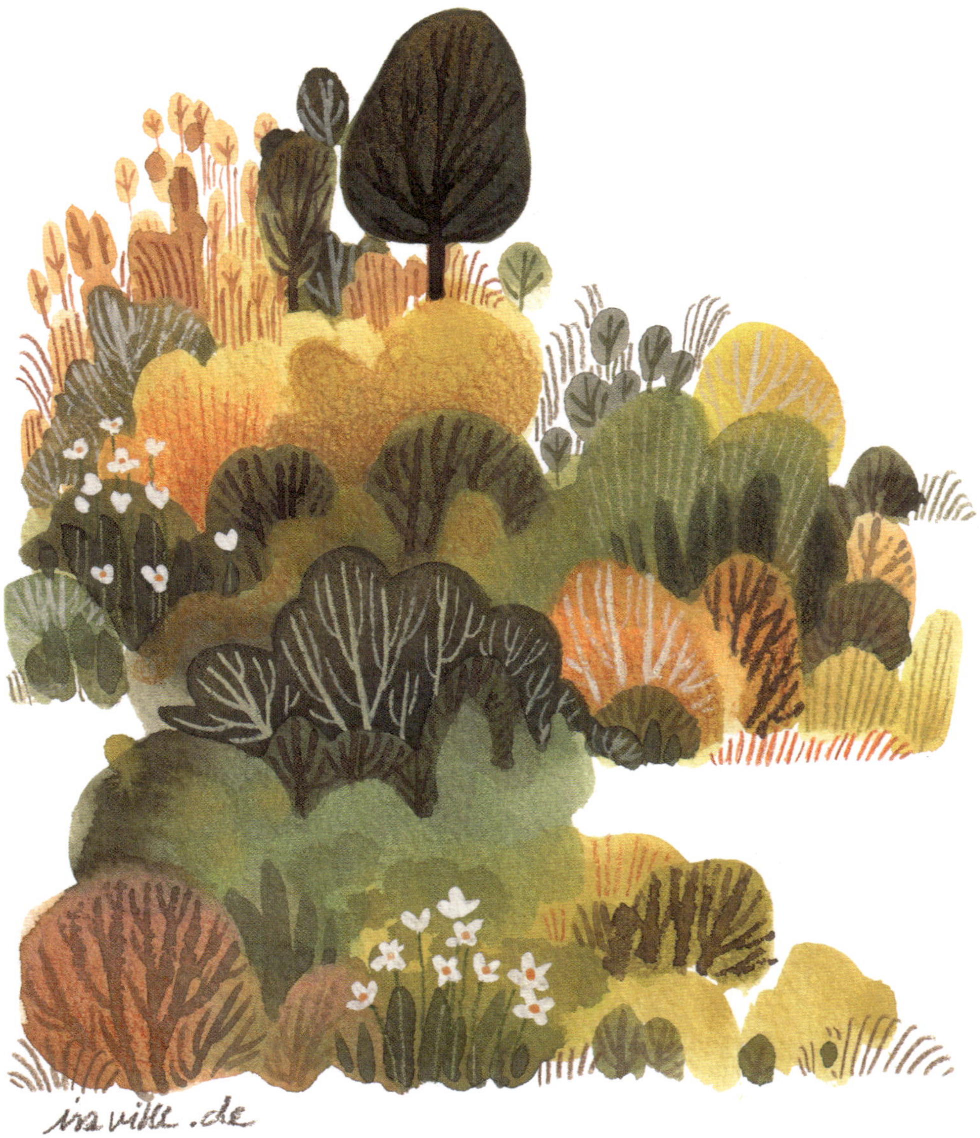

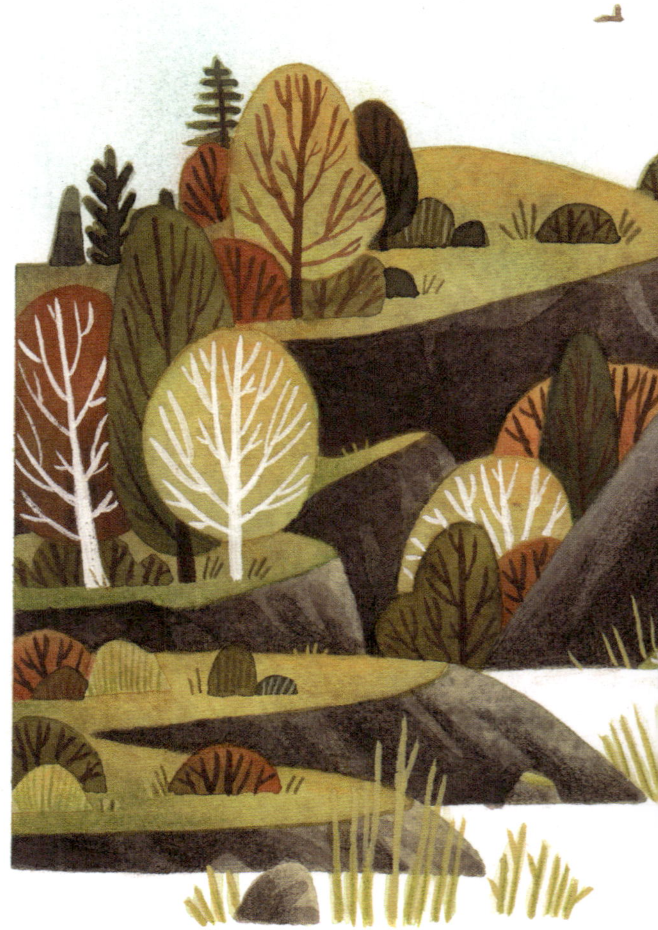

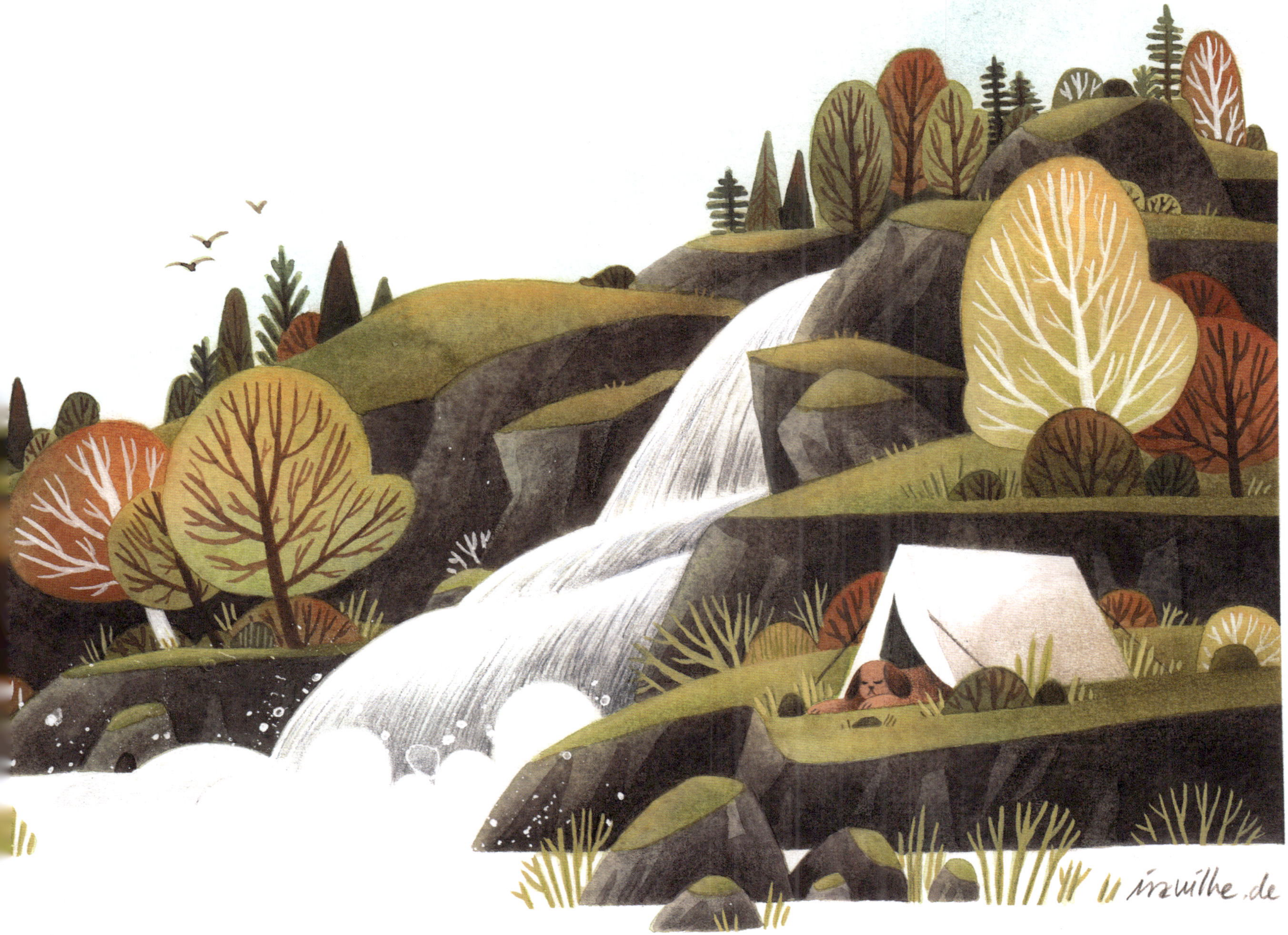
irawilhe.de

IRA'S INSIGHTS

How to find your style

I am often asked how I found my artistic style, which apparently many find distinctive.

First of all, one should know the definition of style. In art – and that is all we are talking about here – style is the way you express yourself. But be careful: this does not mean form alone, which can seem artificial if it does not go hand in hand with the content. Form *serves* the content. In the design world, there are those who say that form follows function, but in art it is a little less technical.

In this context, 'content' is the essence of what you are, what you have seen, what you think, and what you feel.

A great way to break this down is looking at the phenomenon of 'style' from a different perspective, such as literature. I find that it always helps to look at things from various angles, both when drawing and thinking. Haruki Murakami is quite well-known for his distinctive style, but what exactly distinguishes it?

God knows I am no literary specialist, but I noticed that he deliberately uses very simple sentences. His role models include Kafka, Hemingway, and Hammett, and he mixes the real and surreal in his stories. For example, a sheep may speak, or a figure from a painting may suddenly appear in the room. There is usually a melancholy mood, and the protagonists are often average, listless men who like to listen to music, frequent bars, cook simple dishes, and read. Murakami deliberately chooses the appropriate language for his narrative. In interviews, he admits to leading a fairly normal, uneventful life; he worked in a record store, and for a while, he ran his own jazz bar in Tokyo. He knows his story settings well, which he combines with his dreams and imagination.

All of these combined elements make up his style.

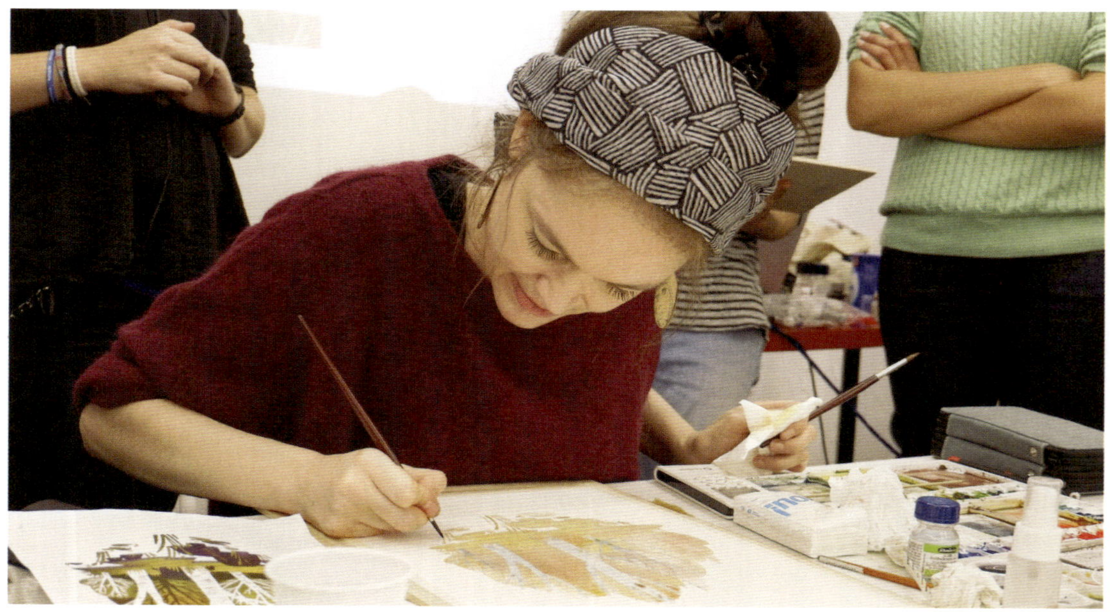

'I find that it always helps to look at things from various angles, both when drawing and thinking'

In visual art, I believe things work similarly. For instance, David Hockney said that he is strongly influenced by Matisse. If Hockney were a minor artist, he would have adopted Matisse's motifs and spent his life trying to copy his work. But Hockney is a great artist for these three reasons: he experimented throughout his life, he paints what he experiences, and he is influenced by more than one person. As far as I know, no one before him took countless Polaroids of a single motif like swimming pools, then arranged them in a way that influenced a new photographic response to Cubism.

These two creators illustrate the difference between 'copying' and 'inspiration'. If Murakami had just copied Kafka, he would never have become famous. To find our own style, we have to find our inner voice, which allows us to express what makes us tick.

I have a connection to the things I draw. For example, I draw Ireland so often because I just love it there. Having visited so many times, I was lucky to take in many impressions. I know how special the light looks, that sheep on steep slopes resemble little white rocks from far away, and how fishing boats look when they sail from a foggy harbour into the sea. Other motifs spring from my mind's eye, which makes me think of Murakami putting his dreams to paper.

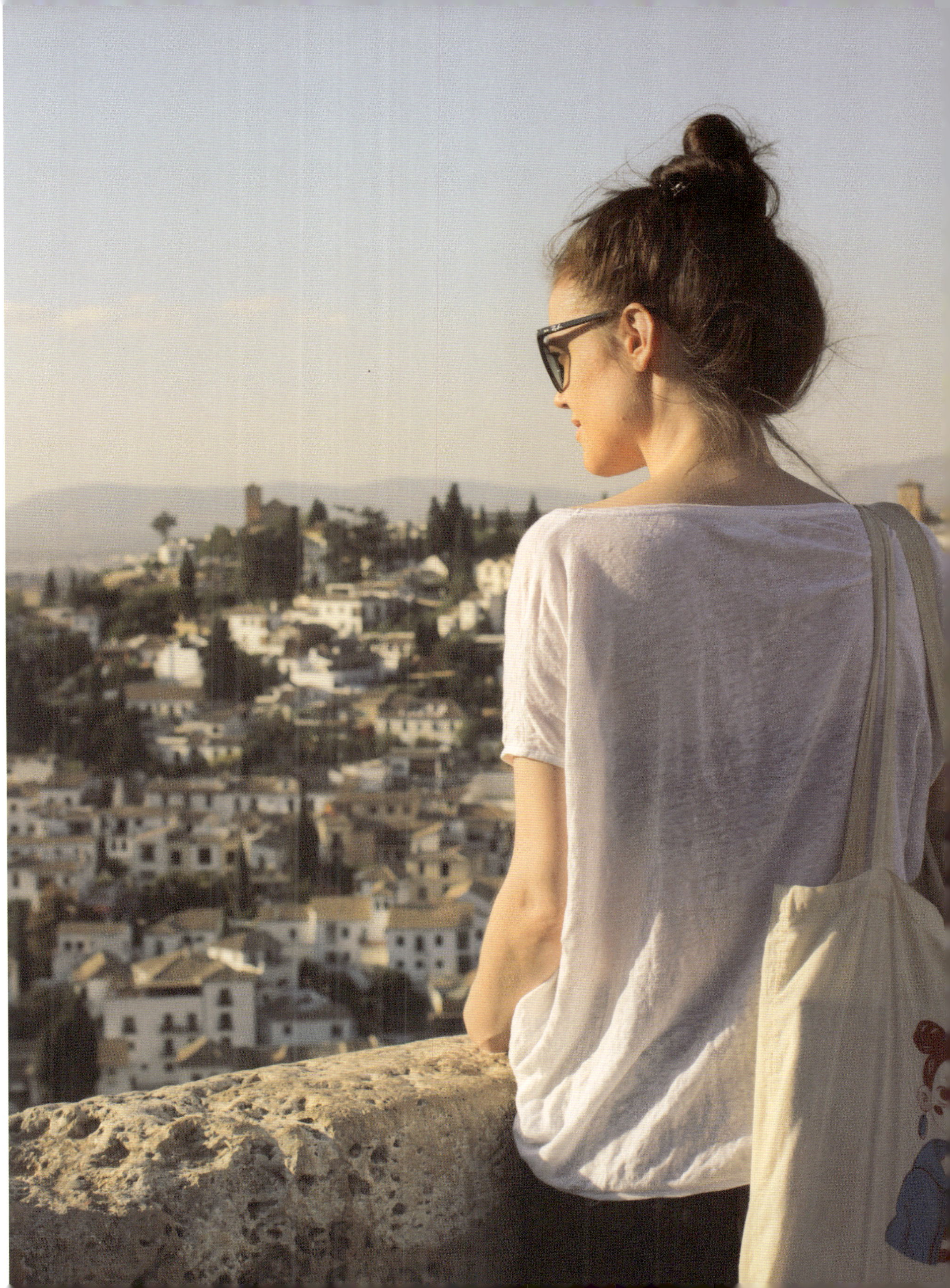

'To find your own style, you have to walk new rocky paths, not the ones already trodden. You have to be a mountaineer, not a tourist'

When drawing, the most important thing is your eye, followed by your head. The hand comes only at the end.

First, you have to learn to see. Then, you must abstract what you see into three dimensions that will look good on a two-dimensional sheet of paper. Finally, what you have thought about in your head is translated through hand movement onto the paper. Of course, it helps to be inspired by other artists, but when you copy a finished painting, you eliminate the first two important steps. Likewise, using a photo as your only reference does not directly help since it is already two-dimensional. It does not allow you to capture the object's entirety, since you can only view it from one perspective. The idea is to have several photos of the same object from different perspectives, as if Hockney had made it into one of his Polaroid collages.

When I draw animals, I usually approach it this way. I look at countless photos of the same species on the internet, from all sides and in different poses until I feel I understand the animal. Then I close the browser window, and try to put my ideas onto a blank canvas. Any other way would just be copying. This way, I can fully understand the shapes and make something new from them.

Artists must be aware that there is a difference between copying and finding inspiration. That is of utmost importance.

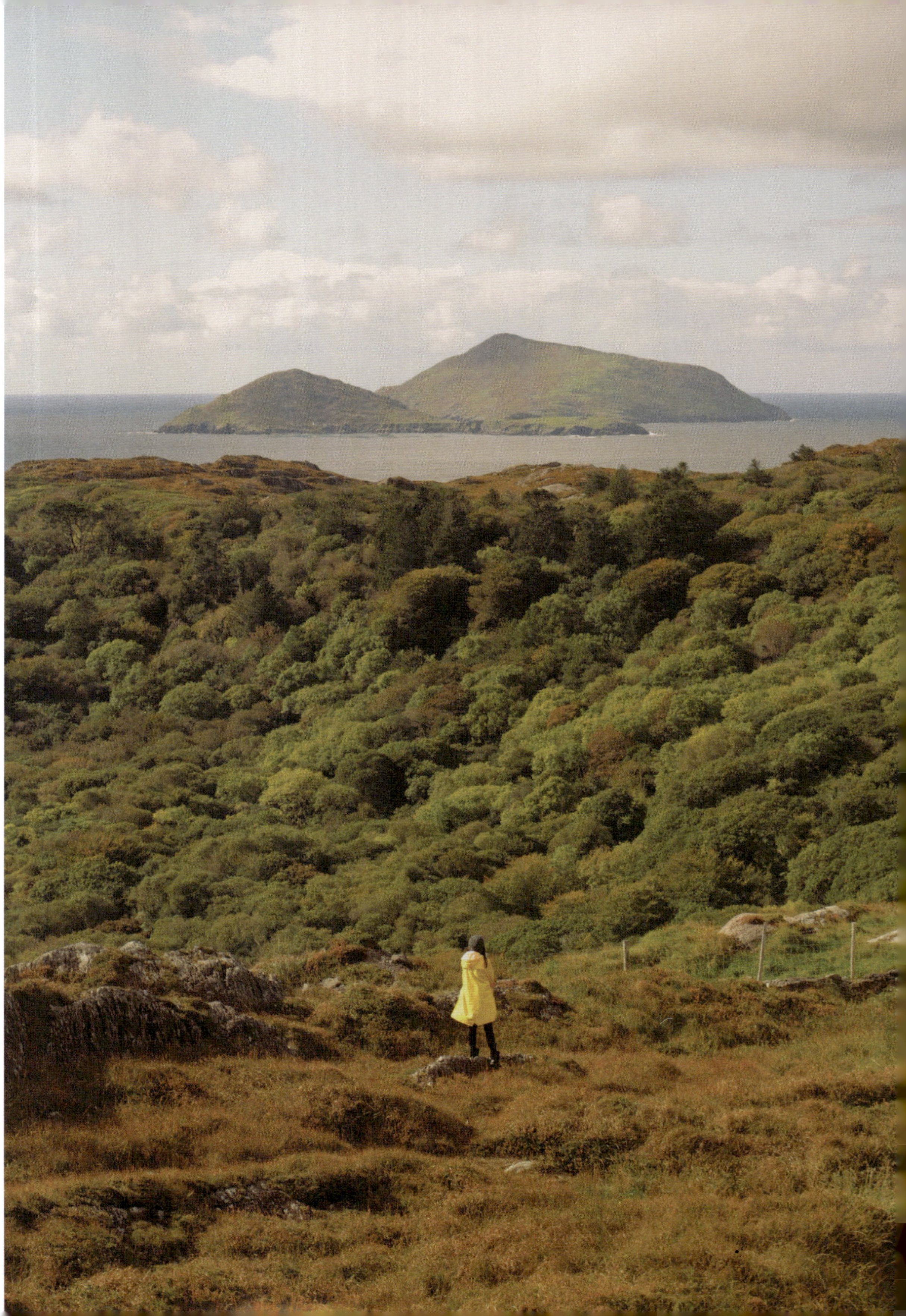

At the very least, you should strive to transform these existing creations into something that is your own. This is why it helps to have more than one source of inspiration. If you copy Hockney, you will just be a second-rate Hockney. You will never find your own style. Why draw Californian swimming pools if it has nothing to do with your life?

To find your own style, you have to walk new rocky paths, not the ones already trodden. You have to be a mountaineer, not a tourist. The same can be applied to form, or the way you draw – it does not help to simply copy others. It is ultimately like your own handwriting. If you keep drawing long enough, your individual style will naturally develop. If you do not, you will only imitate the style of others. Above all, you should not be afraid of making mistakes. They are important because you only learn by making them.

Not long ago, someone wrote to me explaining that my art style was being taught on a course abroad. I am sure that it was meant nicely, and of course, a part of me is pleased that my art is getting attention around the world. But from my point of view, this is exactly what I advise against. Nobody has anything to gain from being a second-rate Iraville.

My hope is to encourage you to take the difficult path of finding your own artistic expression. By choosing this way, you will reach a goal that others have not. It may feel more arduous, and it will take longer (a few years, at least), but it is so much more exciting and satisfying than following someone else's footsteps that have come before you!

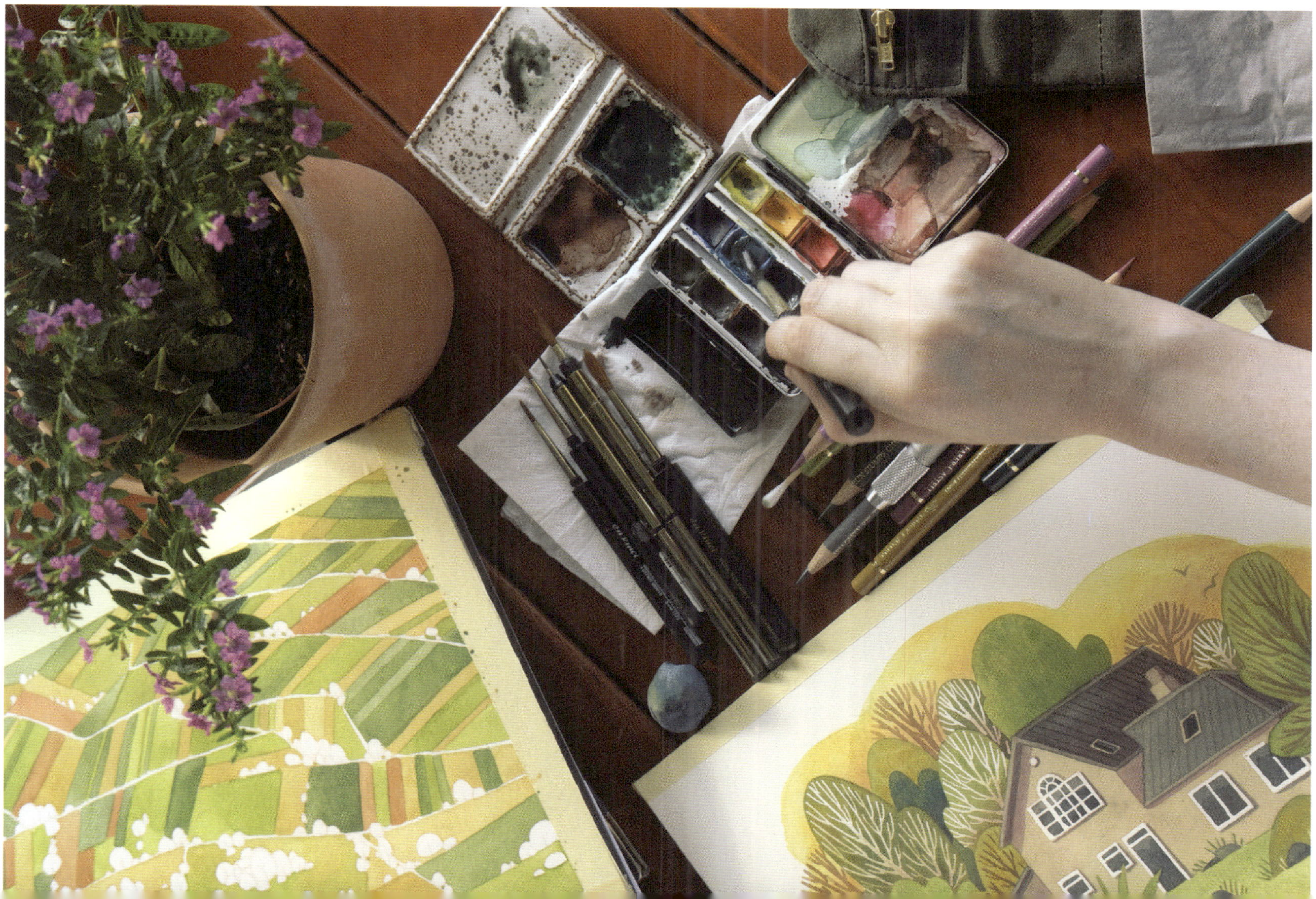

GALLERY

Country life

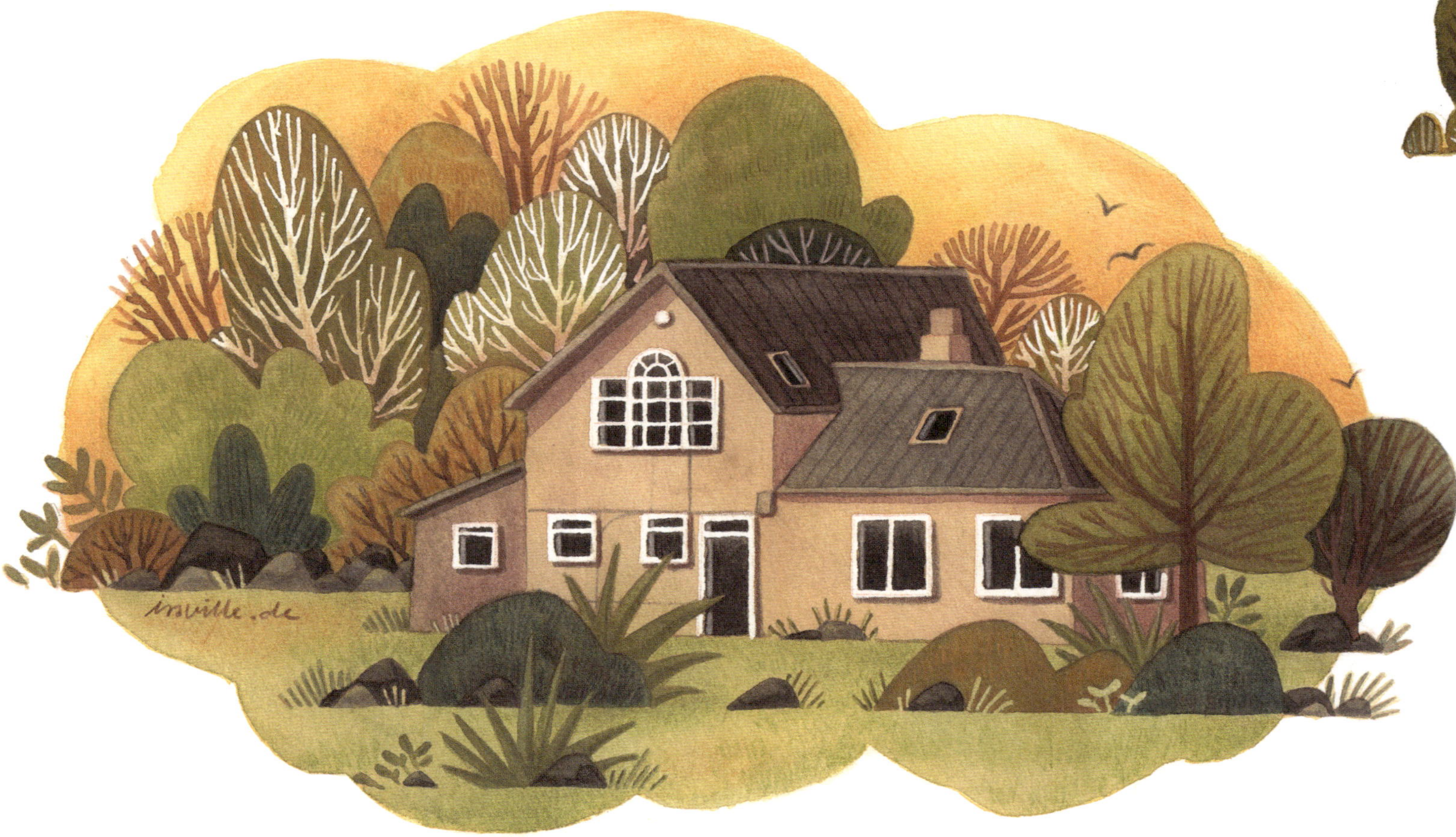

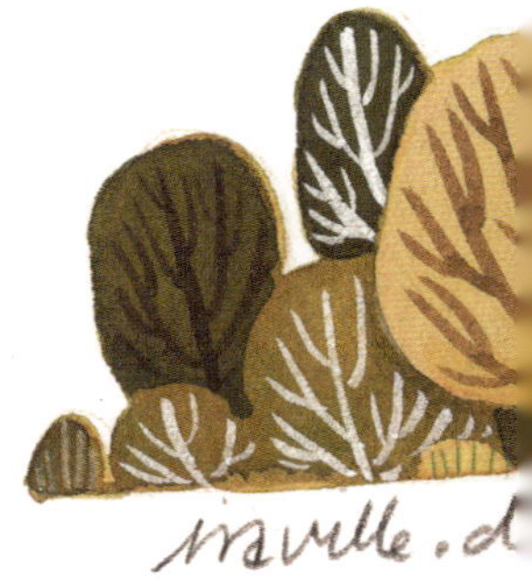

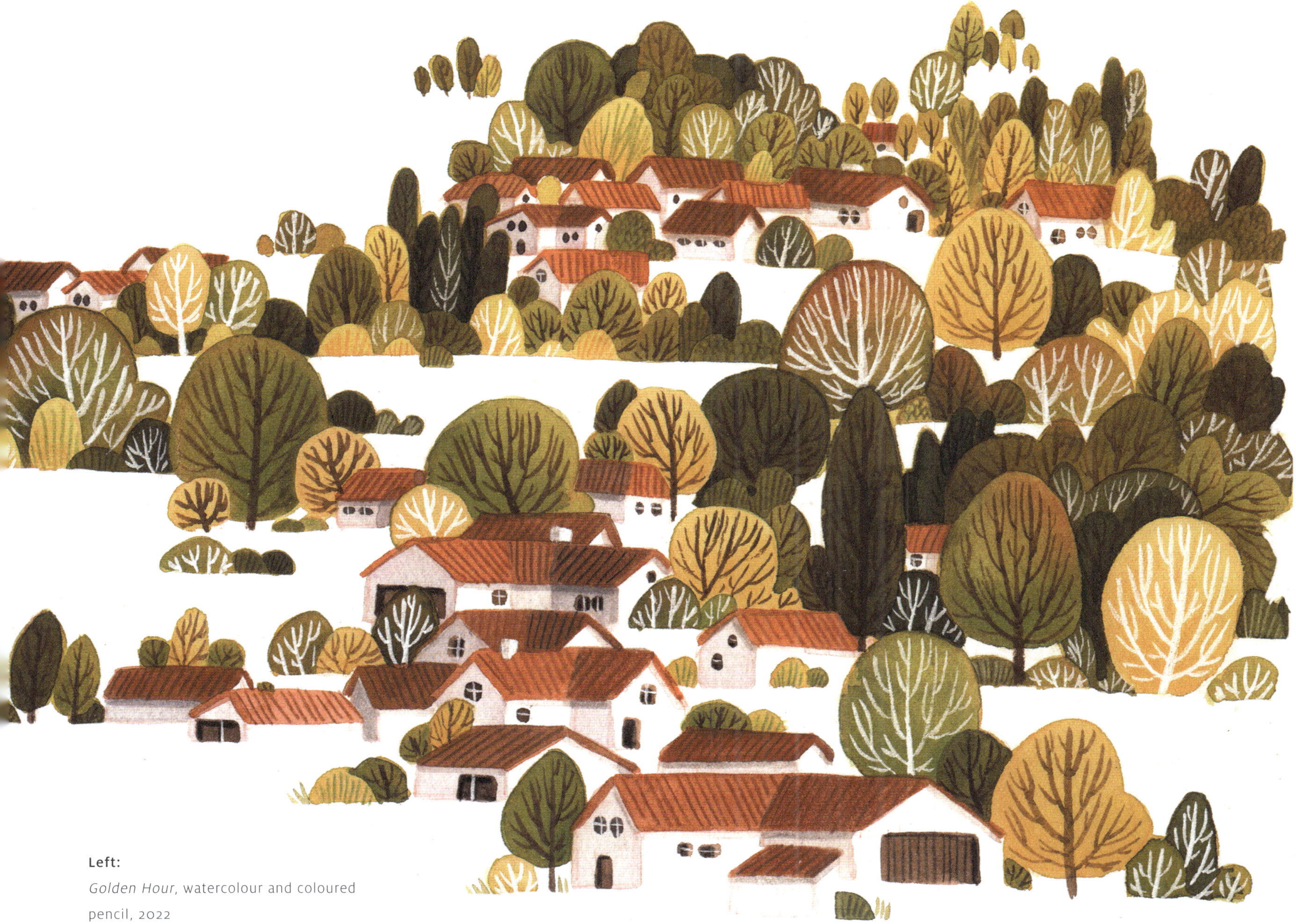

Left:
Golden Hour, watercolour and coloured pencil, 2022

Above:
Village and Trees, watercolour and coloured pencil, 2020

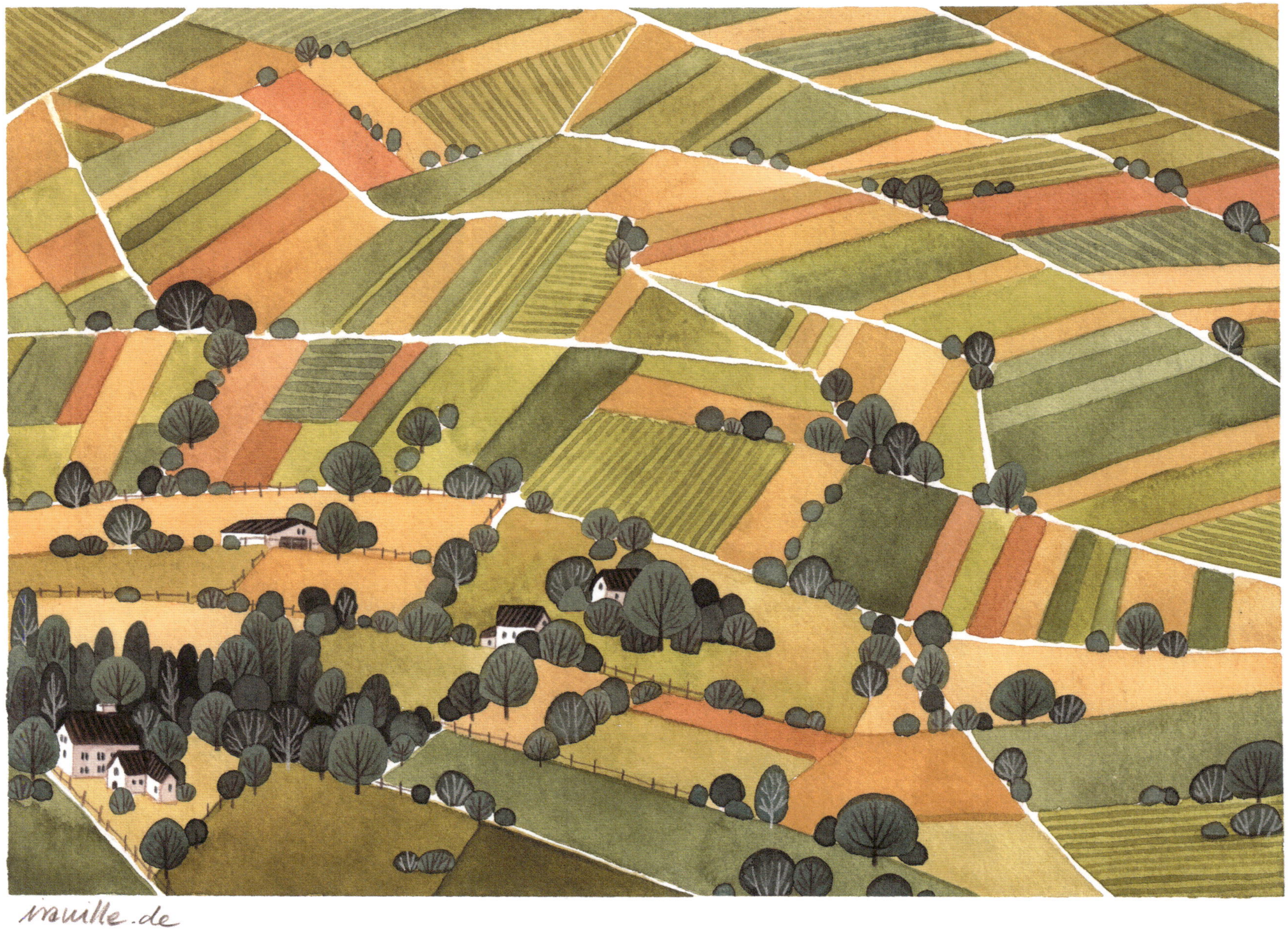

Left:
Fields and Meadows 2, watercolour and coloured pencil, 2022

Below:
Fields and Meadows 1, watercolour and coloured pencil, 2021

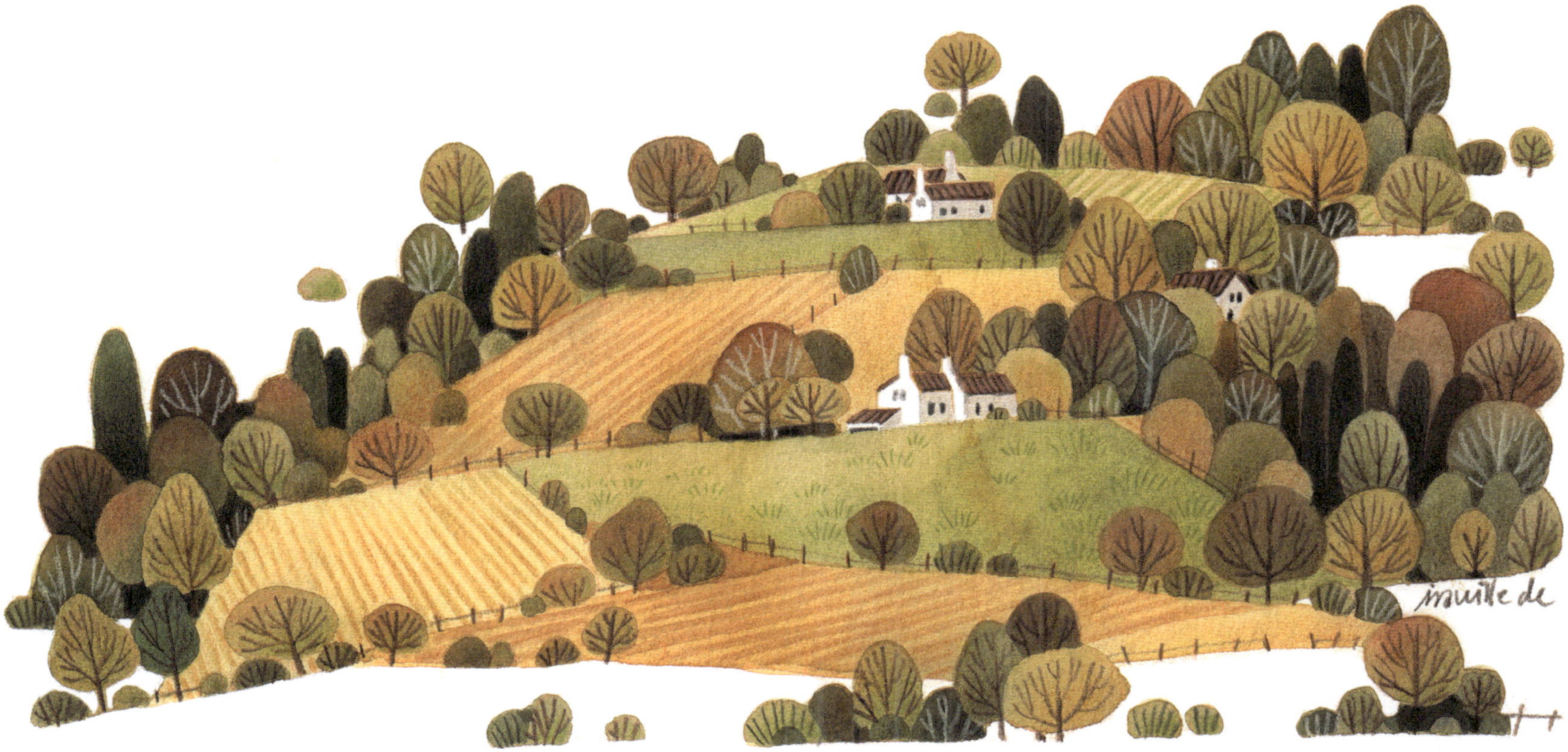

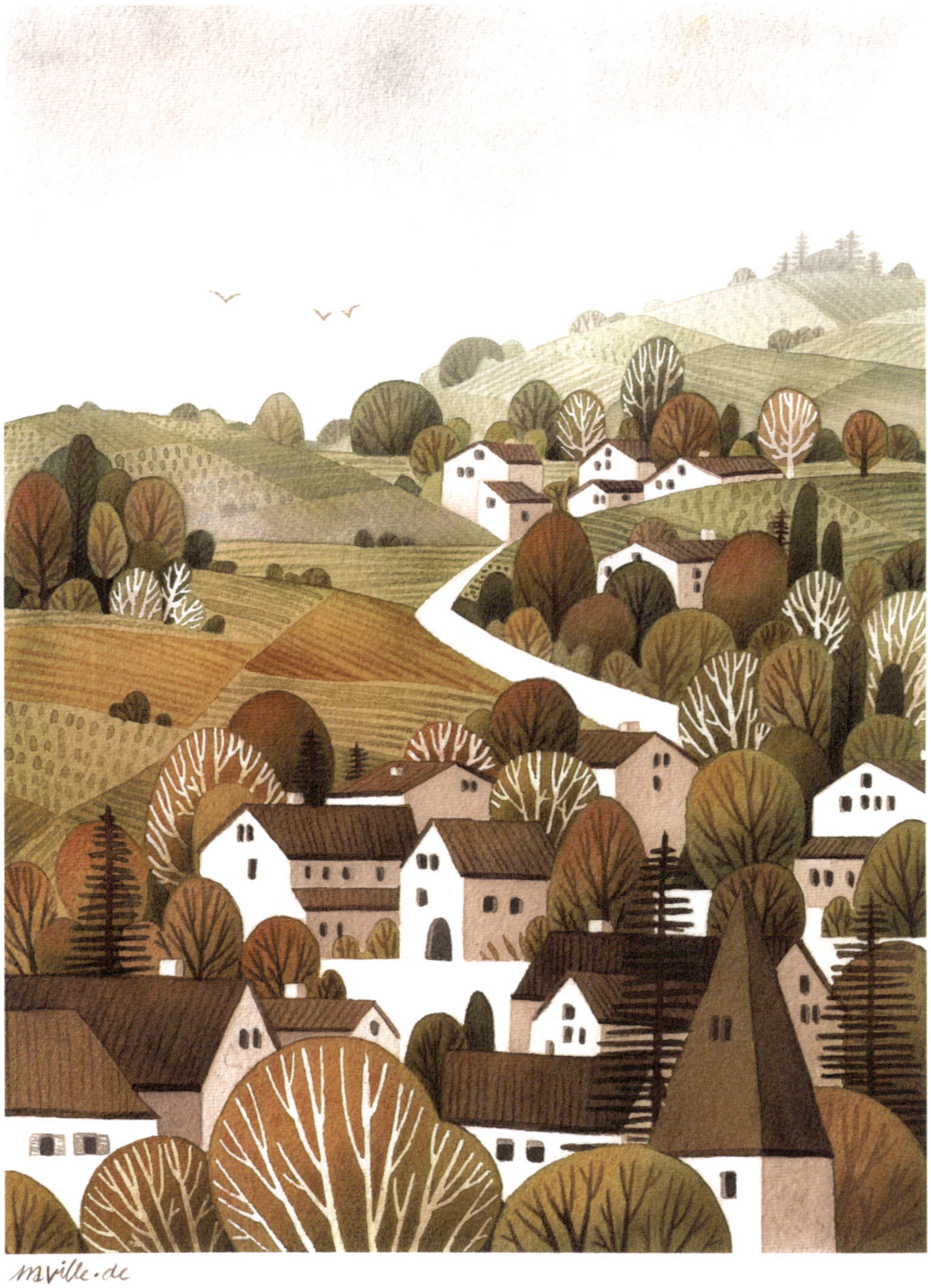

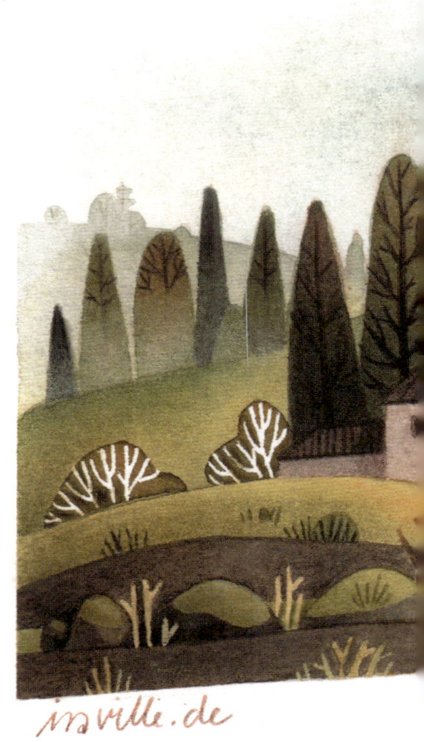

Left:

Autumn Village and Fields, watercolour and coloured pencil, 2018

Right:

Foggy Landscape, watercolour, coloured pencil, pastel, 2018

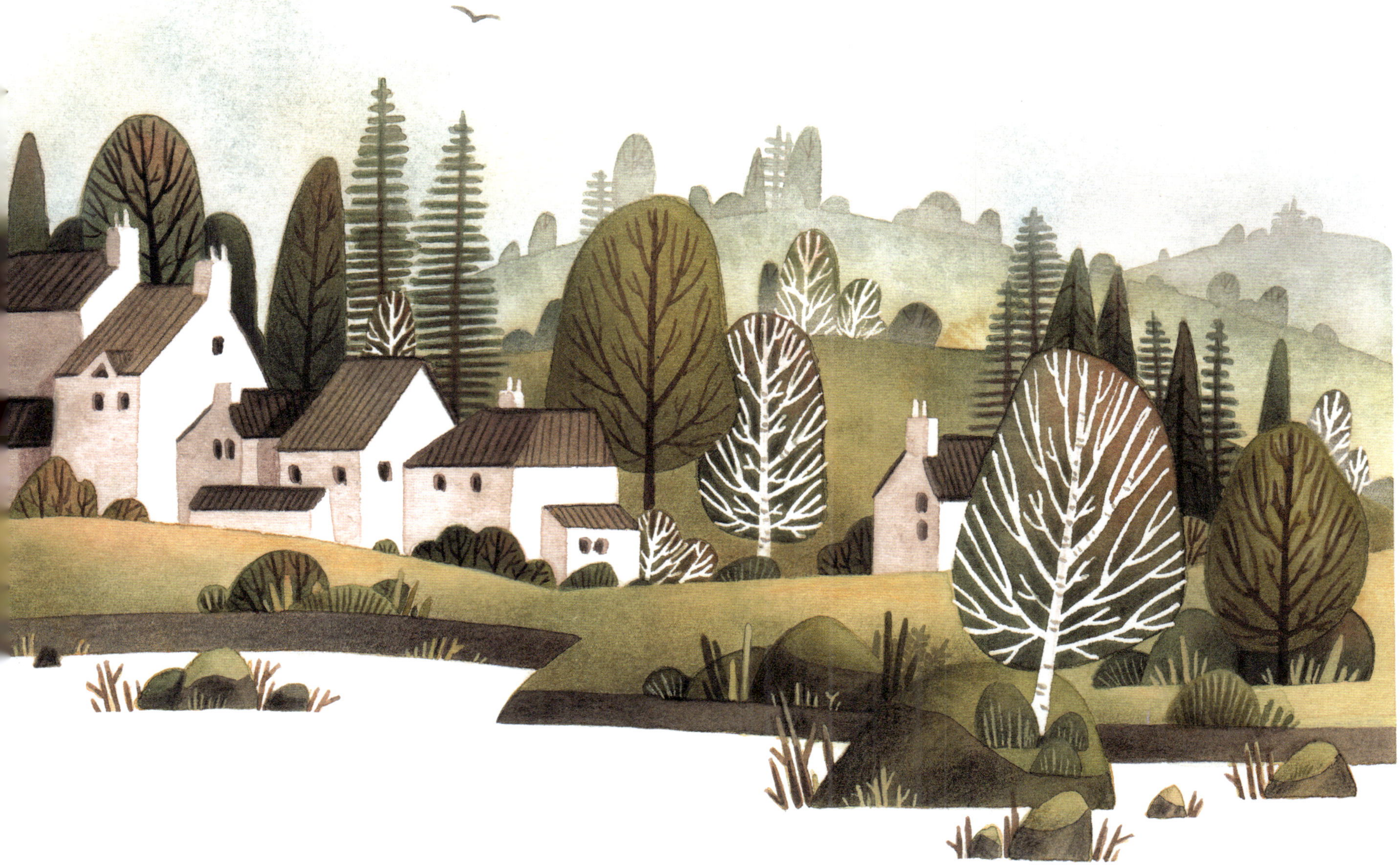

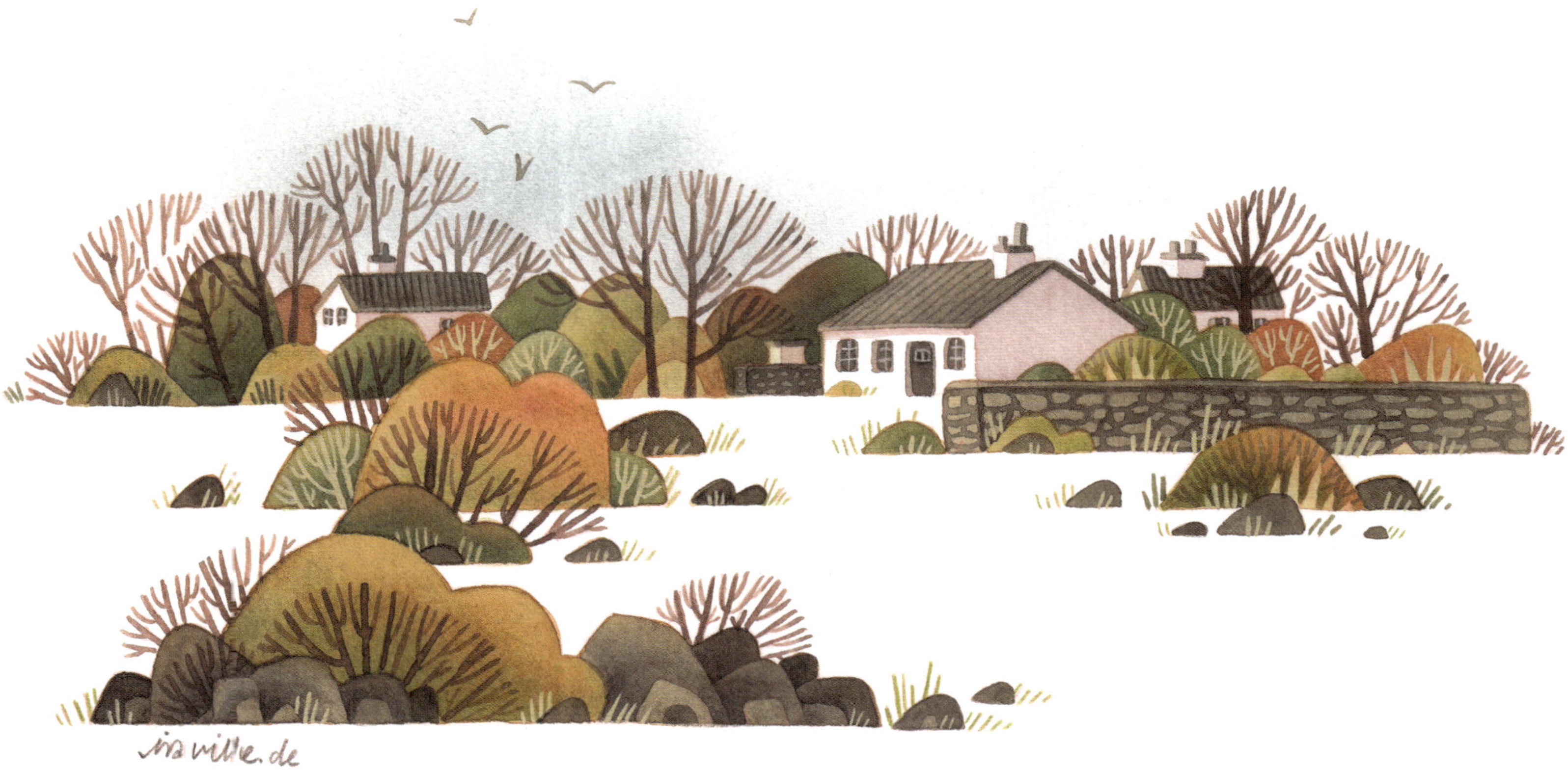

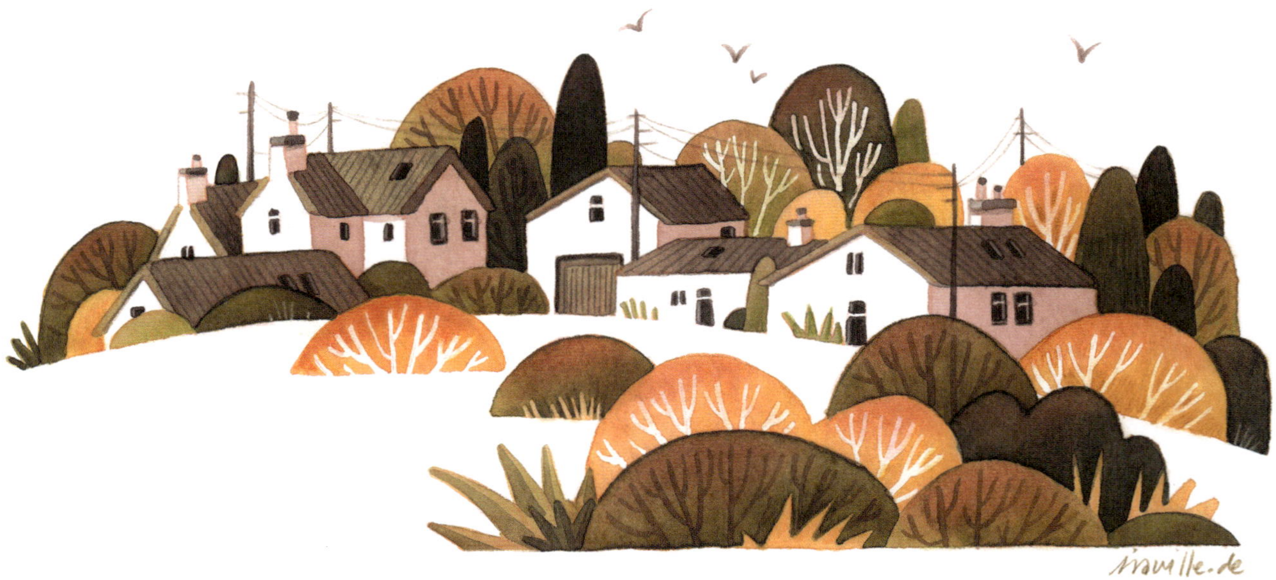

Above:
Irish Countryside 3,
watercolour, coloured
pencil, pastel, 2022

Right:
Irish Countryside 2,
watercolour, coloured
pencil, pastel, 2022

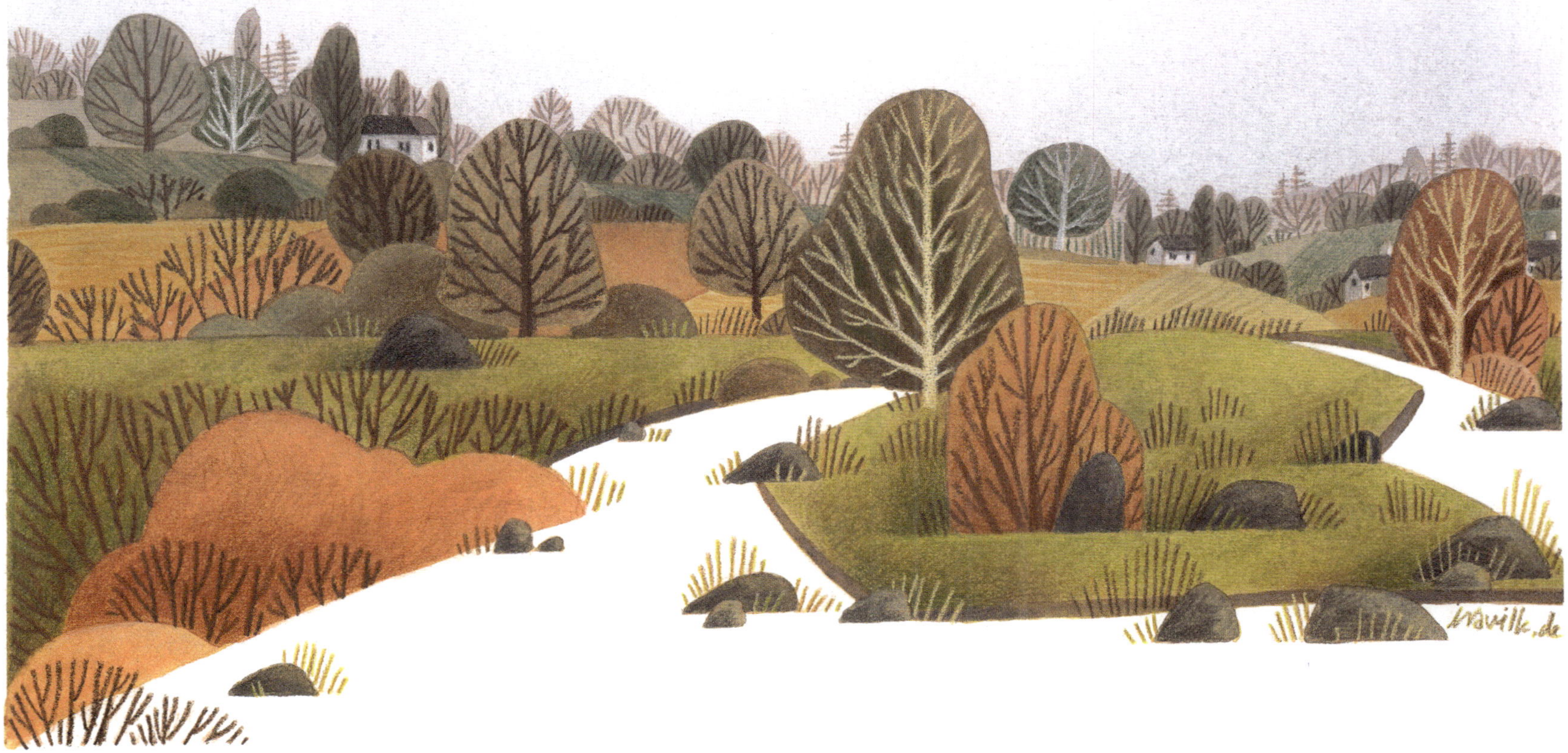

Above:
Irish Countryside 1, watercolour, coloured pencil, pastel, 2022

Right:
Cozy Winter House, watercolour
and graphite pencil, 2018

Sometimes movies inspire me to make a drawing. In this case, it was a rather clichéd movie called *The Holiday*. I have long forgotten the plot, but I liked the production design that included beautiful furnishings in an English cottage, especially the old-fashioned kitchen. I also liked the exterior of the cottage, so it was not wasted time to watch the movie, I believe.

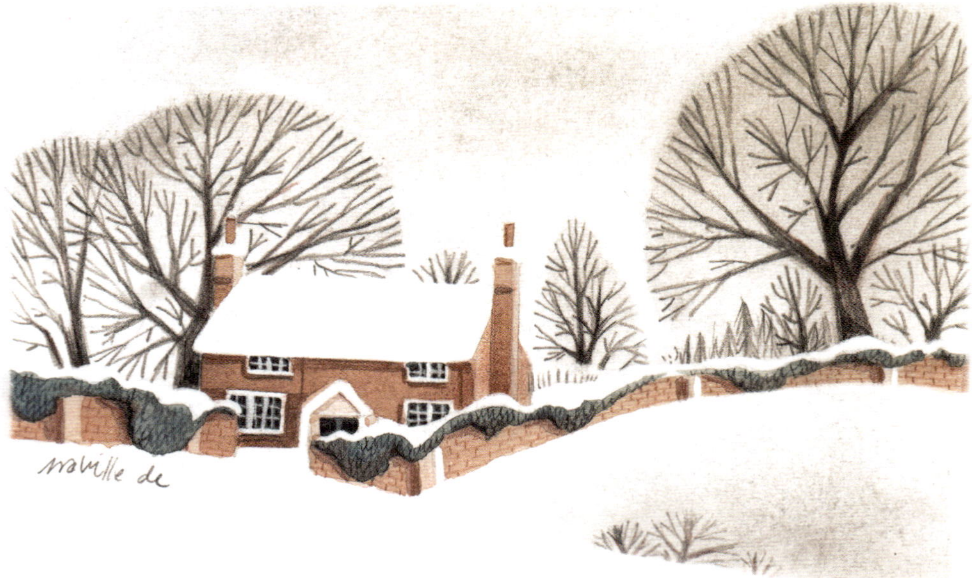

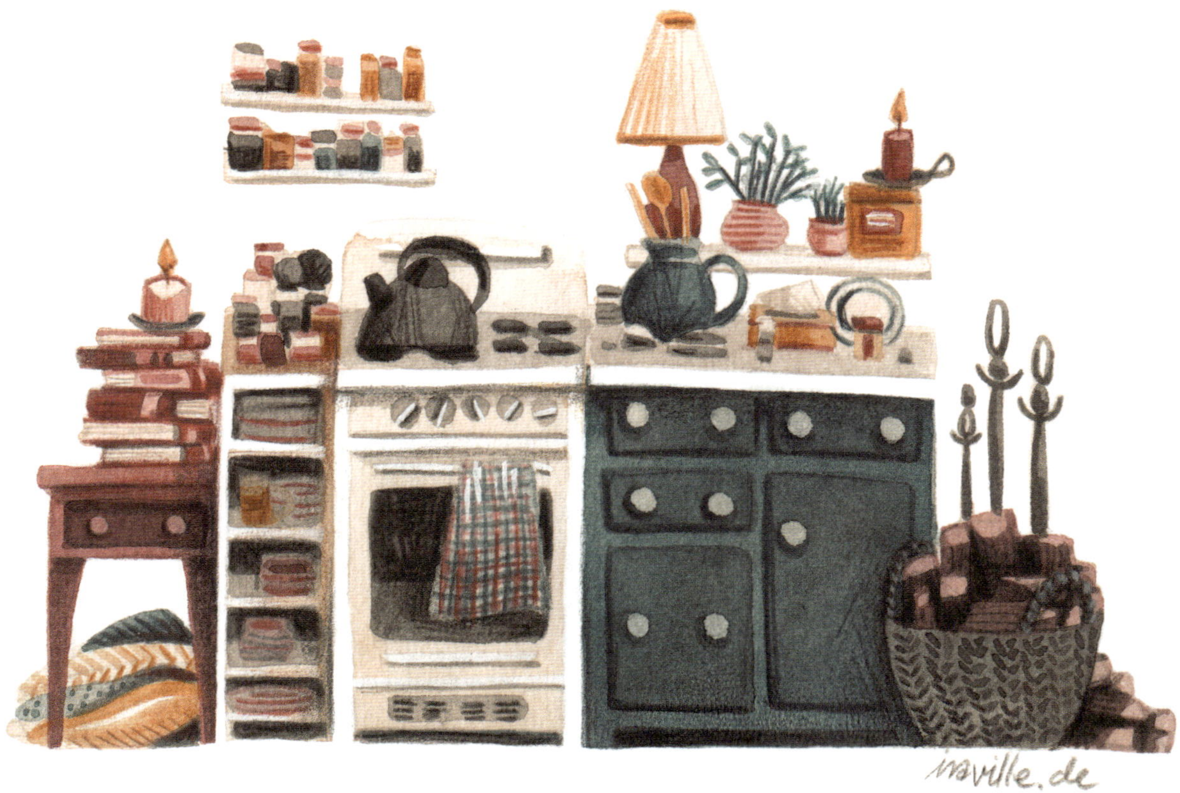

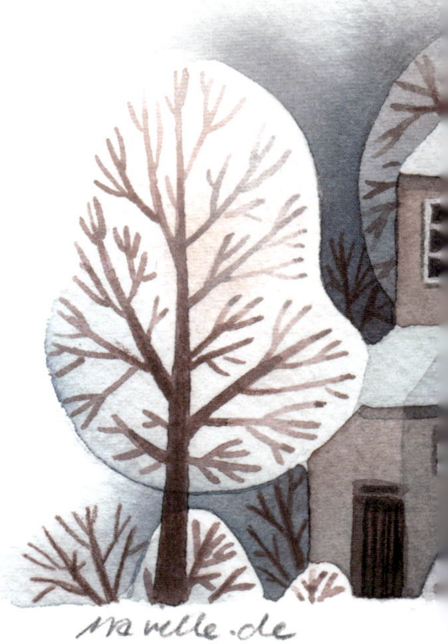

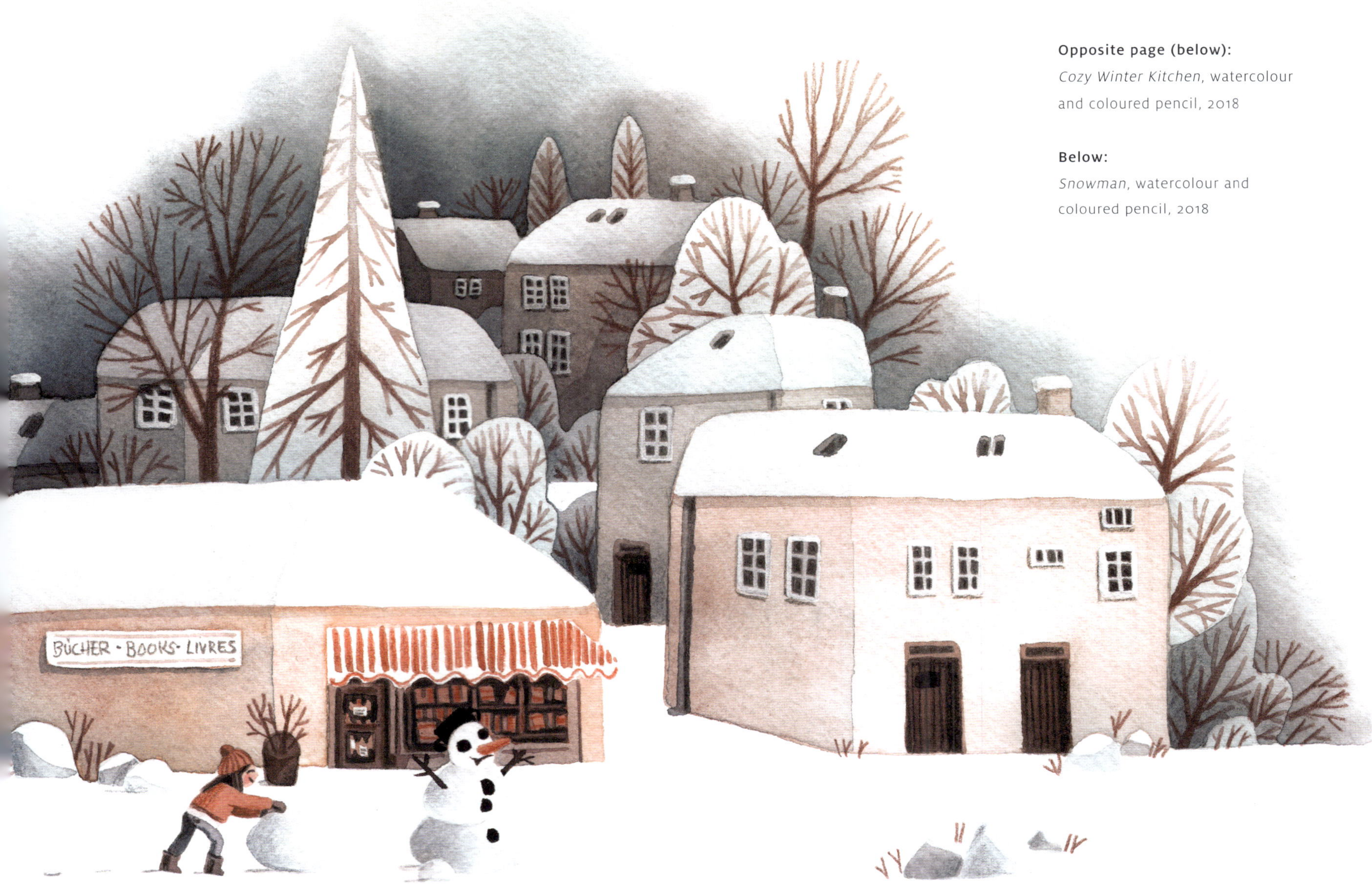

Opposite page (below):
Cozy Winter Kitchen, watercolour and coloured pencil, 2018

Below:
Snowman, watercolour and coloured pencil, 2018

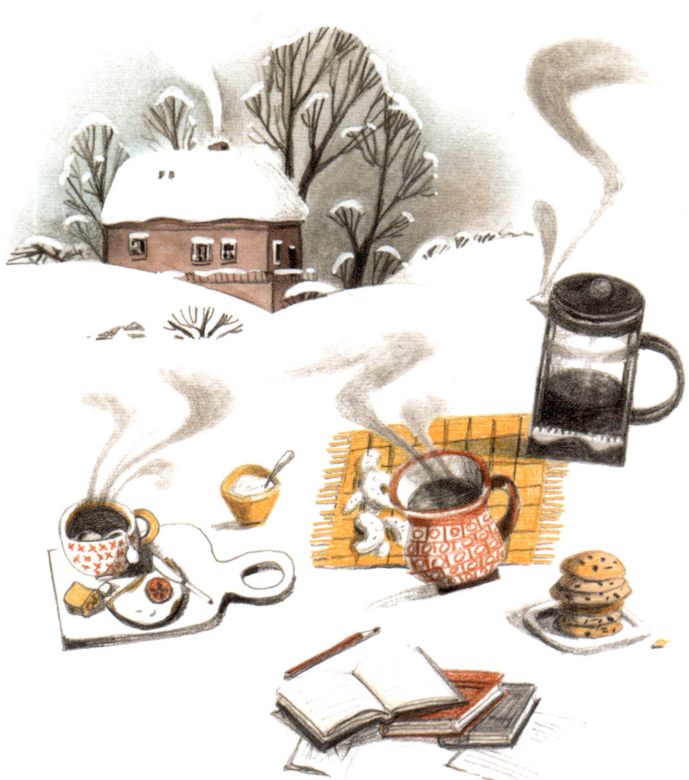

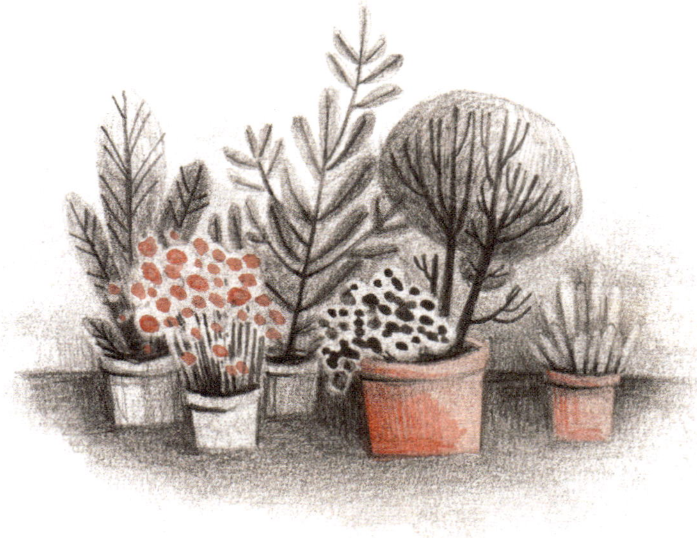

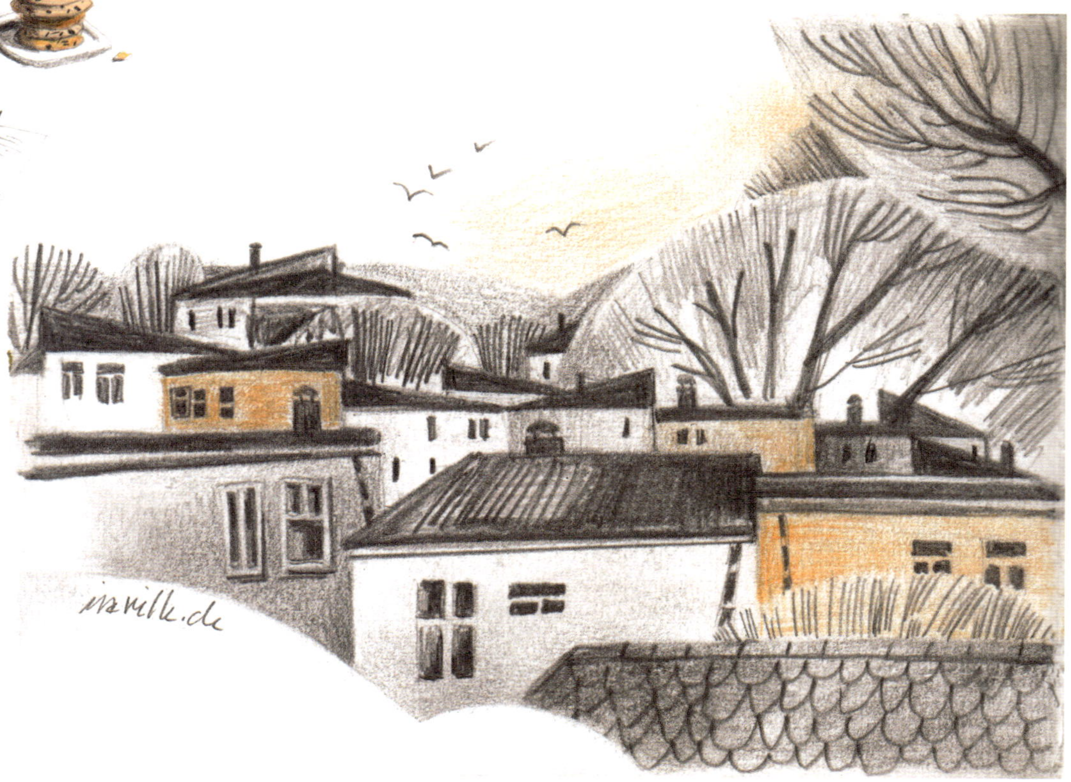

Clockwise from above:
Winter Sketches, graphite and coloured pencil, 2019

Potted Plants, graphite and coloured pencil, 2019

Yellow Houses Sketch, graphite and coloured pencil, 2019

INTERIORS

Right:
Bakery, watercolour and coloured pencil, 2019

Here in Germany, many people are obsessed with bread. It is almost a little bit ridiculous. Traditionally, it is eaten in the morning *and* in the evening. Therefore, there is an incredible number of bakeries that offer a variety of varieties.

You can get all forms of bread there, such as rye, sprout, sunflower, chia, white, and mixed bread. There are also bread rolls, French croissants and baguettes, and Italian breads like focaccia and ciabatta. My husband recently started baking bread himself and it tastes fantastic, especially when it is still warm and fresh. In the drawing, I have painted a more traditional bakery of which there are not so many anymore. I wanted to convey this warm, cosy feeling that you get when you come into a bakery and smell fresh bread.

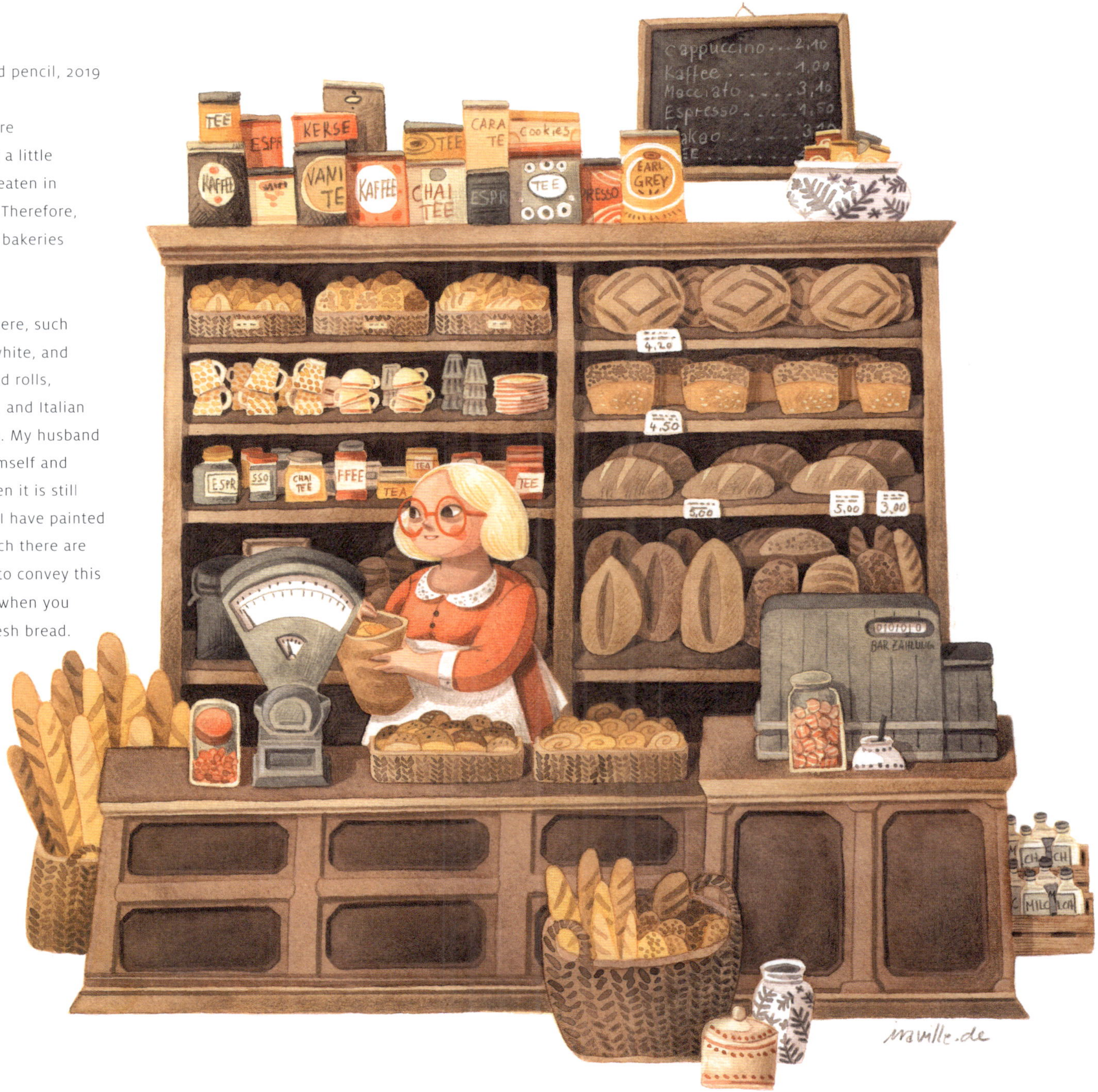

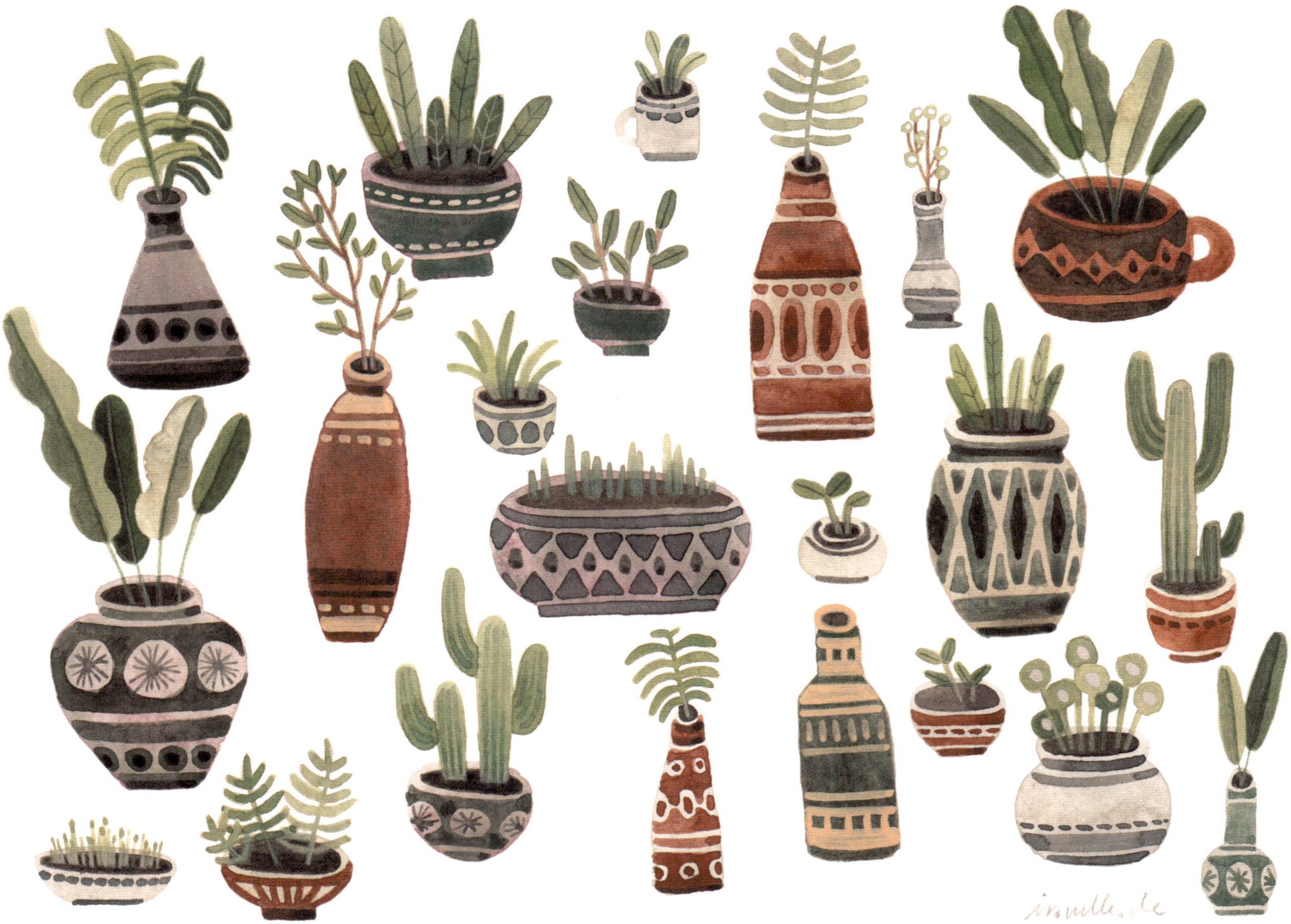

Above:
Vases and Pots, watercolour and coloured pencil, 2021

Right:
Tree Nook, watercolour and coloured pencil, 2023

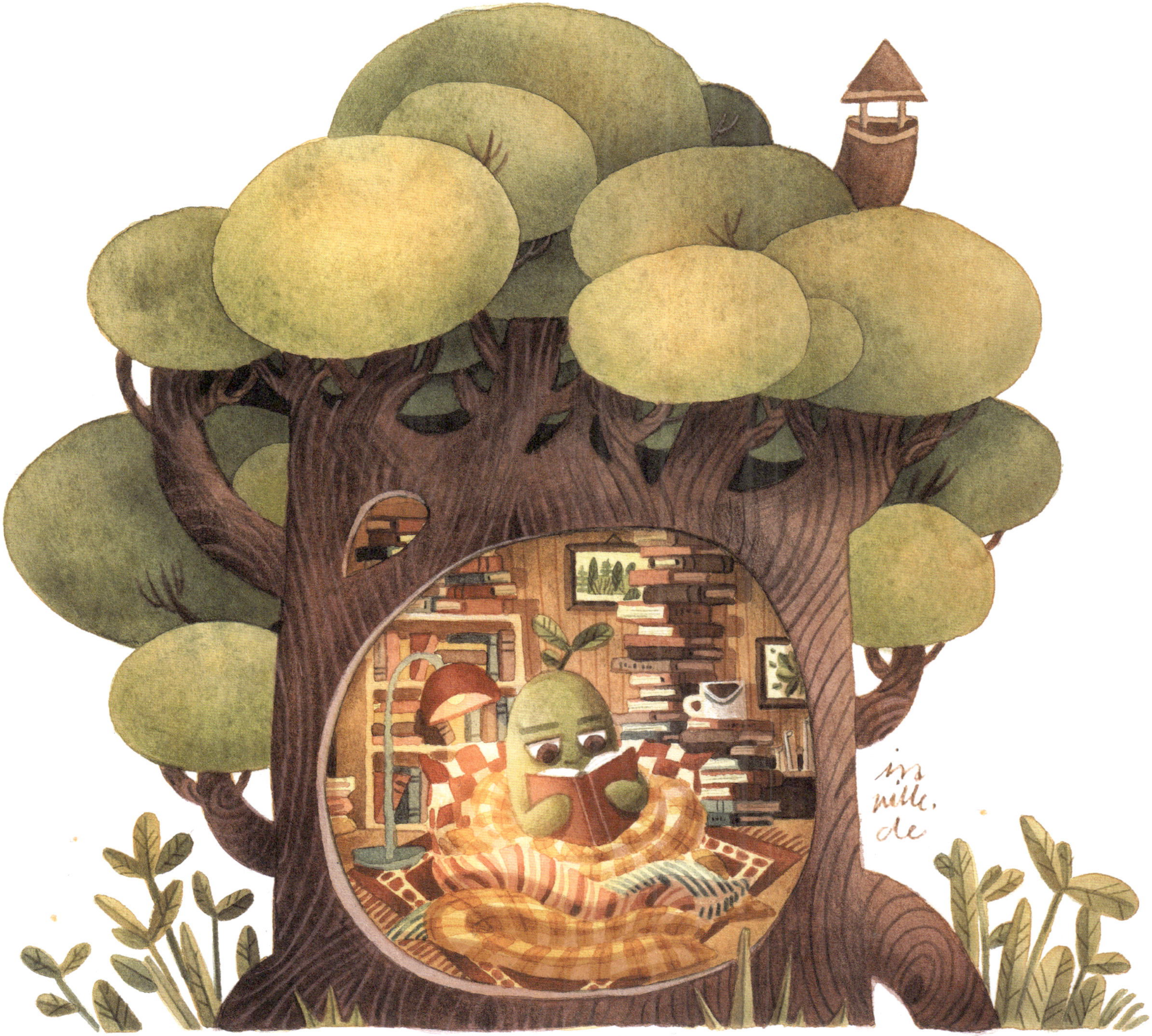

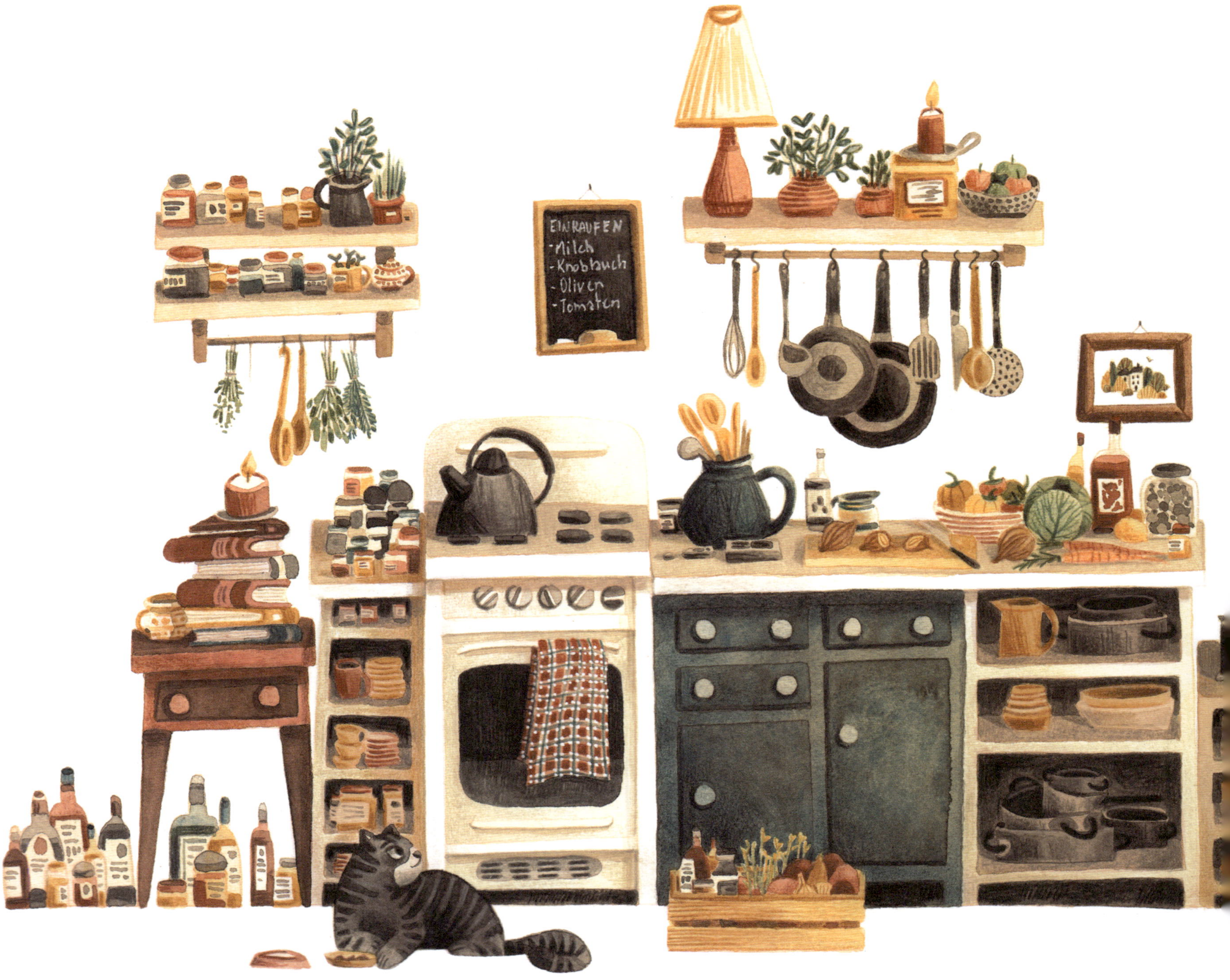
EINKAUFEN
-Milch
-Knoblauch
-Oliven
-Tomaten

JARS

Left:
Kitchen, watercolour and coloured pencil, 2019

Right:
Jars, watercolour and coloured pencil, 2017

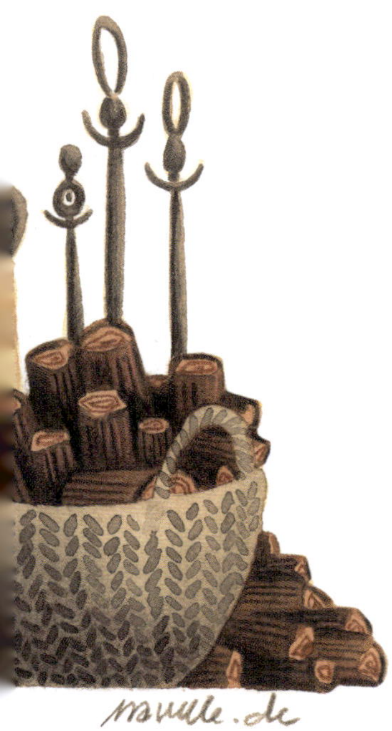

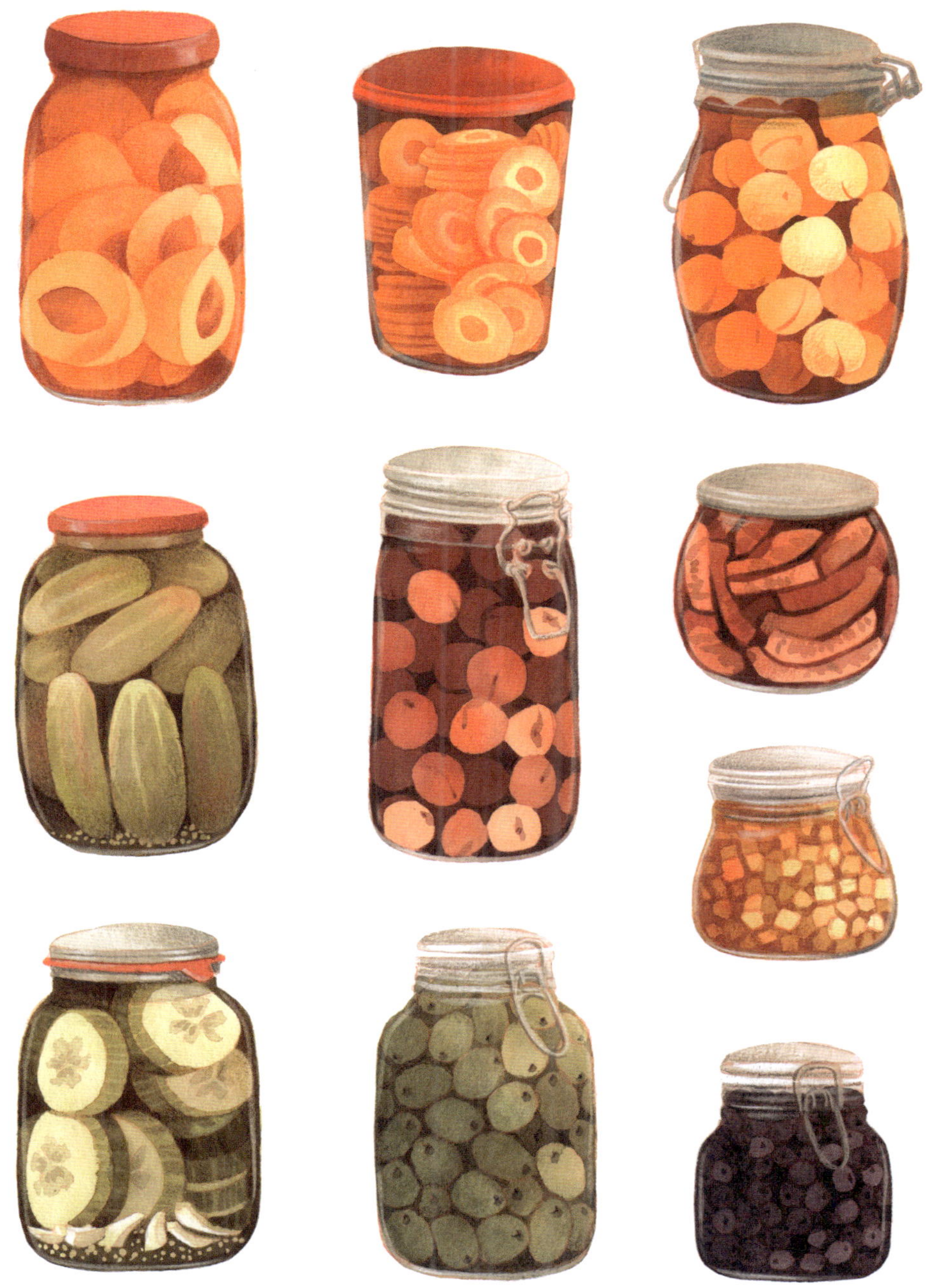

IRELAND SKETCHES

Right:
Irish Countryside Sketch 3, Copic markers and coloured pencil, 2016

Below:
Irish Countryside Sketch 1, Copic markers and coloured pencil, 2016

Opposite page (above):
Irish Countryside Sketch 2, Copic markers and coloured pencil, 2016

Opposite page (below):
Portmagee Sketch 1, watercolour and coloured pencil, 2015

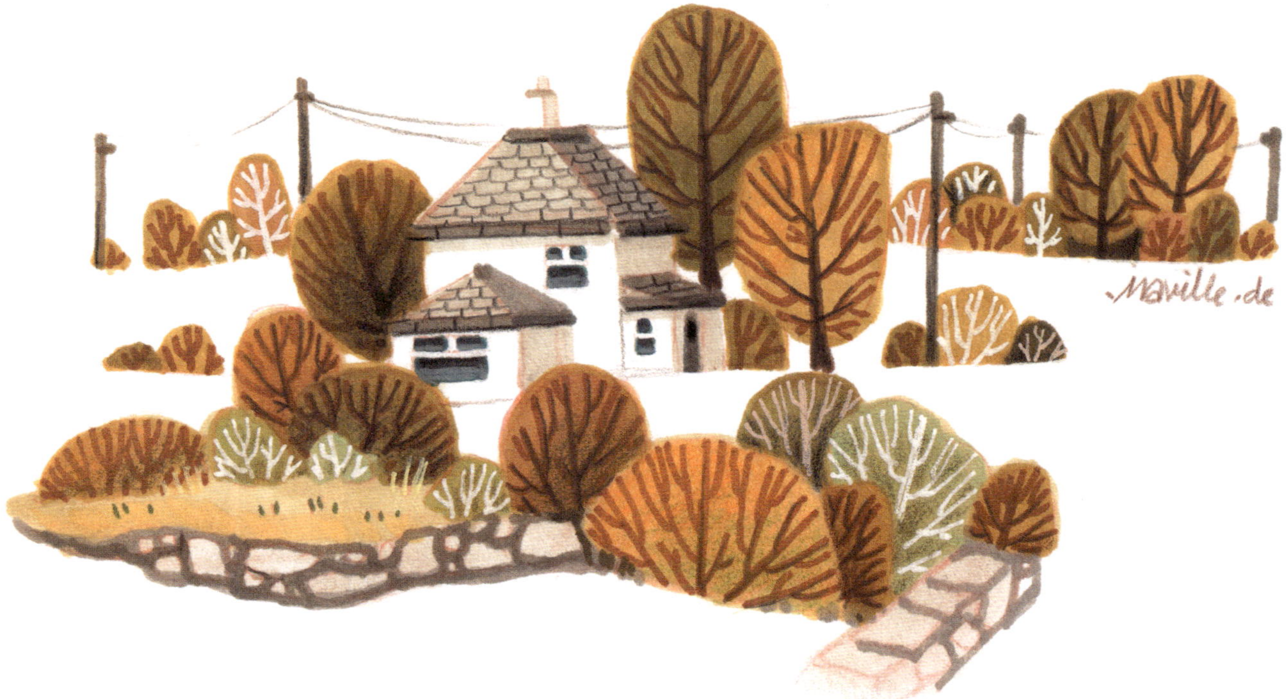

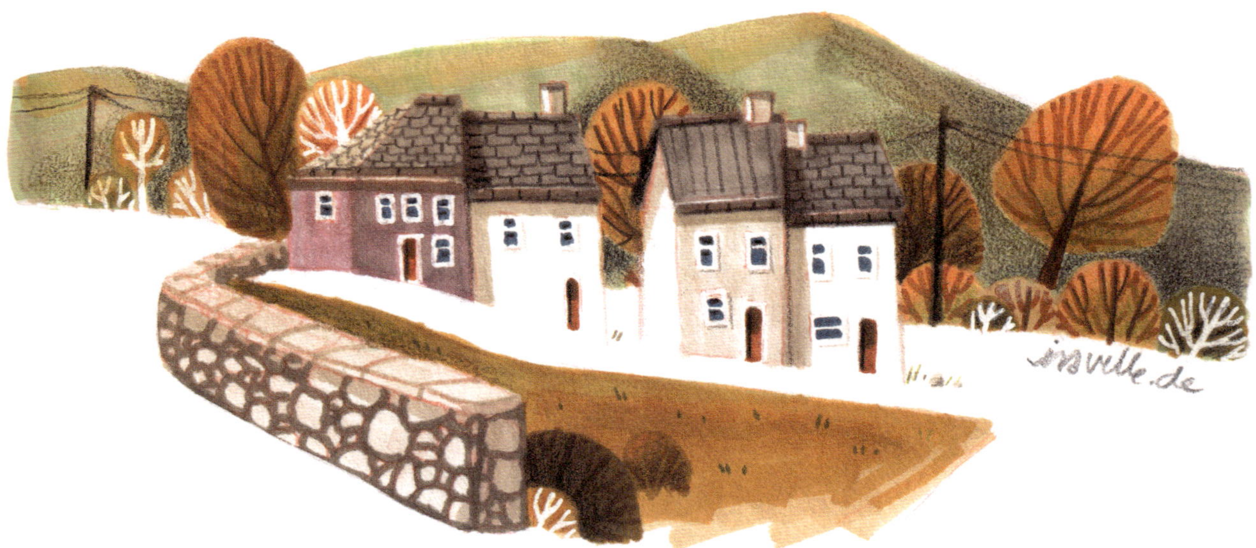

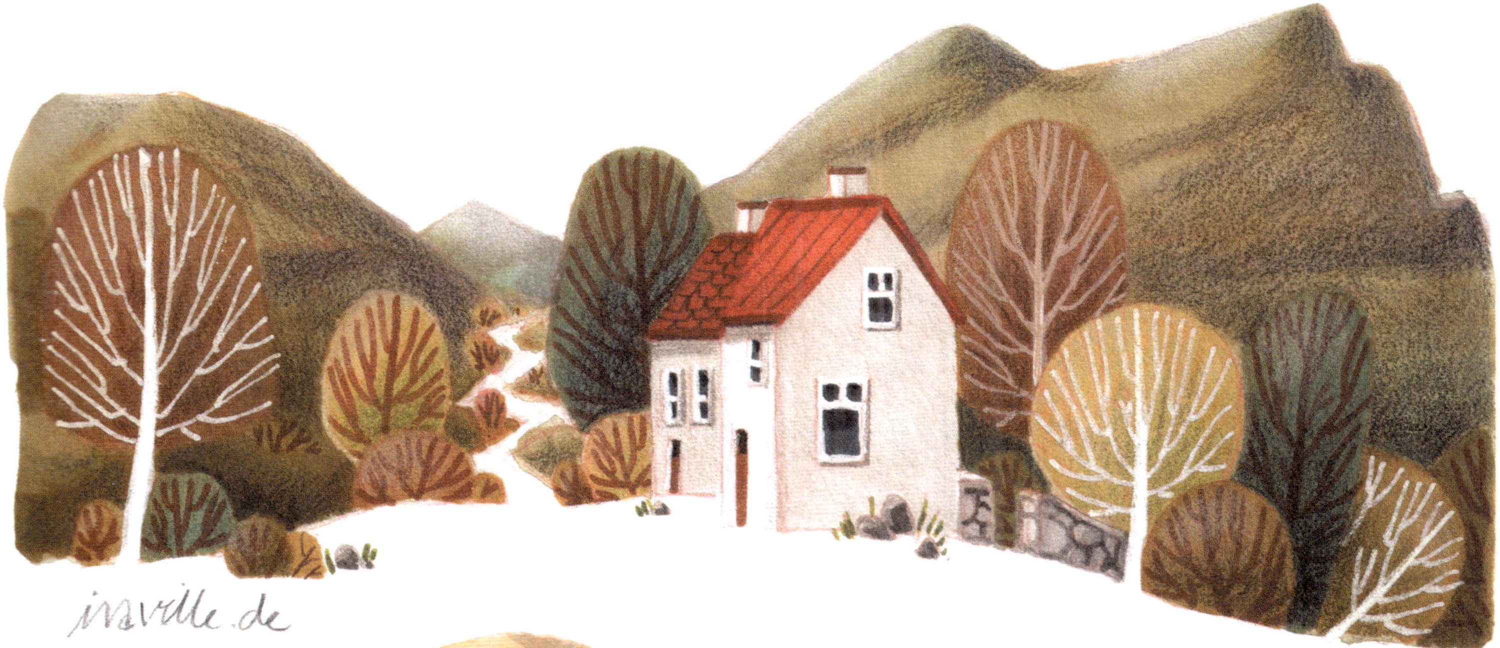

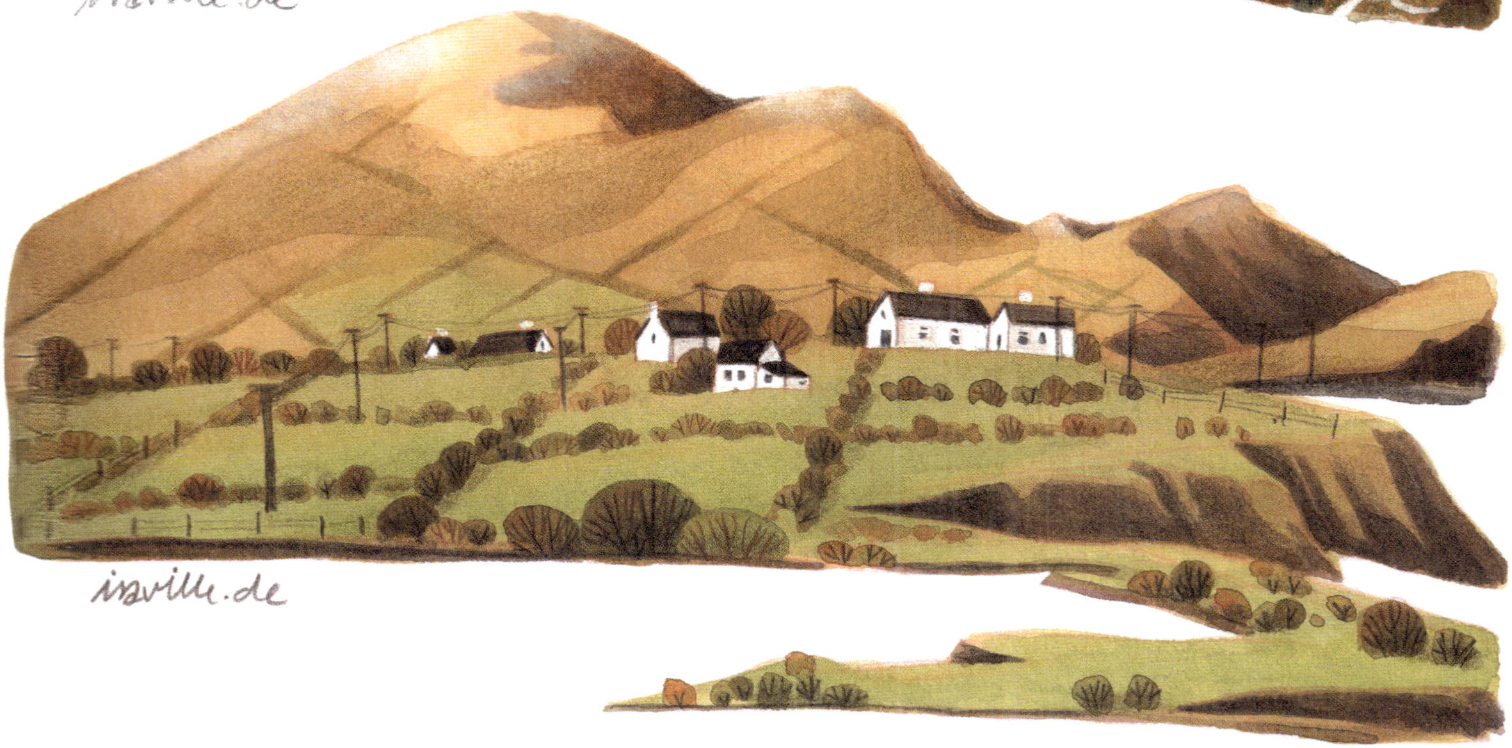

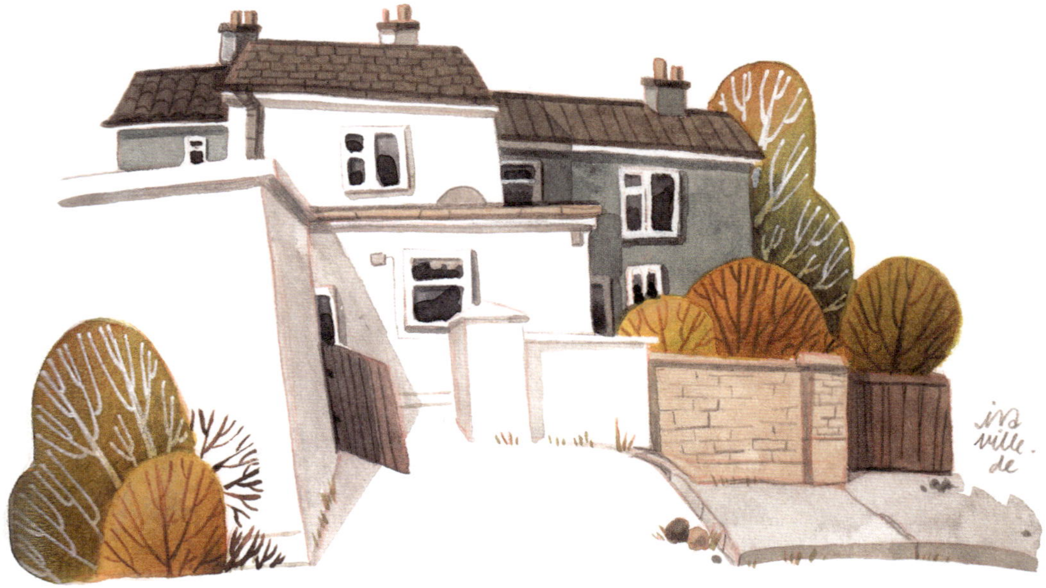

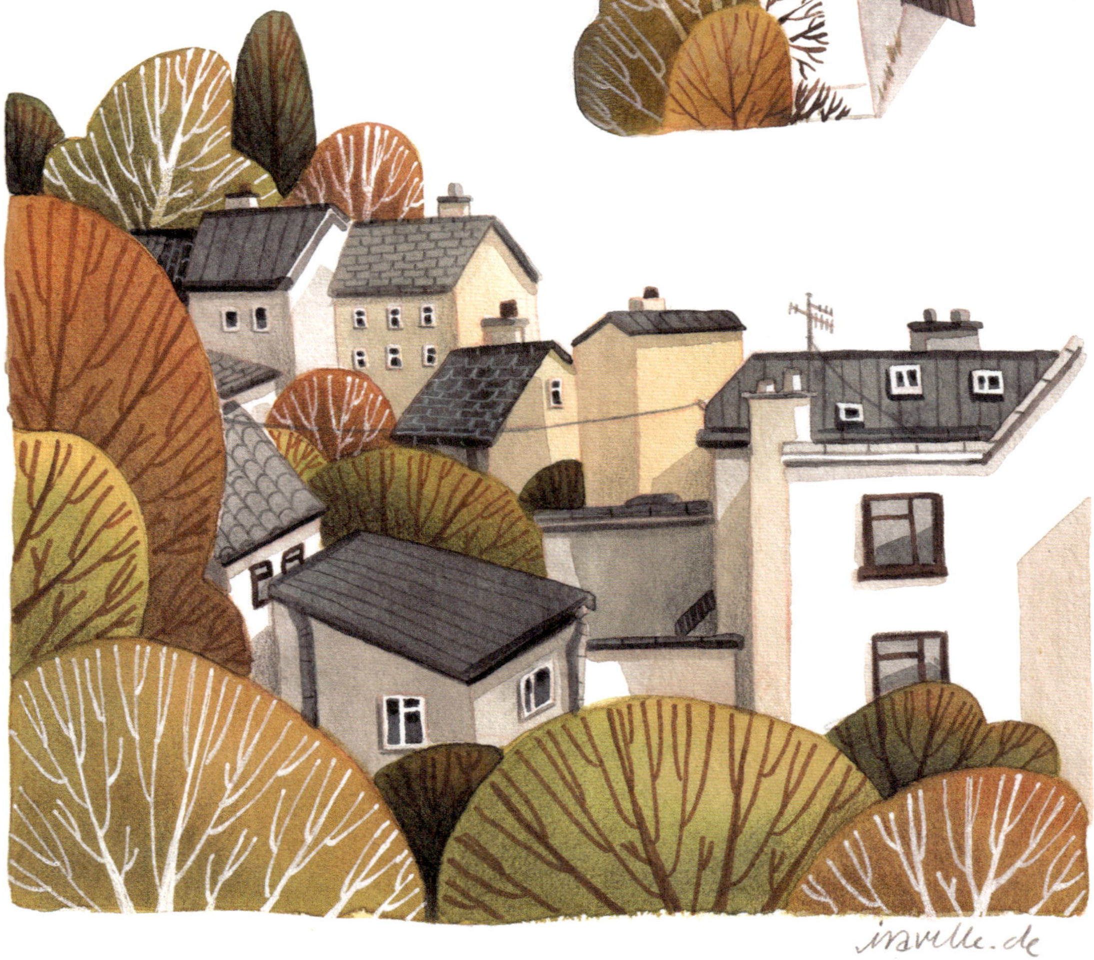

Above:

Portmagee Sketch 2, watercolour and coloured pencil, 2015

Left:

Cahersiveen, watercolour and coloured pencil, 2016

Below:
Fisherman, watercolour and coloured pencil, 2020

I saw this fisherman when I was on holiday in Ireland. He drove his motorboat through thick fog back to the harbour of a small town not far from our holiday cottage. He was accompanied by seagulls that probably wanted to steal his freshly caught fish. As always, everything here is stylized, altered, and simplified. I am not interested in reproducing the reality you see in a photograph. Instead, I focus on the drawing itself by manipulating colours, light and shadow, shapes, and the composition so that a beautiful, two-dimensional image is created in the end. I also try to reproduce mood, and it turned out quite well here.

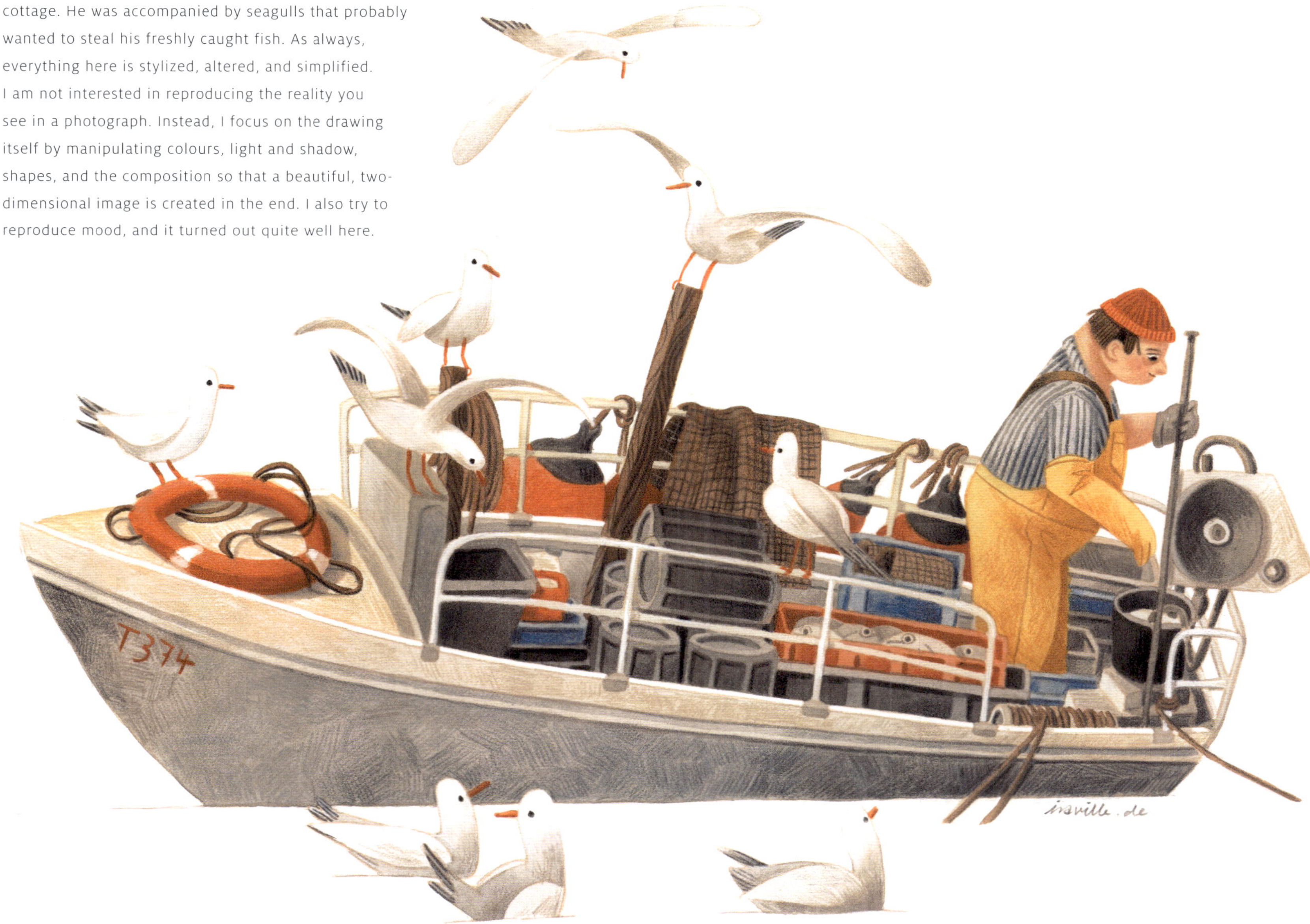

BEHIND THE SCENES

How I usually paint

I love seagulls! The other day, I thought about how much fun I had immortalizing them as the fisherman's companions (see previous page). So, I decided to dedicate a whole watercolour illustration to them, which I could use to show you my painting process.

TOOLS

❶ Watercolour paper

For this painting, I use artist-grade paper with 100% cotton and a thickness of 300 gsm. This particular cotton paper is very absorbent, so it is good for watercolour, especially when there are many layers. The colours also tend to spread nicely.

The surface is hot pressed and the grain is smooth, making it ideal for details using crayon and pencil. However, the downside is that it can be difficult to paint even gradients and layers over them. If you have good-quality hot-pressed paper, the difficulty decreases. To test the mixed colours, I use a small piece of watercolour paper, such as the back of an older artwork that did not work out the way I wanted.

❷ Watercolour brushes

I use good-quality round, tapered, and synthetic watercolour brushes in various sizes. All in all, I prefer synthetic brushes to real-hair options because they are more stable. They do not absorb the water quite as well, but you can paint more precisely with them.

❸ Colours

I always use artist-grade watercolours. For this painting, I choose five different colours: new gamboge, burnt umber, cadmium red/scarlet, Payne's grey, and perylene violet.

❹ Watercolour box

This is my standard pocket box. This time, I only use five pans with my chosen colours.

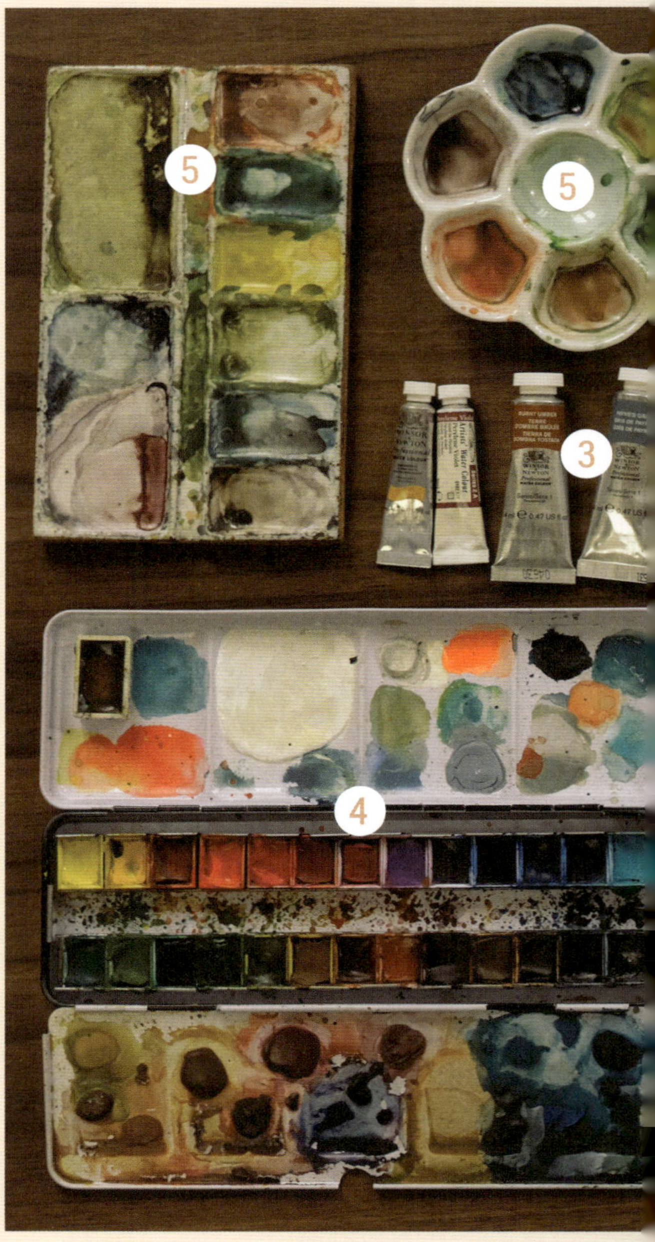

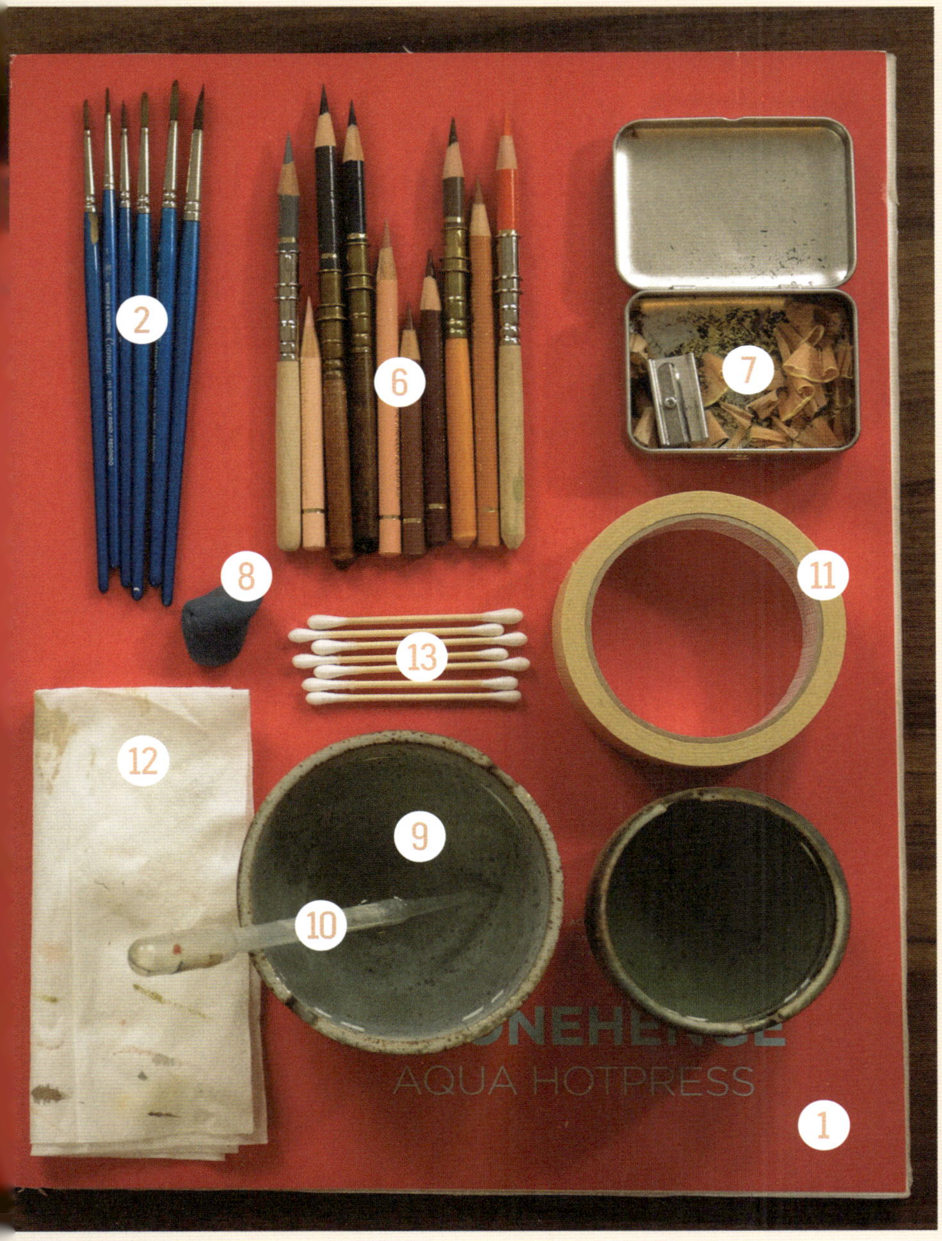

5 Ceramic palettes
Since I mix often, I use two palettes with large wells. This way, I have enough of the colours available while painting. I prefer ceramic palettes over plastic ones, as they are sturdy, will not stain, and are easier to clean. The surface also keeps the pigments from gathering in one place.

6 Coloured pencils
For the first sketch and preliminary drawings on the watercolour paper, I use a red waterproof pencil. The other pencils are for details and texture added at the end of the painting process.

7 Sharpener
I use a long-tip sharpener for the coloured pencils.

8 Eraser
The eraser I use is kneadable. I use it for the preliminary drawing.

9 Water
I use two cups of water. One is filled with clean water, which I use for mixing or adding water directly to the image for the 'wet on wet' technique, or for gradients. The other one can get a little dirty as it is just for cleaning the brushes.

10 Pipette
This is for adding clean water onto the palette.

11 Masking tape
For fixing the watercolour paper to a wood-veneer sheet (which is not shown in this picture).

12 Paper towels
For blotting my loaded brushes.

13 Cotton buds
For blending the texture from the coloured pencils.

PREPARATIONS

01: First, I look at multiple photos of seagulls and harbour scenes taken during my holiday to Ireland, as well as from the internet. Then I make individual sketches in my sketchbook with various poses and objects, such as boxes and buoys where they like to cavort.

I bound the sketchbook myself so I could use watercolour paper of my choosing. You can find a tutorial on how to make your own in my first book, *Cozy Days*. I do not make preliminary sketches for every painting, instead saving it for more complex subjects. On freer works, I will sometimes paint immediately onto the paper.

I make sure the forms look compositionally coherent – not too boring, but not too extreme. The negative space, or space around the painted forms, is equally important to me.

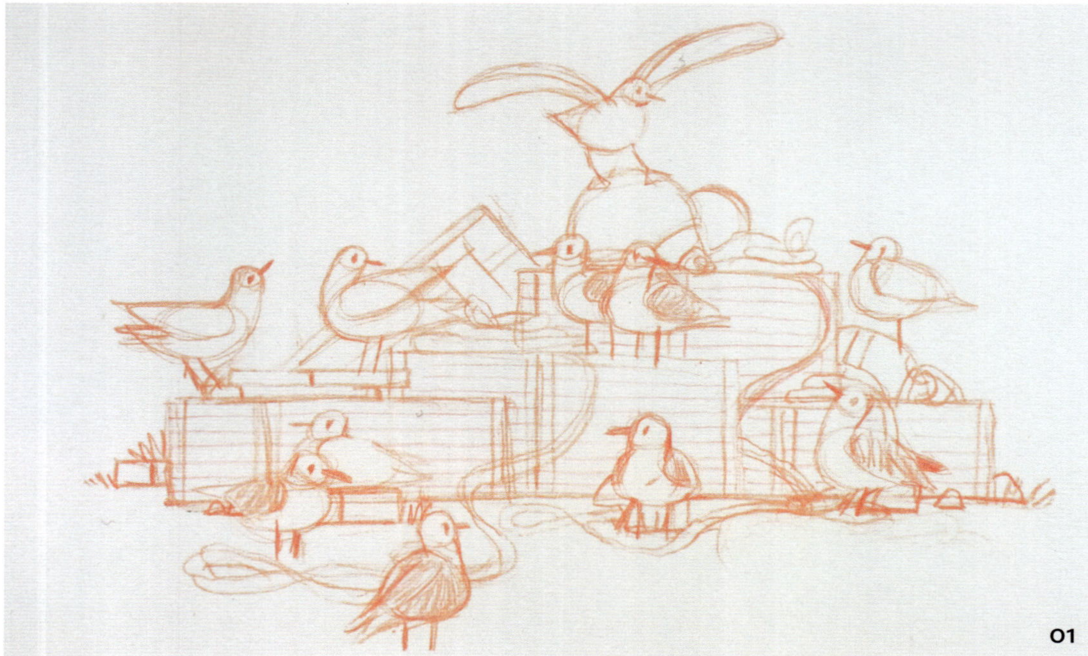

01

02: When I am satisfied with the composition, it is time to consider the colour scheme. In this case, I choose five colours and try out several mixtures in my sketchbook, using various amounts of water. I sometimes do colour trials before beginning, but I also love to override my own plans and mix differently during the process. It does not matter what I had planned – I know better than my past self!

I never use colours directly, because mixing them makes it much more interesting and less flat. But too much mixing can make the colours look dirty, especially with poorer-quality paints. The same goes for pigments that are opaque, as well as ones that have white or black pigments. I therefore avoid these colours. You can use the white of the paper to show white areas or ones with pale, light colours.

Black and grey look much more interesting when mixed from dark complementary colours like dark blue and brown. Doesn't the black look great here? It is just a mix of burnt umber, Payne's grey, and perylene violet.

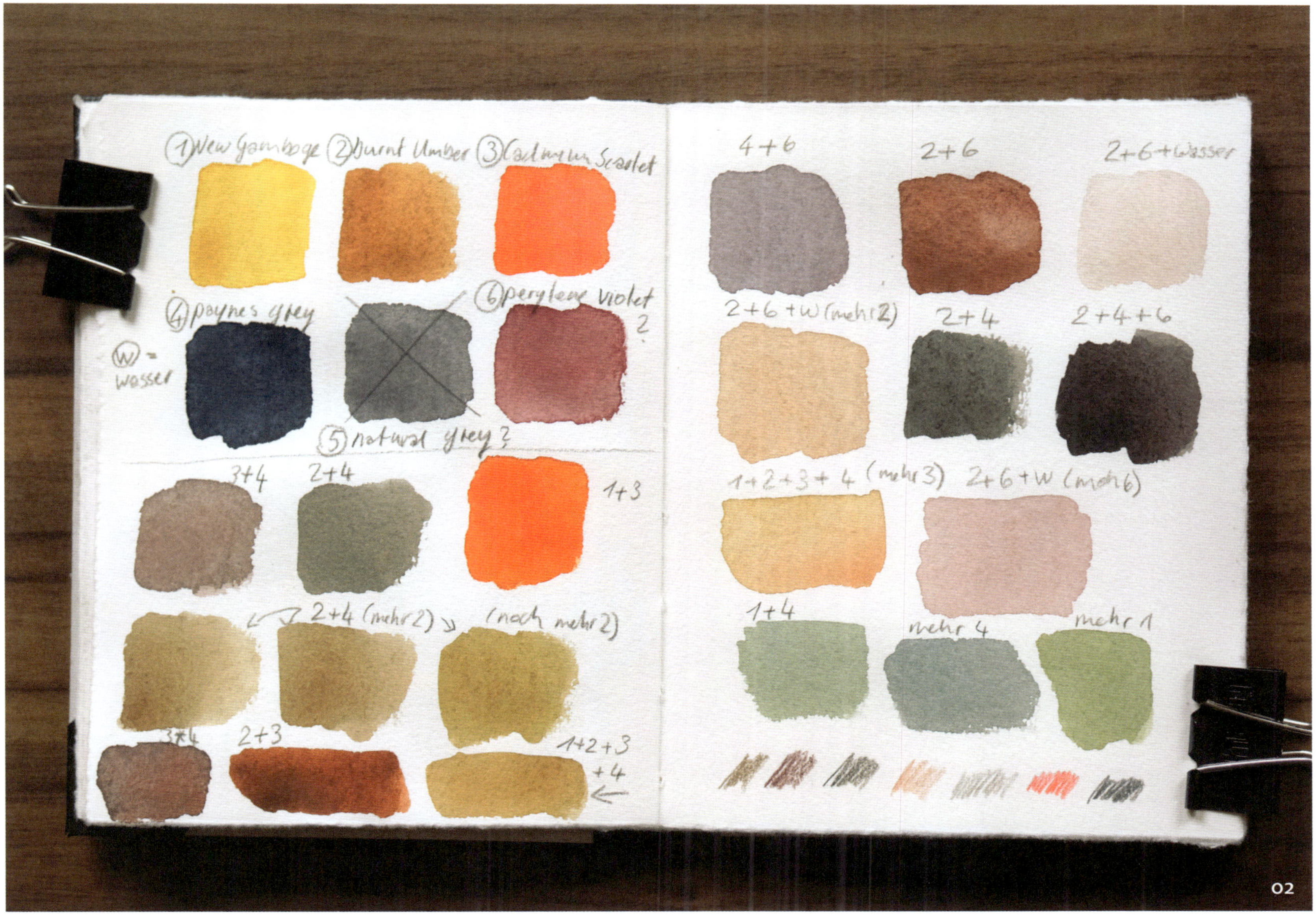

1 New Gamboge
2 Burnt Umber
3 Cadmium Scarlet
4 paynes grey
W = wasser
6 perylene violet
5 natural grey?
3+4
2+4
1+3
2+4 (mehr 2)
(noch mehr 2)
3+4
2+3
1+2+3 +4
4+6
2+6
2+6+wasser
2+6+W (mehr 2)
2+4
2+4+6
1+2+3+4 (mehr 3)
2+6+W (mehr 6)
1+4
mehr 4
mehr 1

02

03: I apply colours to the sketch on a trial basis. Again, I do not always do this, but in this case, it helps me find colours that match each other while creating interesting contrasts. When I do it this way, I am not concerned with the sketch itself looking good. This step will help the final image to look great. I unabashedly write little notes directly on the sketch. In this case, I note (in German): 'Boards from the boxes further apart/less', 'shadows: more Payne's grey', 'beaks: more new gamboge', and 'other form of rope'.

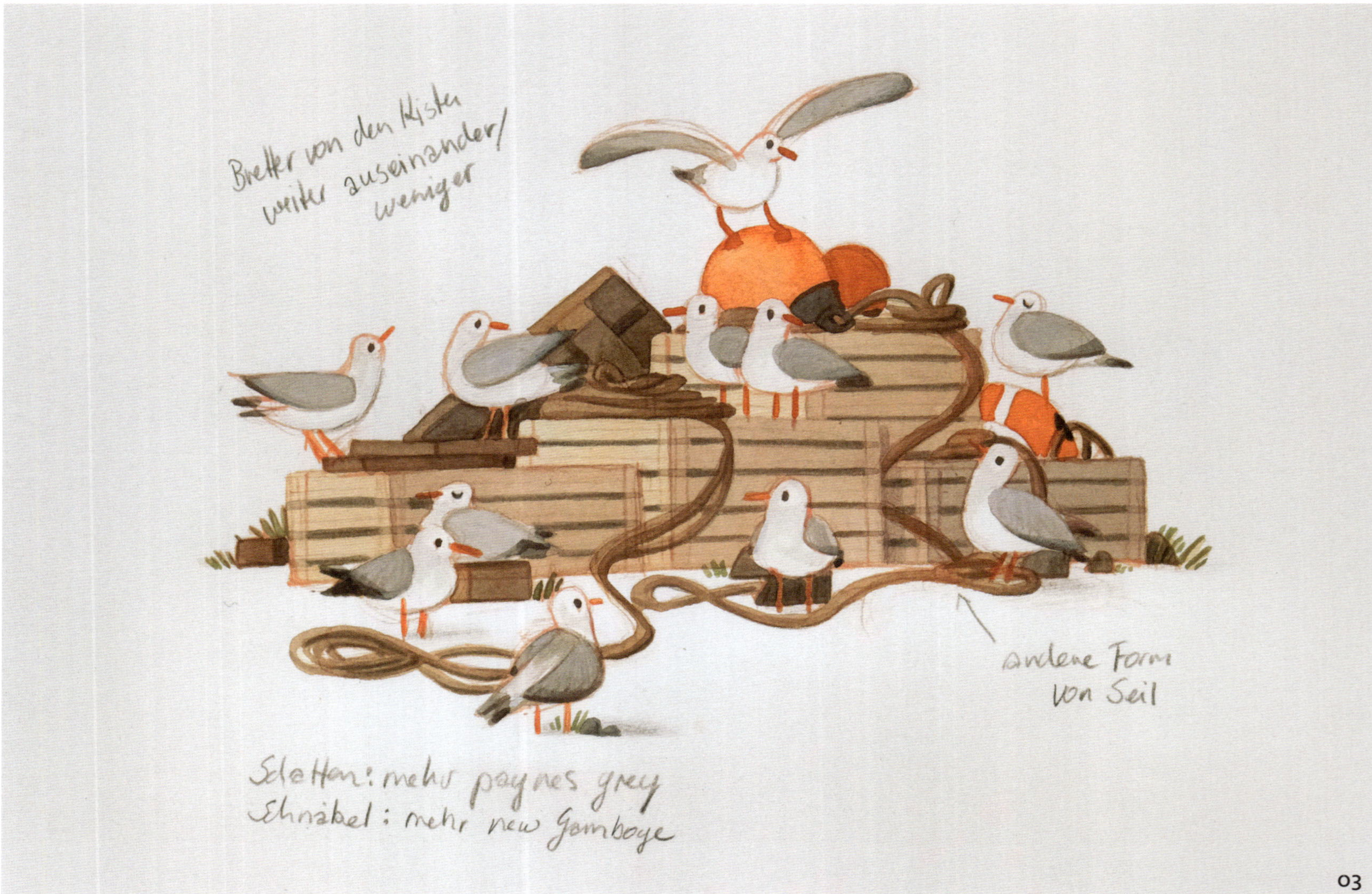

03

04: Having already scanned the original sketch before colouring, I print it out in the size I want. During this process, I adjust the tonal values to get darker strokes that I can use for tracing on my light table with my red waterproof pencil. This creates a large, detailed preliminary drawing, directly on watercolour paper. I always apply the lines delicately so that they will not show in the finished picture.

Sometimes I make the preliminary drawings the traditional way (directly onto watercolour paper), but the digital process is helpful when planning more complex drawings; I do not have to use an eraser that might damage the paper's condition.

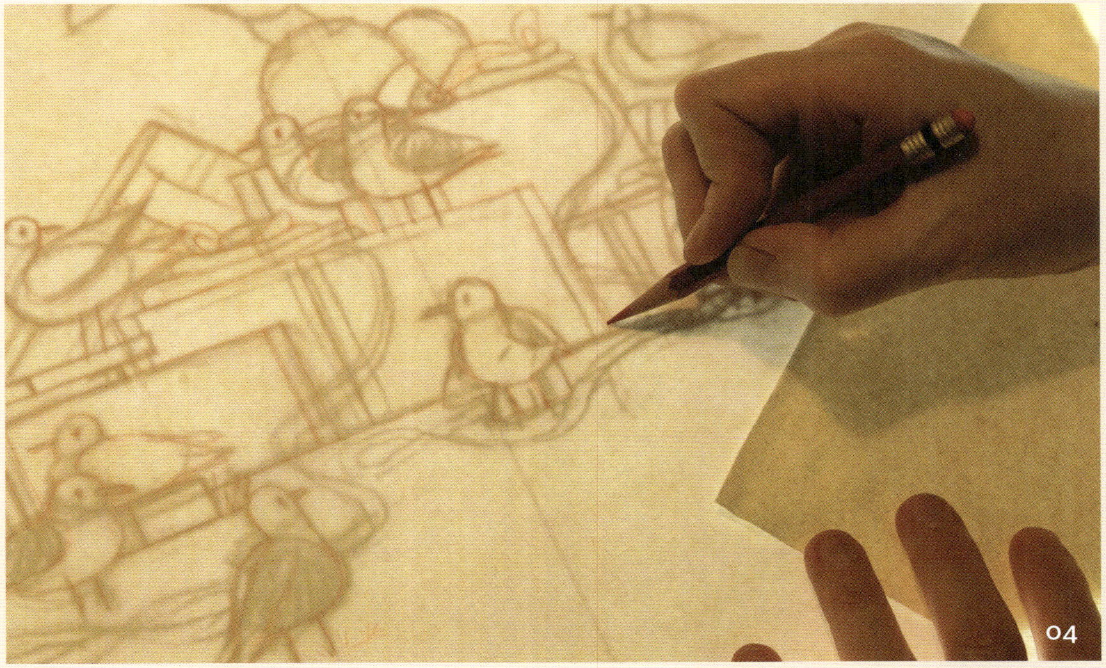
04

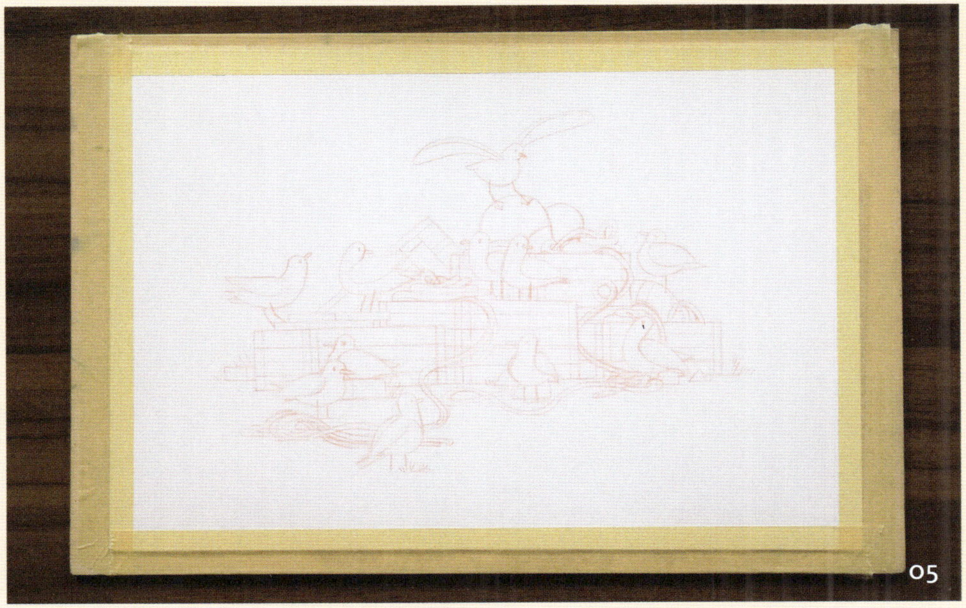
05

05: Using masking tape, I fix the watercolour paper to a wood-veneer sheet so that the paper does not curl while painting. The potential dangers are minimal because there is a lot of free space around the actual motif, and I use relatively thick paper.

THE FINAL PAINTING PROCESS

06: There are two main techniques in watercolour painting: wet on wet (wash) and wet on dry. Additionally, there is dry on wet and dry on dry. All other techniques are based off of these.

In this picture, I mostly use wet on dry, combined with glazing. This means that I will gradually apply very thin layers of paint that partially cover the white of the underlying paper. Depending on the pigment and density – which can be controlled by the proportion of water – a particular colour impression is created. After each newly applied layer, I wait until the colour is completely dry before continuing the process.

As before, I start with a very light first layer for the boxes, ropes, and bricks. For this, I use a mixture of burnt umber and perelyne violet combined with a lot of water. The difficulty lies with making sure the layer is not too light, but also not too dark. If it becomes too light, I may need too many layers. It would not be the end of the world, but the edges would not end up looking as clean as I would like.

If I start with too little water, the boards will look darker than I want, and the image will have failed before it even started. You cannot make a layer lighter if it is too dark. To judge this correctly, you need a lot of experience because you always have to consider relations. A layer that initially seems too dark can appear just right in the overall context of the picture.

07: The next two layers consist of a smaller mixture of colours. I use it for areas on the boxes and bricks that should be darker or further away.

I make the gradient by dabbing a darker mixture with pigment (wet on wet) where it should be dark.

08: For the seagulls' beaks, buoys, and life ring, I apply a mix of cadmium scarlet and new gamboge.

09: I continue to build up the dark areas by adding a reddish-brown tone.

10: Adding two more layers creates the shadows on the boxes, ropes, and the triangular shape towards the back. To achieve this, I mix a slightly colder shade of violet from perelyne violet and Payne's grey.

Mixing black with a large quantity of water creates a very light grey gradient, which makes the seagull bodies look more plastic. I always consider which direction the light is coming from to apply shadows.

For me, composition takes precedence over naturalism, which is why the shadows are often not shown as they would appear in reality. Sometimes, I even omit parts if they disturb the overall impression.

11: I apply the black shade for the buoy and stones. For the latter, I use more water to make them look grey, or dark grey – not black.

12: I add a second darker layer to the buoy and the life ring in the background.

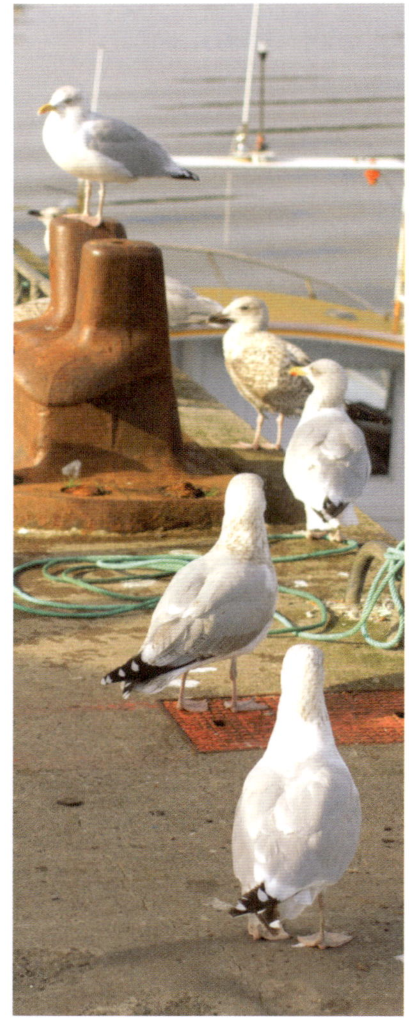

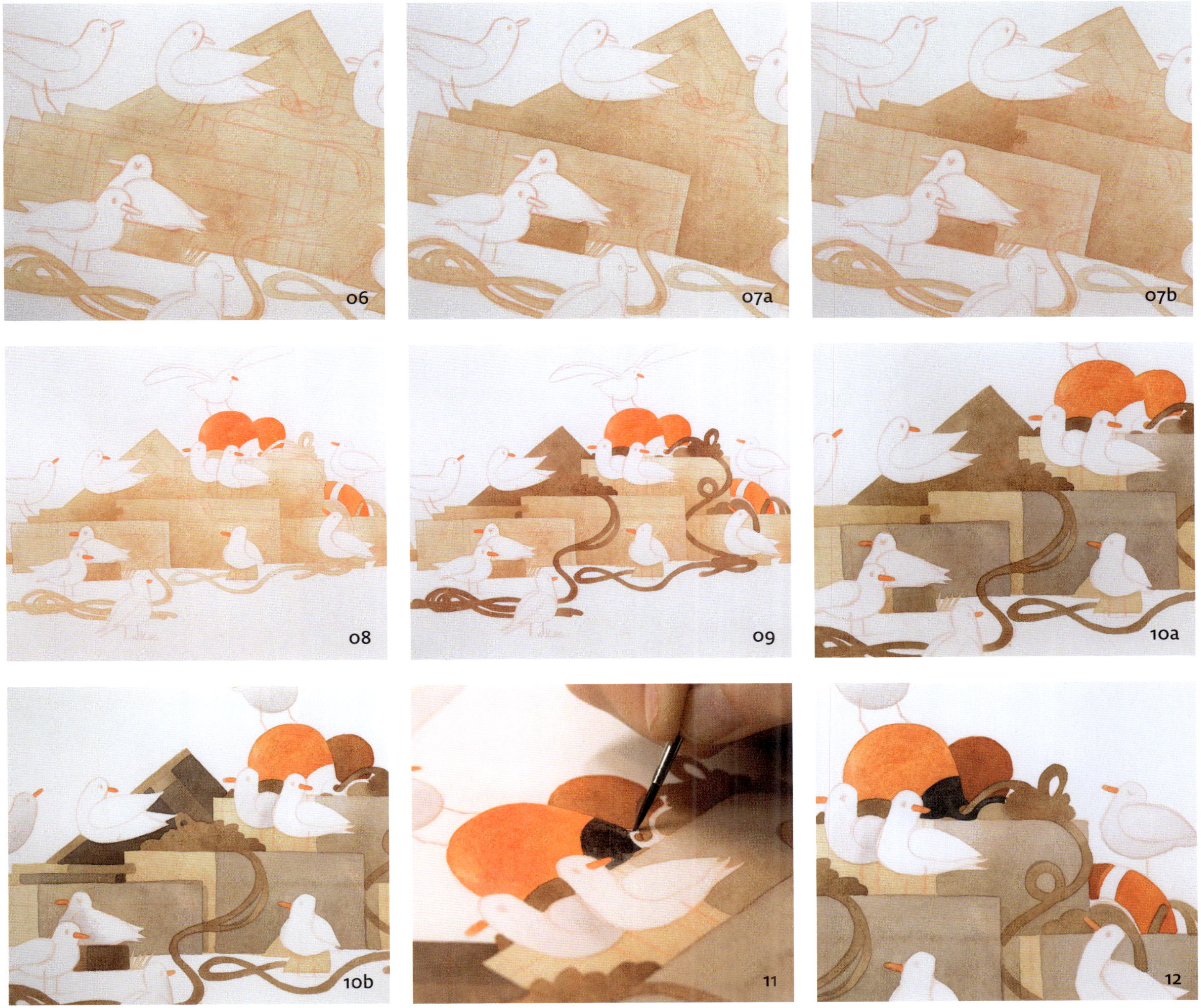
06
07a
07b
08
09
10a
10b
11
12

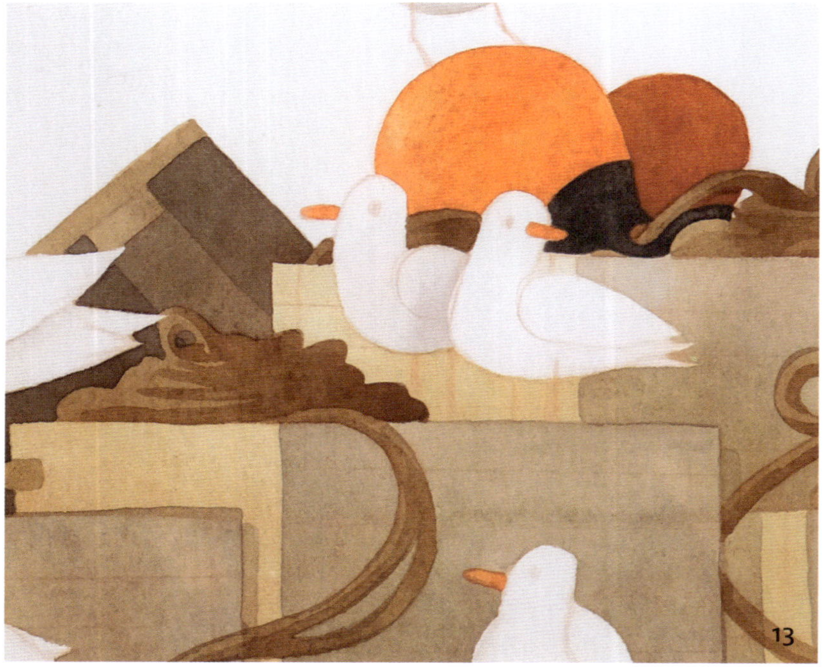

13

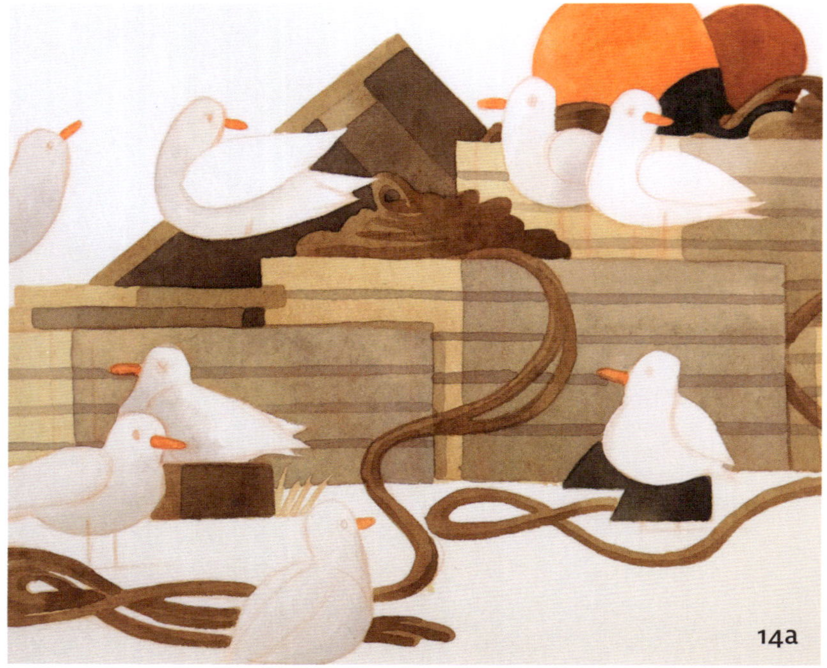

14a

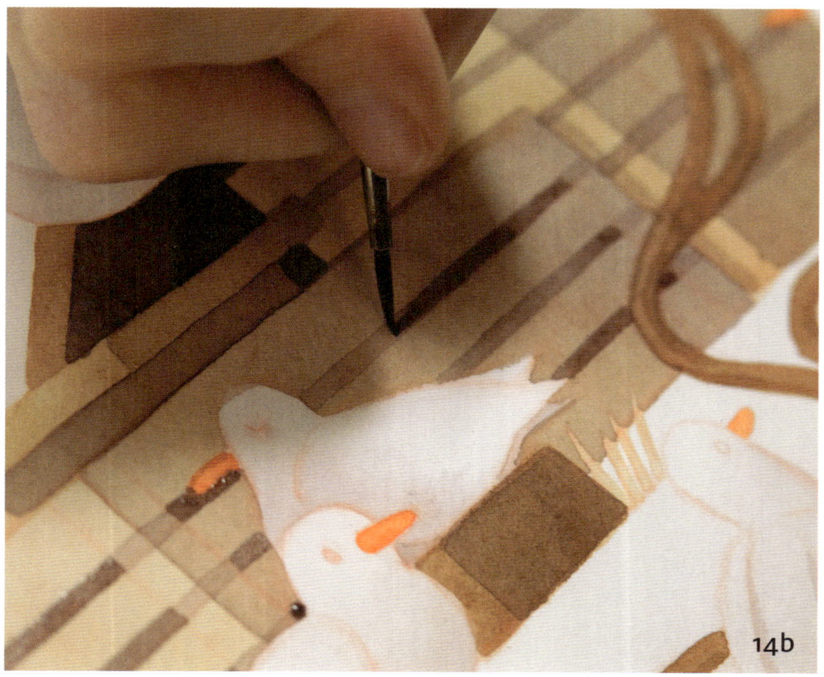

14b

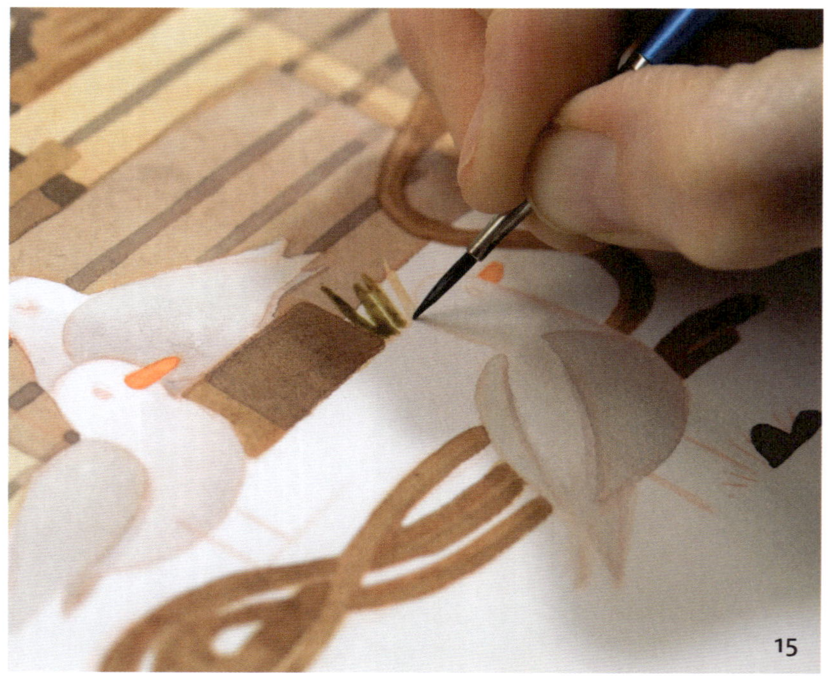

15

13: Another layer in a dark-brown shade creates an appearance of flexibility in the ropes.

14: The darker spaces between the boxes' individual boards are still missing. I apply two layers, one after the other, making sure the second layer only falls in the spaces between the boards. It should be darker than the box corners.

15: The blades of grass get two coats of green paint that I mix from new gamboge and Payne's grey.

16: On the underside of the beaks, I apply another layer of red paint to make it look darker than the top. At the same time, I paint the gulls' legs red. After that has dried, I add another grey layer to their wings.

17: Using a fine, pointed brush, I paint small black dots to represent their eyes.

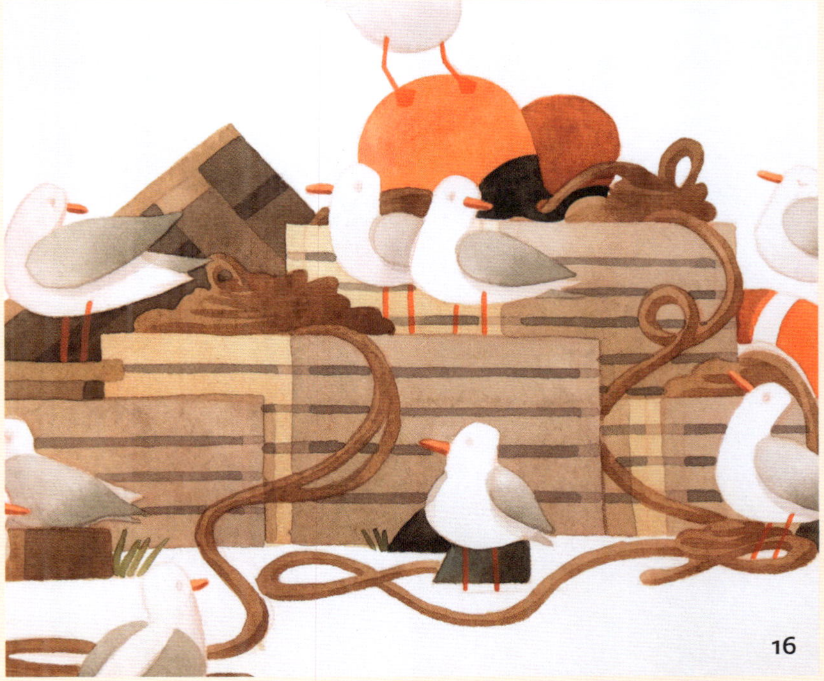

16

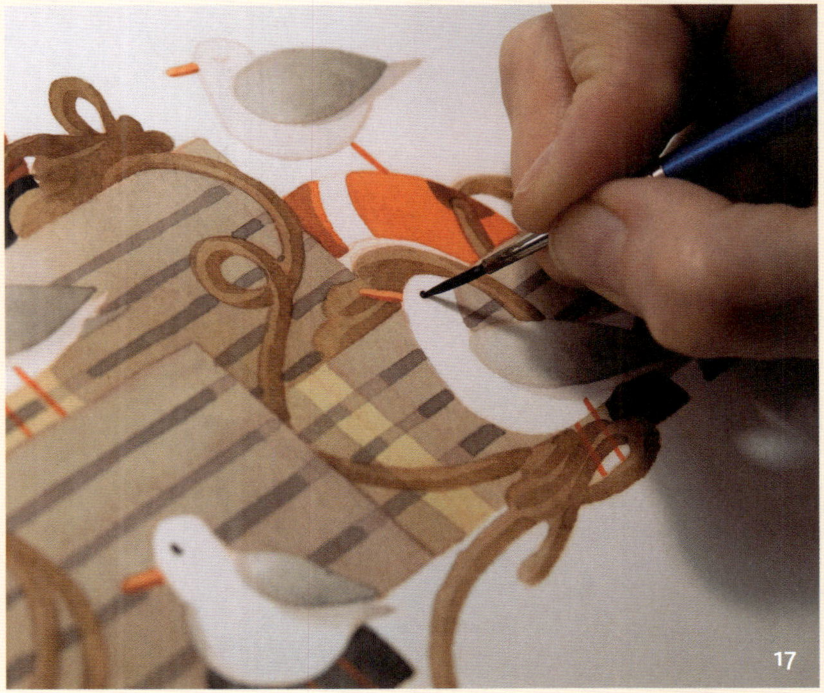

17

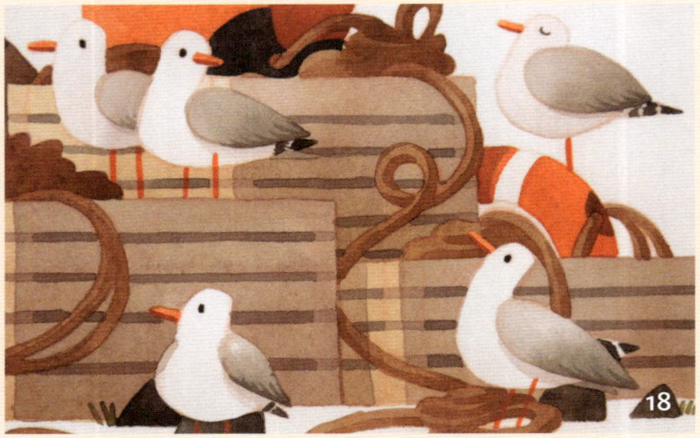

18

18: I add dark-grey details to their wing tips and tails. This completes the watercolour section.

19: Once everything is dry, I add small details with the coloured pencils. I like to mix different techniques. The ropes get their structure this way, and I also hint at individual feathers on the gulls.

20: Now that the painting is finished, I scan it and use an image-editing program to adjust the tonal values and colours to match the original painting. I also erase remaining paper-structure fragments so that they are not seen in the digital version.

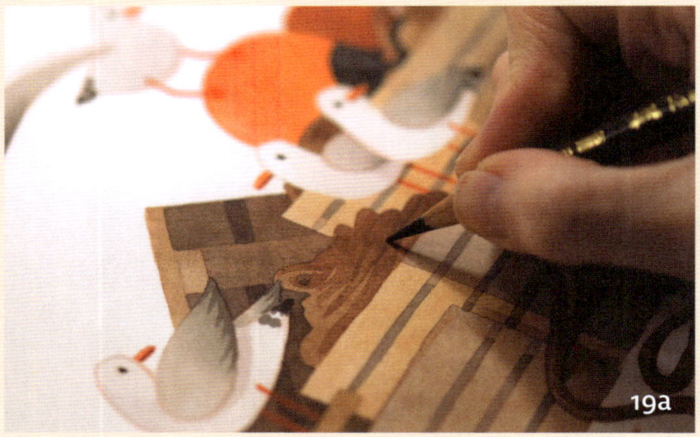

19a

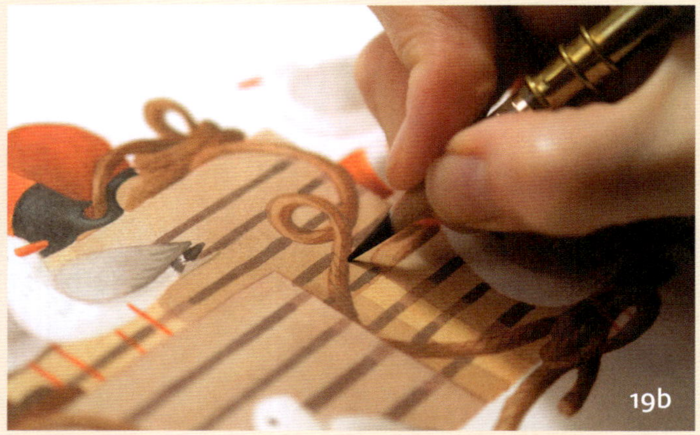

19b

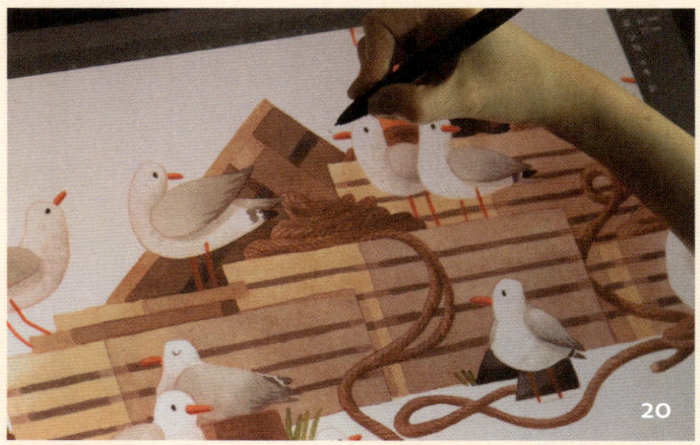

20

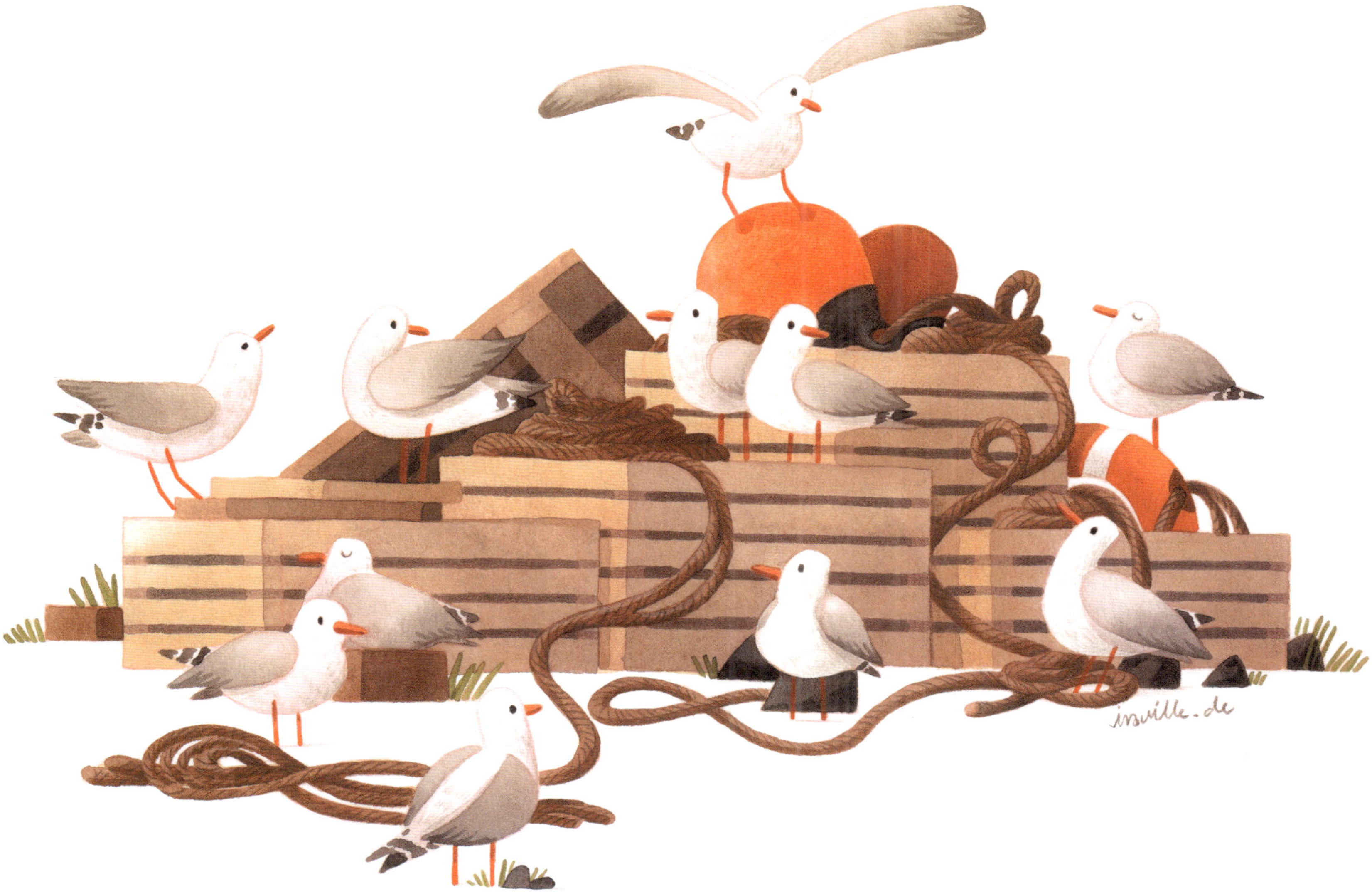

GALLERY

People

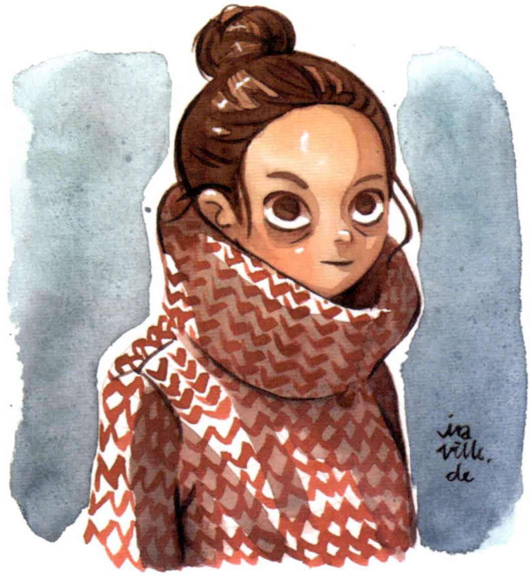

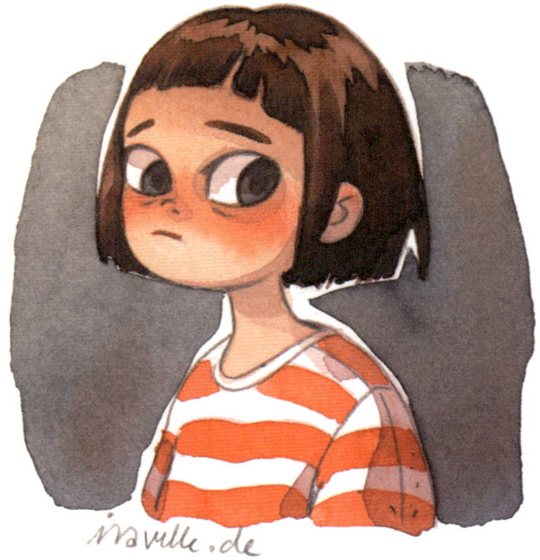

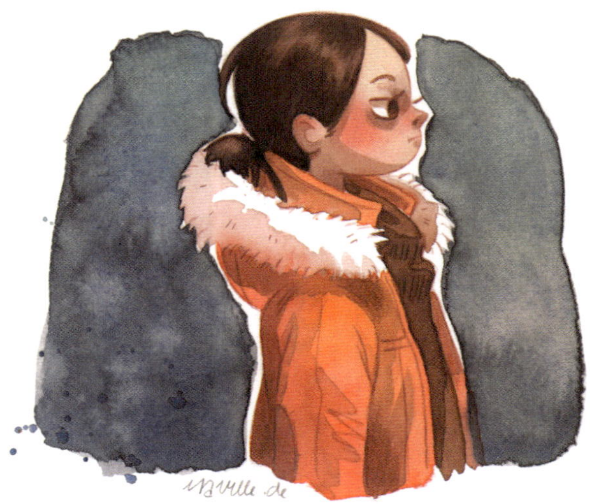

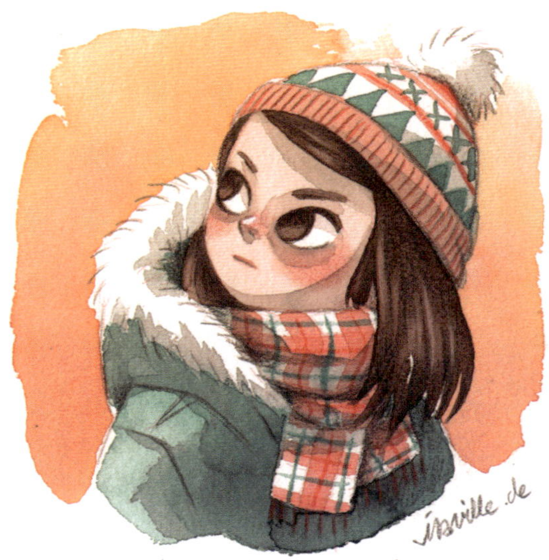

BACKGROUND

Clockwise from top left:
Cozy Turtleneck Sweater Girl, watercolour and coloured pencil, 2015

Sad Girl, watercolour and coloured pencil, 2015

Girl with Scarf and Wool Hat, watercolour and coloured pencil, 2015

Winter Walk, watercolour and coloured pencil, 2016

FLOWER GIRLS

Left:

Flower Girl 1, watercolour and coloured pencil, 2015

Below:

Flower Girl 2, watercolour and coloured pencil, 2015

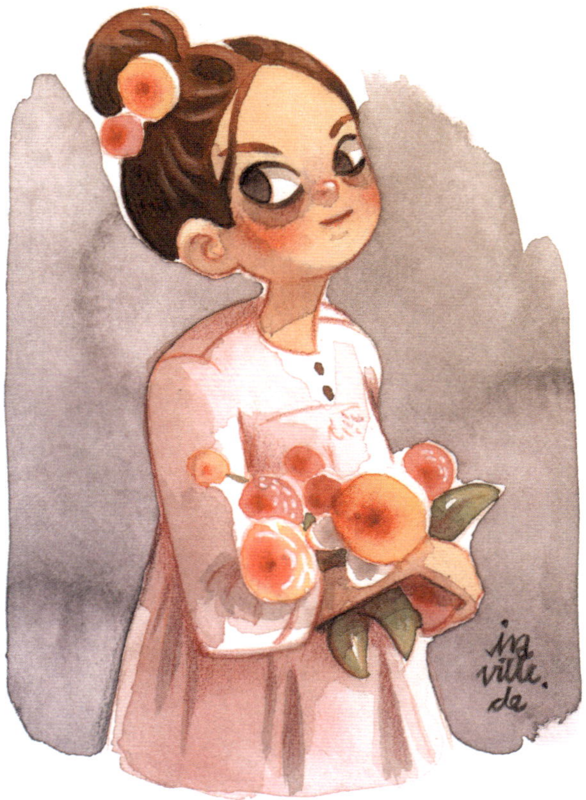

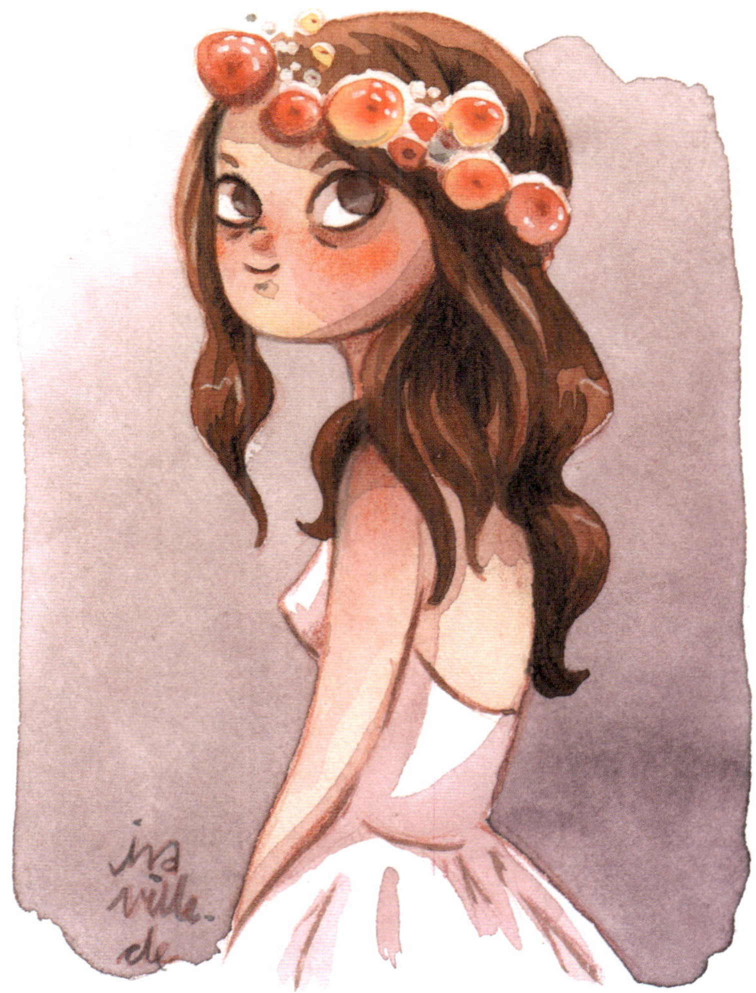

GIRL SKETCHES

This page:
Girl Sketch 1–4, ink and gouache, 2014

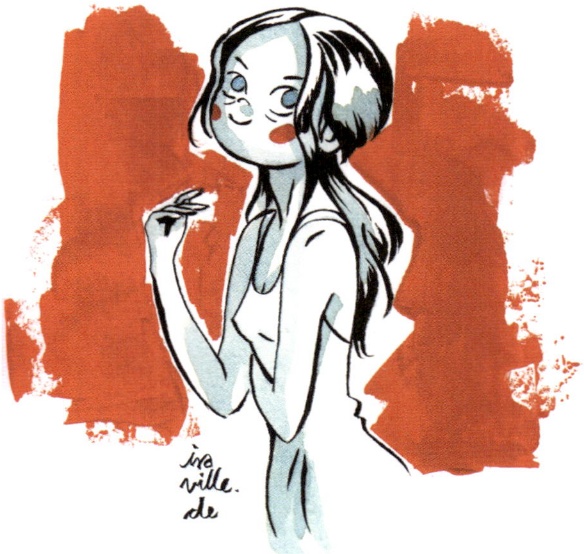

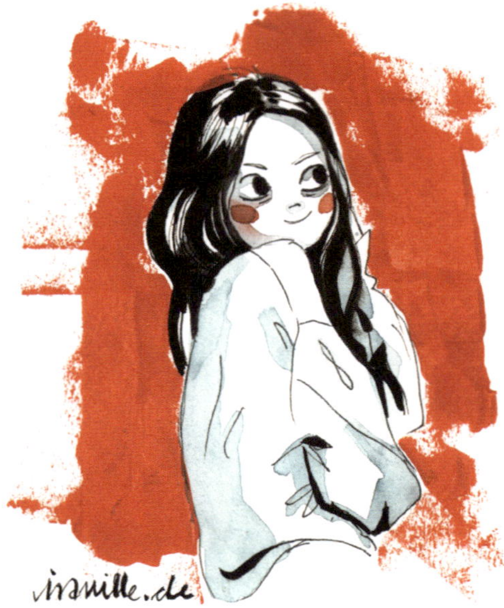

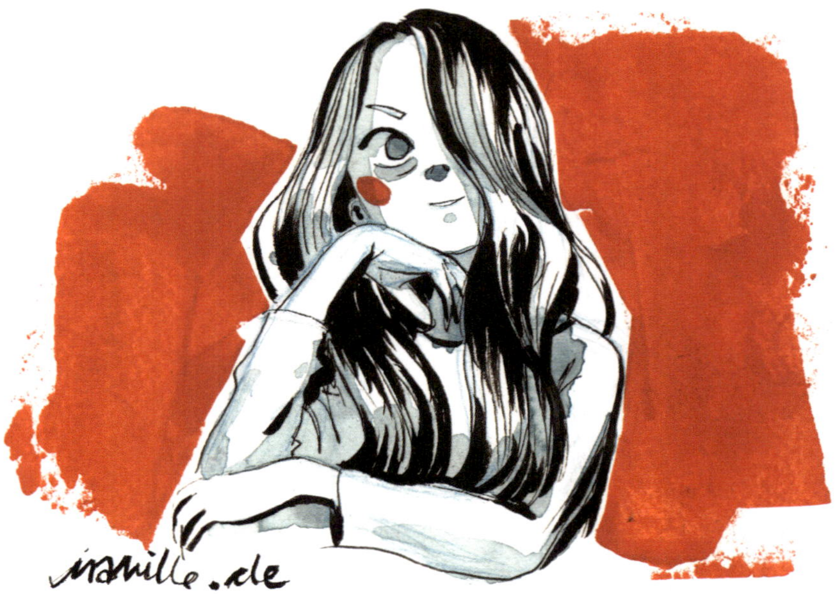

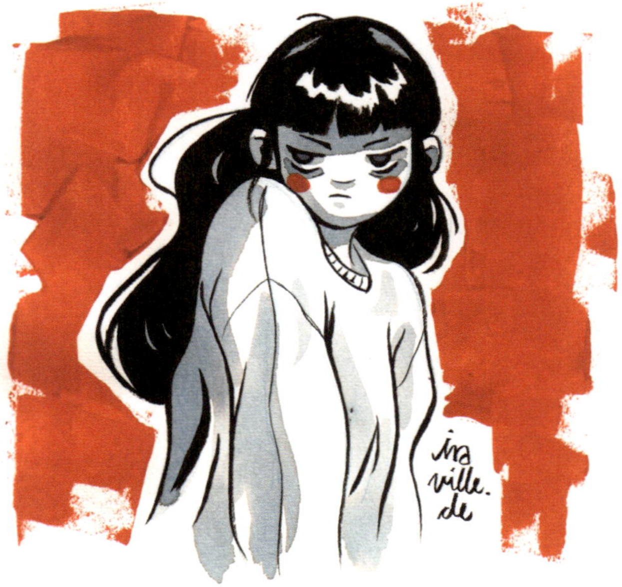

INK

Left:
Angry Girl, ink, 2015

Left (below):
Fire Hair, ink, 2015

Right (below):
Girl with Headband, ink, 2015

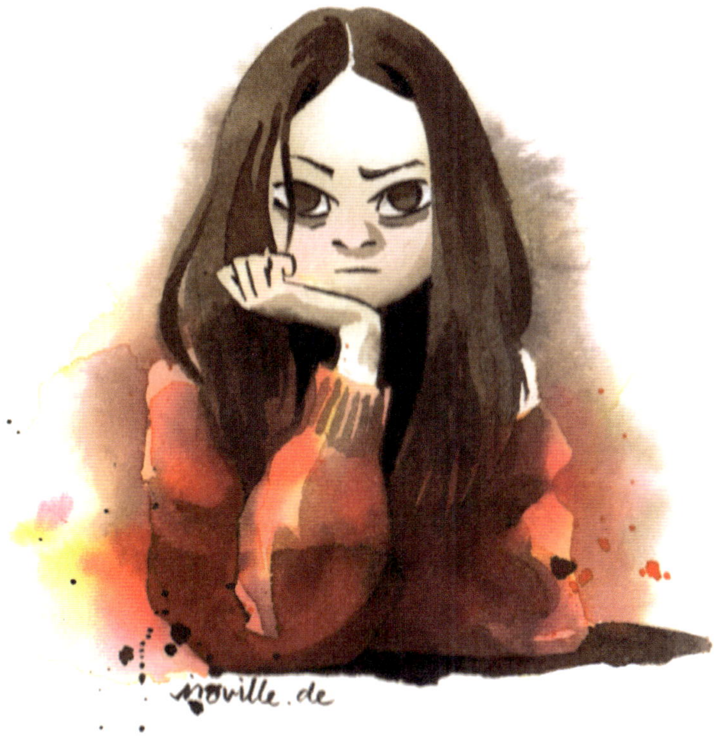

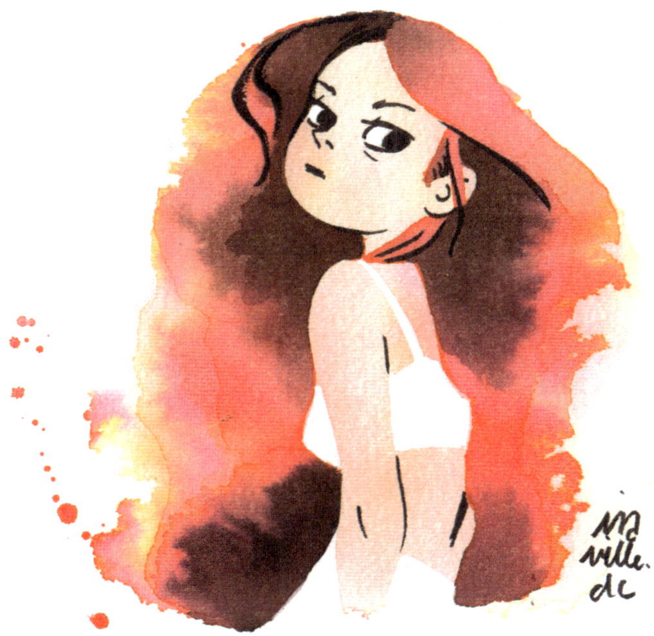

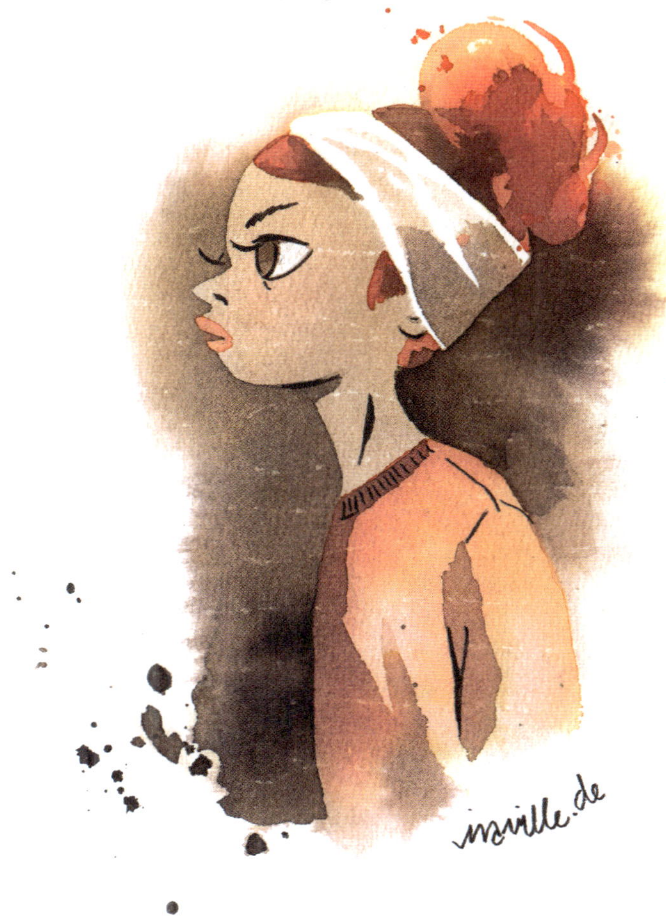

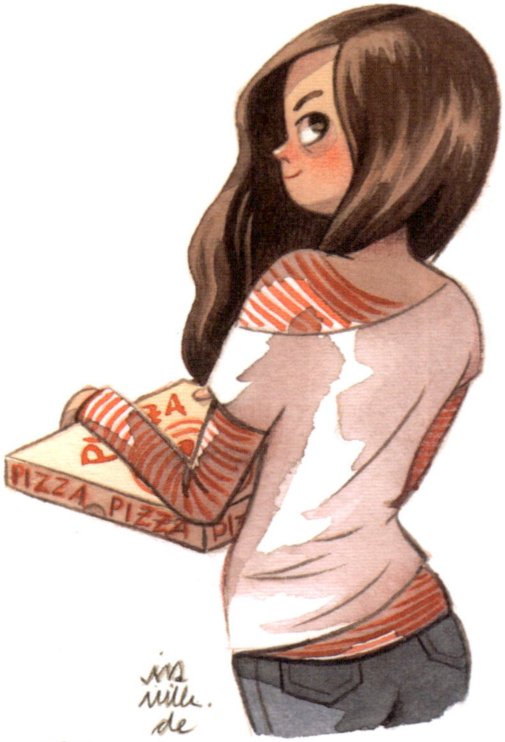

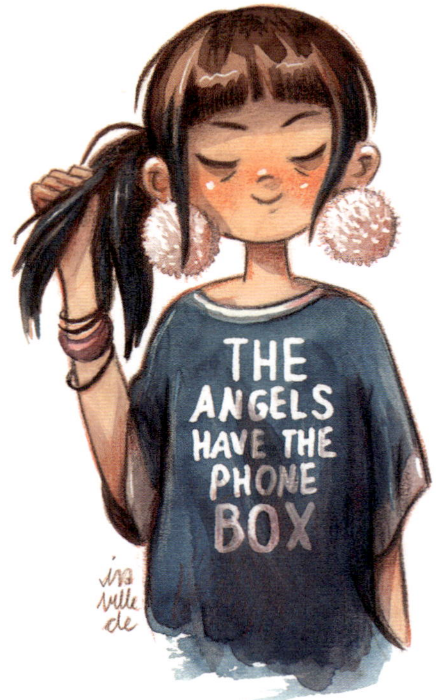

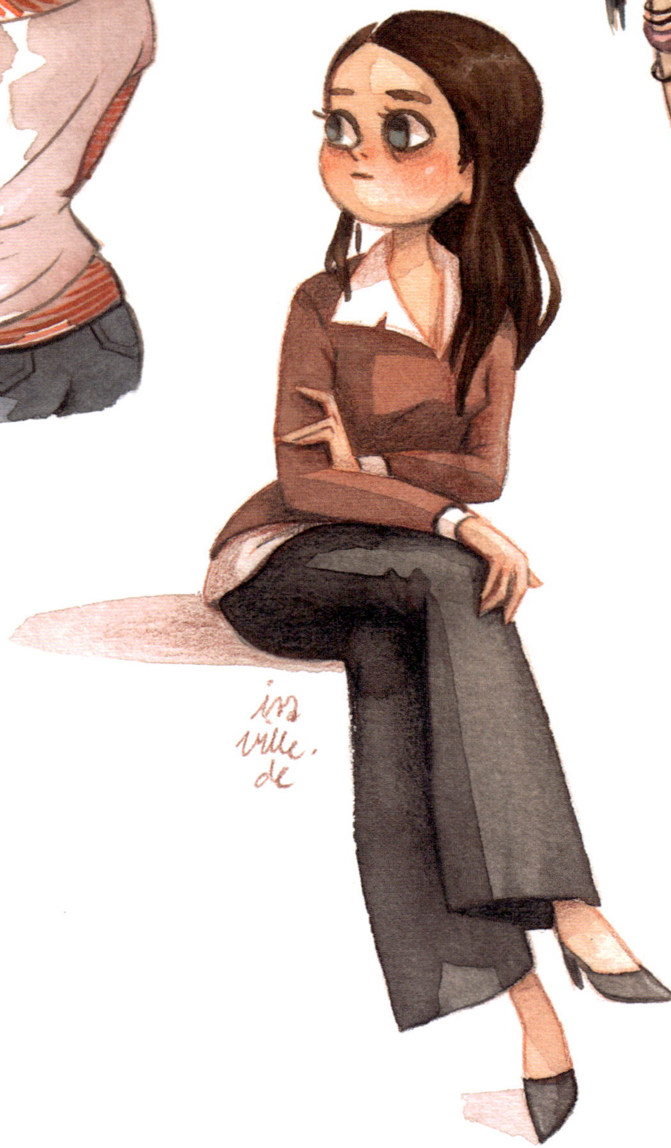

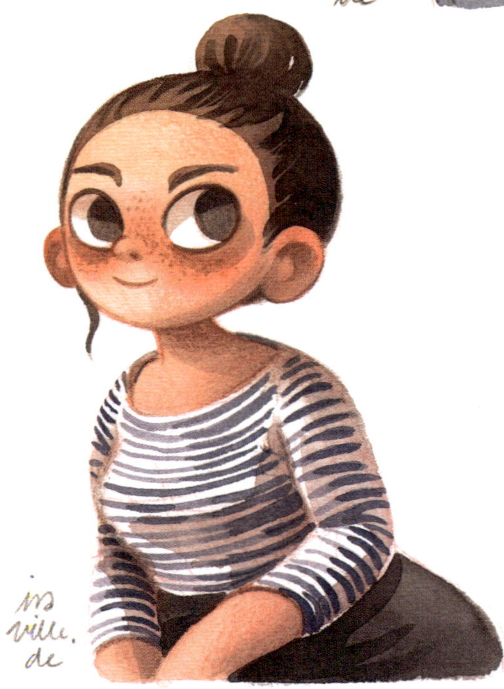

Clockwise from top left:

Pizza, watercolour and coloured pencil, 2015

Don't Blink, watercolour and coloured pencil, 2015

Waiting, watercolour and coloured pencil, 2015

Little Round Lady, watercolour and coloured pencil, 2017

Opposite page:

Head Sketches, Copic marker and coloured pencil, 2022

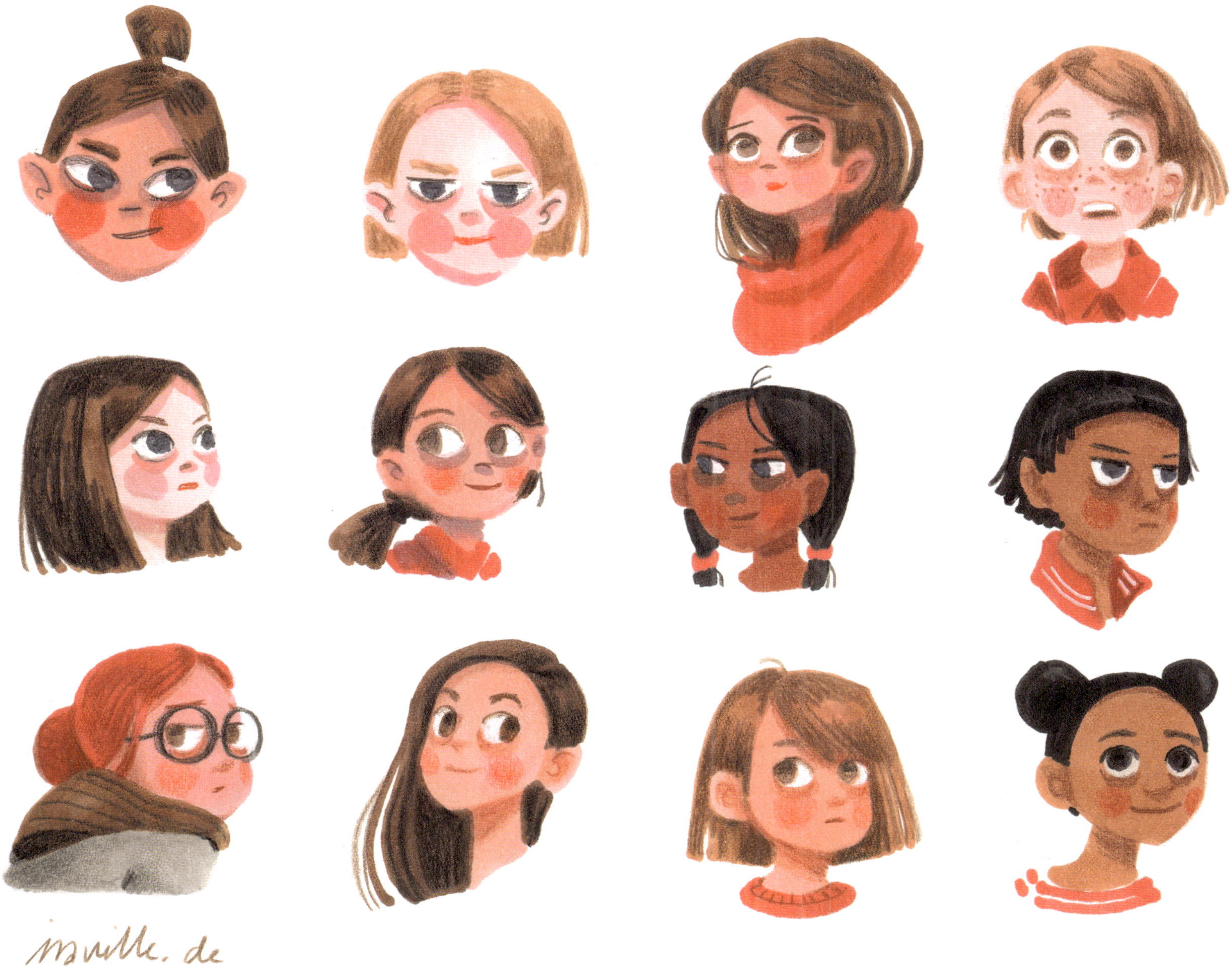

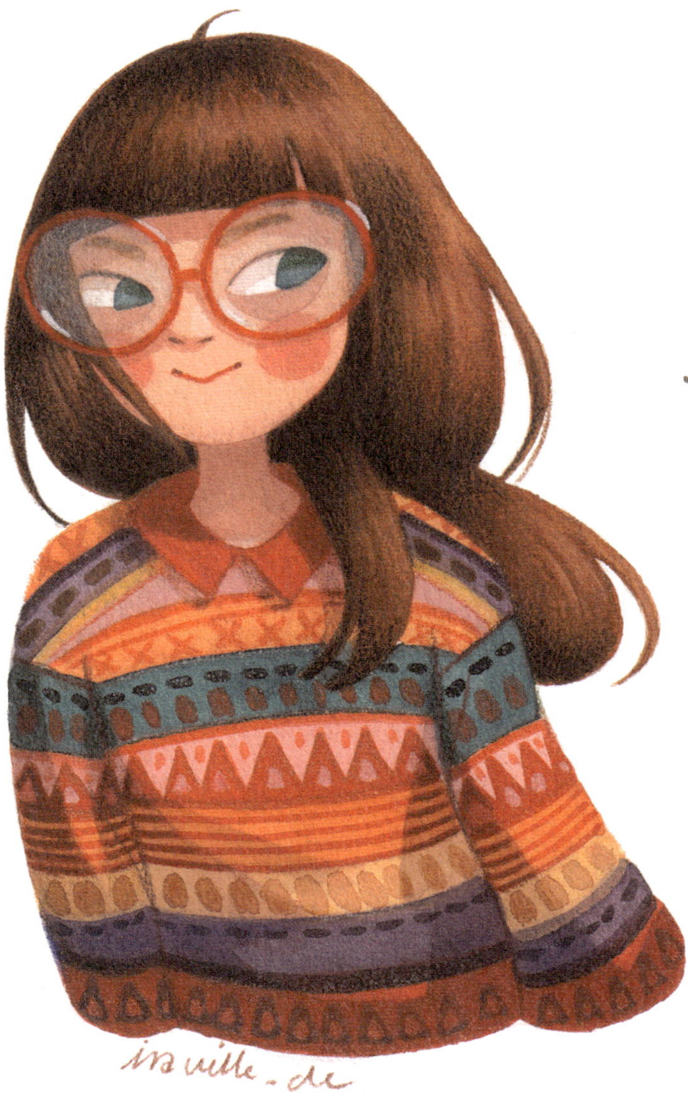

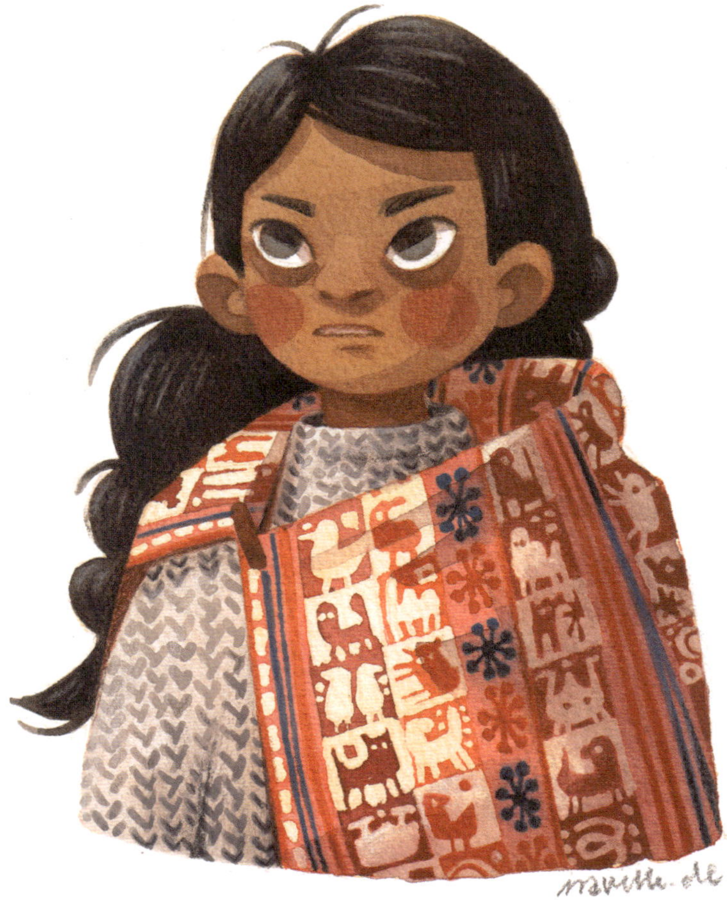

Left:

Girl with Patterned Sweater, watercolour and coloured pencil, 2020

Above:

Peruvian Girl, watercolour and coloured pencil, 2021

I felt like drawing a motif that had patterns in it. Knowing that the traditional costumes of the indigenous Peruvian people are often varied and creatively patterned, I took inspiration from them and came up with my own version of a Peruvian girl. Like many of my characters, she does not just smile sweetly, but looks a bit fierce, or even angry. A strong Peruvian girl.

Clockwise from right:
Happy Floating Girl, watercolour and coloured pencil, 2020

Girl in Yellow Raincoat, watercolour and coloured pencil, 2020

Pattern Girl 3, watercolour and coloured pencil, 2015

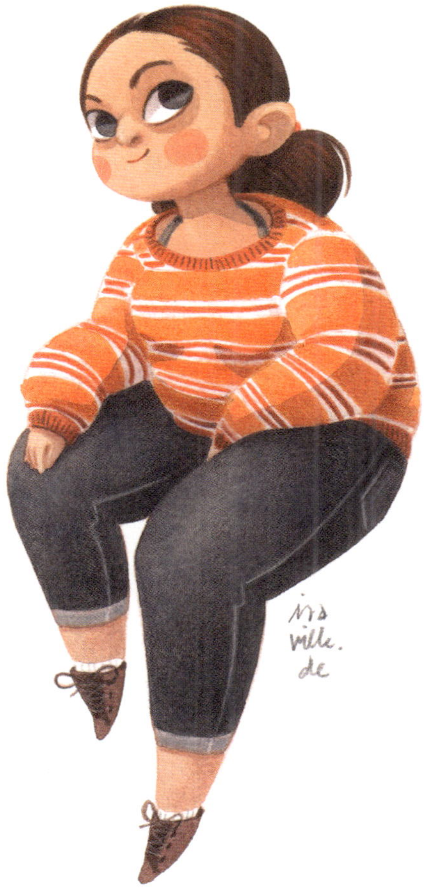

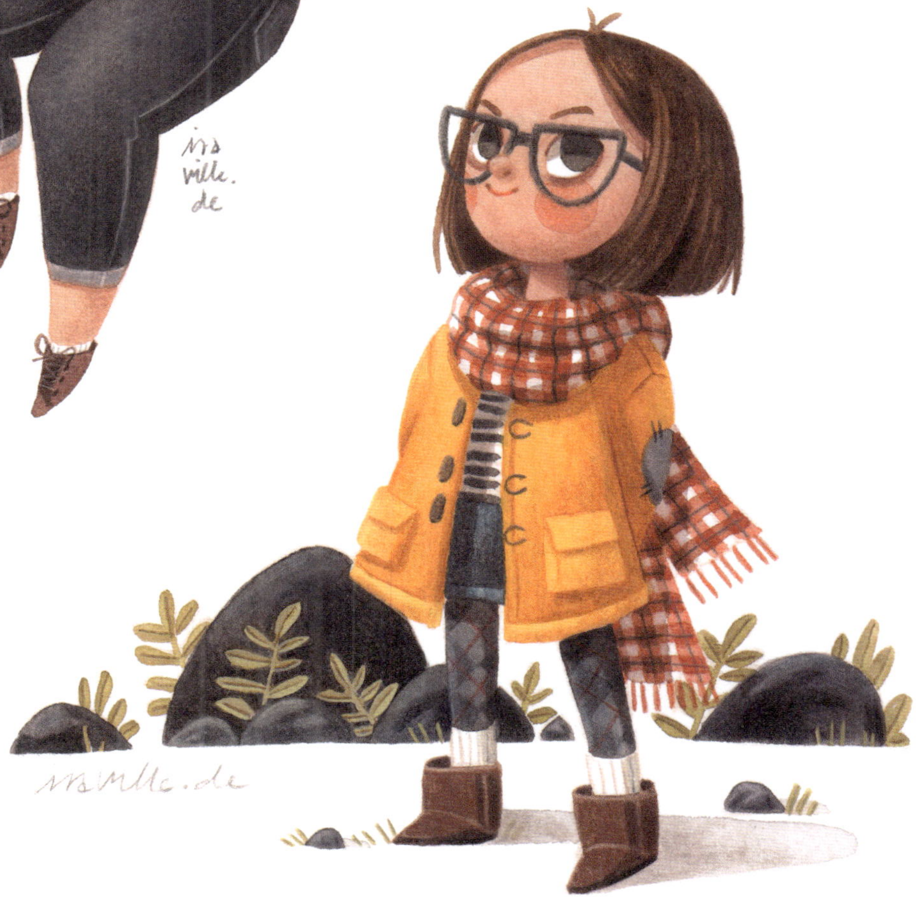

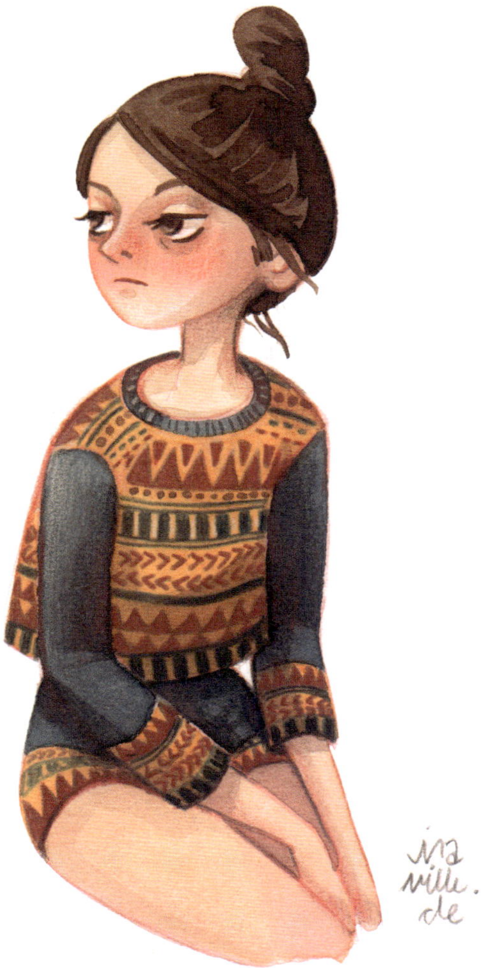

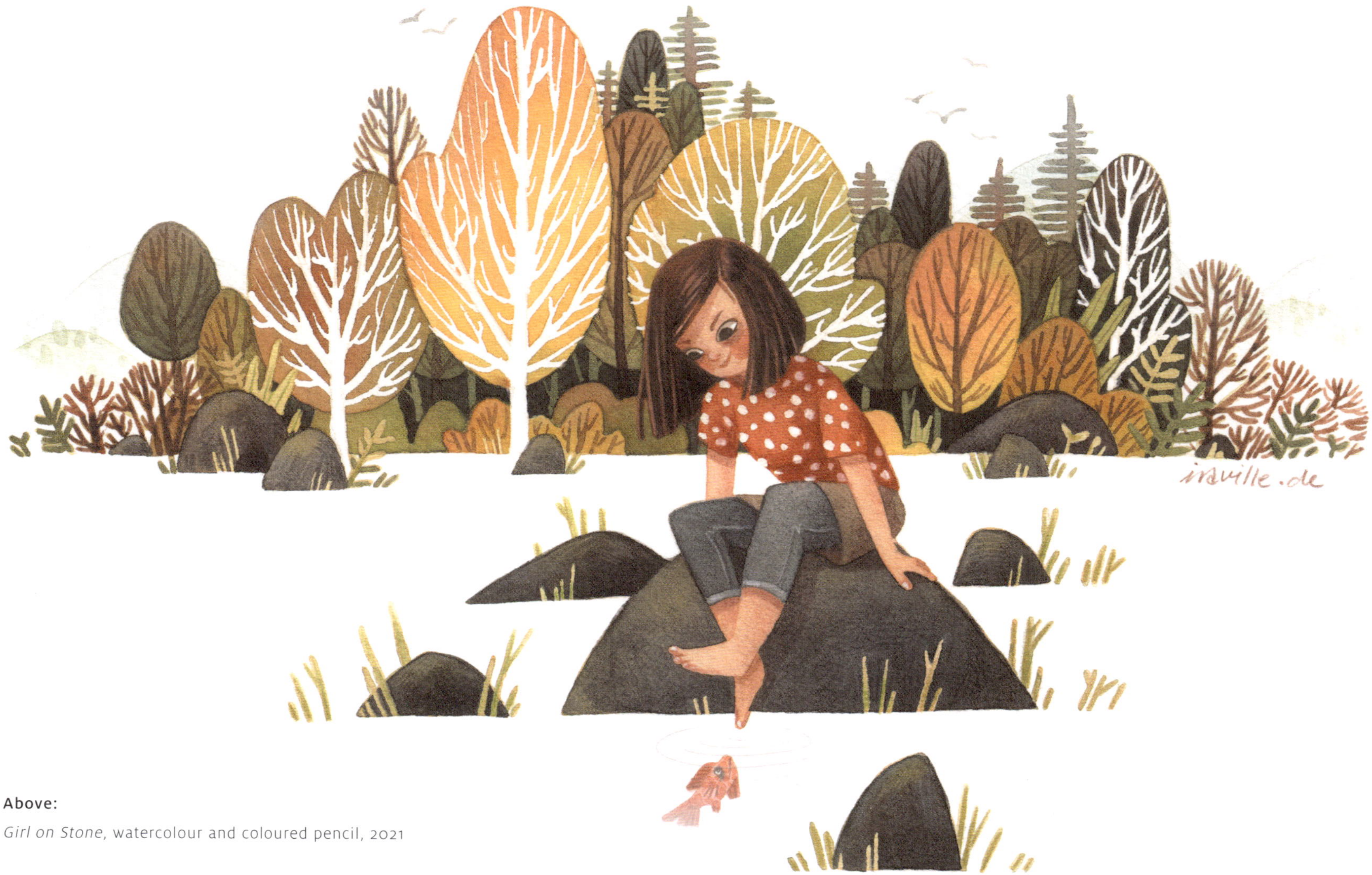

Above:

Girl on Stone, watercolour and coloured pencil, 2021

Opposite page (clockwise from top left):

Flower Girl 3, watercolour and coloured pencil, 2019

Udmurt Girl, watercolour and coloured pencil, 2020

Girl and Bees, watercolour and coloured pencil, 2019

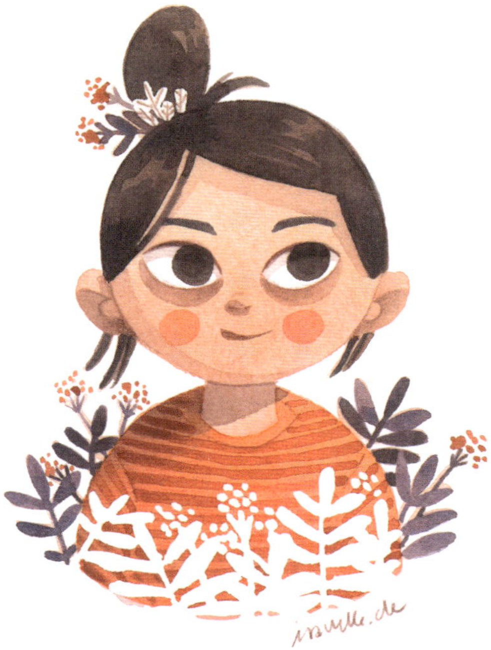

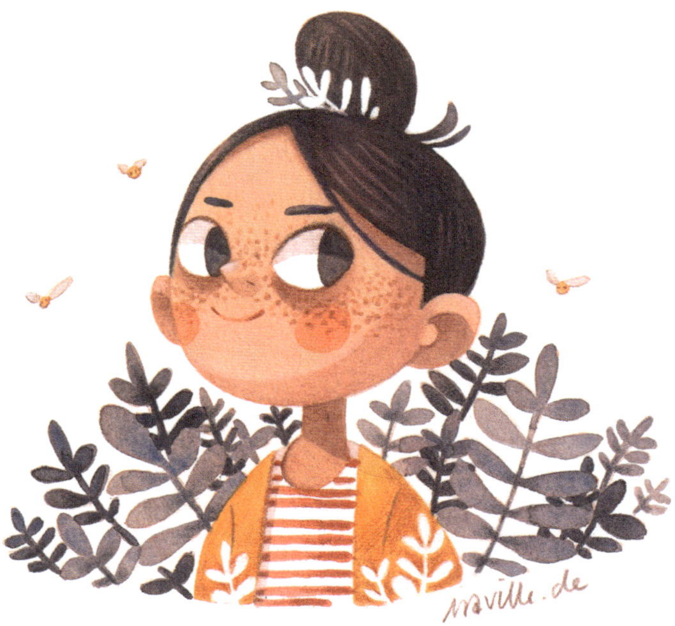

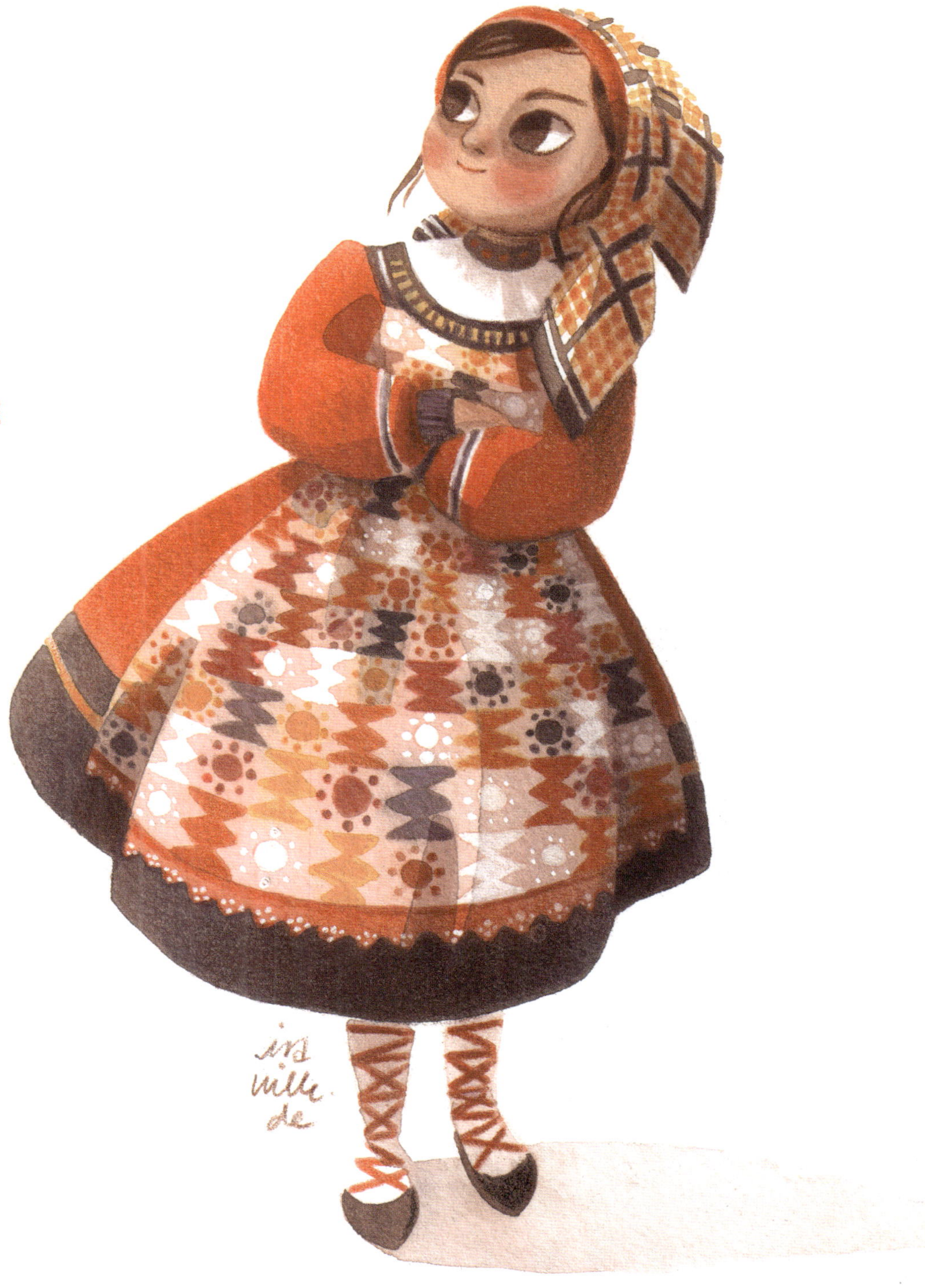

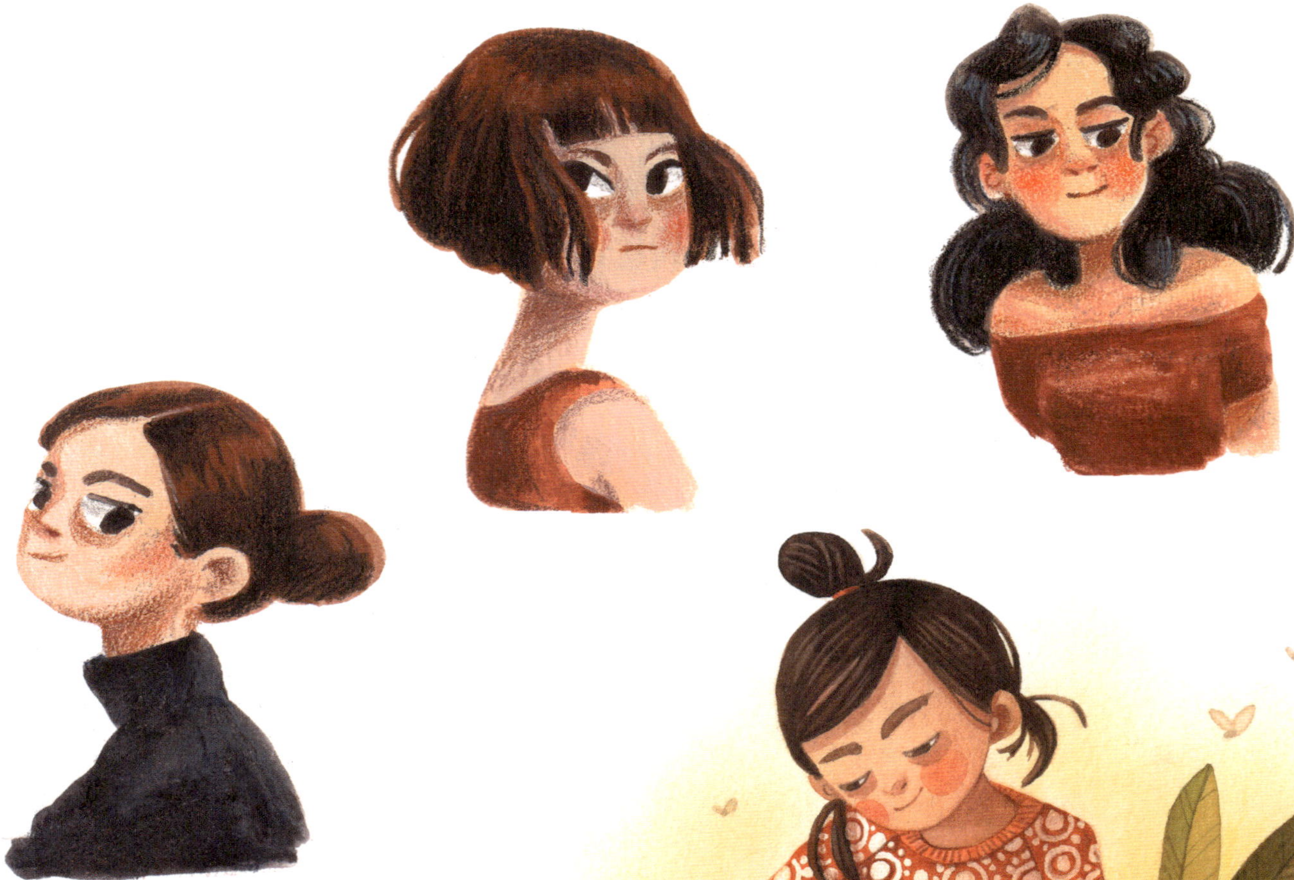

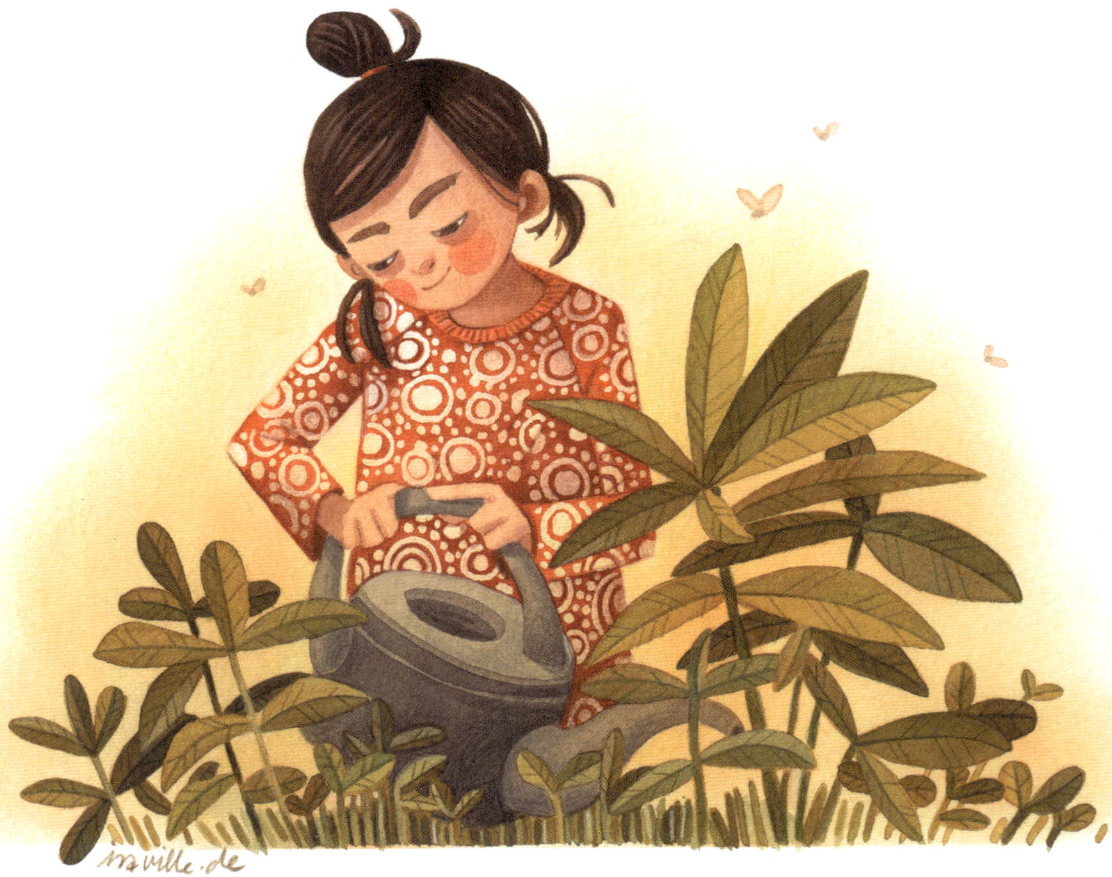

Above:
3 Women Sketch, gouache and wax crayon, 2019

Right:
Girl Watering Plants, watercolour, soft pastel, coloured pencil, 2022

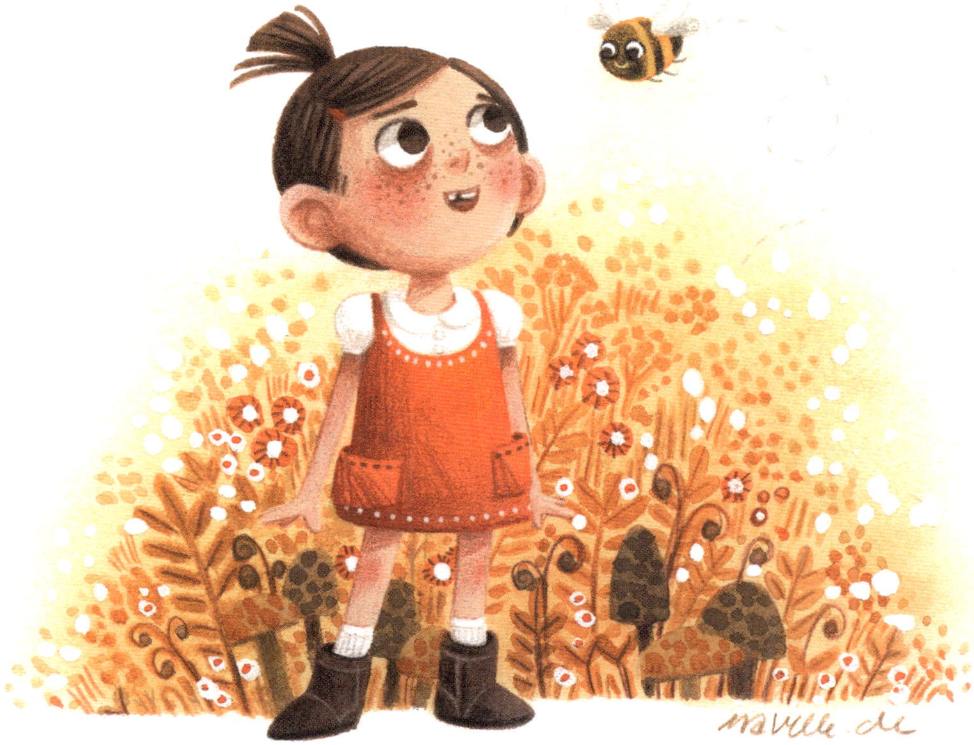

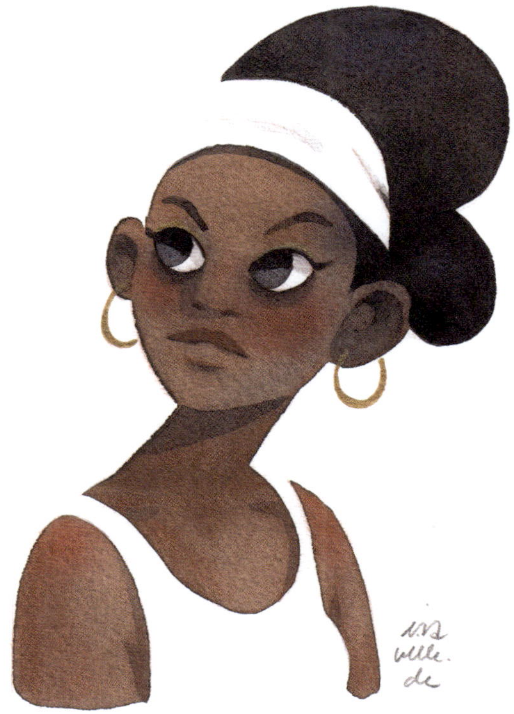

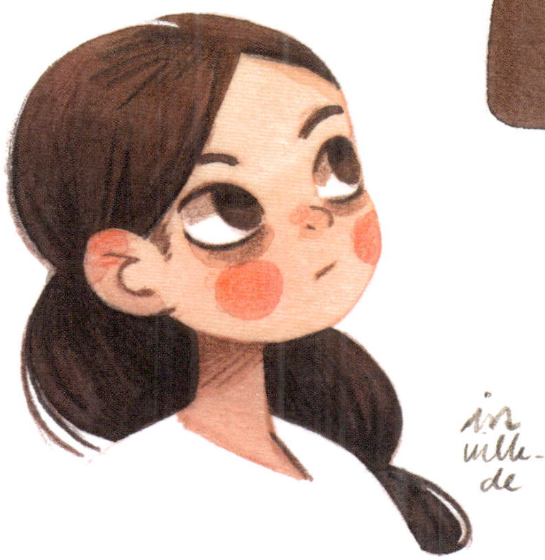

Clockwise from above:

Summer Girl, gouache, watercolour, soft pastel, 2019

Nina 2, watercolour and coloured pencil, 2022

Looking Up, watercolour and coloured pencil, 2018

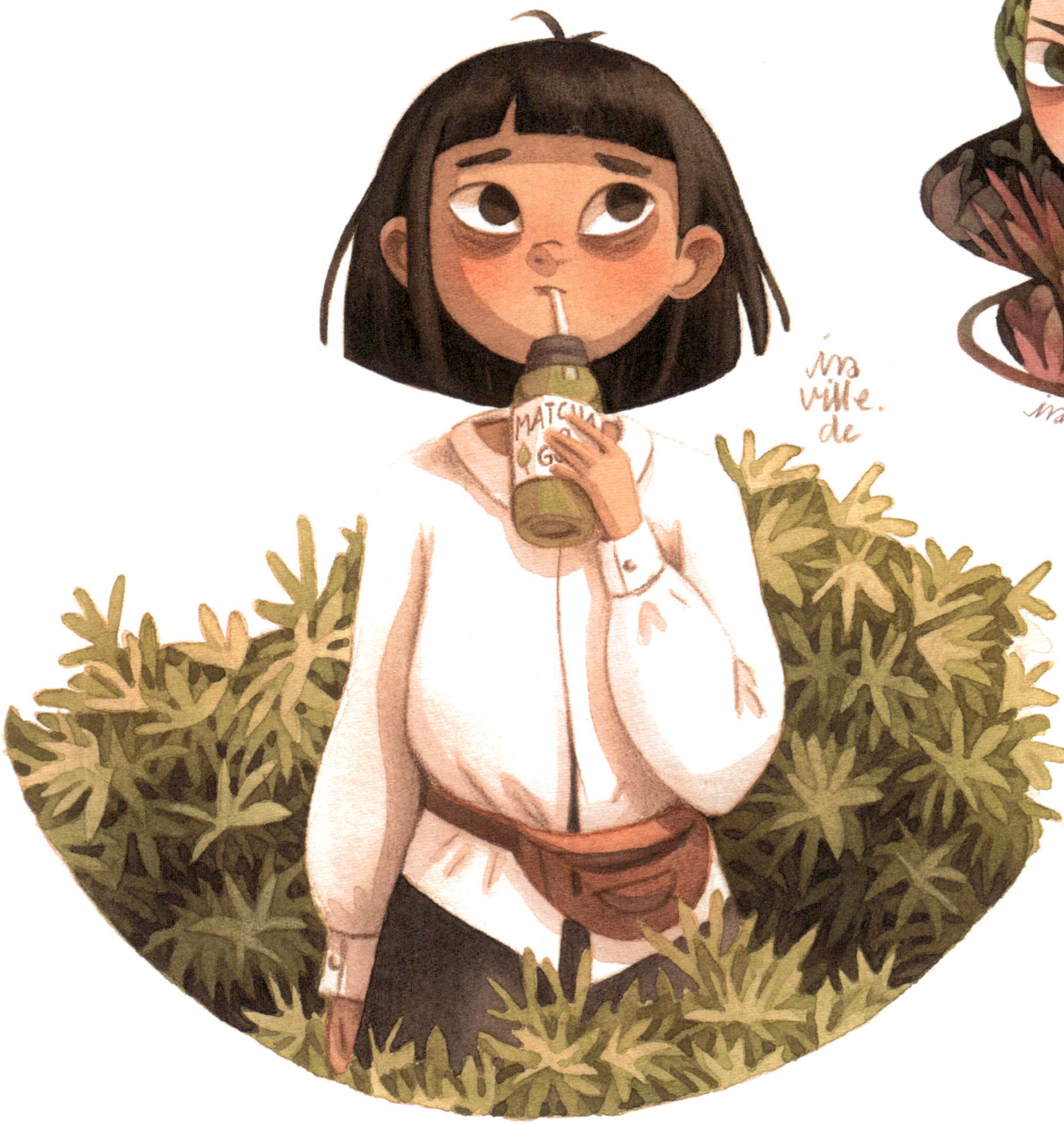

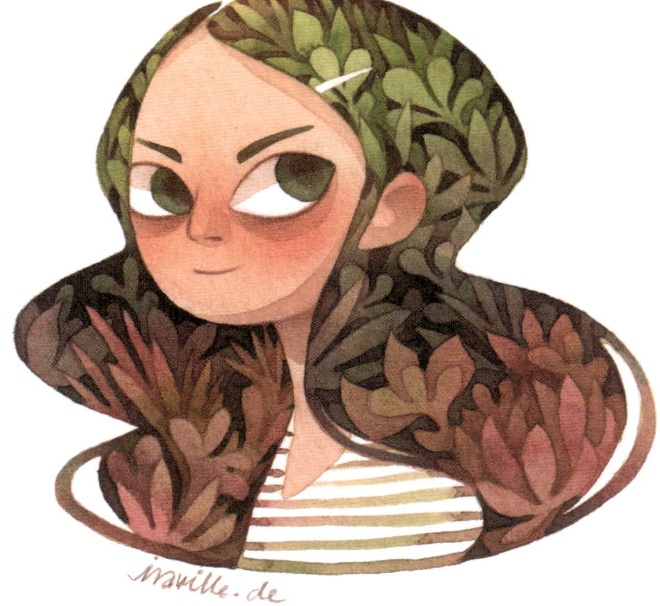

Left:
Matcha Girl, watercolour and coloured pencil, 2019

Above:
Green-pink Plant Hair, watercolour and coloured pencil, 2019

Left:
Thinking Girl, watercolour, coloured pencil, soft pastel, 2018

Right:
Two Character Portrait Sketch, coloured pencil, 2017

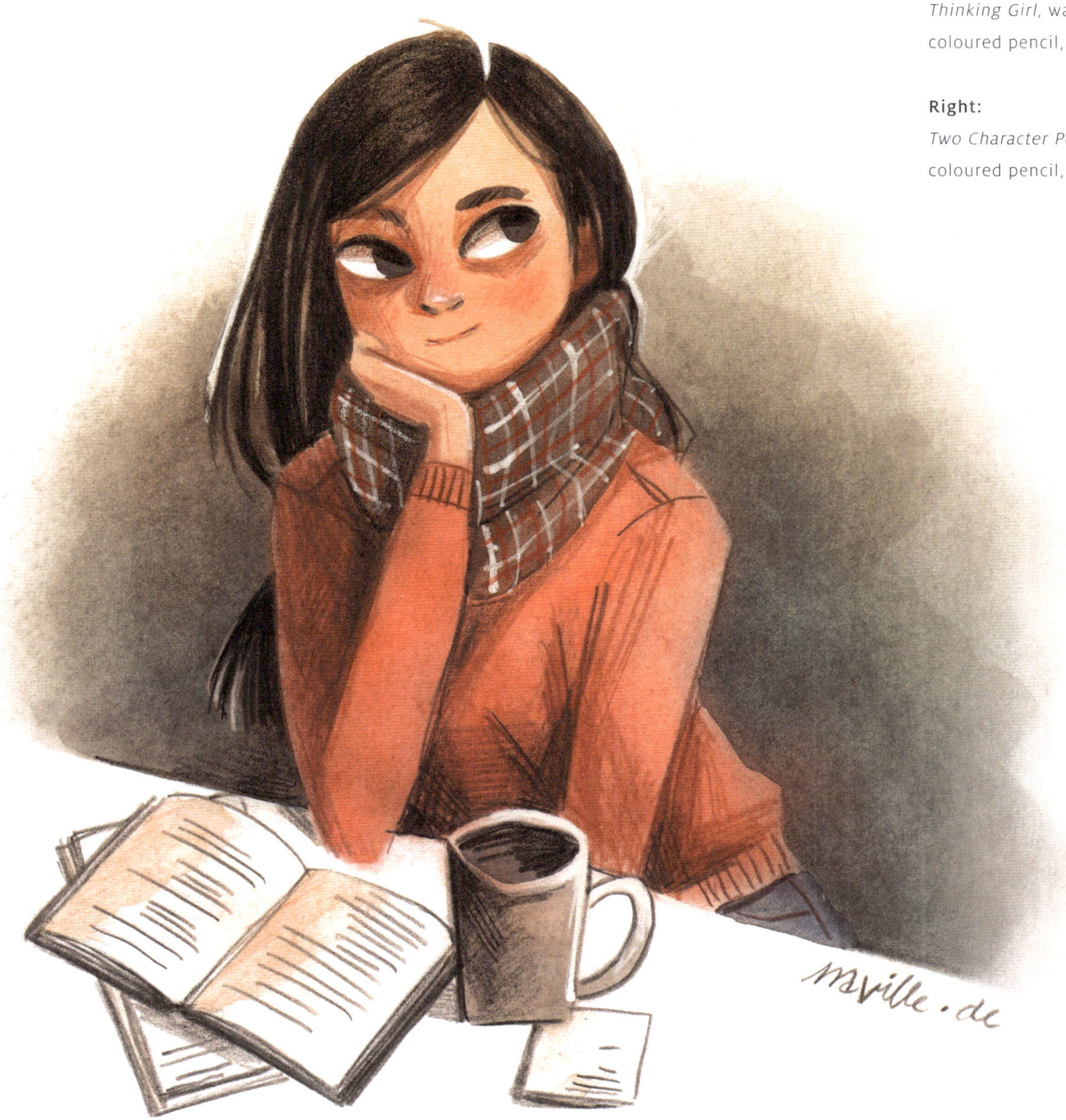

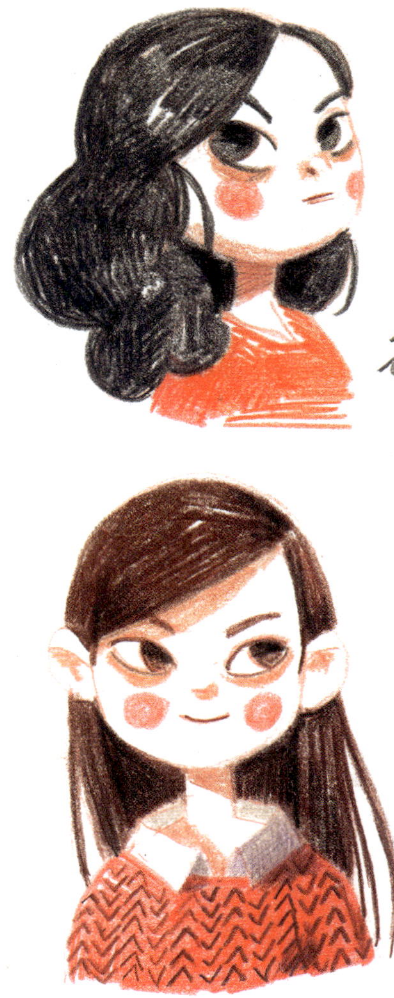

Experiments

I LOVE TRYING OUT NEW THINGS.

When cooking, I do so intuitively and never use any recipes. I find inspiration from TV shows or the odd cookbook, but I always end up changing ingredients or preparation methods. Of course, this means the result changes too.

The unfortunate downside is that these altered recipes are sometimes inedible. But that is what you have to live with when you try something new. Fortunately, it rarely happens. Most of the time the taste is passable, or even good. I'm generally not the best cook because as the food sizzles on the stove, I often find myself lured over to my drawing table. However, there are occasions when the result is terrific!

I take a very similar approach when visiting a foreign city. I do not head for the top sights advertised in travel guides, and prefer to live spontaneously, exploring the city off the tourist-beaten track. It is much more exciting to travel into unknown places this way. Narrow, winding alleys are much more interesting than the well-known boulevards. I am drawn to the parts of the city where real life happens. That way I can discover the hidden gems, such as restaurants where the locals eat and drink – everything normally tastes better in these kinds of places. You will be rewarded for not relying on your phone all the time when you choose to explore the world with open eyes.

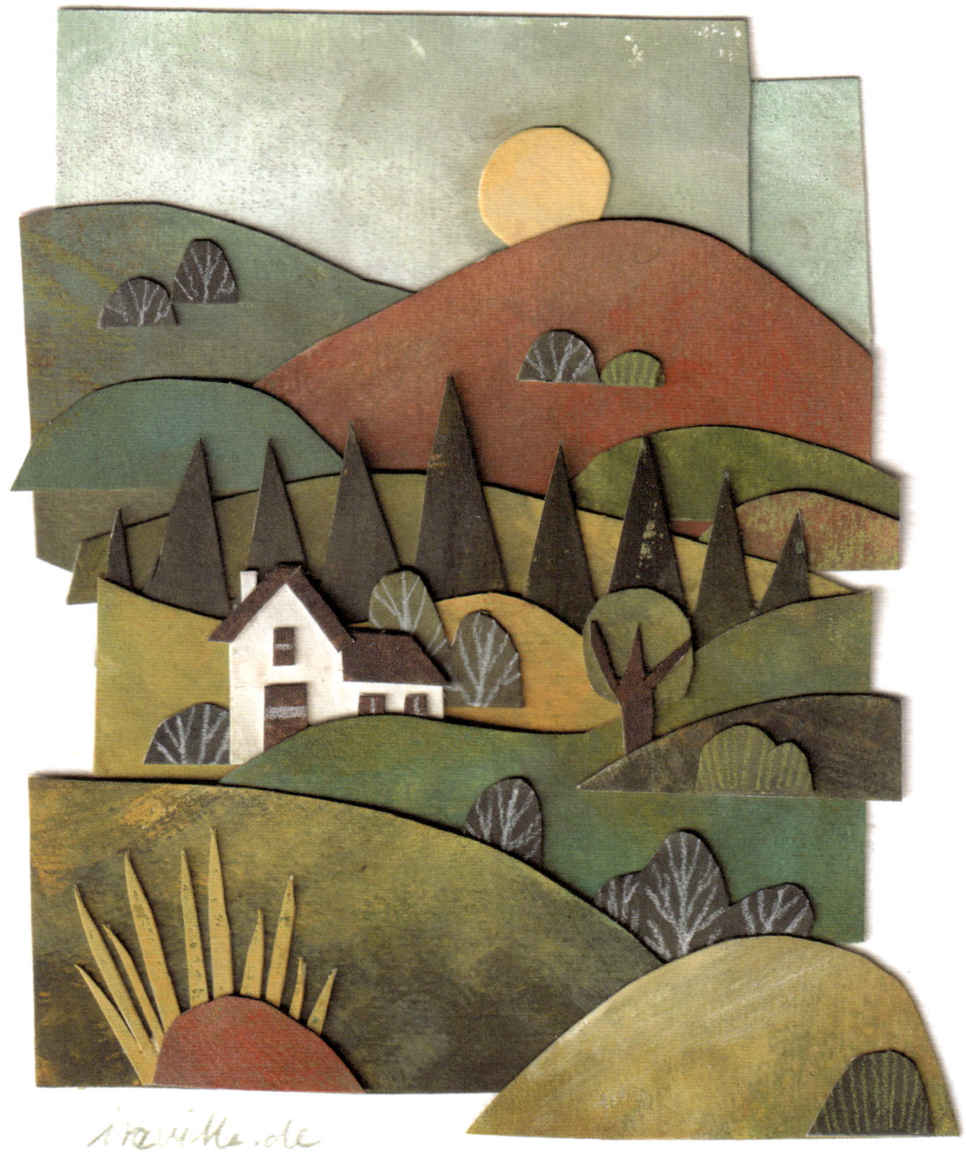

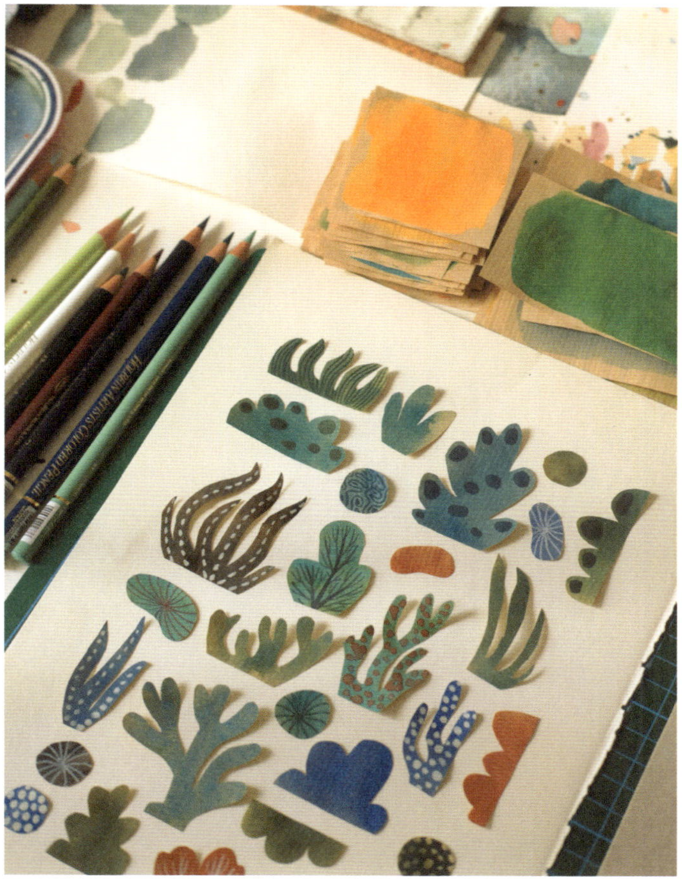

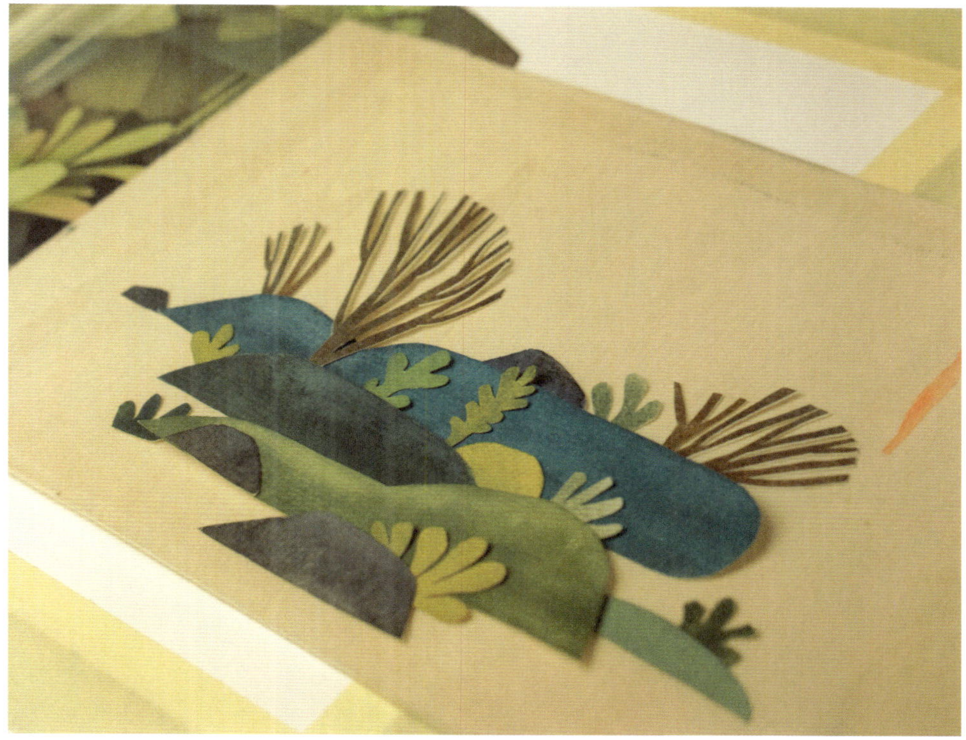

ART IS MUCH THE SAME FOR ME.

I love trying out new materials or techniques outside my beloved realm of watercolours, which I taught myself. I never took any classes and I was not trained in those techniques in school or college either. And you know what? I don't think it's necessary to be professionally taught. All you need is a brush, some paper, and three to four colours to begin painting. Over time, you will learn how to use different tools, pigments, and materials that will affect the result. You will also learn how to use water to create various effects. There is no right or wrong way. You can simply try things out and discover what materials and techniques work best for you over time. It may take a while, but it is more fun, and leads to better, more personal results.

Although I have a favourite method, I like to experiment with other painting and printing techniques. I couldn't care less if a traditionalist were to tell me I couldn't do something.

For example, I have explored *suminagashi* (the art of Japanese marbling), stencil printing, cyanotype, and paper cutting. I've also tried out gouache, as well as oil and soft pastel. In addition to these, I have made pottery palettes, scooped watercolour paper, produced watercolour paints from pigments, and have bound my own sketchbooks. The tutorials for the last two can be found in my first book *Cozy Days*. It is helpful to understand the materials you are using.

In this chapter, you will find the results of my many excursions into previously unknown terrain.

Papercut Stone Landscape, soft pastel and watercolour, 2022

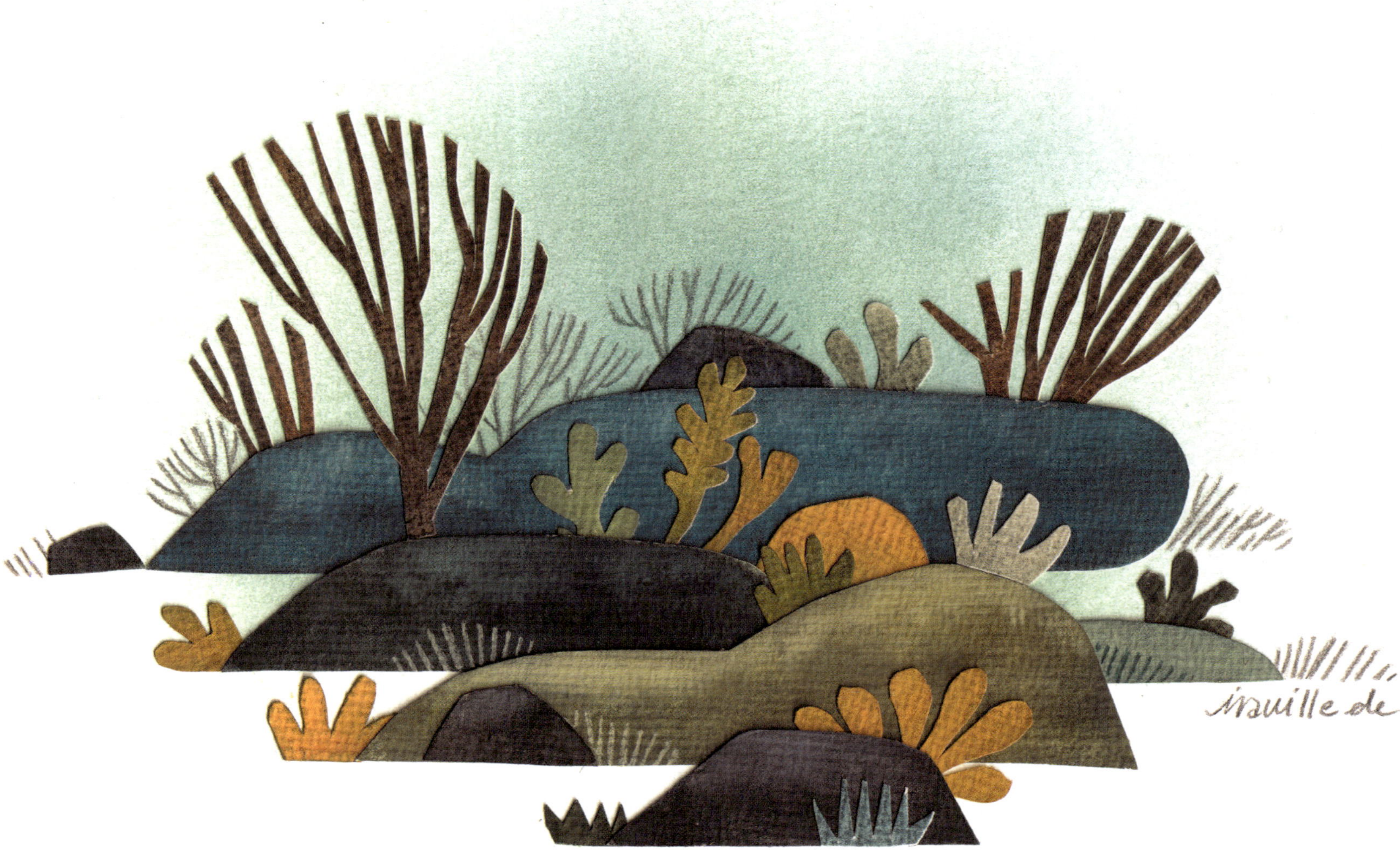

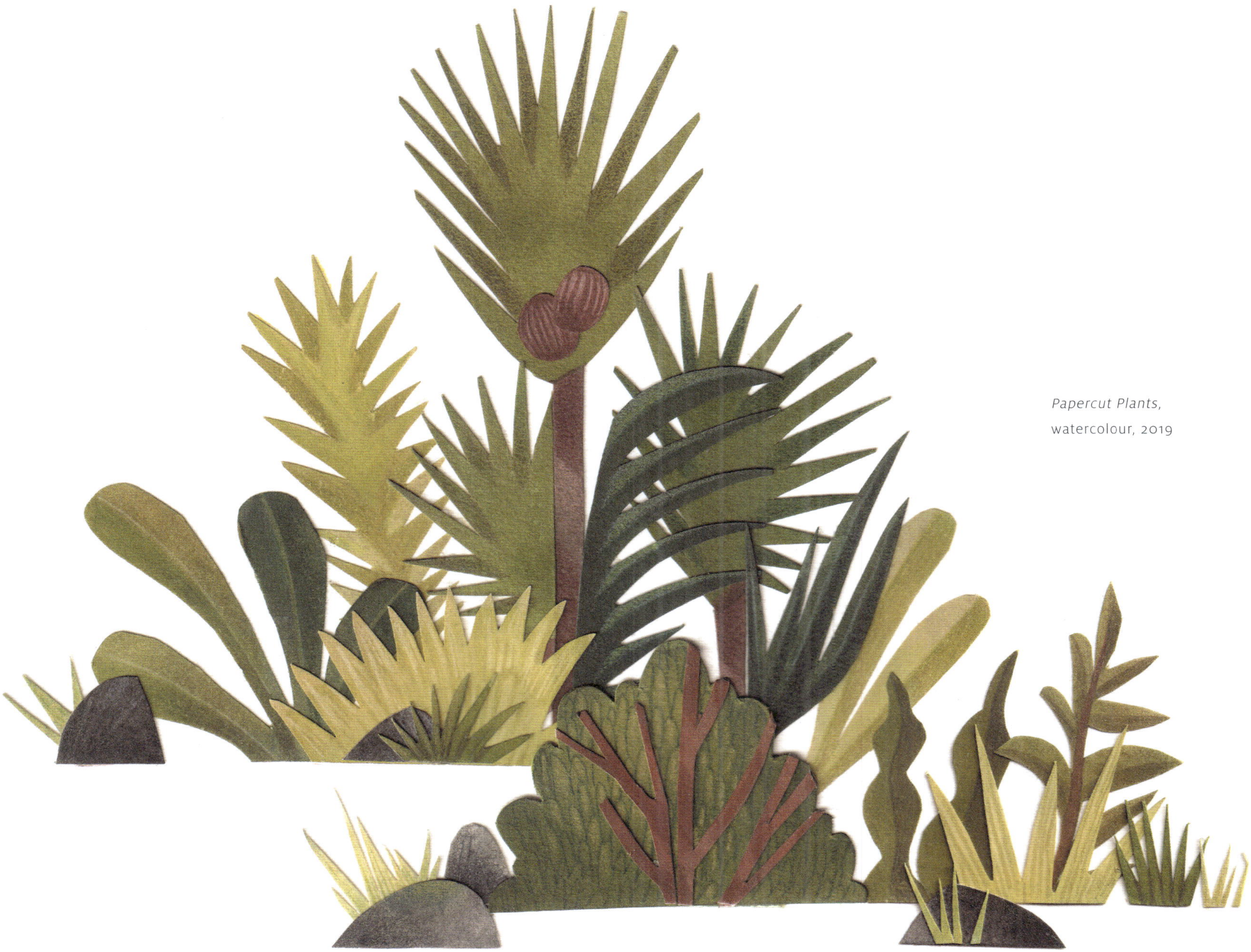

Papercut Plants,
watercolour, 2019

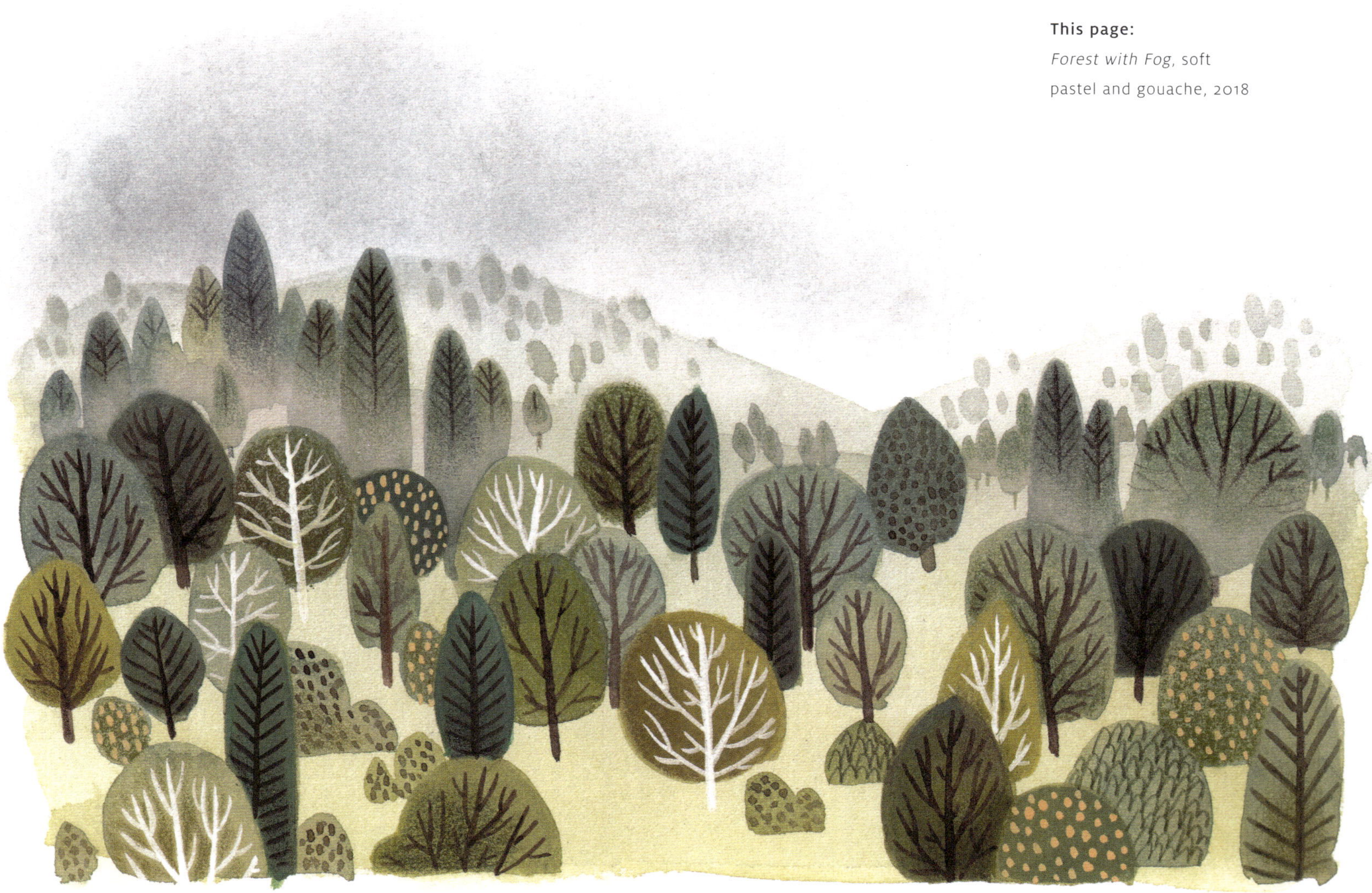

This page:
Forest with Fog, soft pastel and gouache, 2018

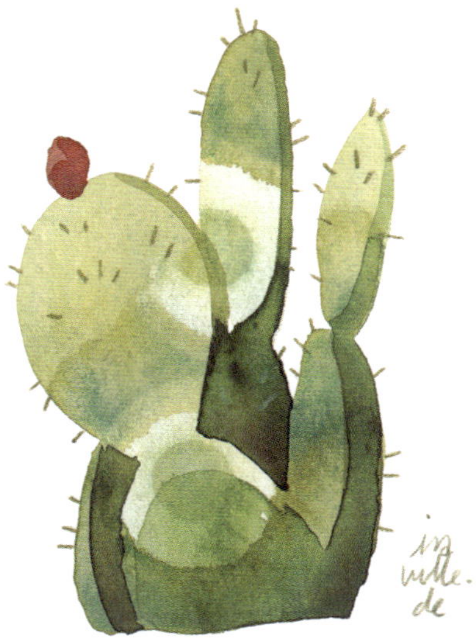

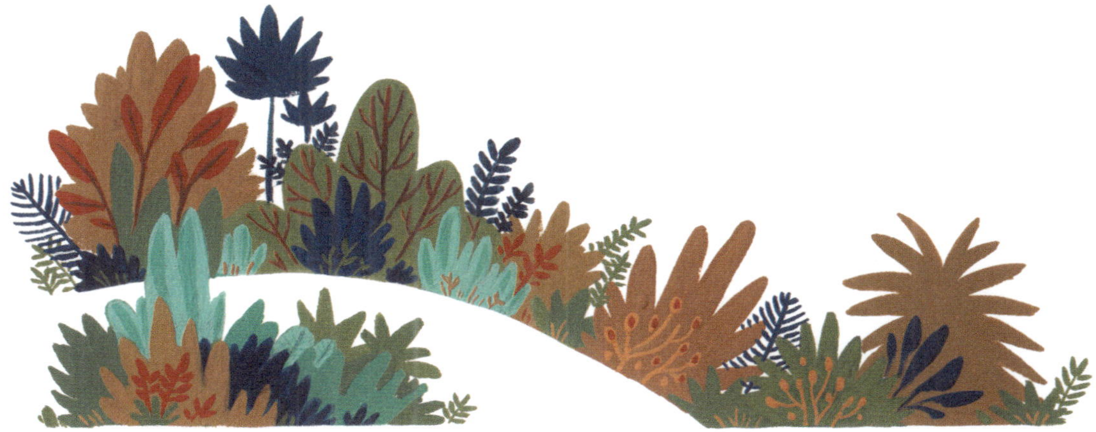

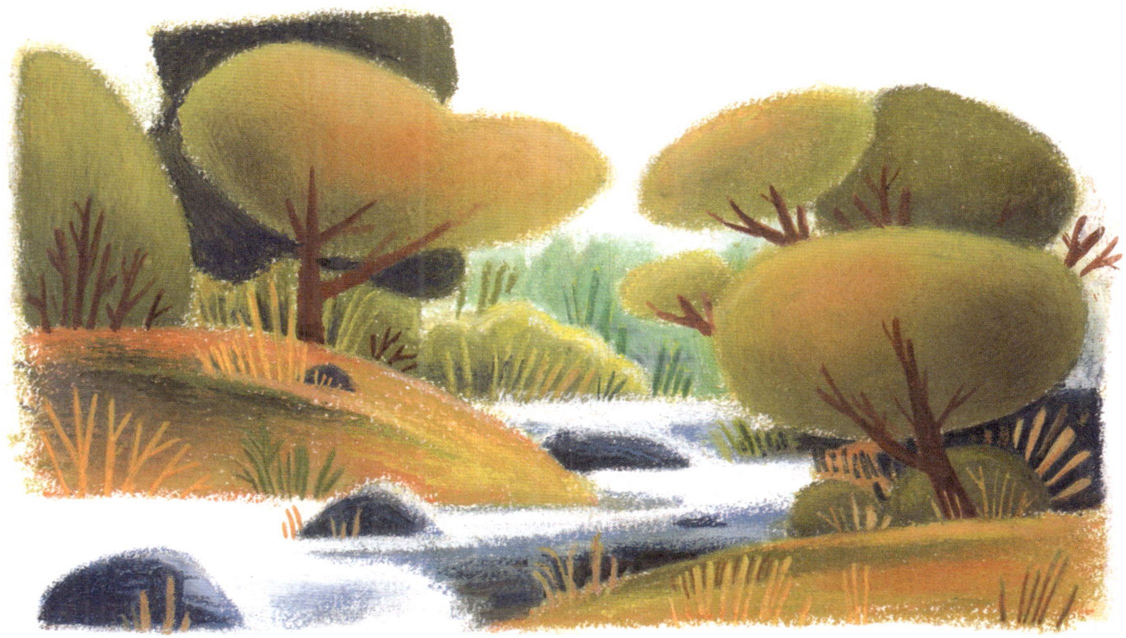

Above:
Cactus Experiment, watercolour and ethanol, 2017

Top Right:
Colorful Parkway, gouache, 2018

Right:
Autumn River, oil pastel, 2019

CYANOTYPE

Right:
Manatees, cyanotype, 2020

Opposite page (above):
Sperm Whales, cyanotype, 2020

Opposite page (below):
Blue Whale, cyanotype, 2020

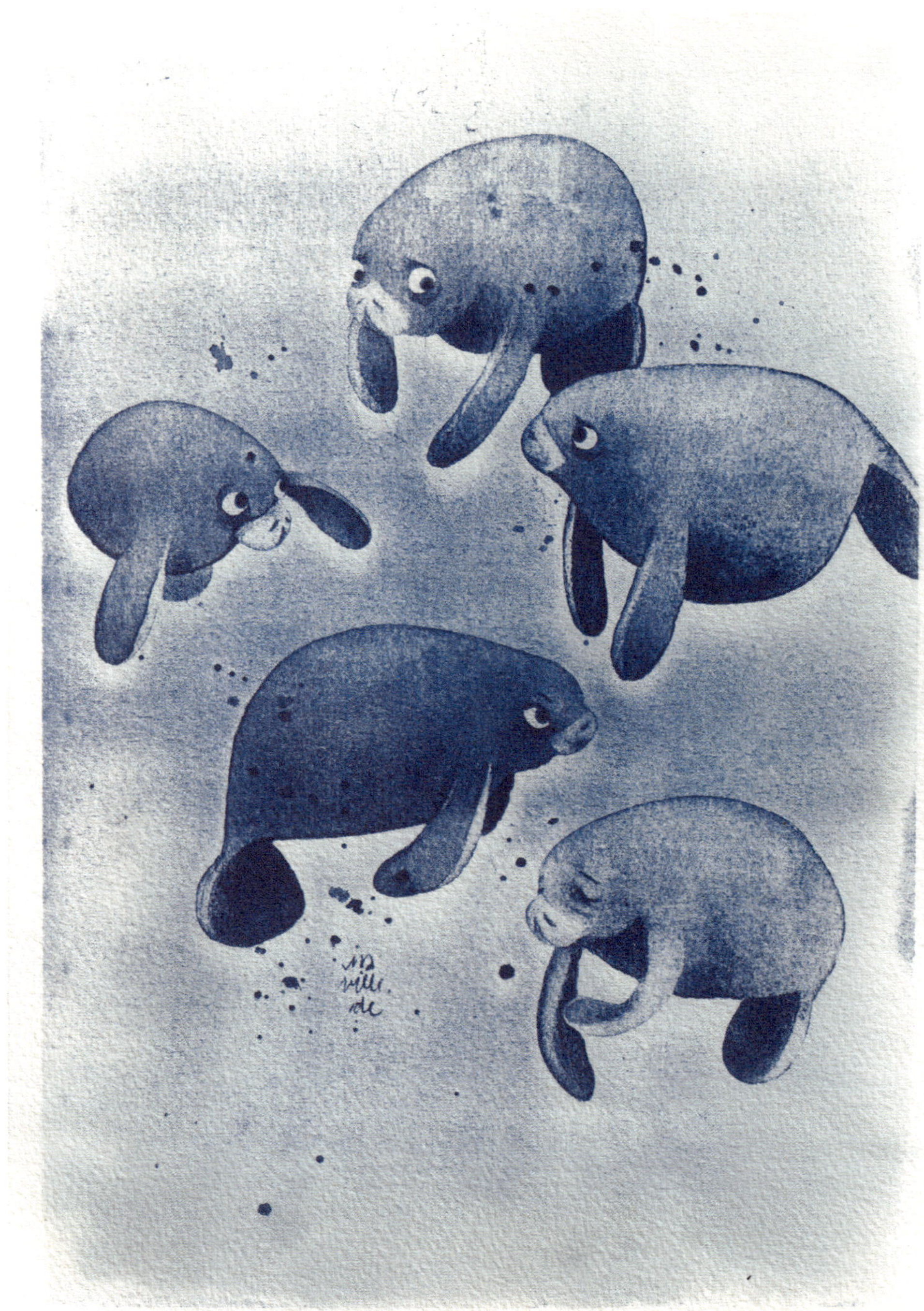

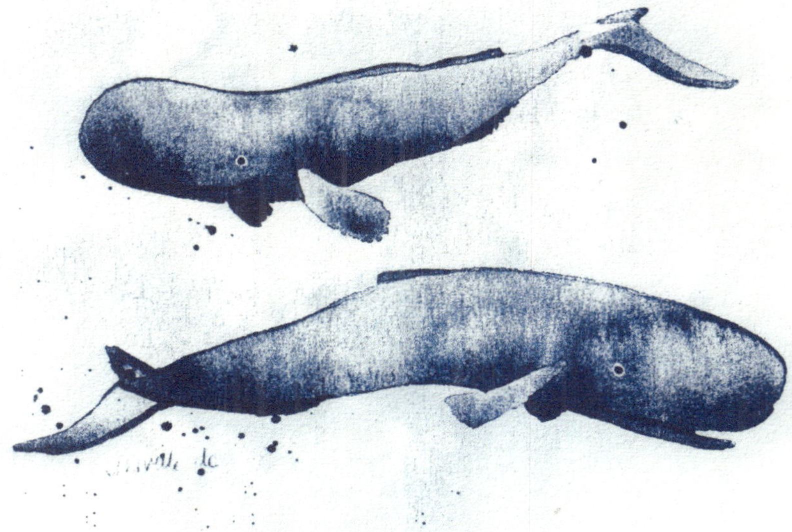

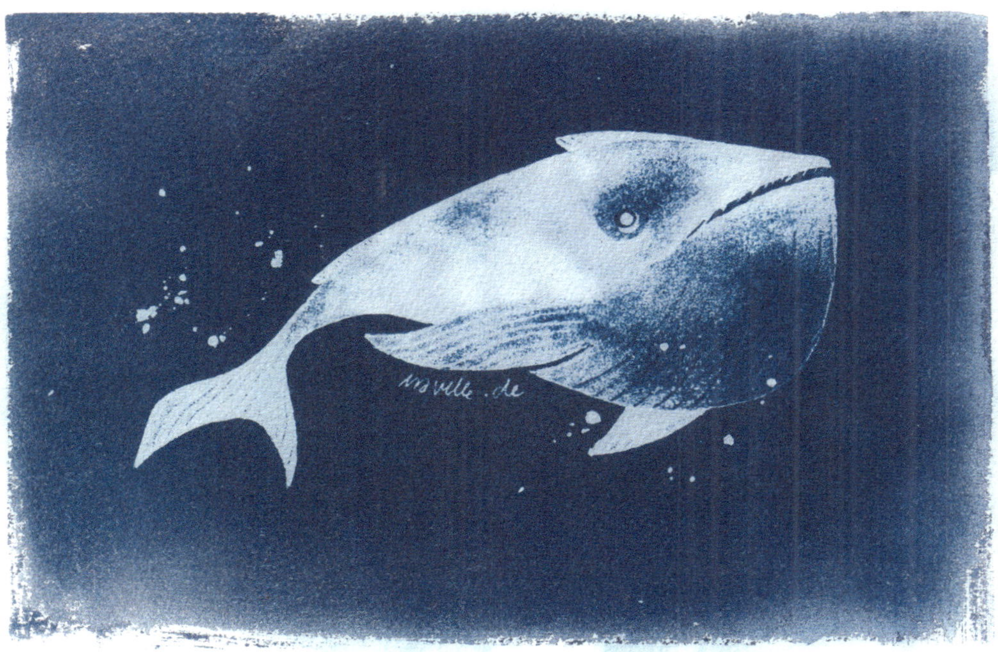

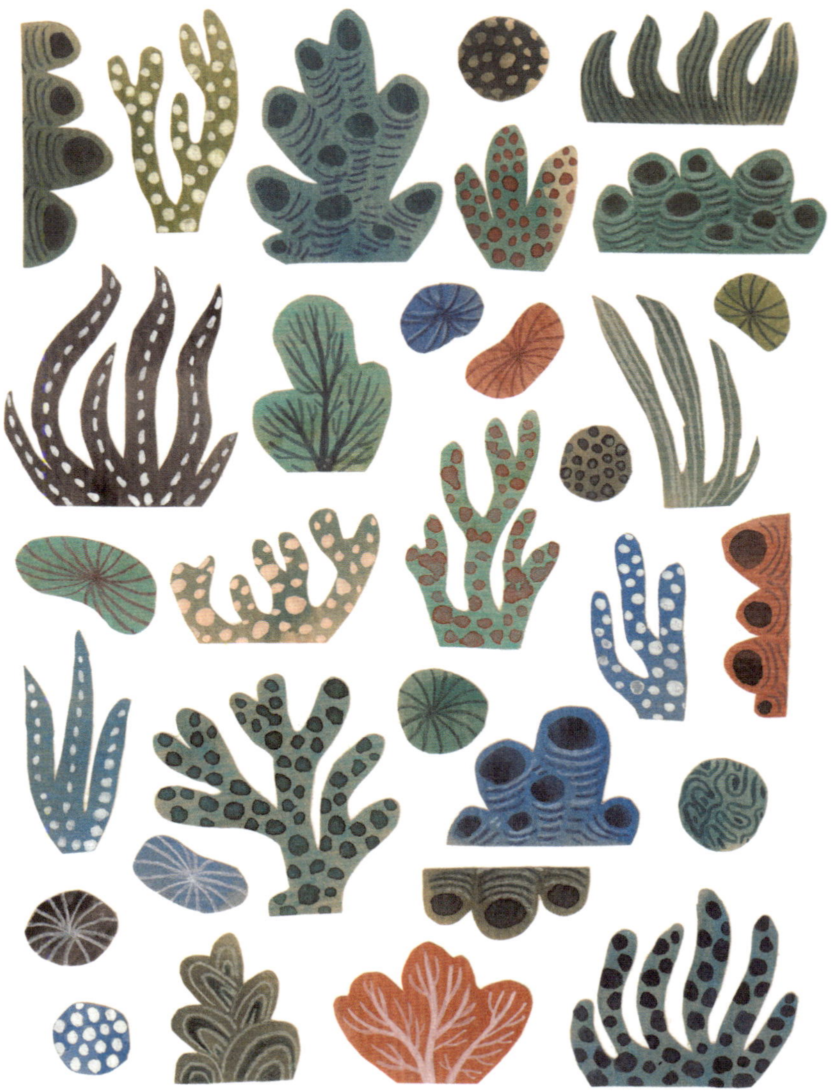

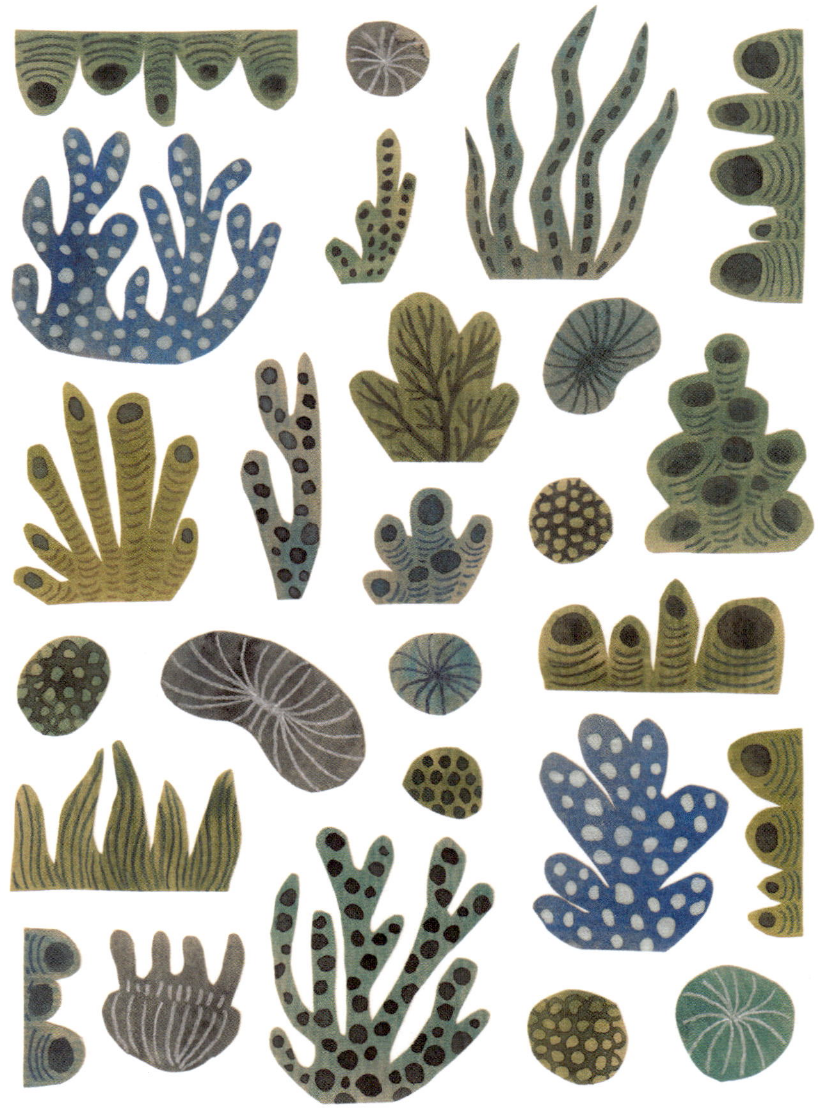

COLLAGE

Underwater Plants Collage 1, watercolour and gouache, 2022

Underwater Plants Collage 2, watercolour and gouache, 2022

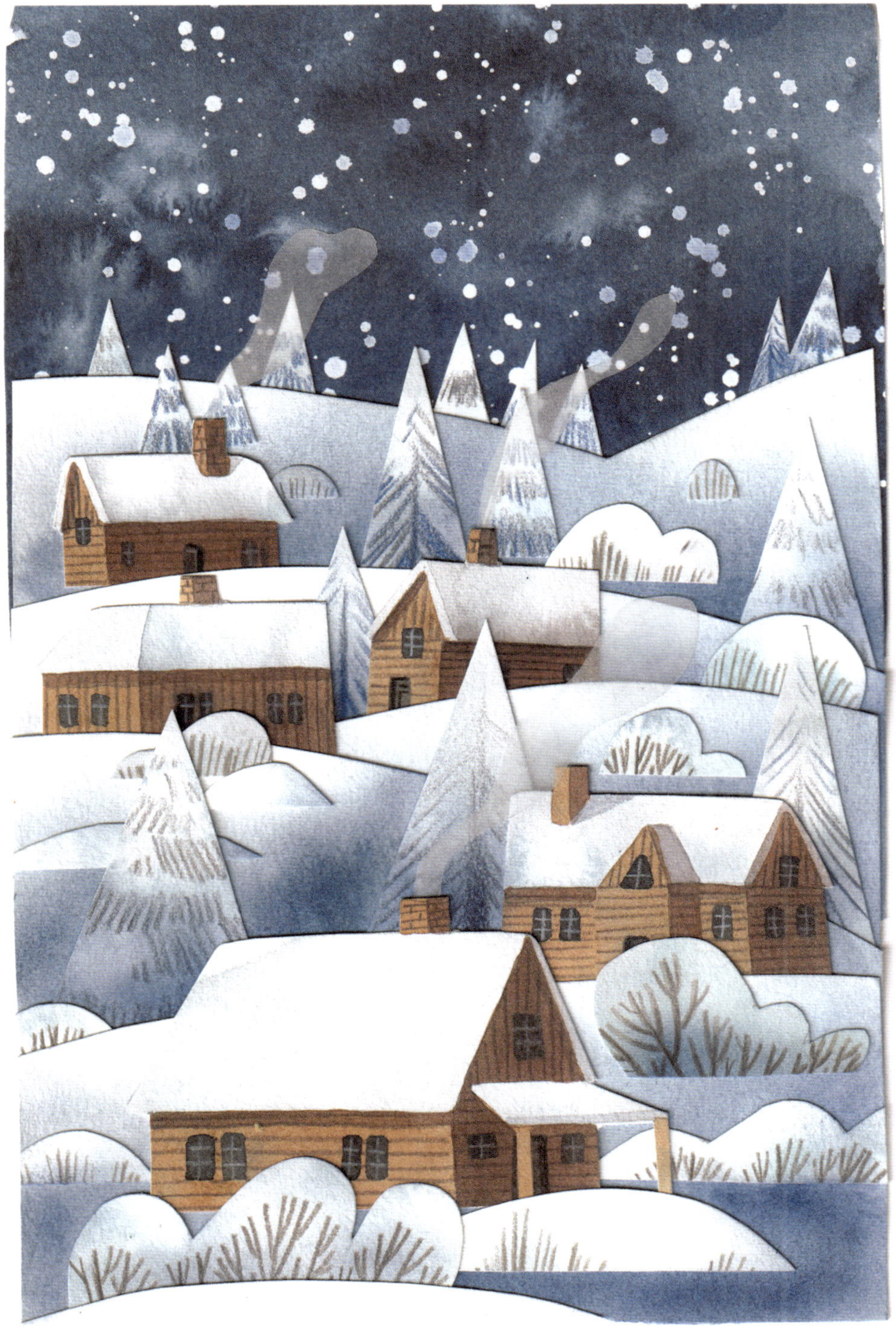

Snowscape Papercut,
watercolour, 2021

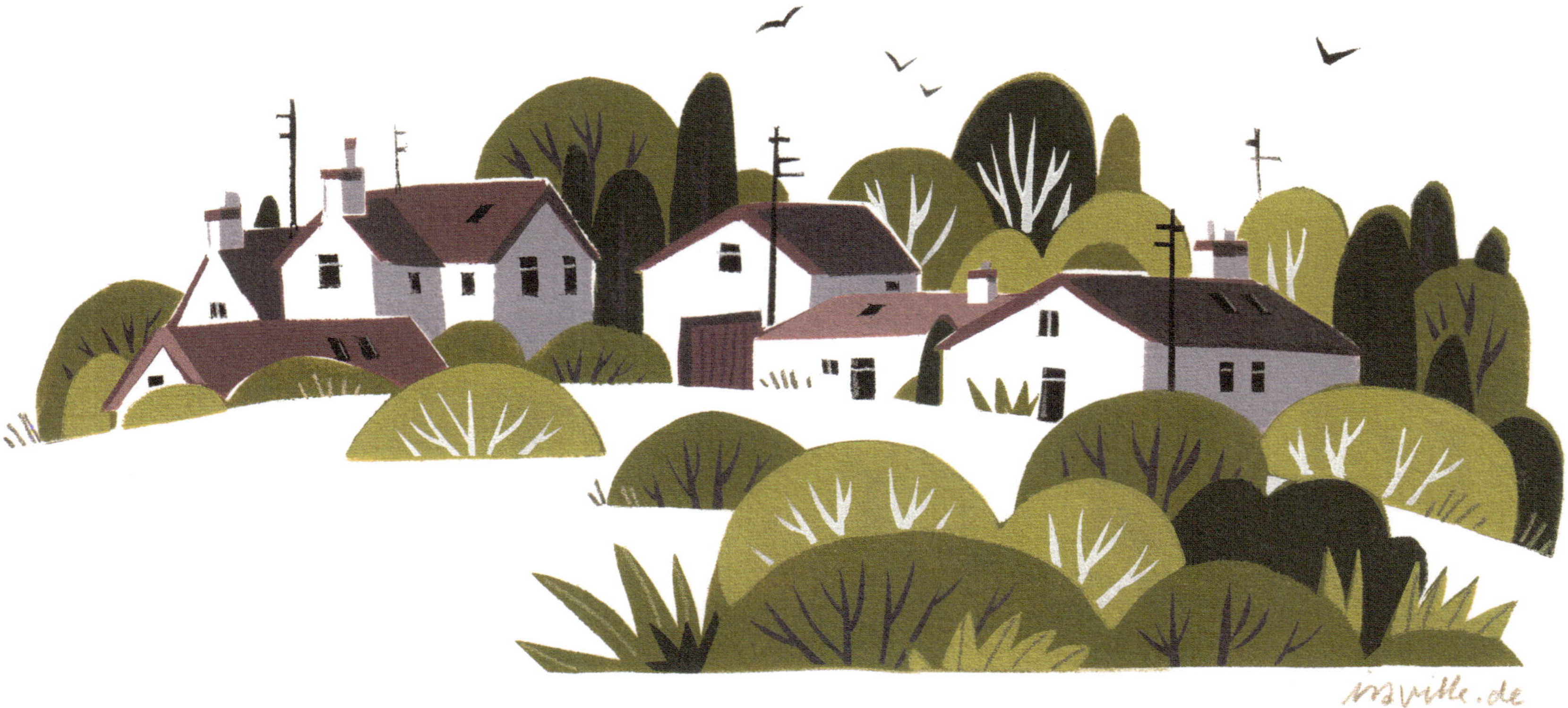

STENCIL

Above:
Irish Countryside 2, stencil version with relief ink, 2023

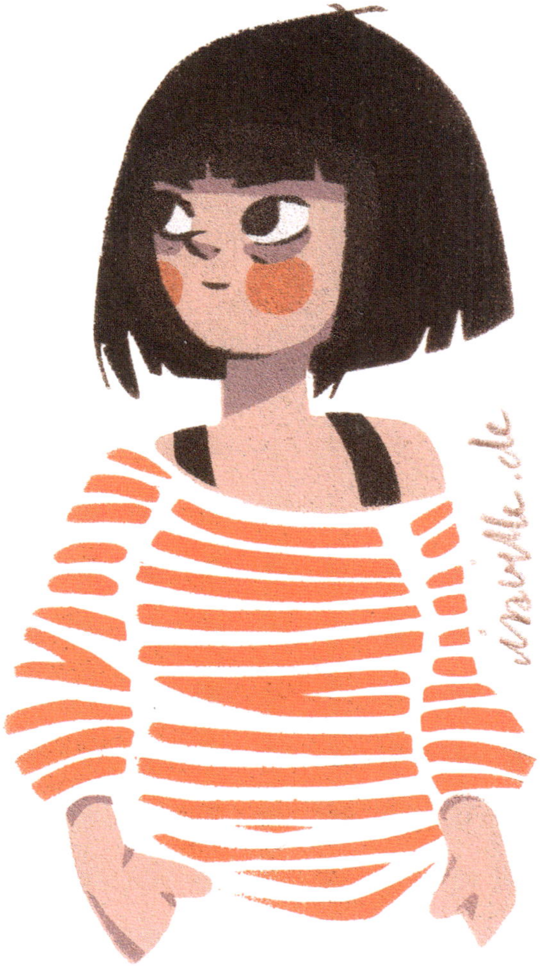

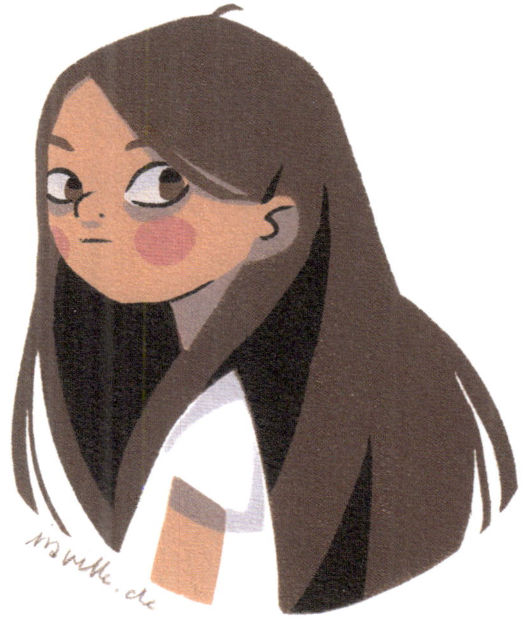

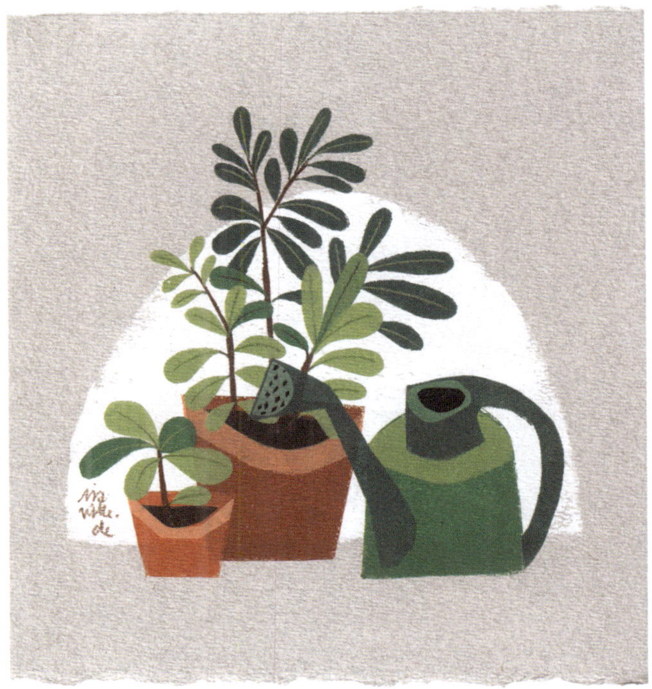

Above:

Girl with Red Stripe Shirt, stencils with relief ink, 2023

Top right:

Stencil Girl, stencils with relief ink, 2023

Right:

Potted Plants, stencil technique, silk screen ink, 2022

GALLERY

Towns & buildings

Below:
English Historical Town, watercolour and coloured pencil, 2021

One day during the pandemic when I could not travel, I was rummaging on a shelf and happened to find a coffee-table book from the eighties that I had borrowed from my parents years ago. I discovered a photo of Stratford-upon-Avon, well known as being the birthplace of Shakespeare, which I liked very much. I found other images of the town online, and in the end, I came up with this very free interpretation. Of course, I would have preferred to be there myself. But so what? Shakespeare was never in Denmark and still wrote *Hamlet*.

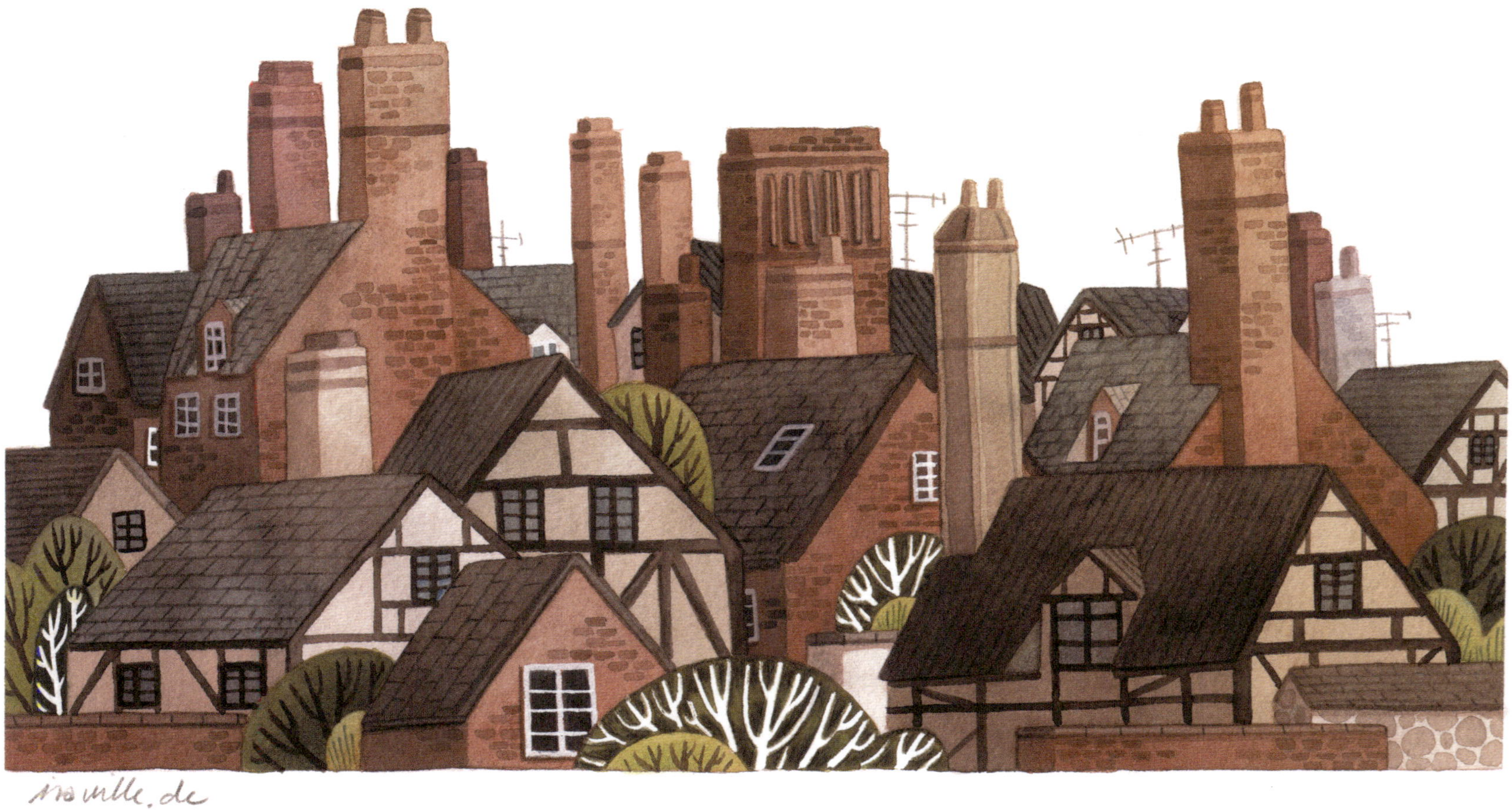

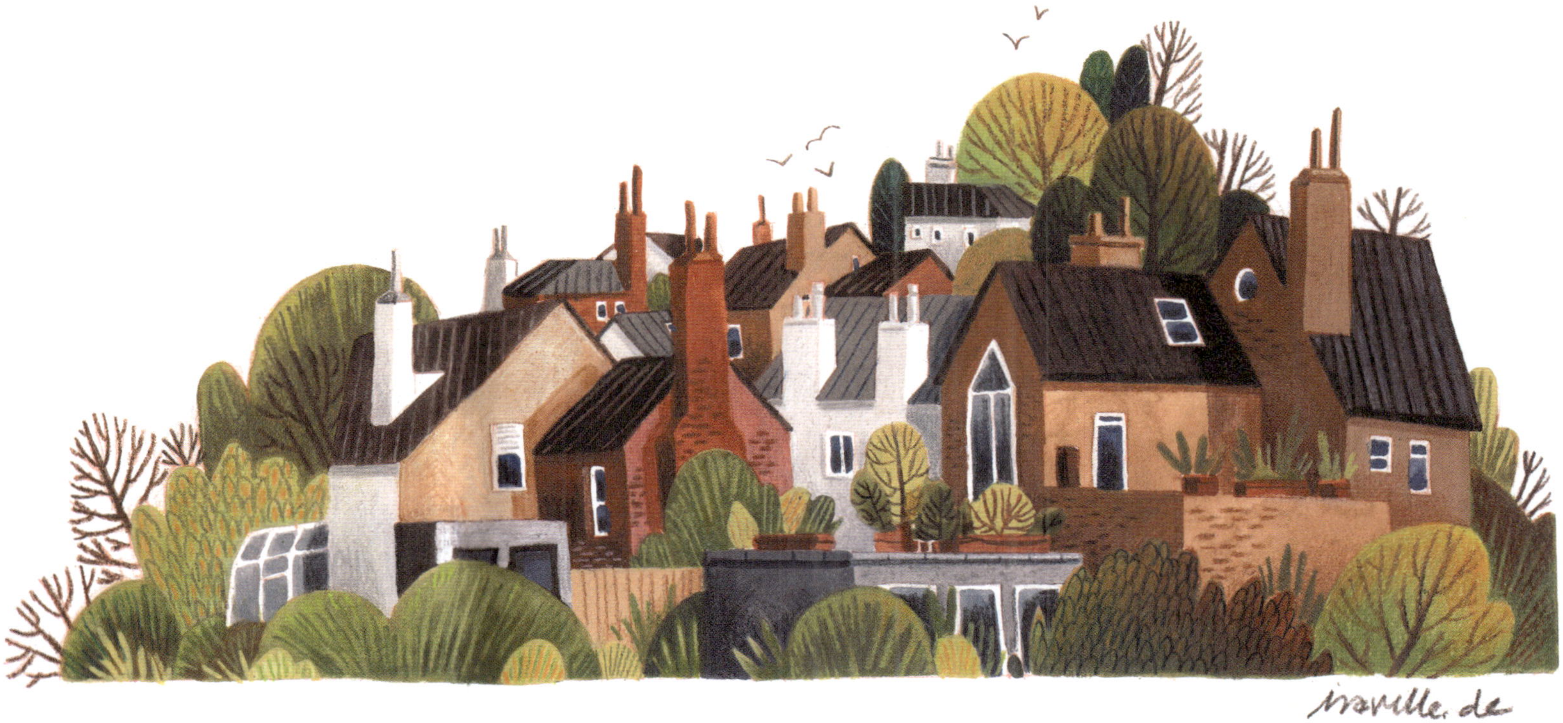

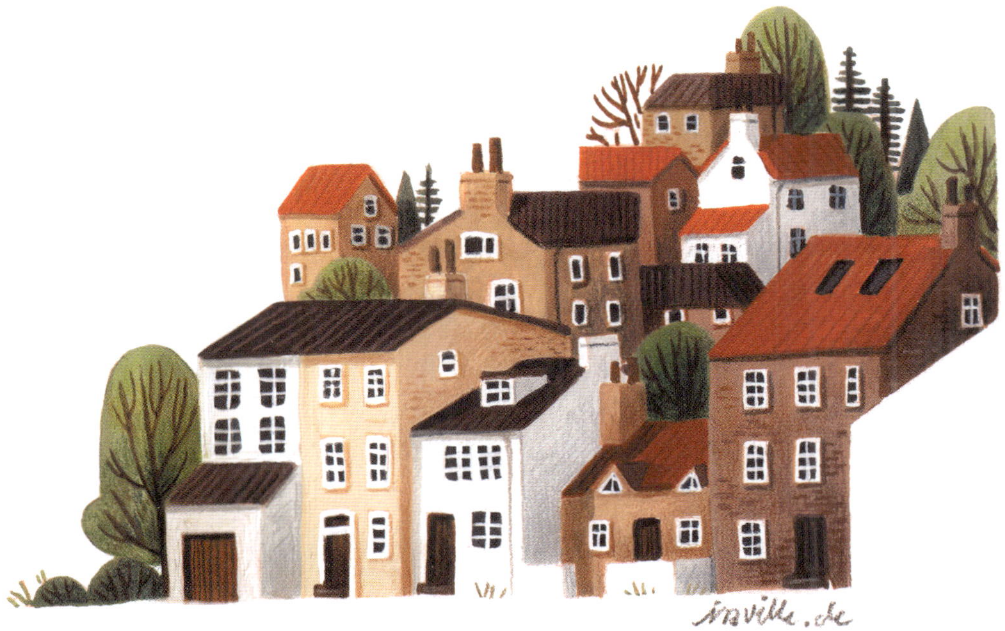

Above:

Dublin Houses, gouache and wax crayons, 2019

When I visited Dublin with my husband some time ago, we strolled from our hotel along the Grand Canal and discovered a row of small houses. They were beautifully nested and surrounded by lots of greenery. I took a few photos and started this drawing that same evening, which – as always with me – was loosely inspired by the houses. I added the houses in the background and even more greenery, but also changed the foreground quite a bit. To my surprise, one of my Instagram followers realized the location. He must have had a pretty good eye and known the area well!

Left:

Little English Harbour Town, gouache, coloured pencil, wax crayons, 2019

Right:
London Houses Sketch,
gouache and wax crayons, 2019

Below:
Castle, watercolour and
coloured pencil, 2017

Opposite page:
Irish Town, watercolour and
coloured pencil, 2020

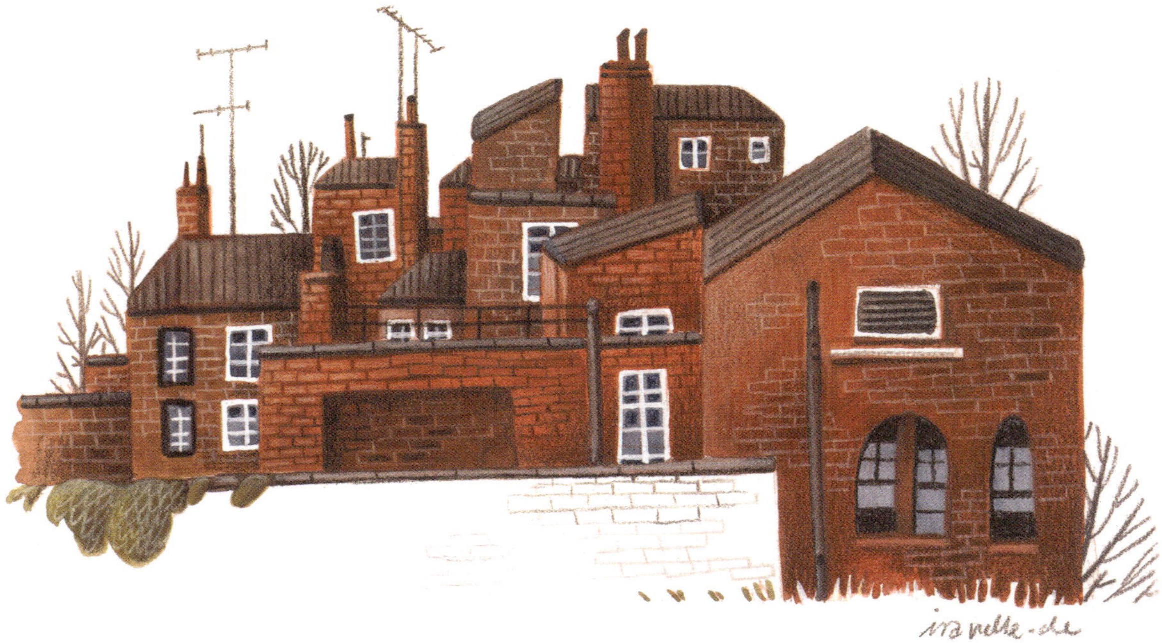

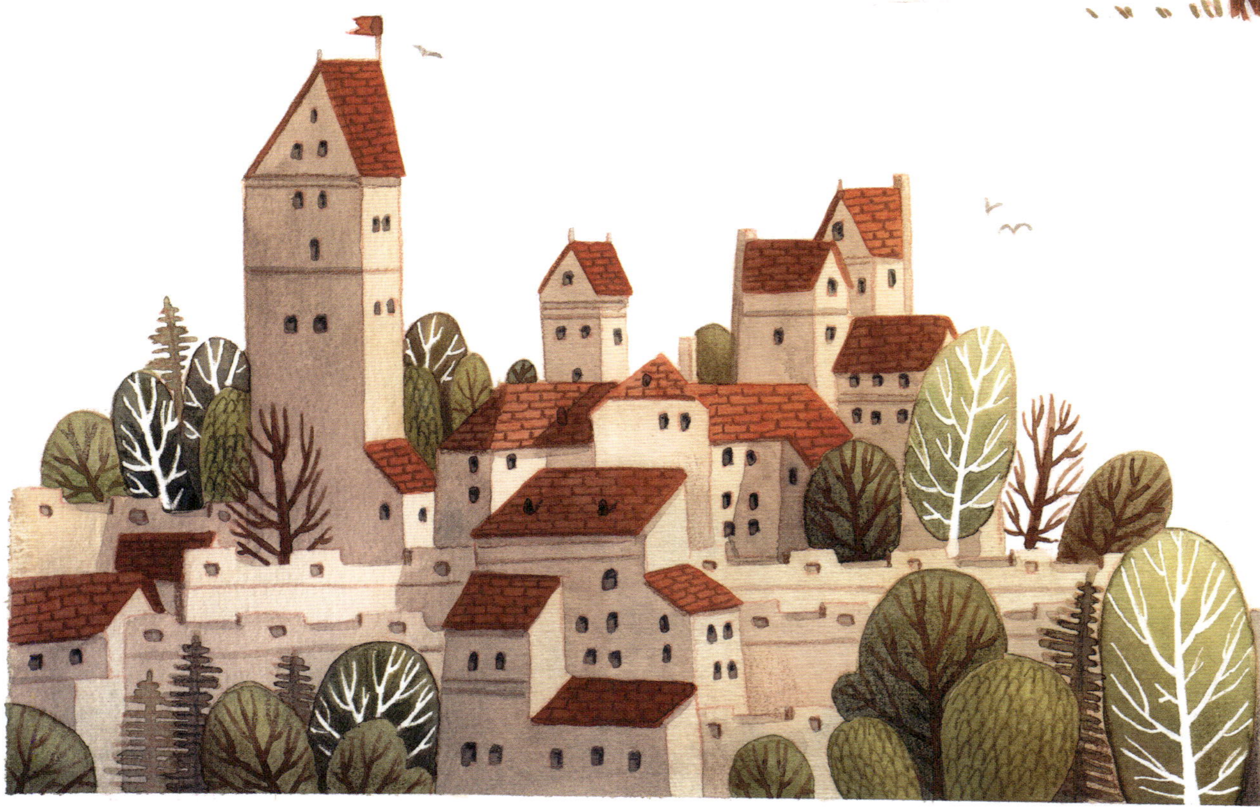

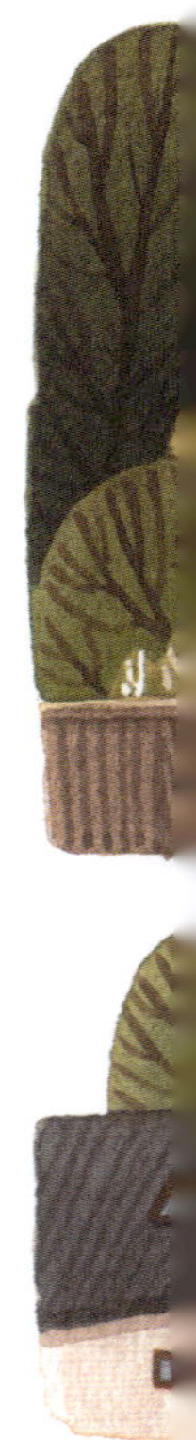

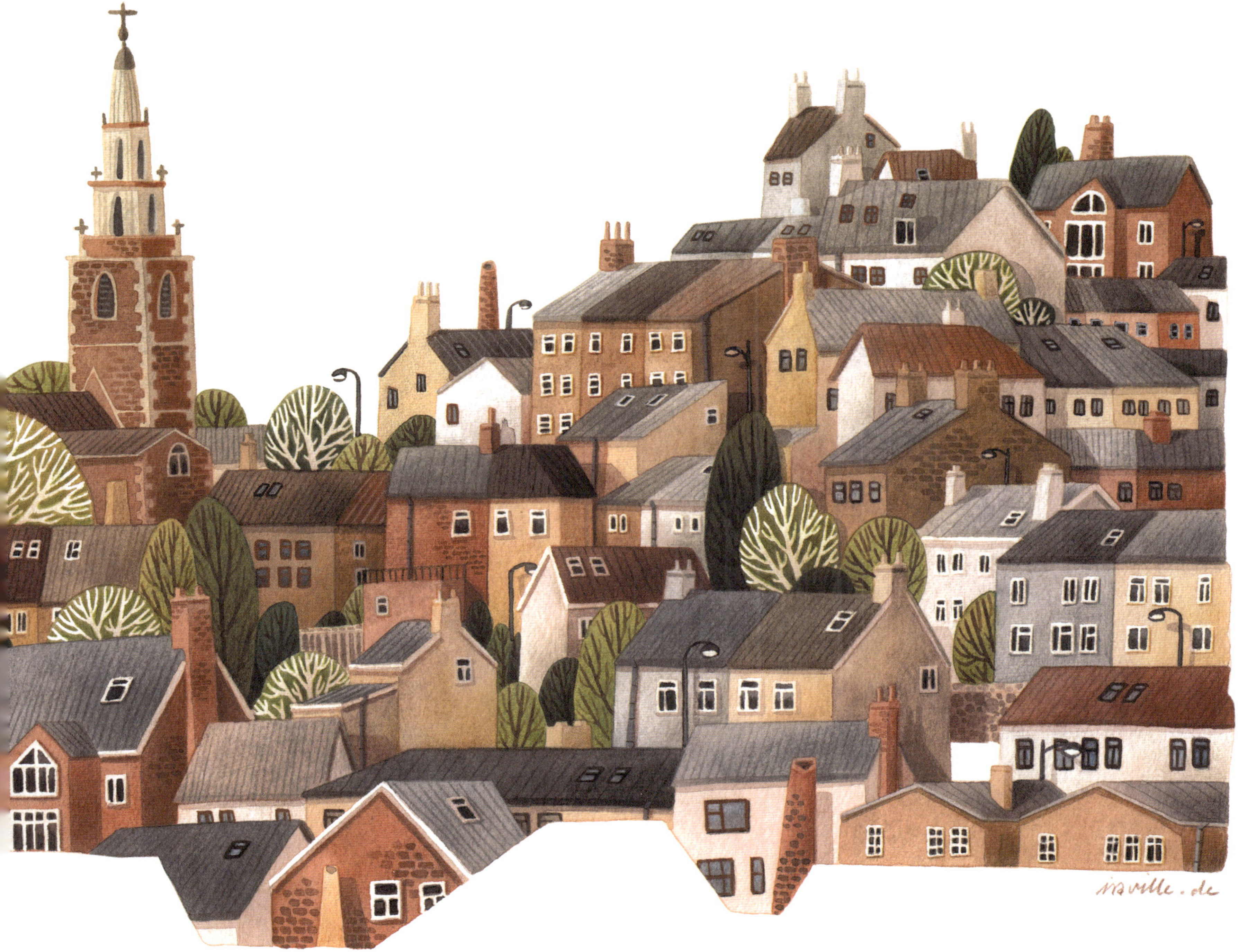
naville.de

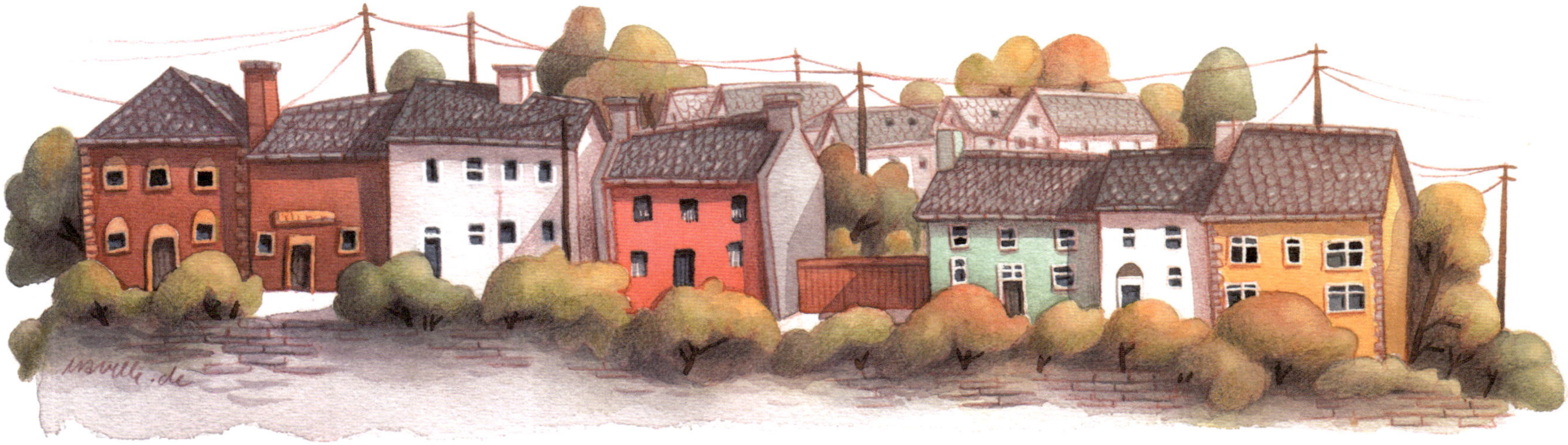

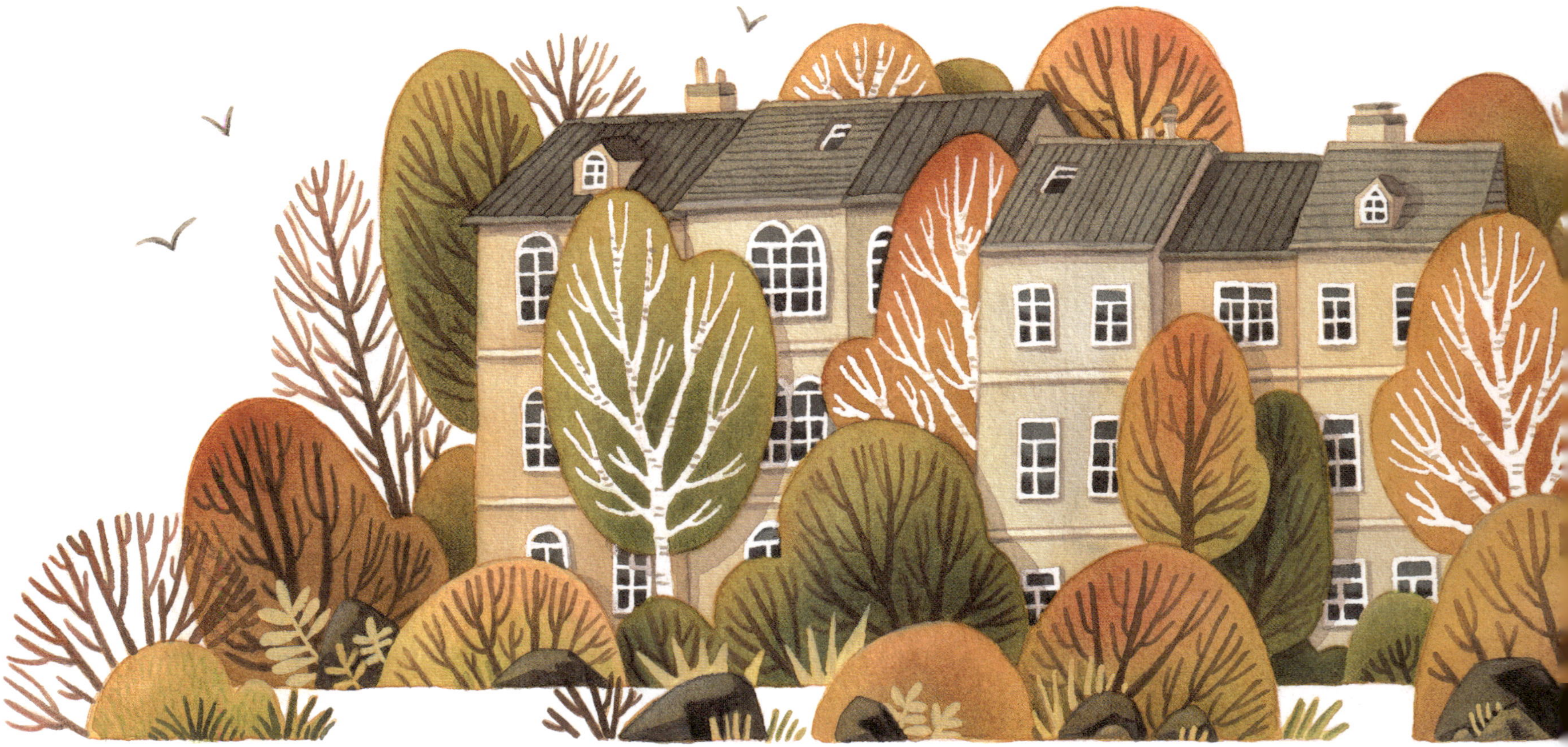

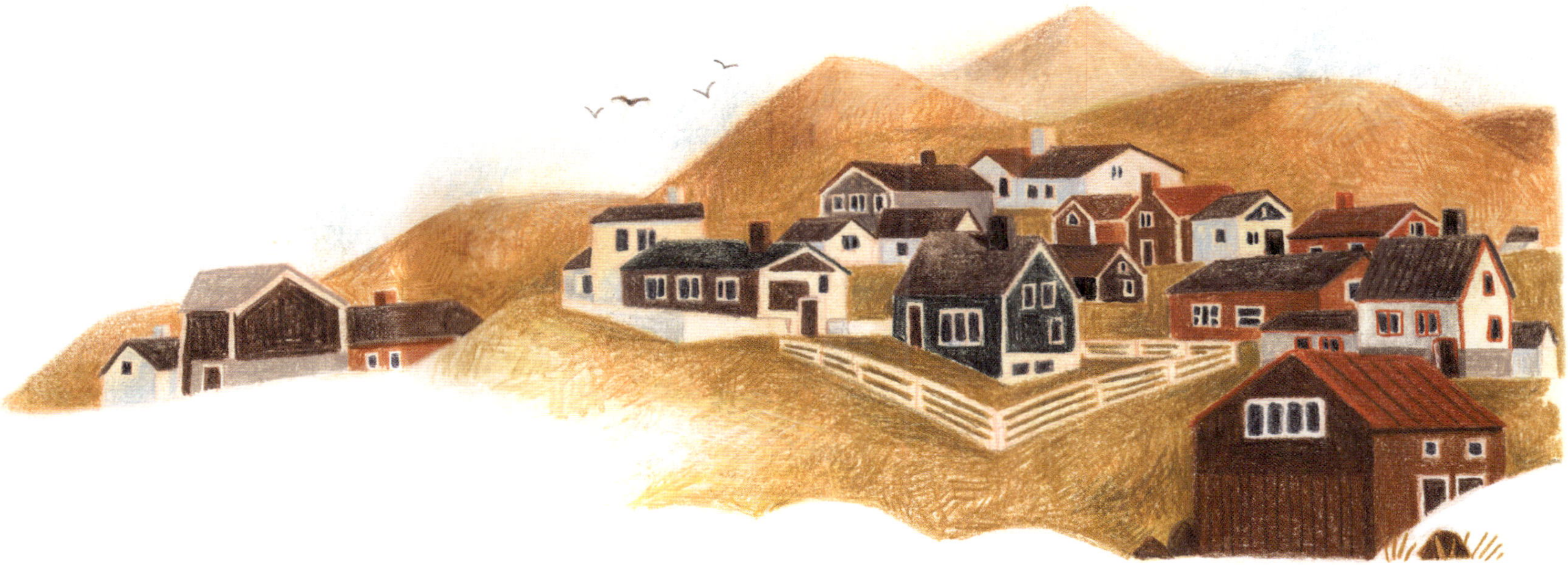

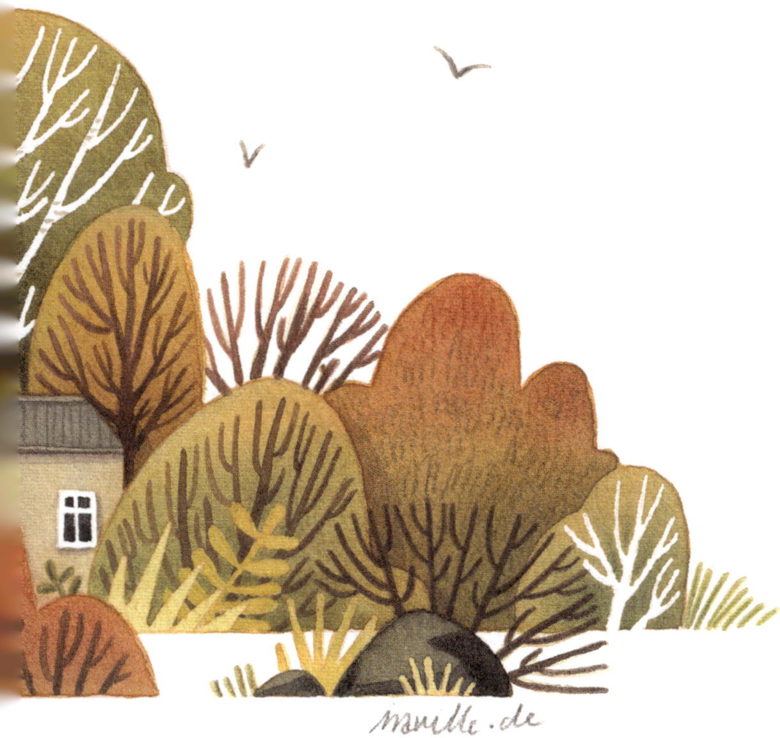

Opposite page (top):
Portmagee 1, watercolour and coloured pencil, 2015

Left:
Munich Isar View, watercolour and coloured pencil, 2022

Above:
Danish Village, watercolour pencil, 2019

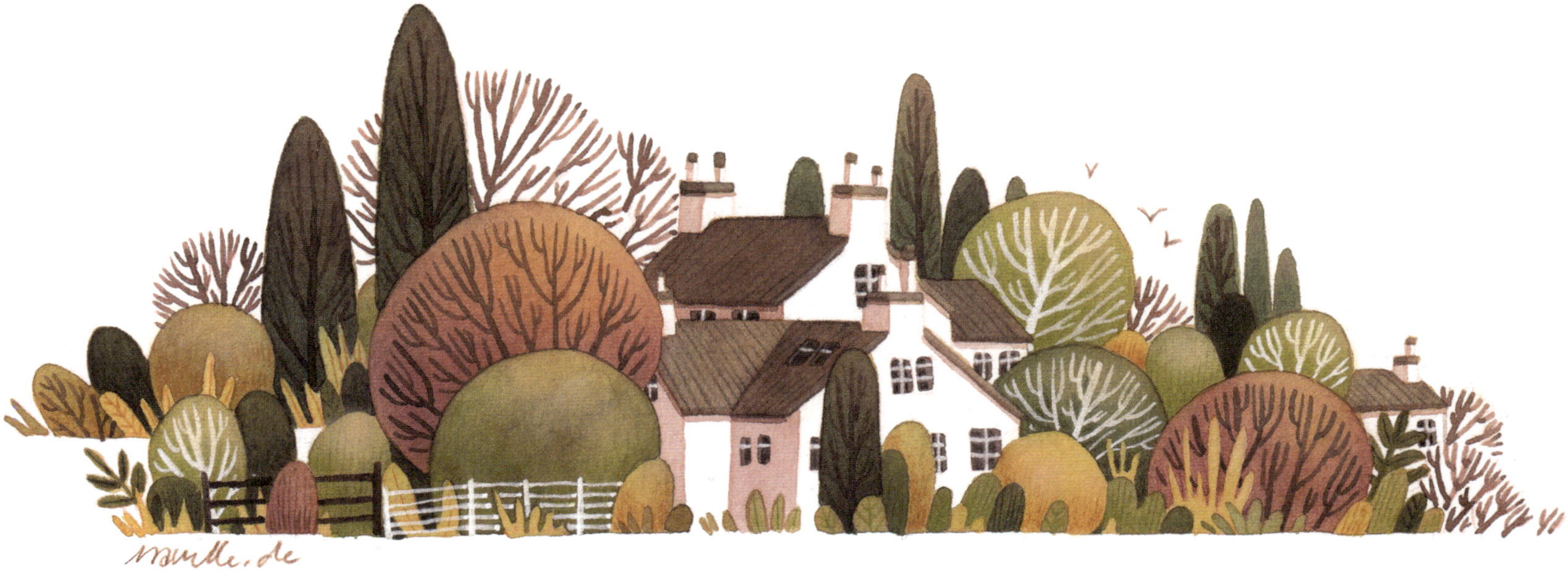
maulle.de

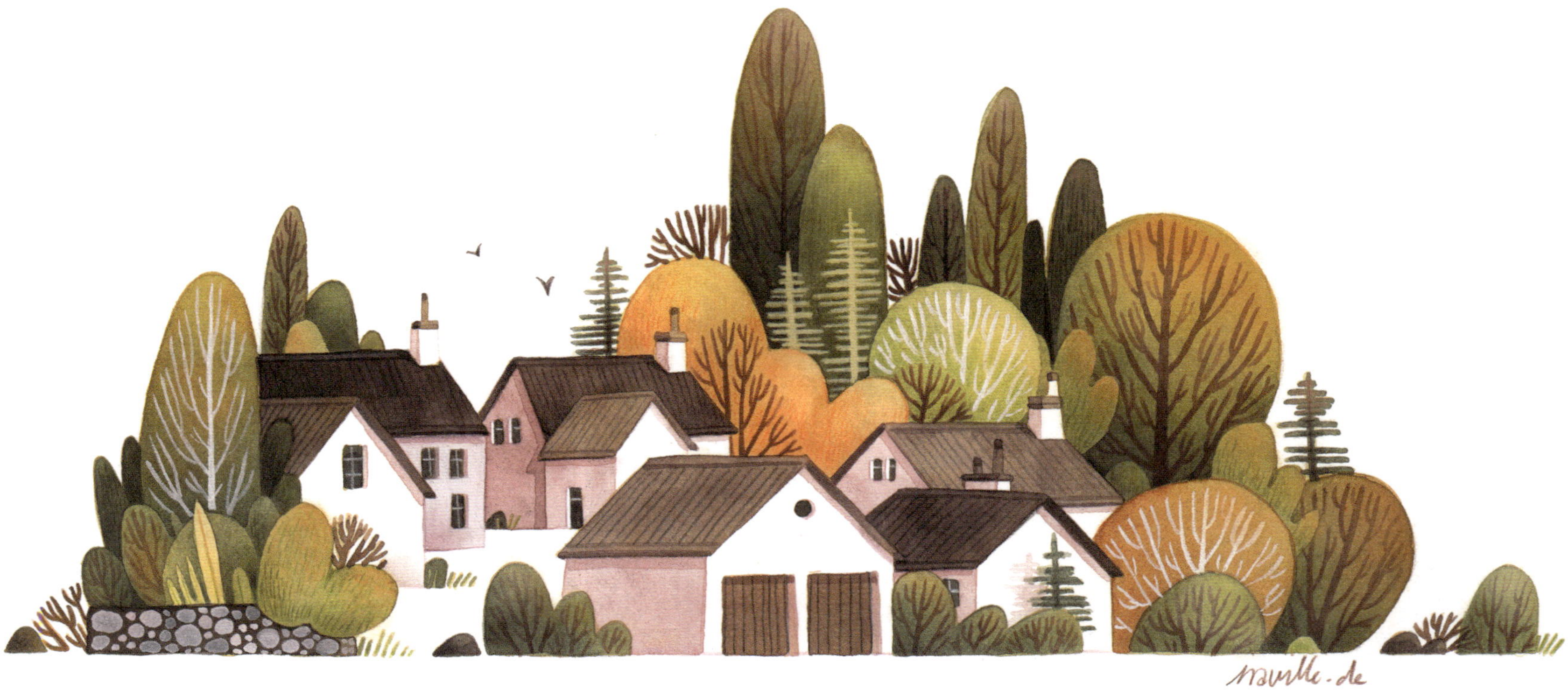
maulle.de

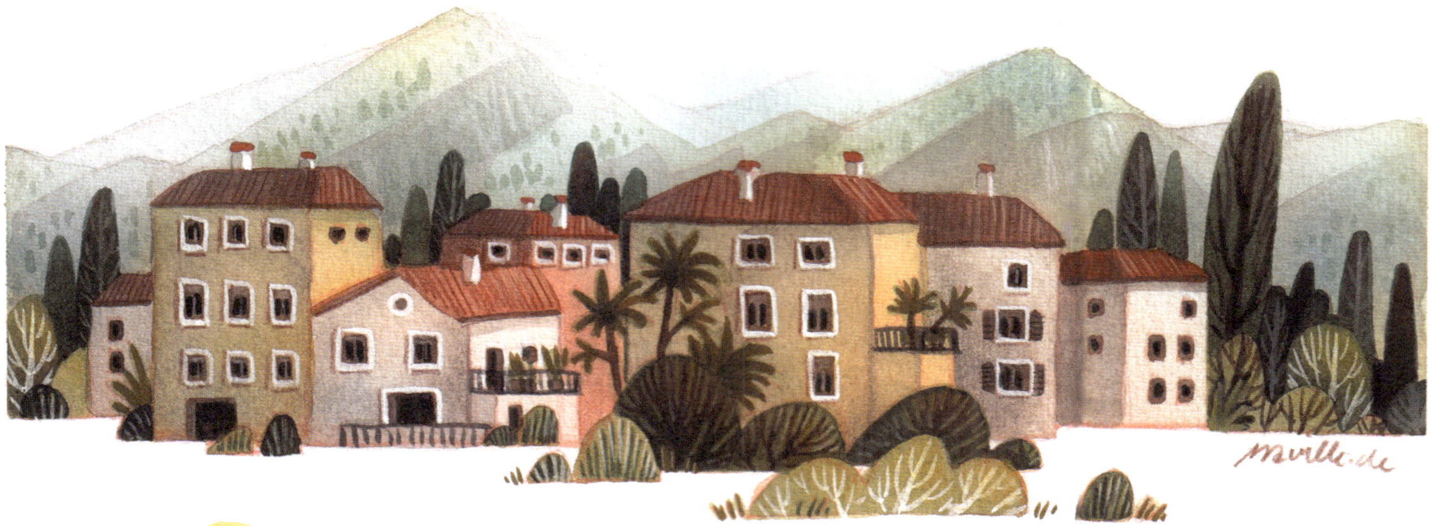

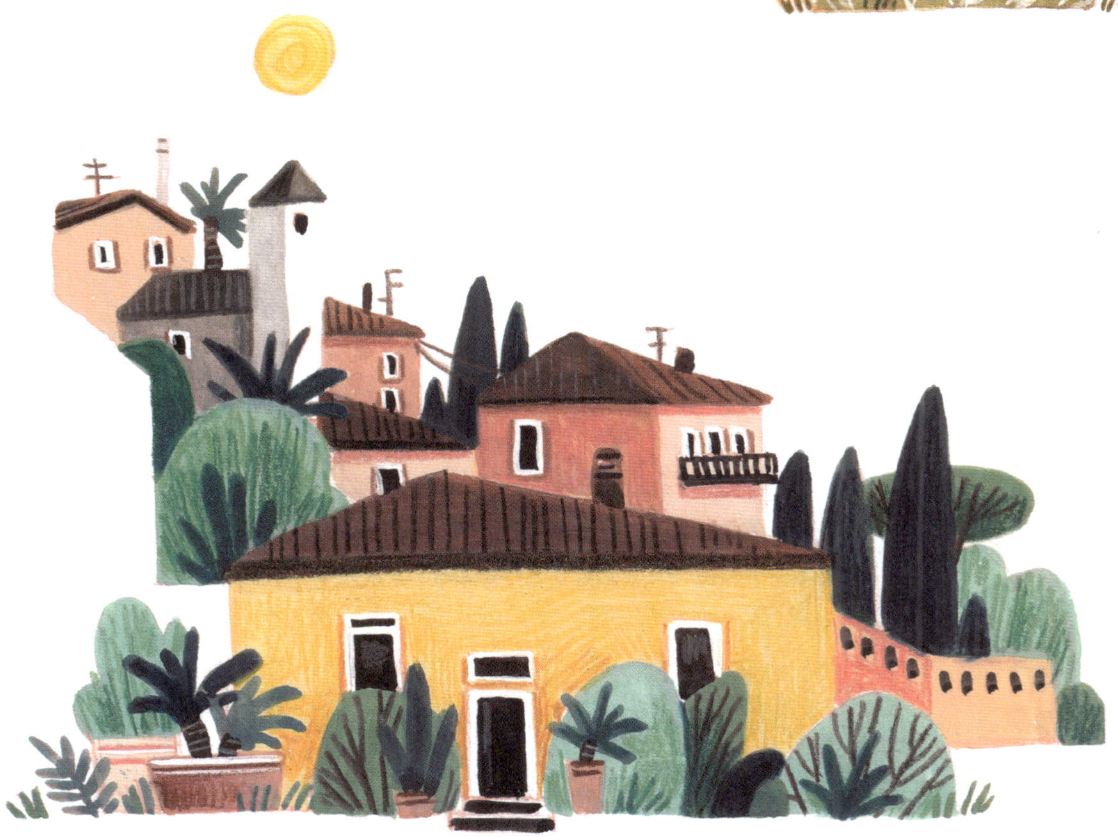

Opposite page (above):
Irish Houses and Trees, watercolour and coloured pencil, 2023

Opposite page (below):
Irish Houses and Trees 2, watercolour and coloured pencil, 2023

Above:
North Italy Sketch, watercolour and coloured pencil, 2018

Left:
Sunny Day in Italy, gouache and wax crayons, 2019

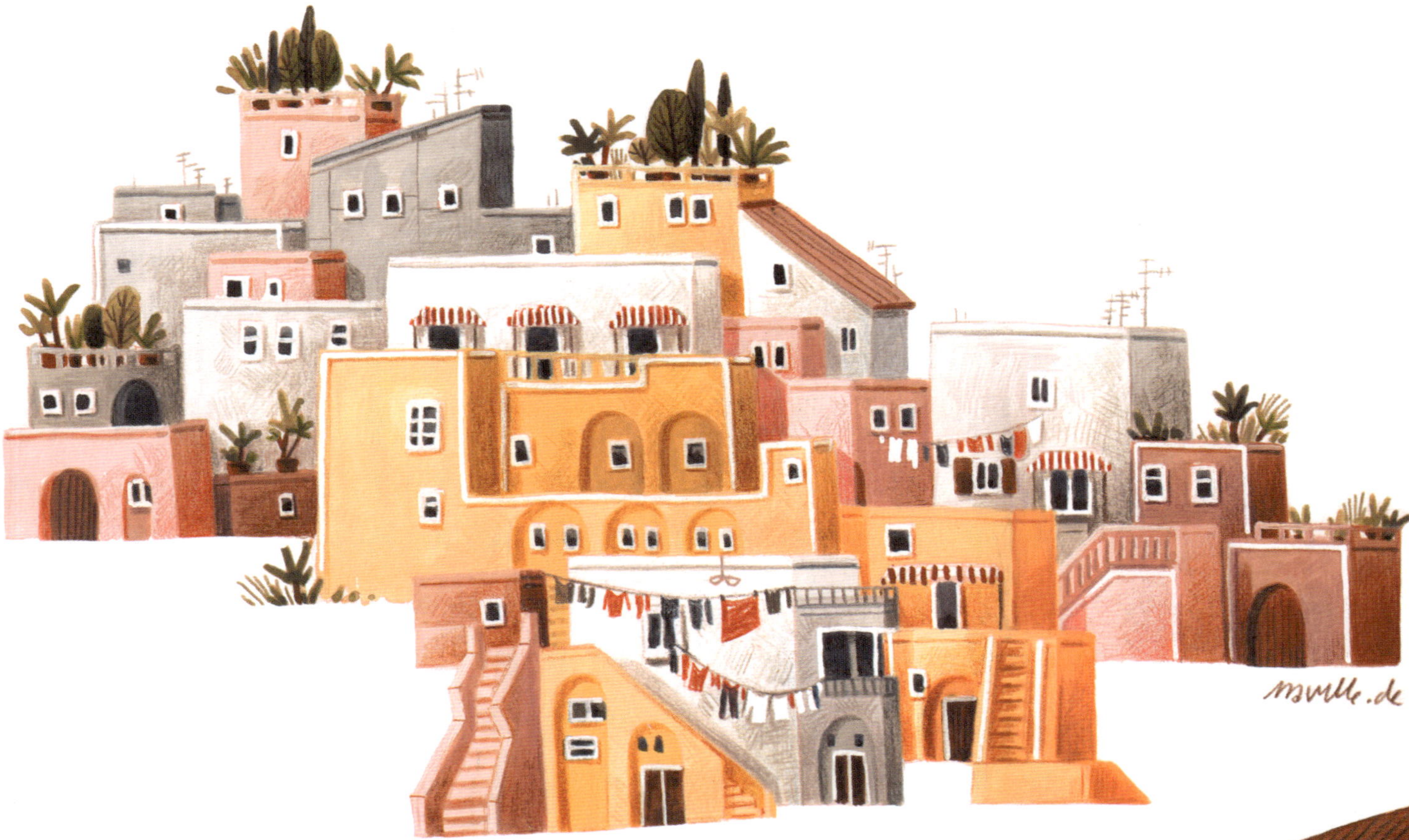

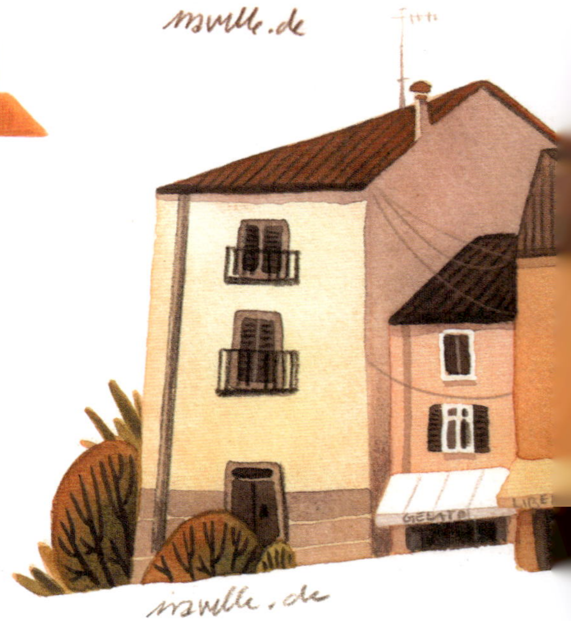

Above:
Italian Rooftops, gouache and coloured pencil, 2019

Right:
Italian Town, watercolour and coloured pencil, 2018

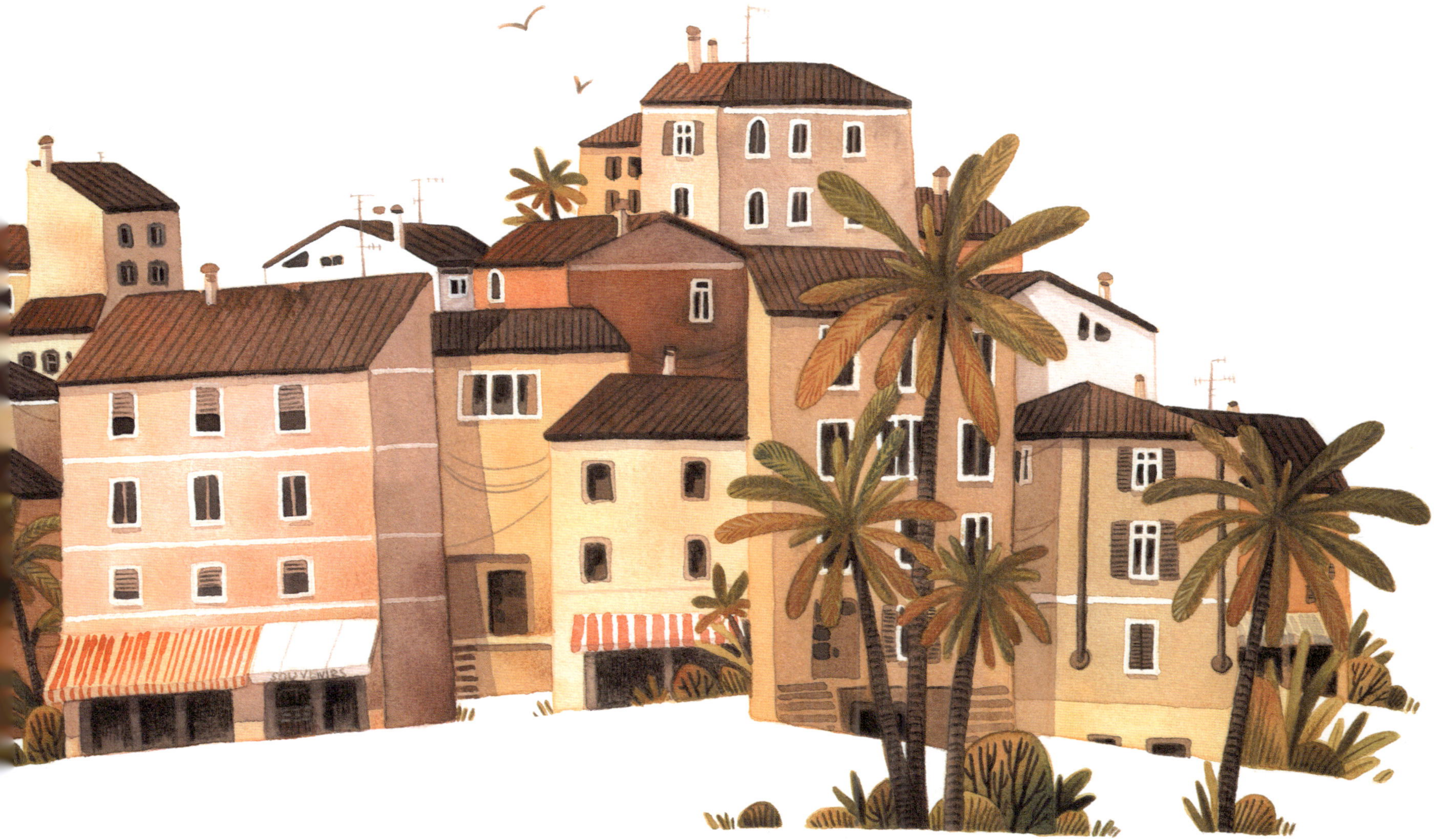

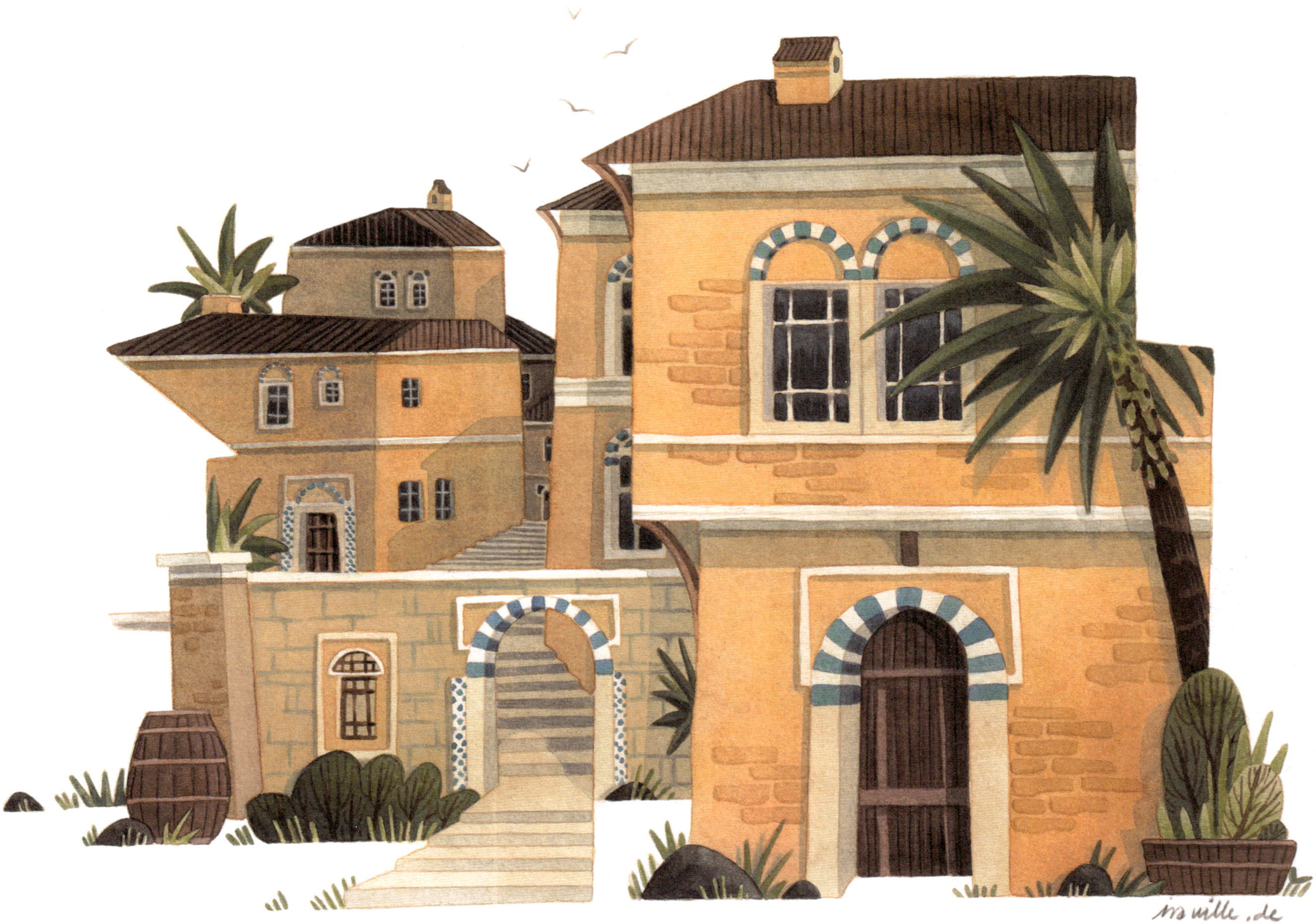
isawille.de

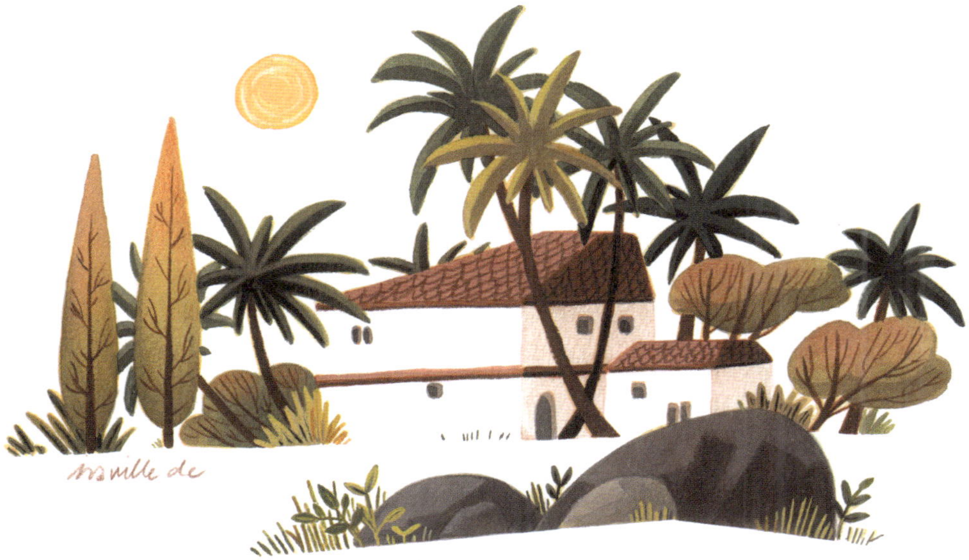

Left:
Moorish Houses, watercolour and coloured pencil, 2022

Above:
Mediterranean Houses, watercolour, gouache, coloured pencil, 2018

Right:
Yellow Roofs, watercolour and coloured pencil, 2019

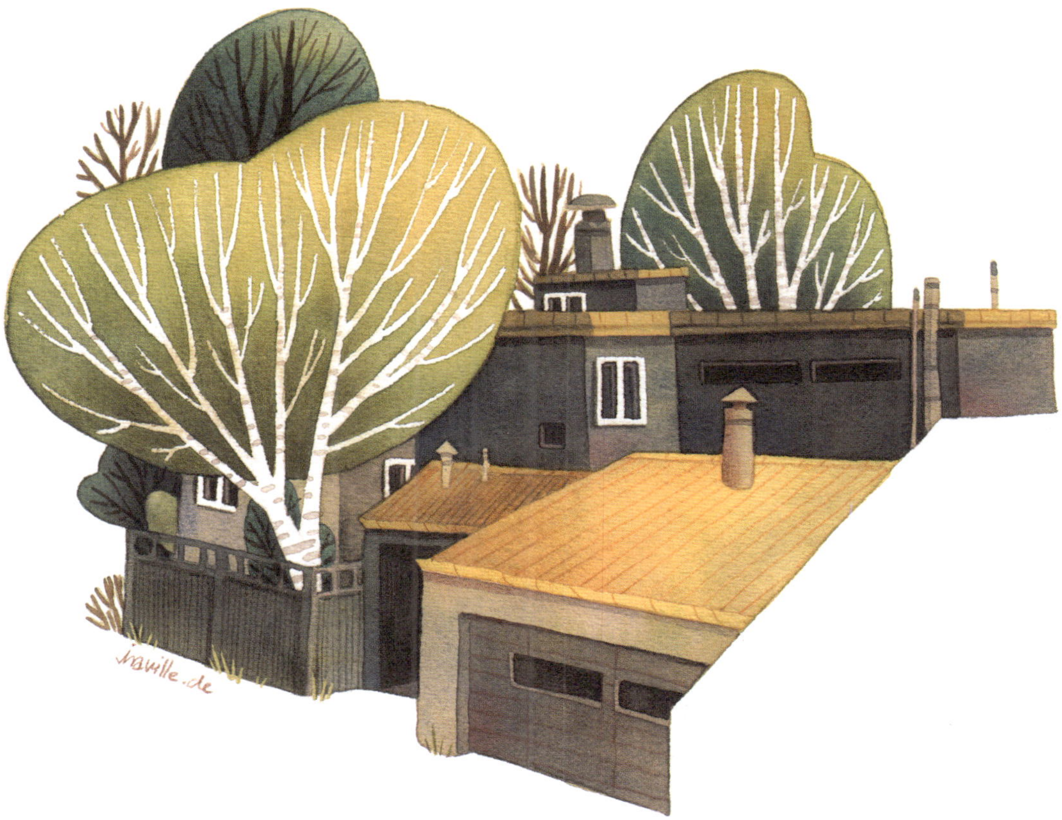

BEHIND THE SCENES

How I use colour

I cannot imagine a world without colours. To put it another way: I do not want to imagine it. That world would be a nightmare.

For me, colour is the world, and in quite a literal sense too. Natural pigments derive from the earth, whether that is through metals, minerals, plants, or even animals. Maybe that is one of the reasons why I love to use watercolours to depict life.

Colour is the first thing I consider when starting a new artwork. It is an important part of determining the overall composition – it has to serve it. Everything is about the final image itself. I do not intend to use colour 'correctly' all of the time, just like I intentionally paint false perspectives.

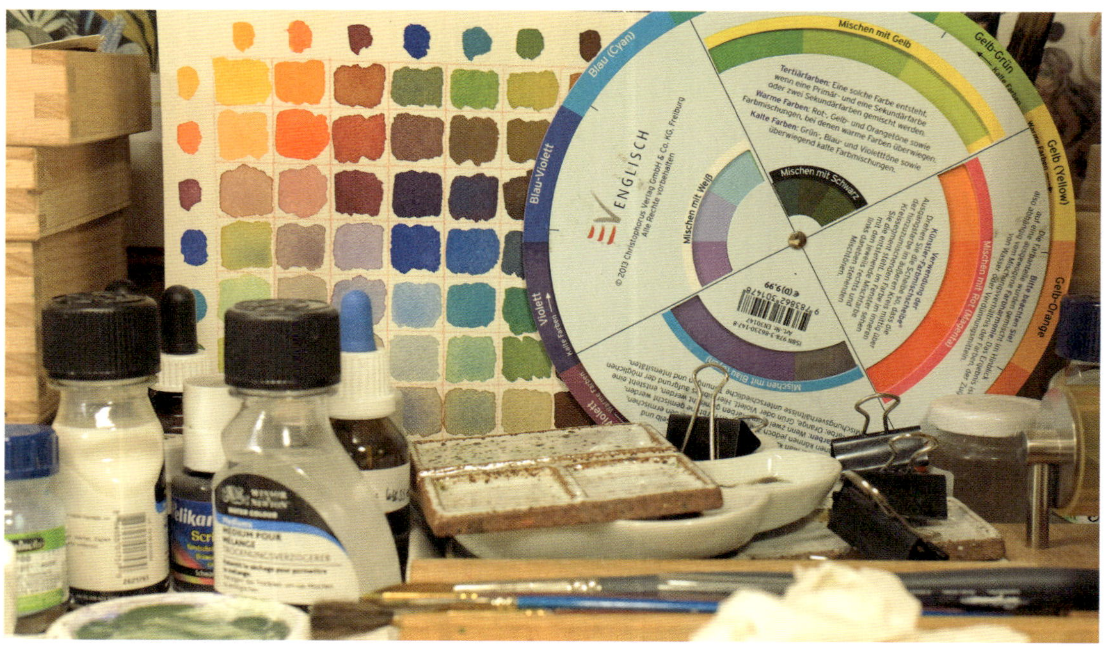

All colours influence each other, so I always look at them in relation to each other. Sometimes the result can be harmonious or contrasting, depending on the desired effect. For example, since I rarely draw outlines, I often use colour contrasts – complementary, or nearly complementary ones (besides value contrasts) – for separating forms. I even look at the ratios when doing so. Normally, I would not paint a yellow area beside a blue area in the same size because the ratio between contrasting colours should work well together.

I never use paints directly out of the tube or pan, but rather mix them on my palettes, paper, or both before applying them. I mix them through overlays, using many transparent layers of paint to get more depth. This makes the colours much more interesting and less flat.

As mentioned on page 56, it is also important not to mix too much because the colours can appear dirty, especially if they are poor quality. Certain pigments can make colours appear muddy as well, like opaque colours or ones containing black or white pigments. Therefore, I usually use very few base colours from which all other shades can be mixed, even black.

When I determine those colours, I tend to add at least one granulating colour, which will create interesting textures on the paper.

Let me show you some examples of how I mix colour.

EXAMPLES

GREENS

Here, you can see how I mix different green hues from a few basic colours. Cobalt turquoise light is a granulating colour. Check out the texture it creates – isn't it lovely? I love those details.

Please be aware that this is just an example as you can choose other basic colours.

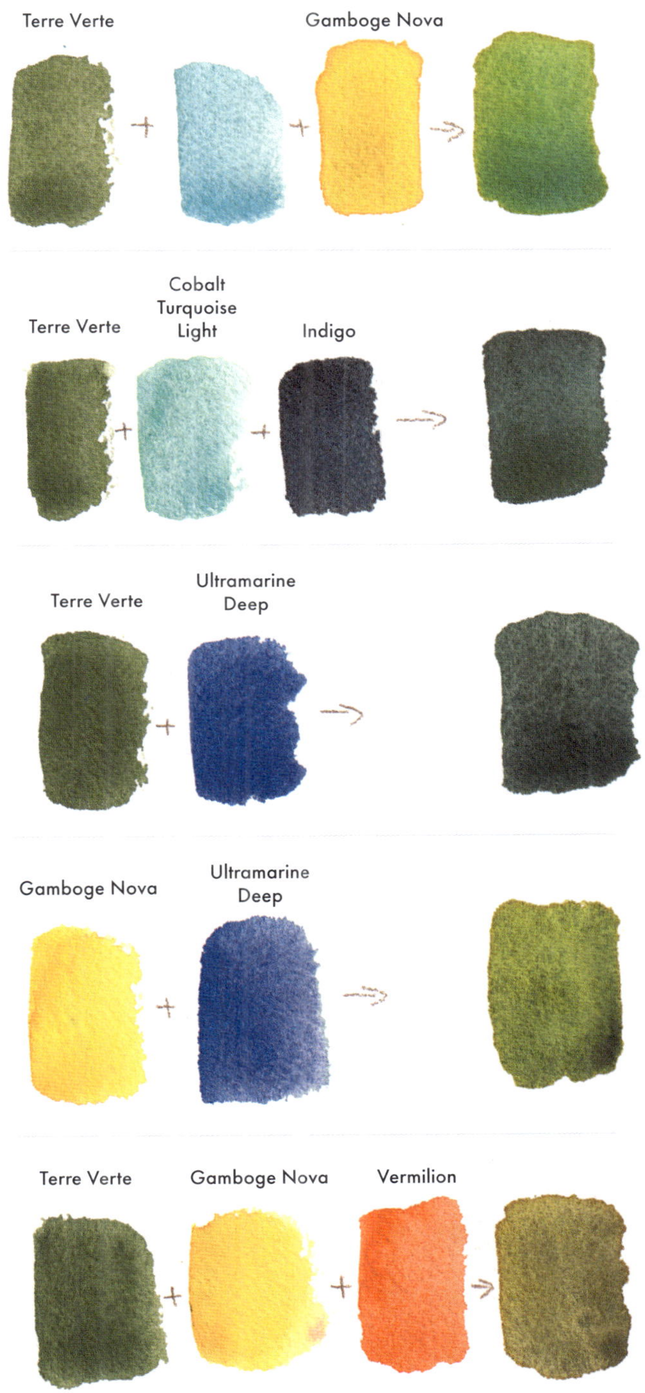

VALUES & TRANSPARENCY

This chart shows how I would play around with one of the greens (the mix from the first row on the previous page). If I want it to be colder and lighter, I add more cobalt turquoise light with water. If I want it to be colder and darker, I add indigo. But I could also make warmer and lighter greens by adding more gamboge nova and water, or warmer, darker tones by mixing it with burnt umber.

Another way to change the tonal values is to adjust the amount of water. The more water used, the lighter the colours.

The other way to get darker tones is to add black. But remember: black pigments do not work well. That is why I mix my black first before adding it (as you can see in the last row).

VALUE EXAMPLE FOR ONE OF THE MIXED GREENS

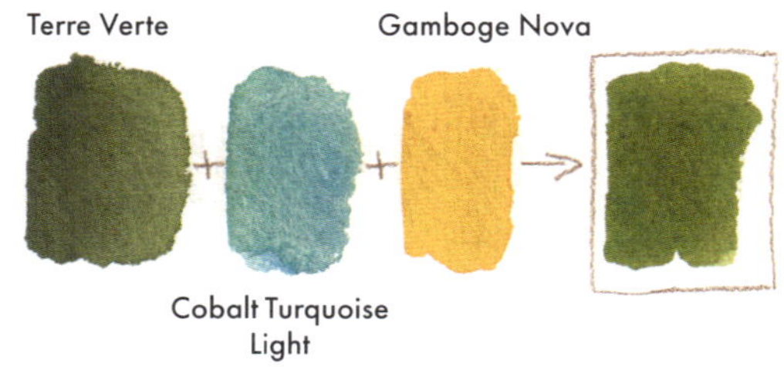

COLD SEQUENCE

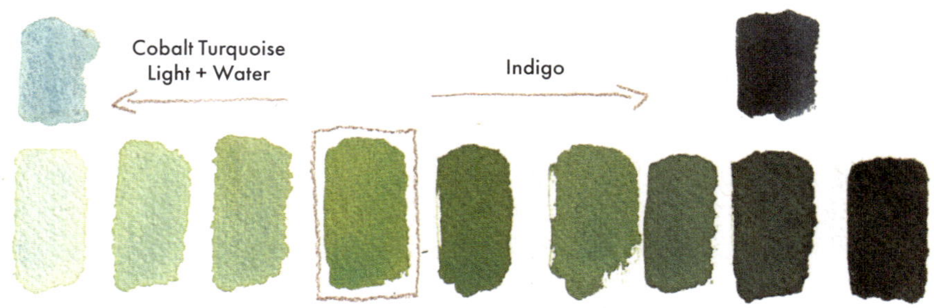

NEUTRAL SEQUENCE

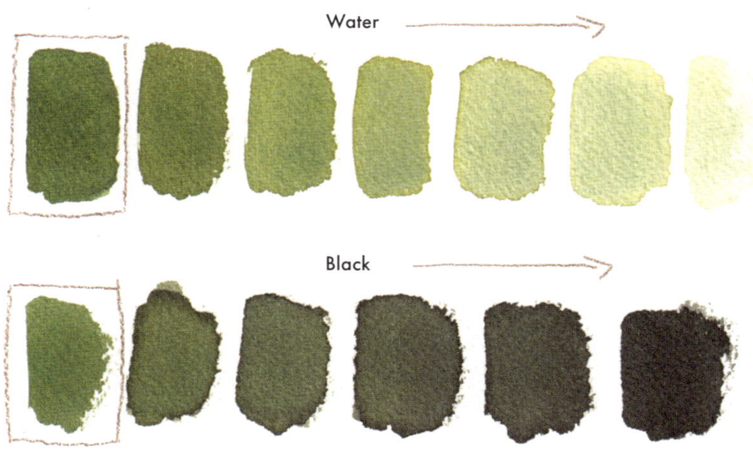

WARM SEQUENCE

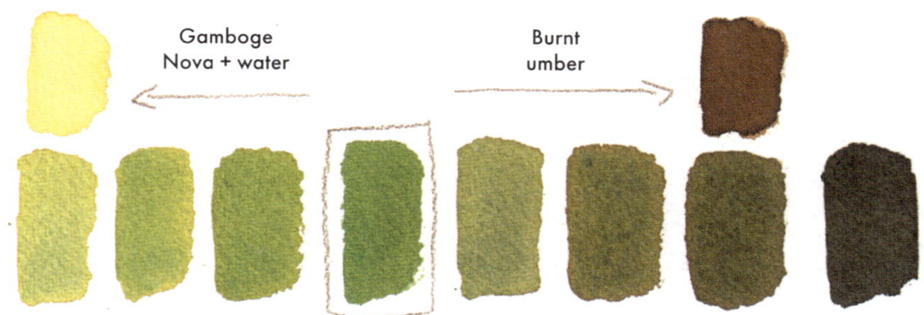

BLACK

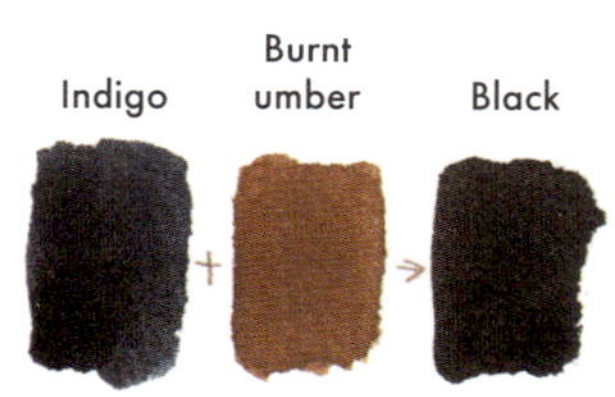

NEUTRALS

Thankfully, there are many ways to mix neutral tones to avoid a muddy black pigment. In the example image below, I like the mixed grey tones because you can still see separate colour pigments in them (if one of the colours is granulating).

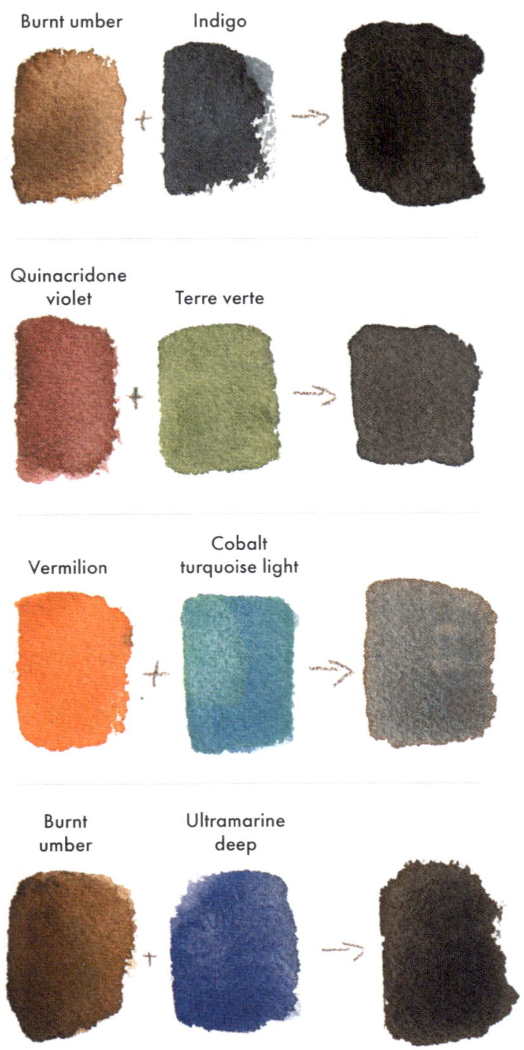

SHADOWS

Here, I demonstrate how I mix colours for shadows. In real life, shadows are not just grey. The colour depends on the surface they appear on. I tend to use a lightened or darkened violet for shadows, combined with a colour that is complementary to the layer beneath.

If you are interested in trying out watercolours for yourself, a colour wheel can help with determining contrasts and harmonies. You can try out different mixing techniques and base colours. It helps to write down the colours you used, as well as the mixing results in swatches, in your sketchbook like I did here. Have fun trying it out! There are endless possibilities!

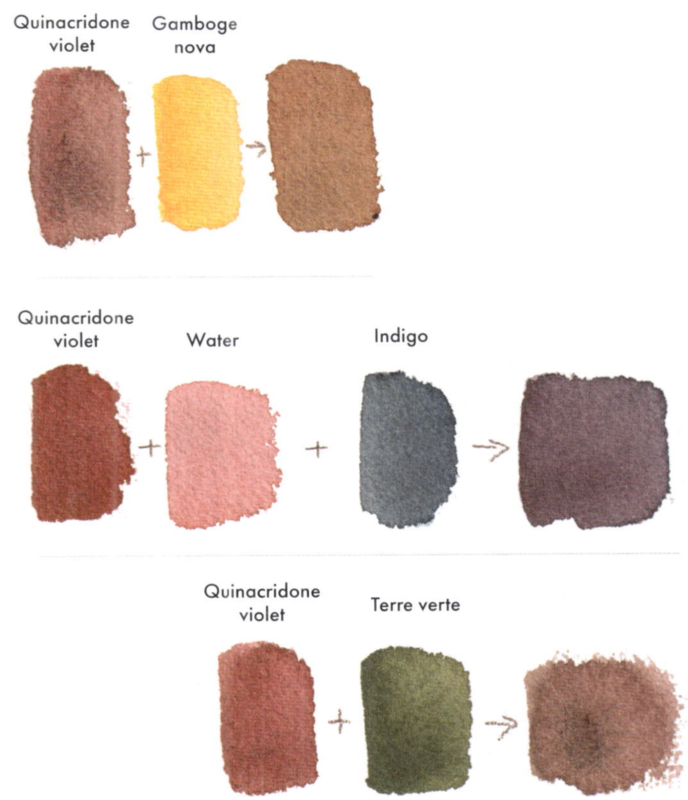

IRA'S INSIGHTS

What Japanese aesthetics taught me

I admire Japan for its long and rich artistic traditions.

Two theories that underlie traditional Japanese aesthetics correspond quite well to my conception of art: *wabi-sabi* and *ma*. I am not an expert in these theories, but their respective principles have always made sense to me. If I understand correctly, *wabi-sabi* refers to the non-obvious beauty that is hidden in the imperfect and ageing/transient.

For people like me who grew up with a European conception of art, this is a revolution. Unlike antiquity, which has shaped the beauty ideal in the West, perfection, symmetry, completeness, and direct visible beauty do not occupy the Olympus of art; instead, it is the opposite: imperfection, asymmetry, irregularity, modesty, intimacy, and simplicity … the hidden beauty. But what does that really mean, especially in relation to today? And what does it have to do with my drawings?

Every so often, I receive a comment that reads, 'Simple, but beautiful', and I smile each time I see it. After all, my drawings are deliberately simplified and stylized. I strive for the right degree of simplicity. You will find that 'simple' is often better when you move through the world with open eyes.

One of the reasons the comic strip *Peanuts* became world-famous is because the characters consisted of just a few ingenious strokes. Some of them are slightly spidery, but try drawing Charlie Brown – it is harder than you think. Only Charles M. Schulz could make these simple strokes the same way. Aside from the simplicity, the human factor made the drawings so fantastic. Sometimes less is more, and the imperfect can be beautiful.

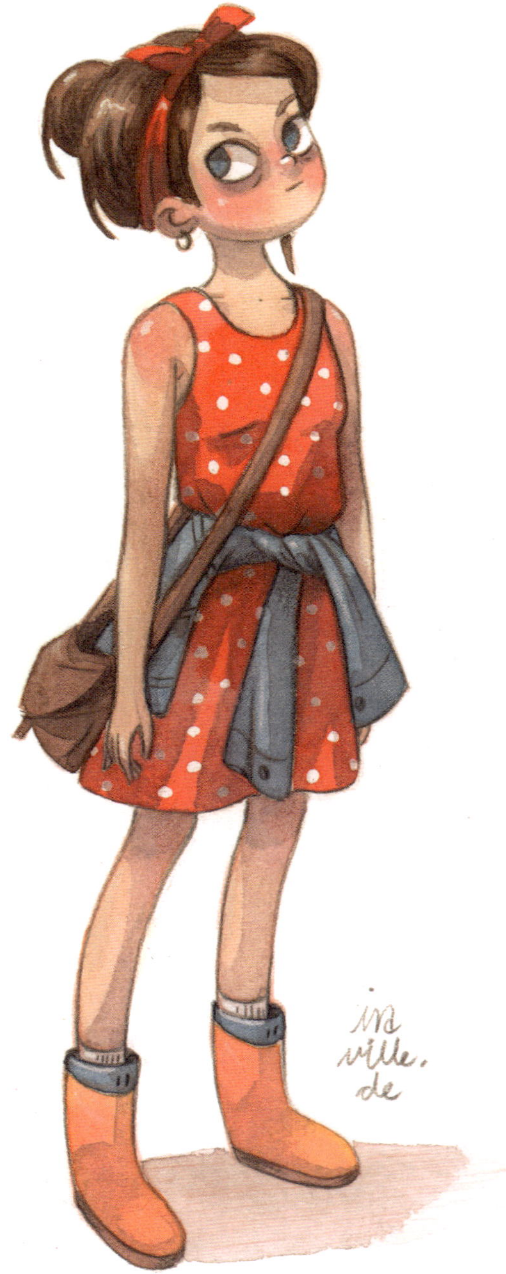

'Sometimes less is more, and the imperfect can be beautiful'

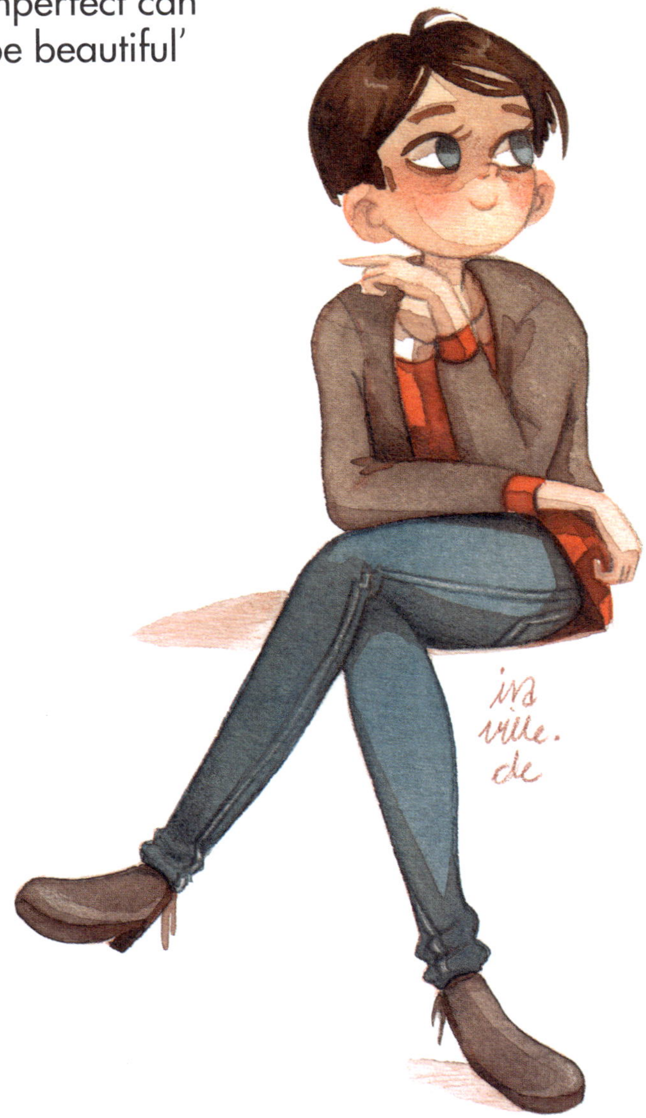

A good example is stop-motion animation. I feel that it can sometimes have more charm than computer-generated 3D animation. I have nothing against 3D animated movies – I even love some of them! In the end, it is just a matter of taste, and it is good that there are many different ones. However, the handmade, slightly imperfect nature of *Wallace and Gromit* – despite the stop-motion mastery – brings a human factor to the animation that makes the films particularly endearing. Wes Anderson uses stop-motion for the same reason, even for animated scenes in real-life films, such as *The Grand Budapest Hotel* or *The Life Aquatic with Steve Zissou*. I even like the aesthetics of the old, hand-painted episodes of *The Simpsons* way better than the new, computer-drawn ones (I will not go into how the scripts were also better back then!). In all of these examples, the greatness lies precisely in their imperfections.

What about the beauty of ageing in *wabi-sabi*?

I also see parallels there when I look at my artworks, an example being my preference for autumn, the season of slight melancholy. This also applies to the houses and towns I paint. My houses are never straight or accurate, as if they had just been newly built. Quite the contrary, it is obvious that their best years are now long behind them. But they have a special sort of beauty because they have history, and their age is shown through lopsided areas, crooked chimneys, and extensions.

The other great principle of traditional Japanese aesthetics, *ma*, is the emptiness and space between things or time, like in music. It refers to all aspects of life, but in painting, it is primarily the recognition that space and non-space (or emptiness) are related and equally important.

Many of my drawings are surrounded by negative space. During the preliminary drawing phase, I think about the space around the forms and try to create a balanced, interesting relationship. My drawings always have deliberate open spaces, like when I draw a group of animals, or when a wall fades into nothingness.

Since white space in layouts is important to me as well (like the relationship between text and open areas), I will wrap up my superficial thoughts on this beautiful topic before the writing takes up too much space. I would rather take a long tea break, and perhaps I will leaf through an old *Peanuts* volume while sipping it.

BEHIND THE SCENES

Negative painting

This tutorial shows you how to use the negative-painting technique. In this method, darker areas are painted around lighter objects, which become indirectly formed by their surroundings.

The basic principle is the same as my earlier *Behind the scenes* chapter (page 54). Layers of paint are gradually applied (wet on dry), and I wait until each layer is completely dry before applying another. However, the difference is that I don't fill in the shapes like I did with the buoys. Instead, I fill in their surroundings.

I am often asked about this technique, and the final picture shows the principle well. Keep in mind that you do not have to apply this method for the whole image.

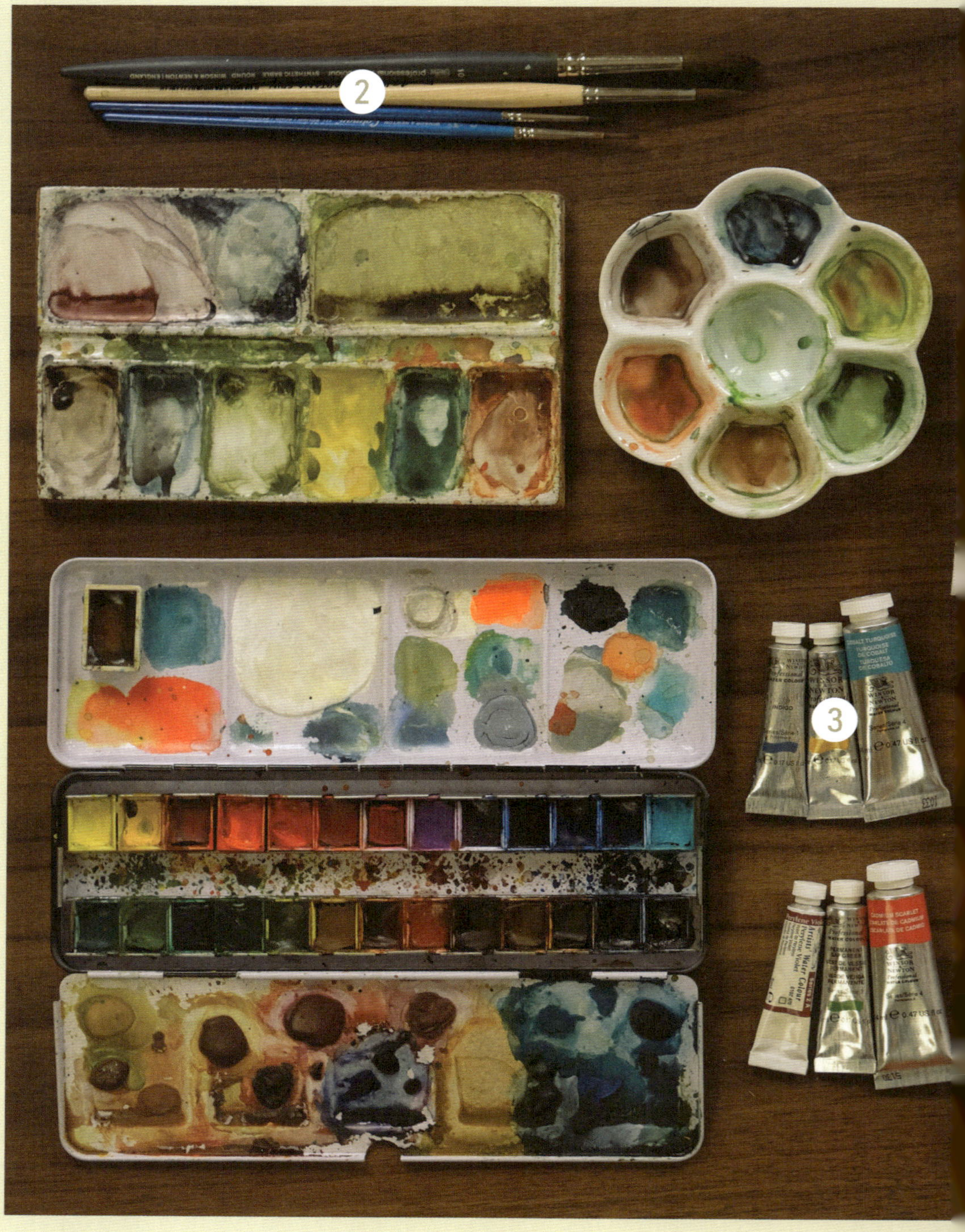

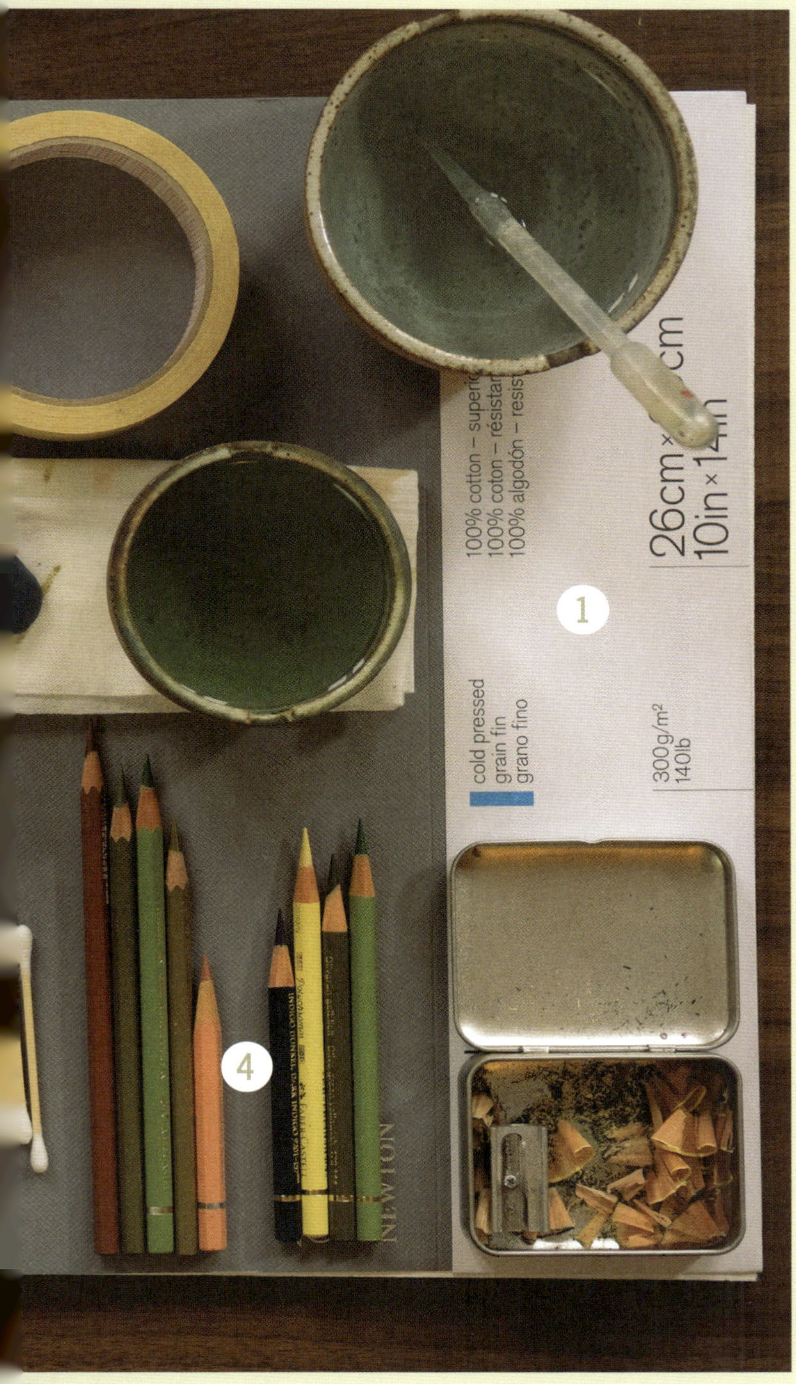

TOOLS

❶ Watercolour paper

As before, I use artist-grade paper made of 100% cotton with a thickness of 300 gsm. However, this time it is cold pressed instead of hot pressed. The surface of cold-pressed paper has more structure, and therefore it is more absorbent and allows for even more layers.

❷ Watercolour brushes

The watercolour brushes are all synthetic, but the style is somewhat different: I use a very large brush with a very long, thin tip.

❸ Colours

I choose artist-grade watercolours for this painting in permanent sap green, new gamboge, cobalt turquoise, cadmium scarlet, perylene violet, and indigo. I use the first four as base colours from which I mix most of the colour shades. The other two are used for darkening. Cobalt turquoise is a very granulating colour and will create a lot of texture.

❹ Coloured pencils

This time I use watercolour pencils (left) in addition to normal coloured pencils (right). I make sure to choose colours that match the motif. I will use the watercolour pencils to pre-draw over the watercolour layers, while the other coloured pencils will be used for details and textures at the end.

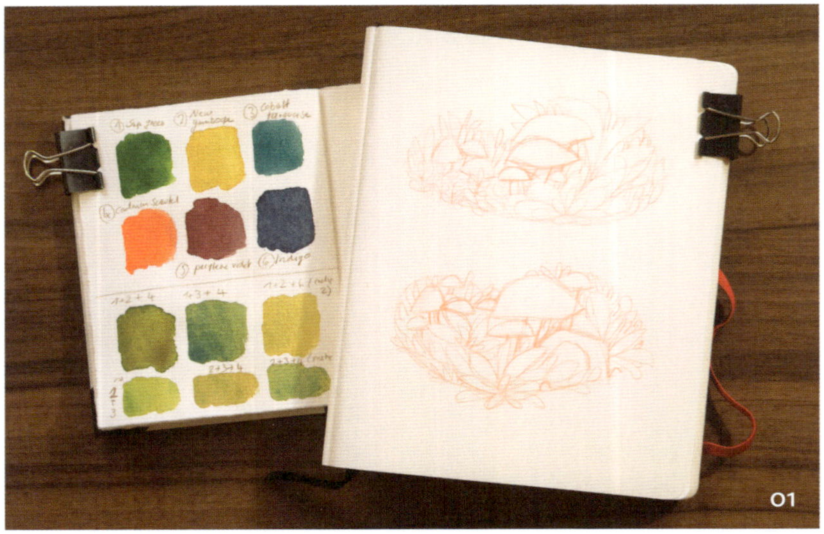

01

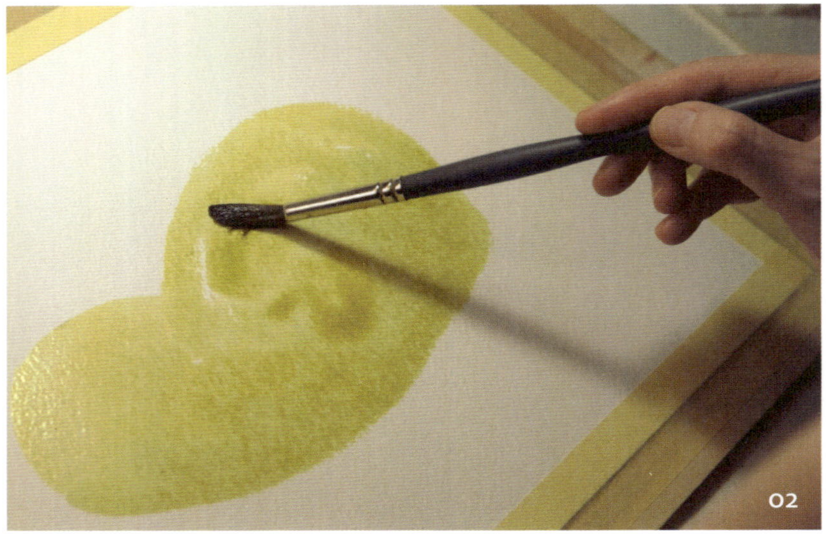

02

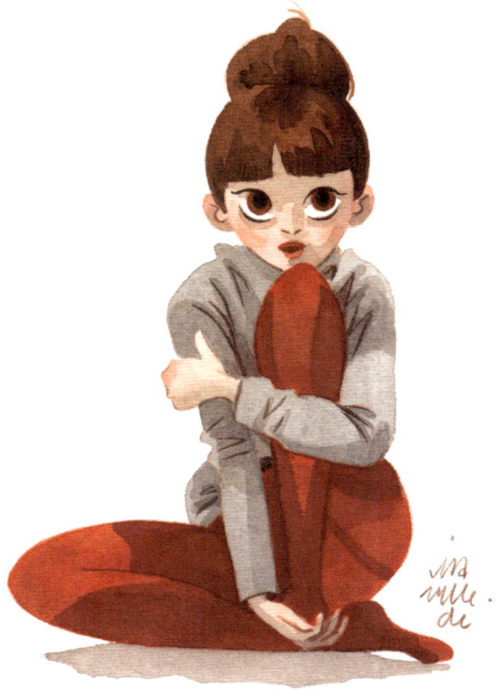

01: This painting is a still-life of imaginary mushrooms, ferns, grasses, and leaves. I make two rough sketches to determine the composition of the painting. Next, I draw a few colour swatches in my sketchbook; the six colours and accompanying mixtures will result in different shades of green and yellow.

02: First, I fix the watercolour paper with masking tape to a wood-veneer sheet to prevent it from buckling during the painting process.

Since I want to improvise with this motif, I do not make a preliminary drawing on the watercolour paper. Instead, I start immediately with a bright primer. Using a large brush, I apply a mixture of new gamboge, some permanent sap green, and some cadmium scarlet, diluted with a lot of water.

03: With the pointed brush, I pull up a few corners from the primer. A few leaves should stick out now.

04: I dab some cadmium red into the wet primer to create beautiful colour gradients – something watercolour is perfect for. At the same time, the green adopts an interesting contrast from the red hue. The mushrooms will be painted here later, so it helps that this area is getting warmer.

05: Along the edge of the primer (and also in the middle), I deliberately let a few random splashes of dark green and red drip from the brush to further emphasize the image's improvised character. In other words: I do it because I find it beautiful.

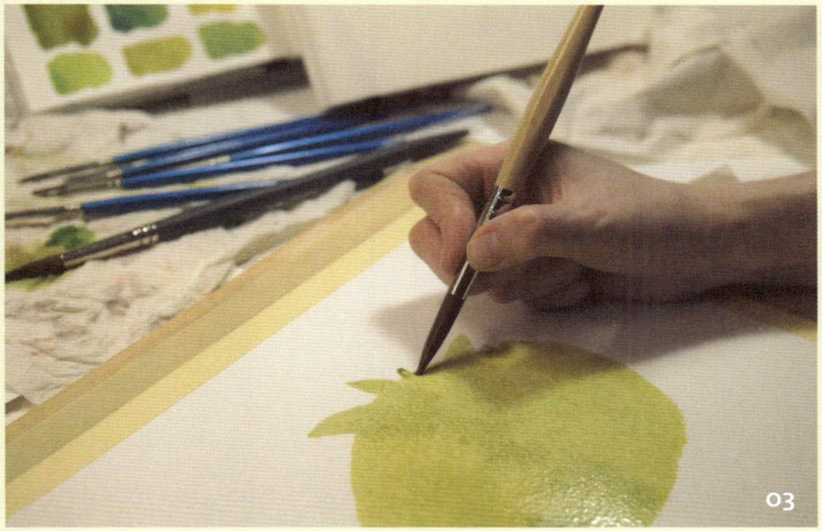

03

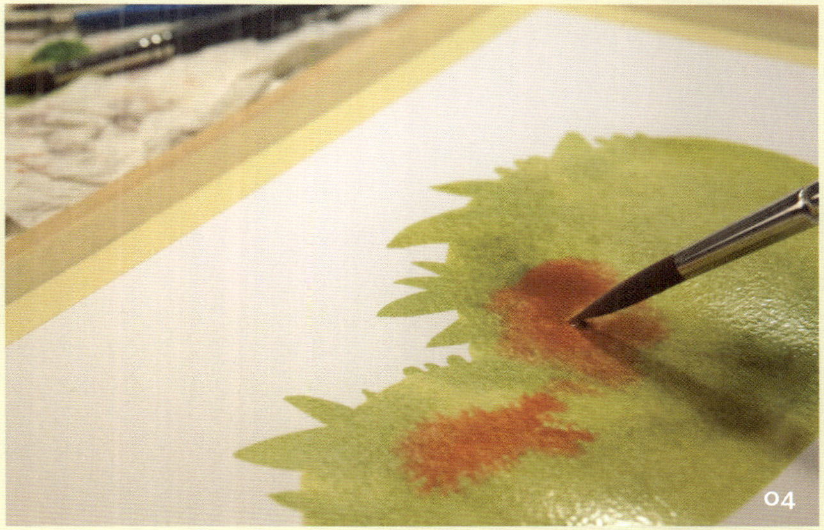

04

05

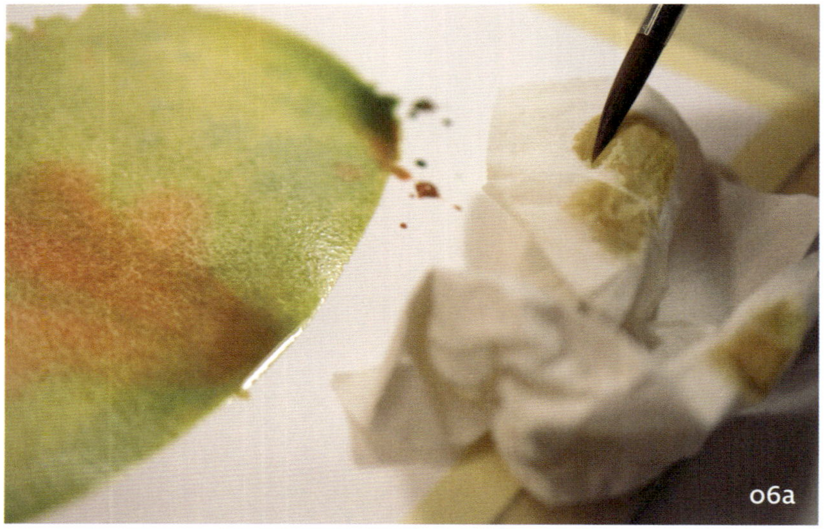

06a

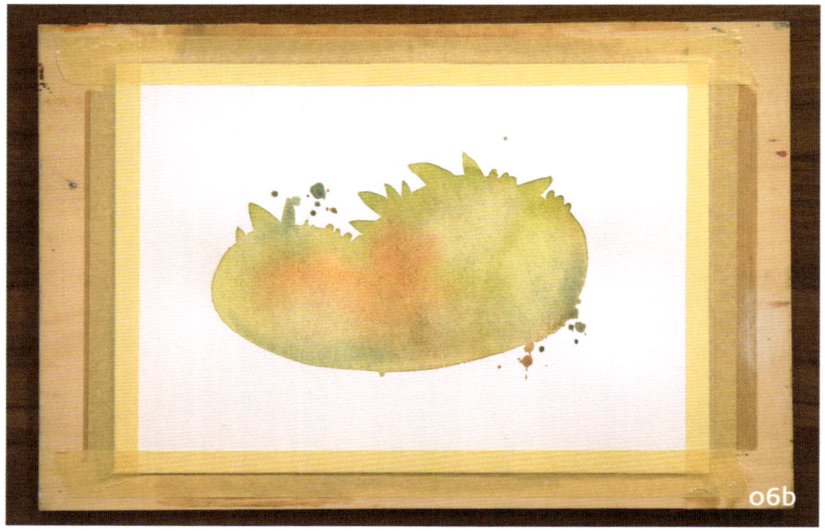

06b

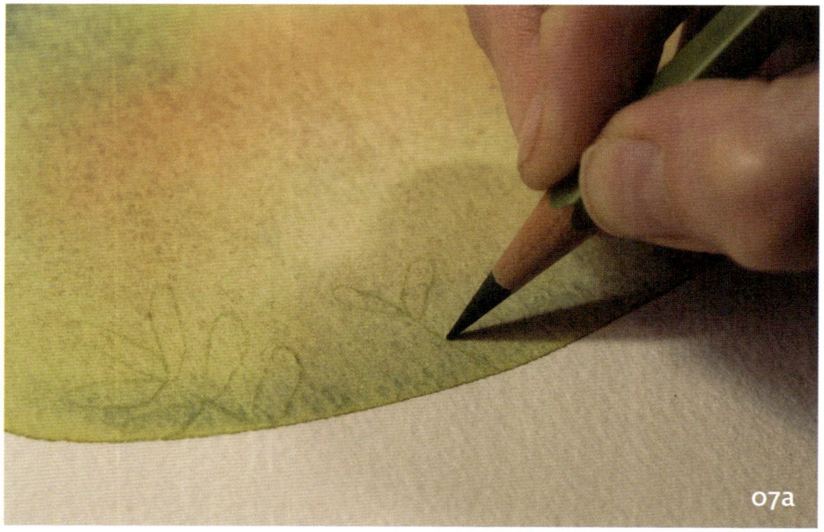

07a

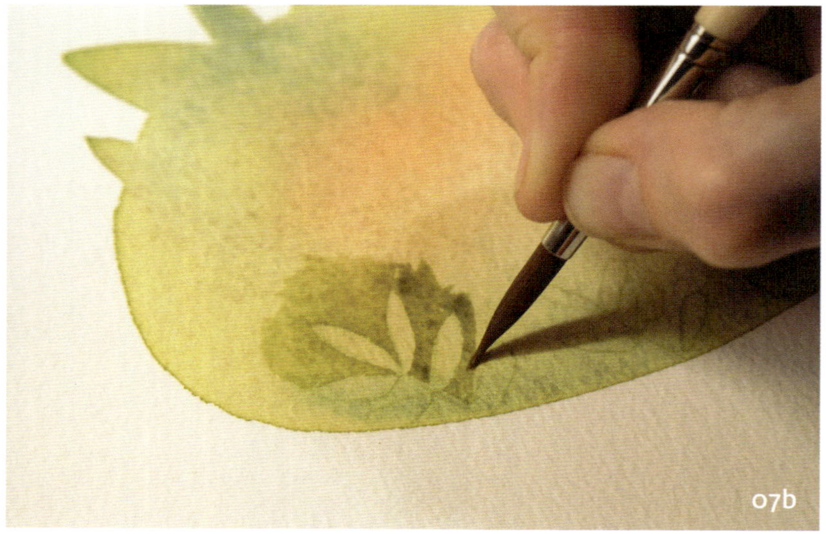

07b

06: Using a dry brush, I absorb water and pigments where too much of it has accumulated. This prevents the edges from becoming too thick after the painting dries. I also do not want too many watercolour blooms.

07: On the bone-dry primer, I draw my first row of plants with watercolour pencils, starting from the bottom edge. With the pointed brush, I apply a warm green colour layer around these outlines, then add clean water towards the outmost edge because I want the colour to bleed transparently in those areas. Whenever any water or colour edges appear there, I dab them with tissue.

08: After this new layer has dried, I repeat the steps: I pre-draw another row of plants that stick out behind the first row and fill the areas outside their outlines with a new layer of green paint. Again, this should fade out transparently.

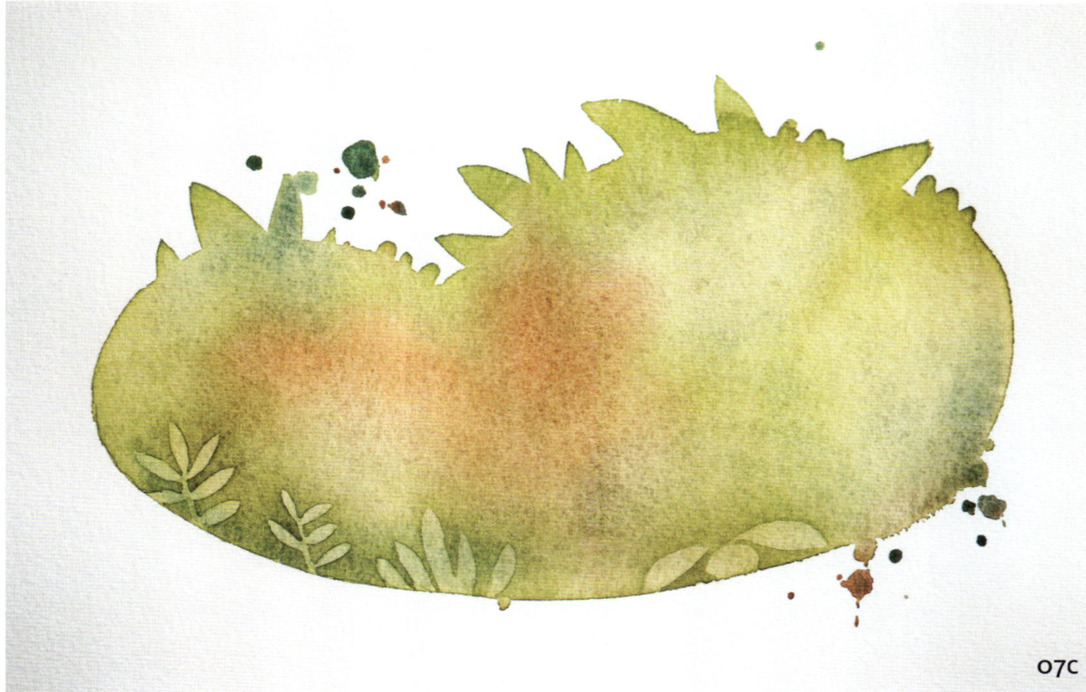

07c

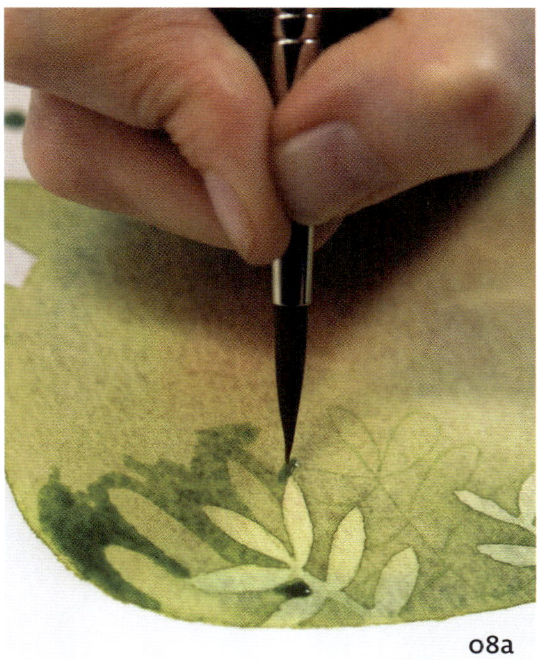

08a

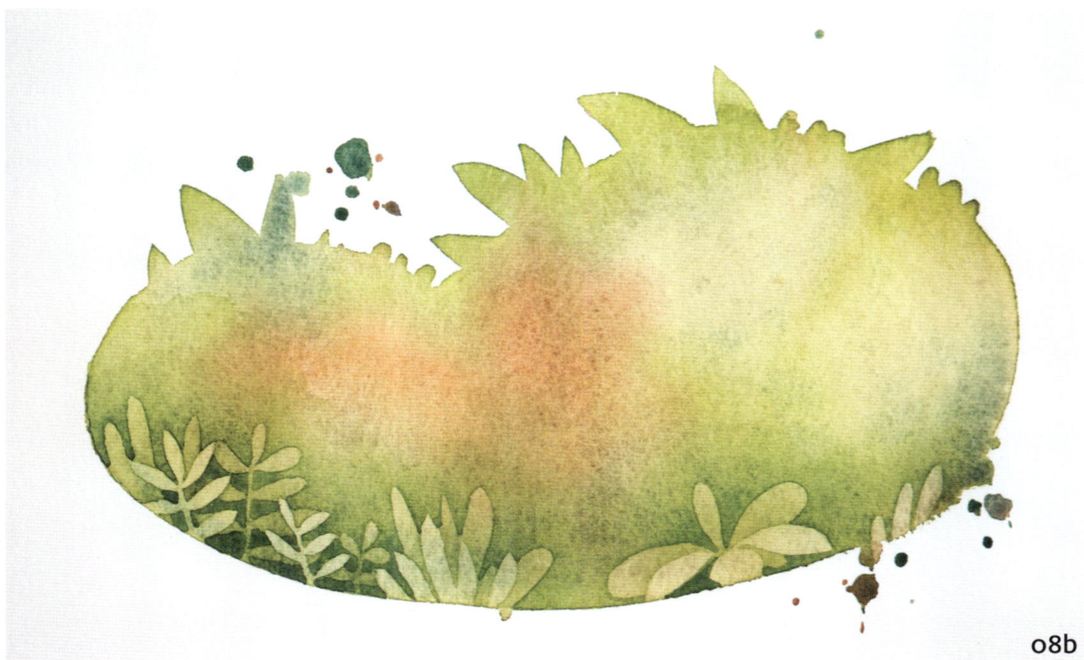

08b

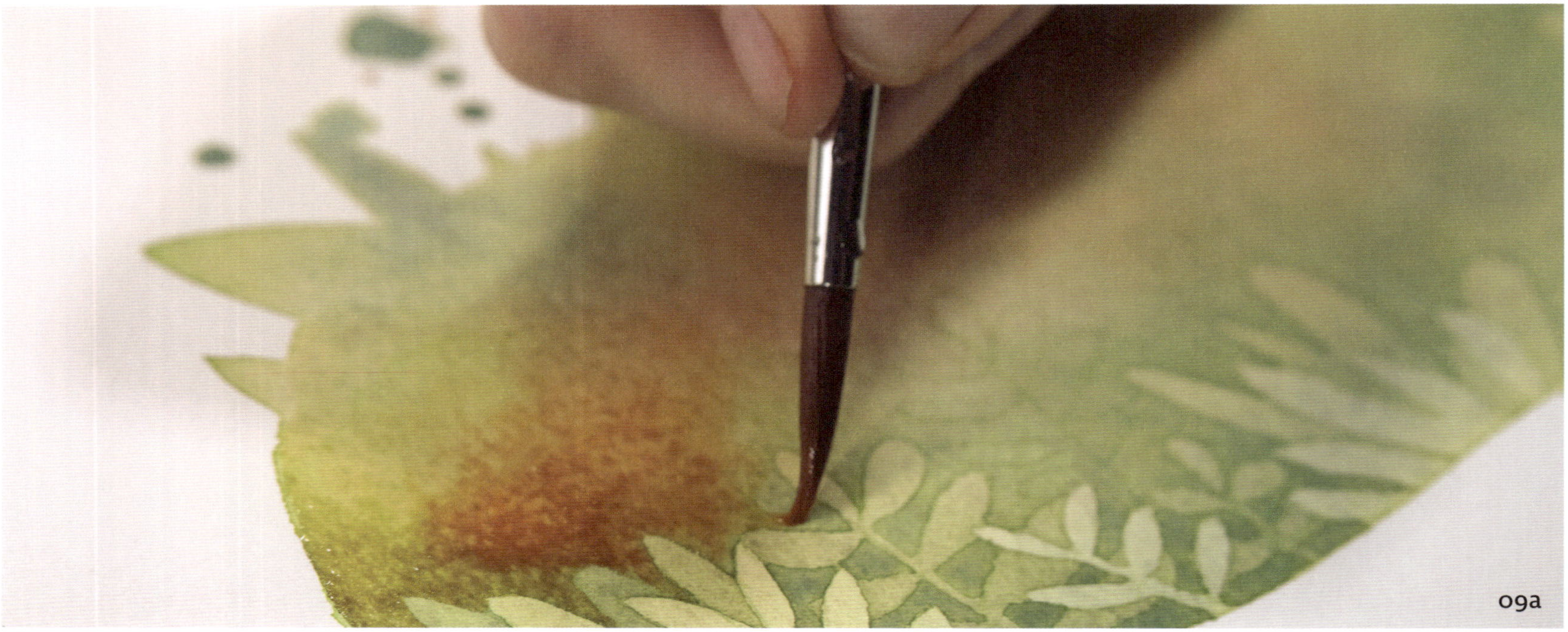

09a

09: I repeat the steps again. However, this time I add a bit of red to the wet paint to once again create beautiful colour contrasts and gradients. This brings some much-welcomed tension into the painting.

10: I find this way of painting (building everything little by little, layer by layer) very relaxing! There is something meditative about it. You do not have to think too much about it.

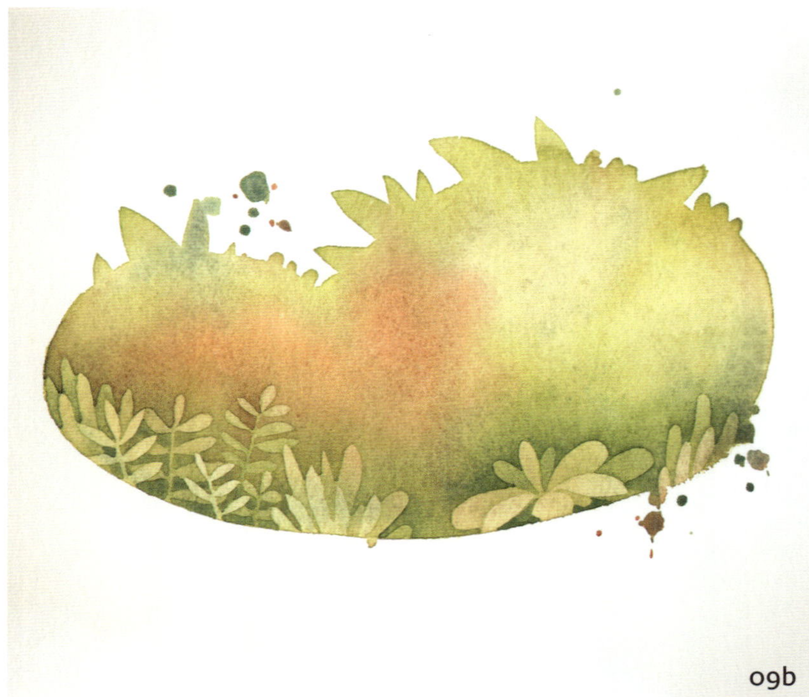

09b

10a

10b

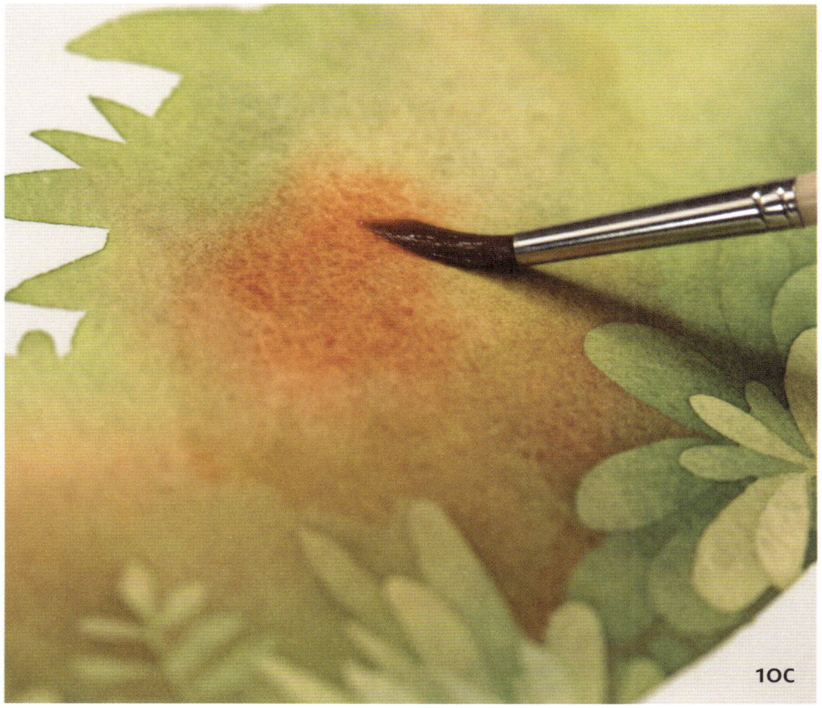
10c

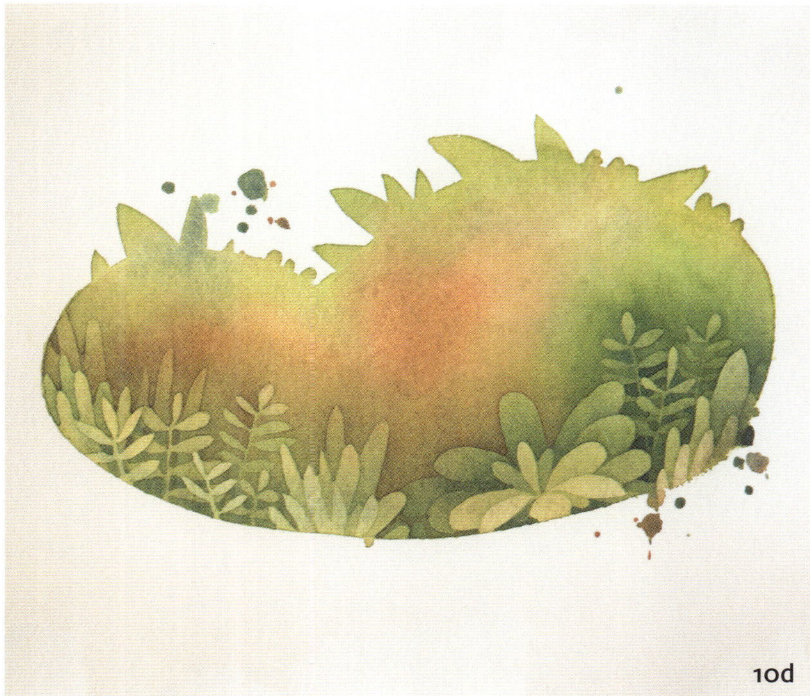
10d

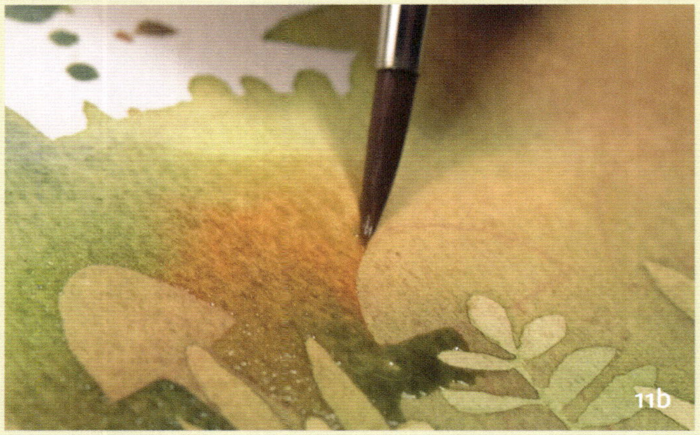

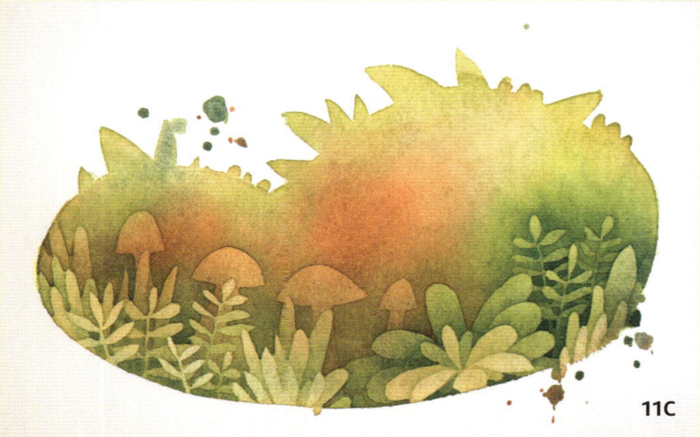

11: Now it is time for the mushrooms. I sketch them using a red watercolour pencil, then apply a layer of paint around their shapes.

12: I paint another mixed row of plants and mushrooms behind the existing mushrooms. I make sure that the colours I apply are mixed with a lot of water, so the background does not look too dark with all the layers.

13: I also repeat this step, making sure the plants at the top of the image match the bulges that I created in the primer stage at the beginning.

14: Now, it looks as if they were growing organically our of the inner form.

15: When each plant and mushroom is on the paper, I paint the details. I start by filling the dark underside of the mushroom heads and stems with a mixture of perylene violet and indigo.

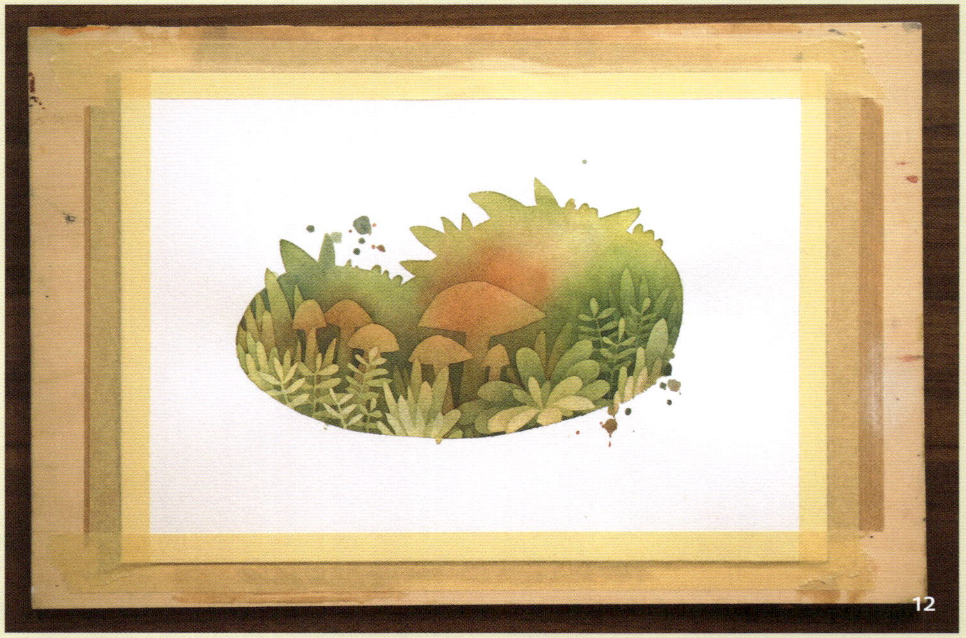

13a

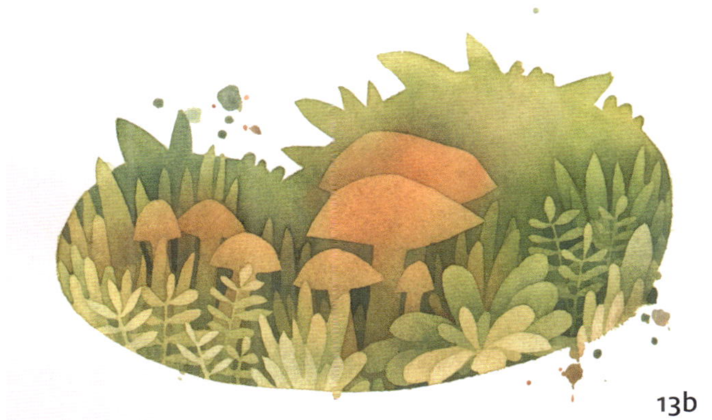

13b

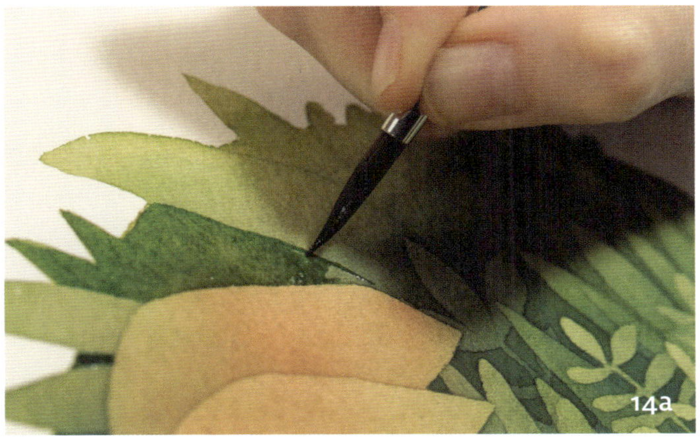

14a

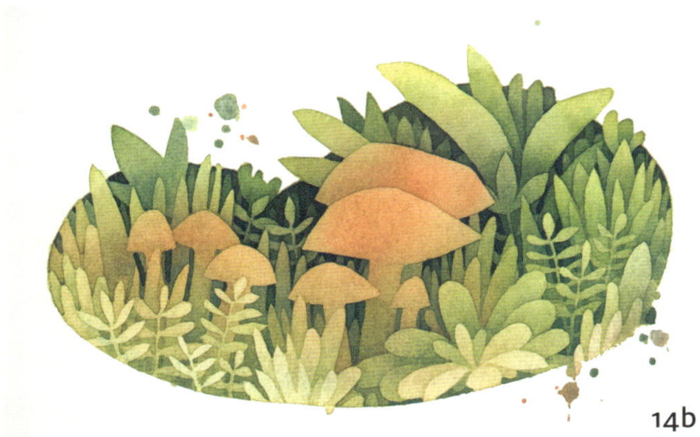

14b

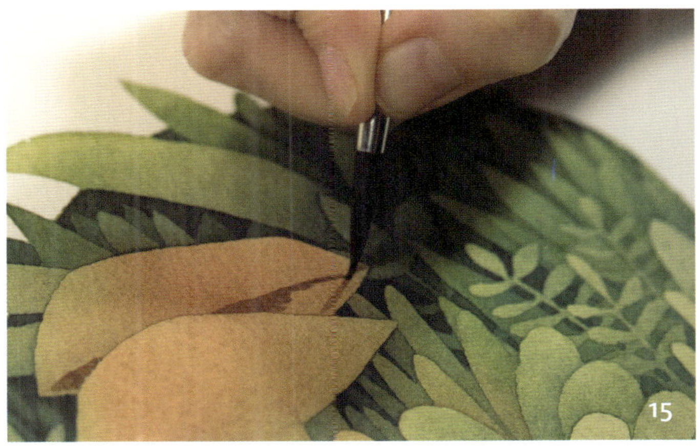

15

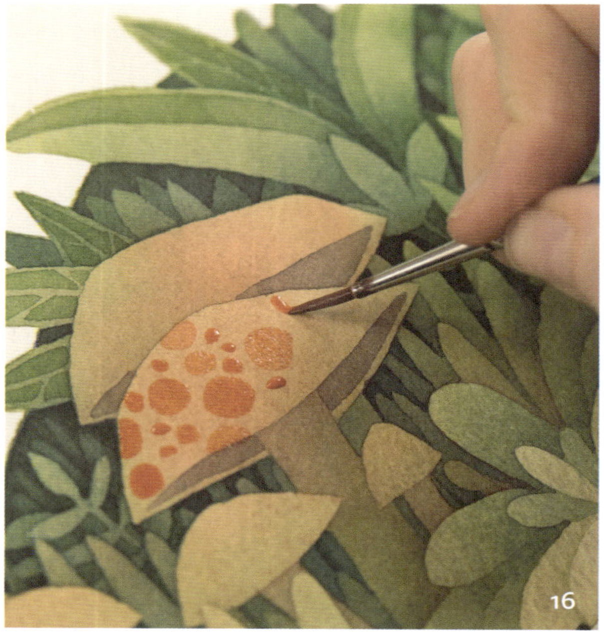

16

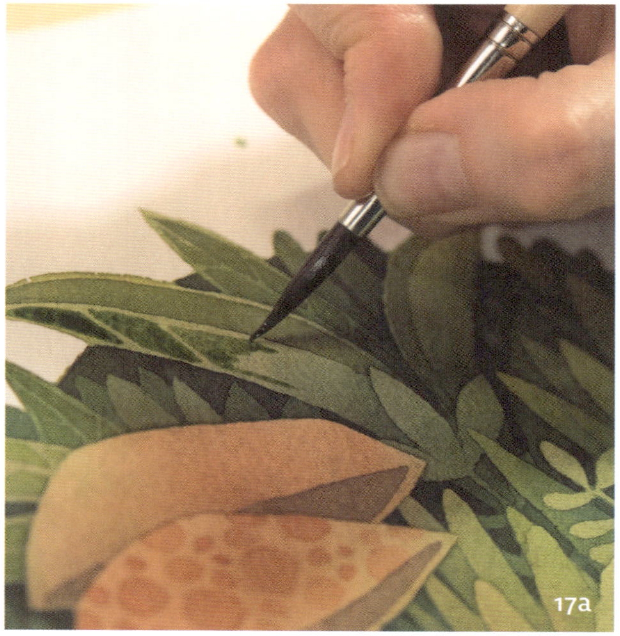

17a

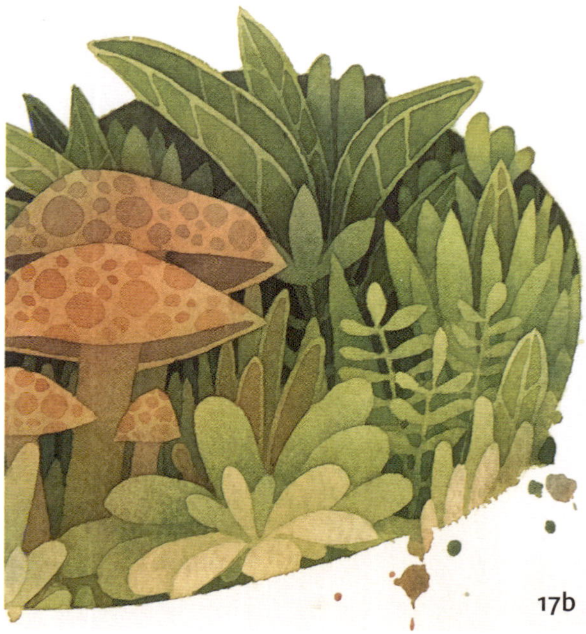

17b

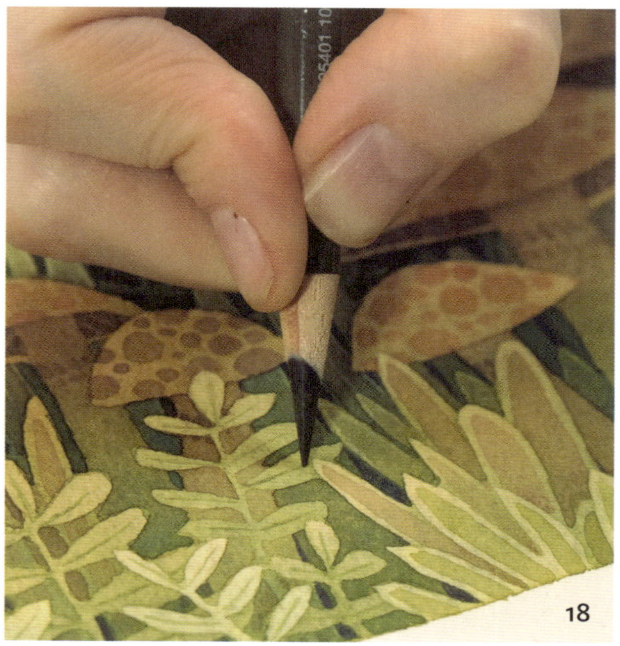

18

16: Now, I paint the mushroom caps with random red spots. I have no idea whether such a mushroom species really exists, or if it is poisonous. Good thing I am just painting them!

17: The leaves also get some details.

18: Finally, I add some details to the very small subjects using coloured pencils, enhancing highlights and emphasizing depths.

The last steps are the same as the *How I usually paint* chapter (page 64): I scan the image, adjust the colours and tonal values until they match the original, and remove any visible paper structure.

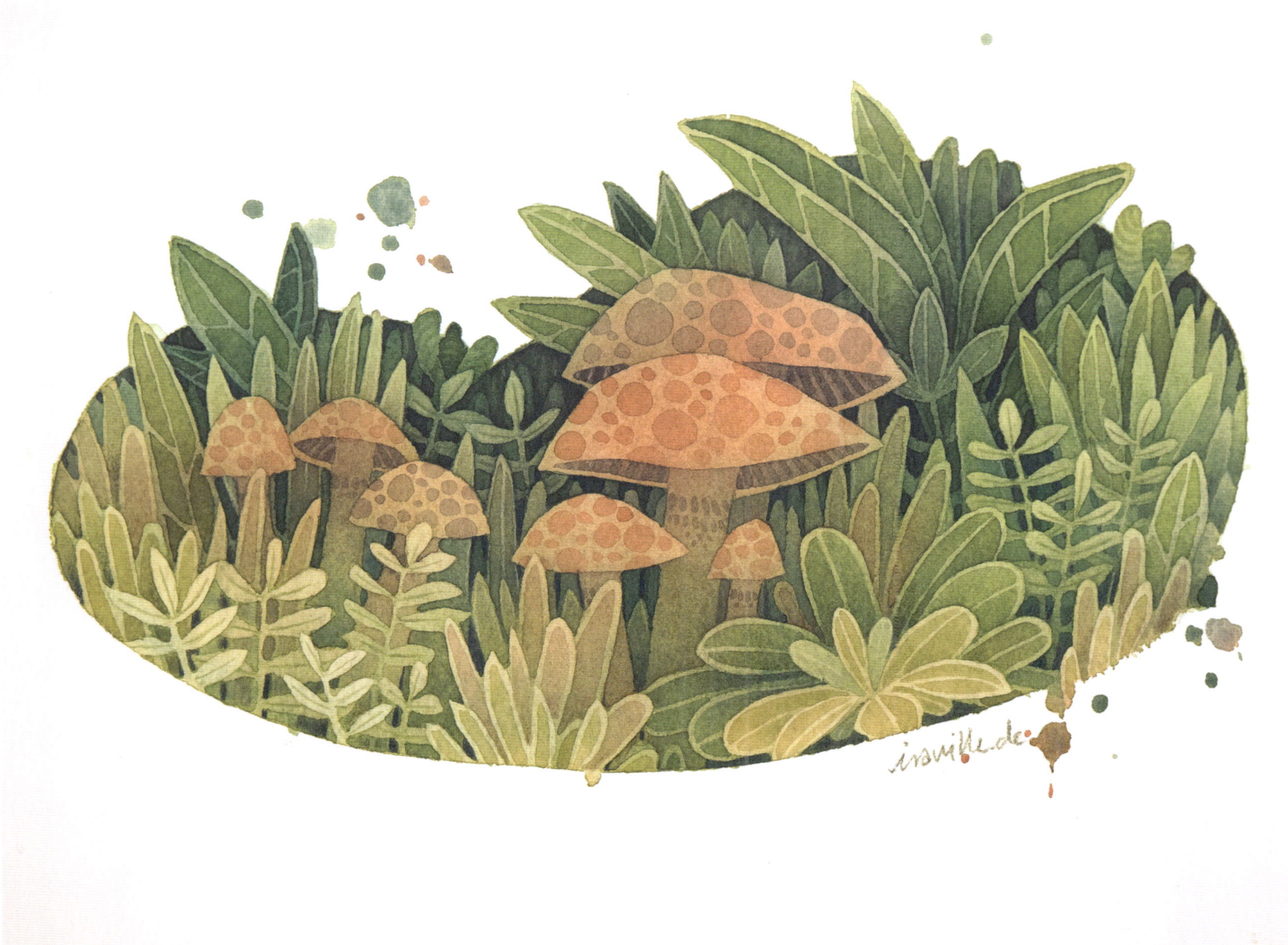

Of course, you can use this technique with other shapes, or just in certain parts of a painting. There are no limits to your imagination. If you want to try it, let your ideas proliferate like the plants and mushrooms in my picture.

GALLERY

Flora & fauna

UNDER THE SEA

This page:
Under the Sea 2, graphite, gouache, coloured pencil, 2018

Opposite page:
Under the Sea 1, soft pastel, gouache, coloured pencil, 2018

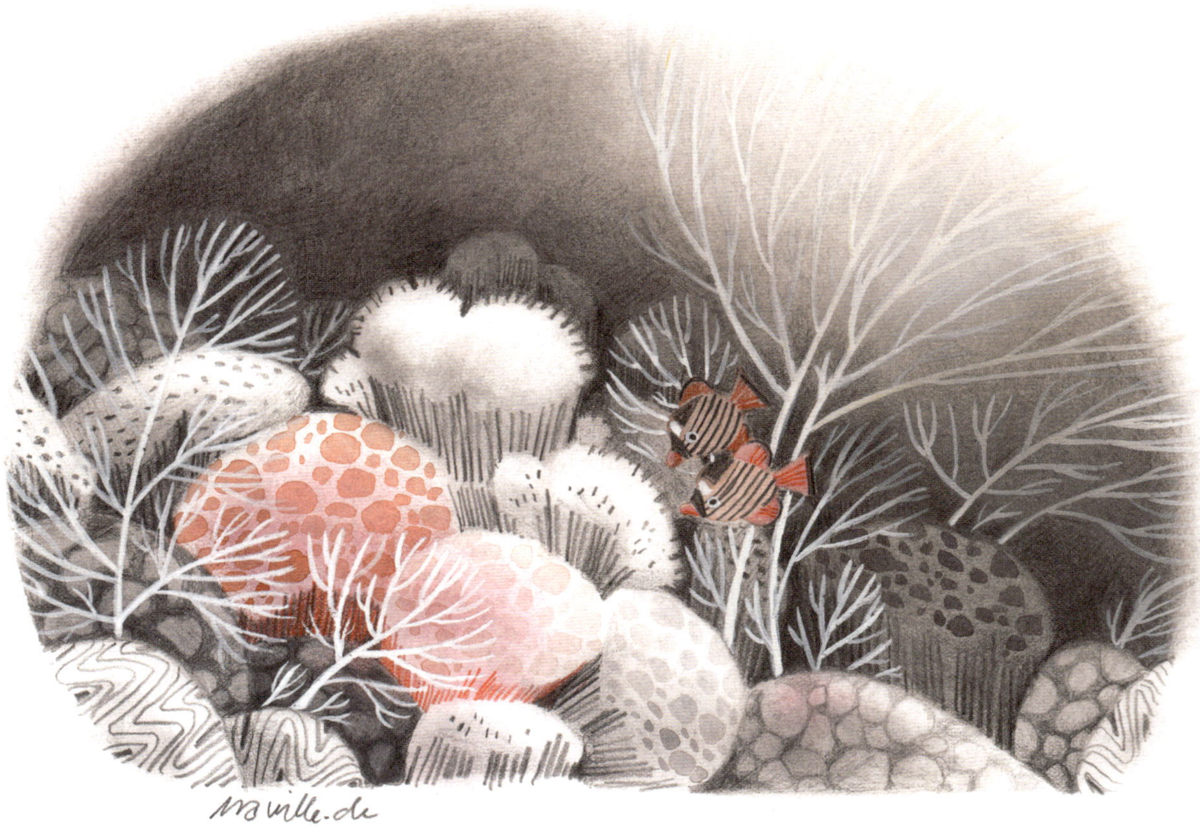

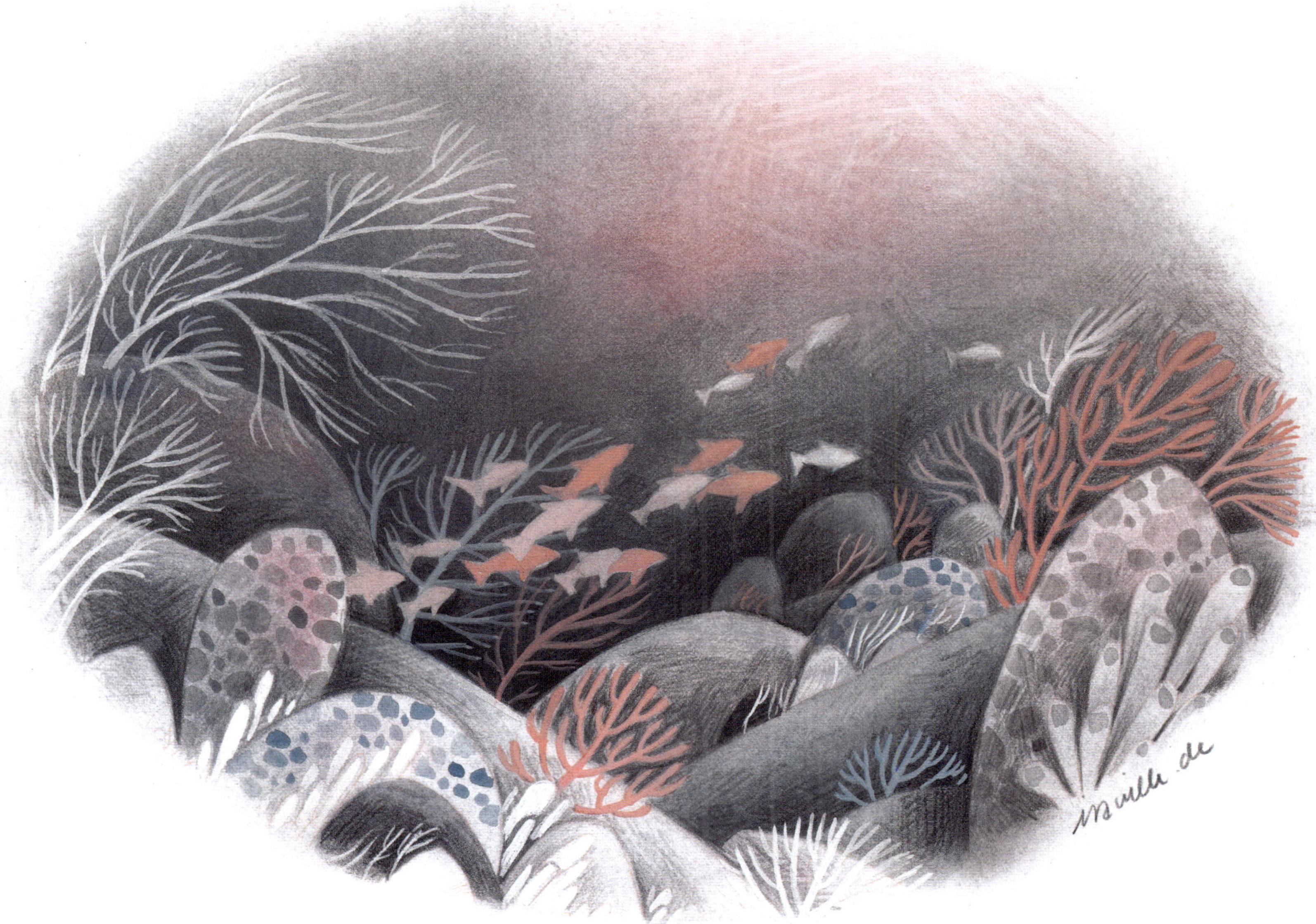

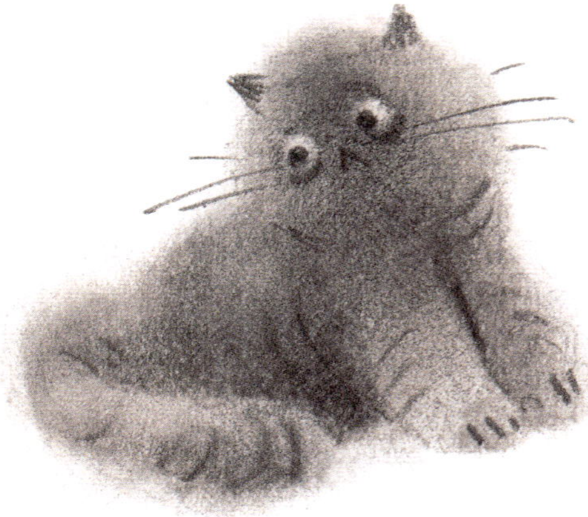

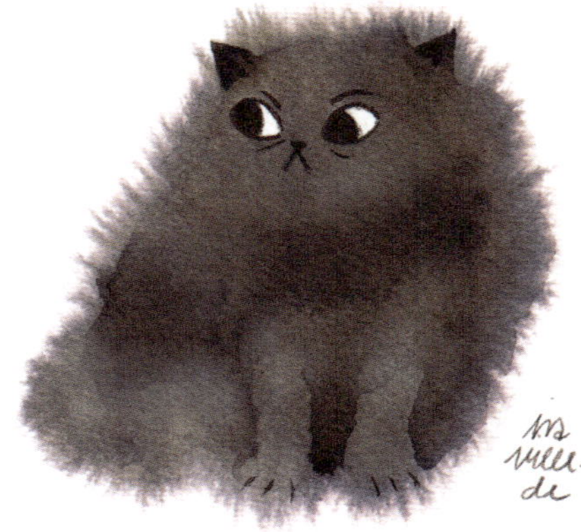

SKETCHES

Above left:
Cat Sketch, graphite, 2019

Above right:
Exploded Cat, ink, 2016

Right:
Dog and Cat Sketches, graphite, 2019

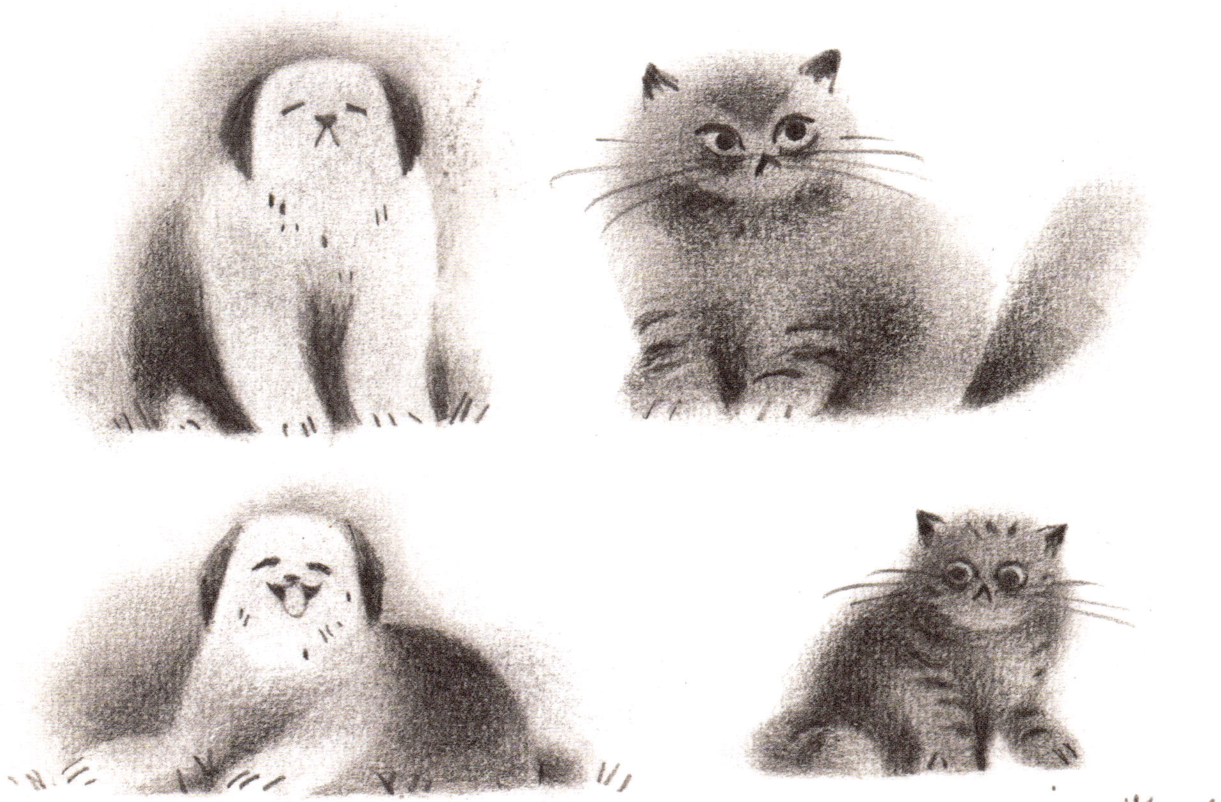

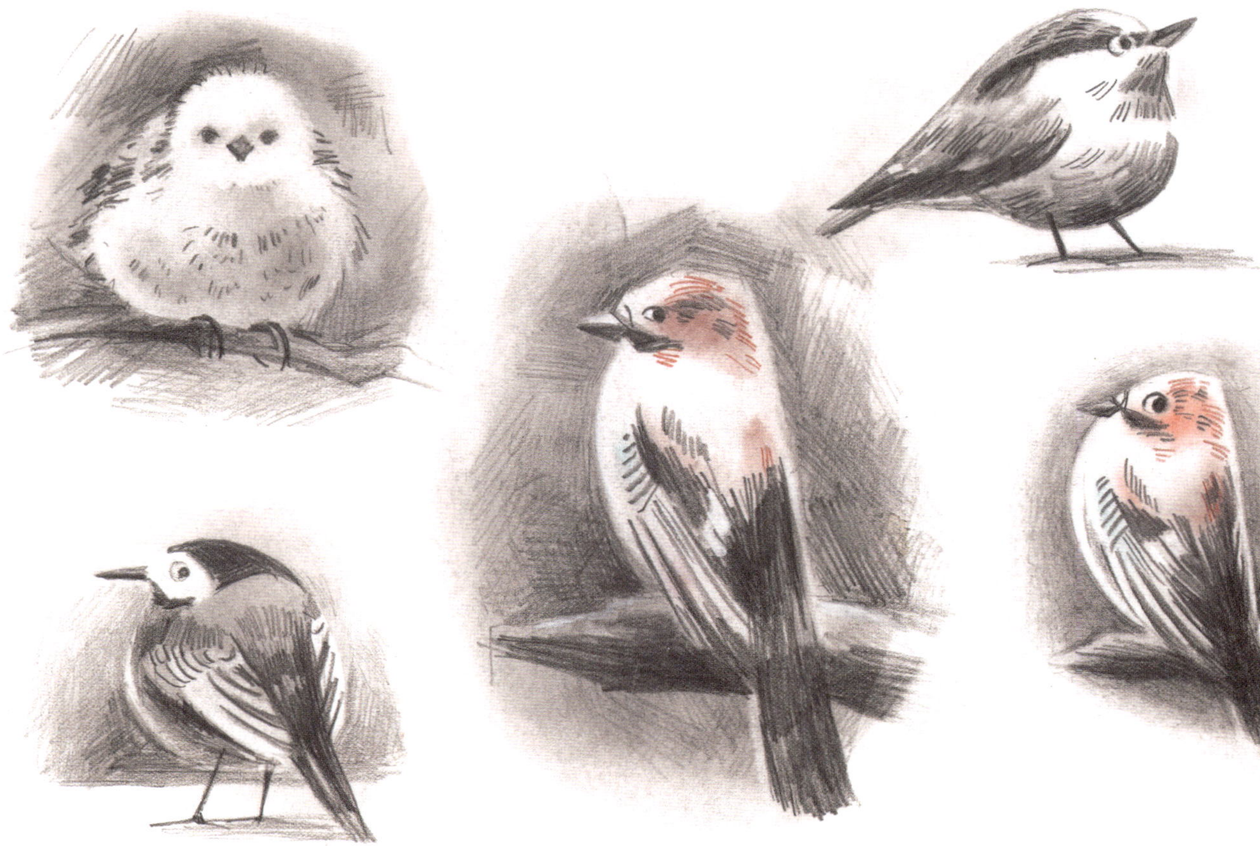

Above:
Bird Sketches, graphite and coloured pencil, 2019

Right:
Smooth Robin, watercolour and coloured pencil, 2016

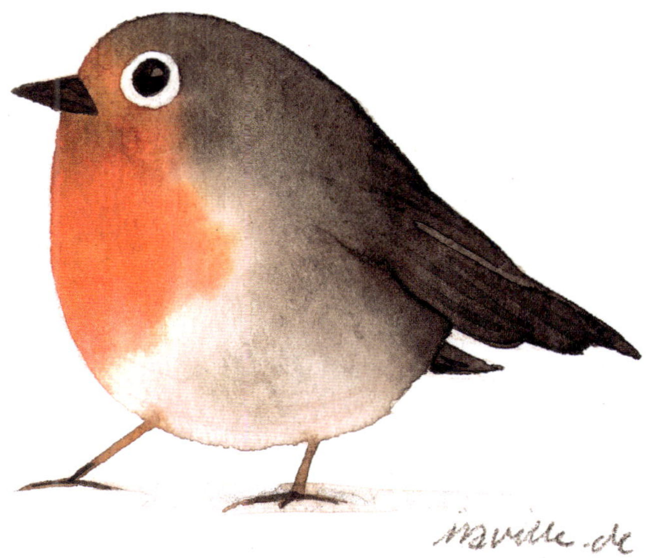

FAUNA

Below:
Meerkats, watercolour and coloured pencil, 2018

Opposite page:
Seals, watercolour and coloured pencil, 2018

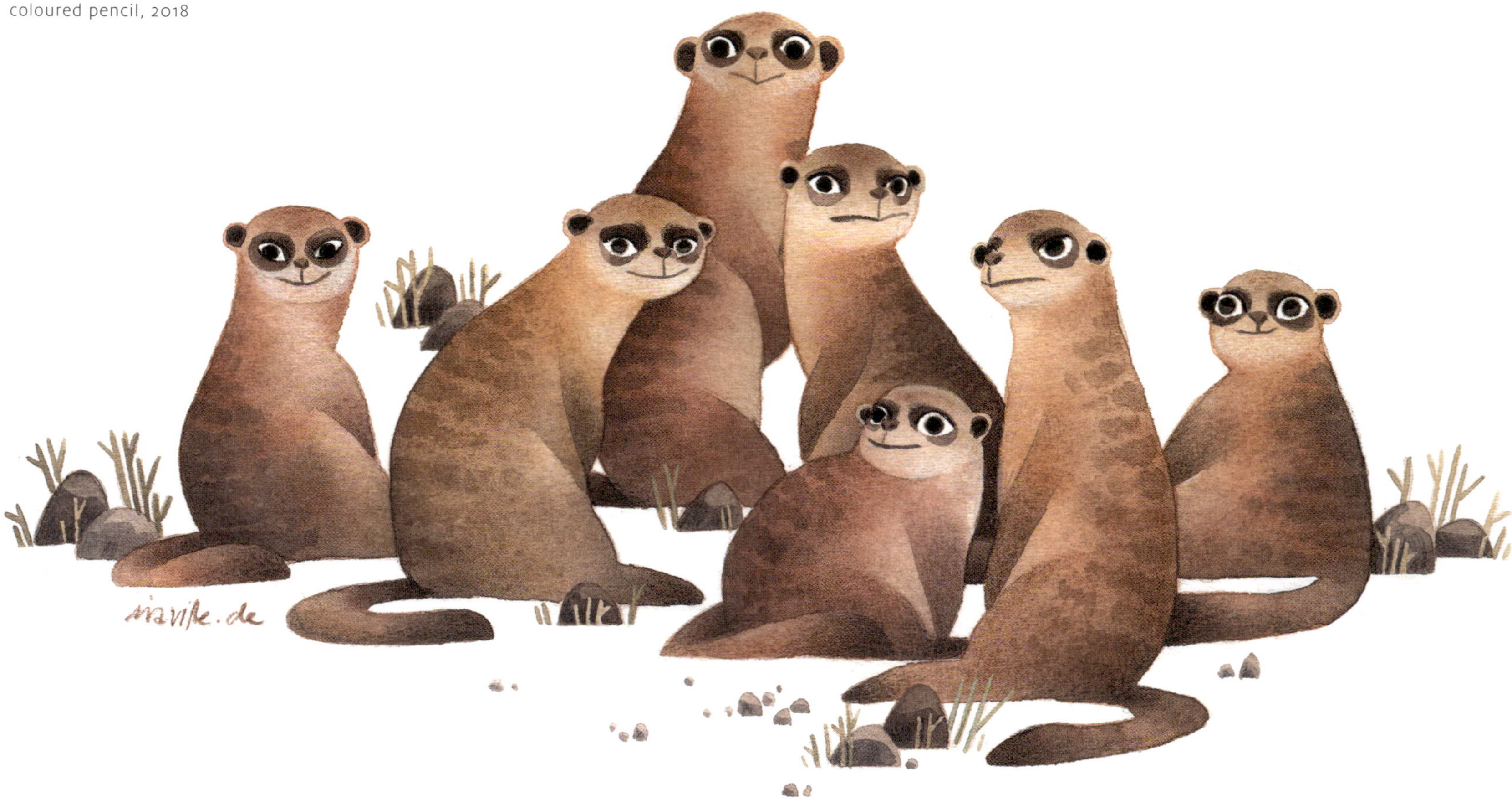

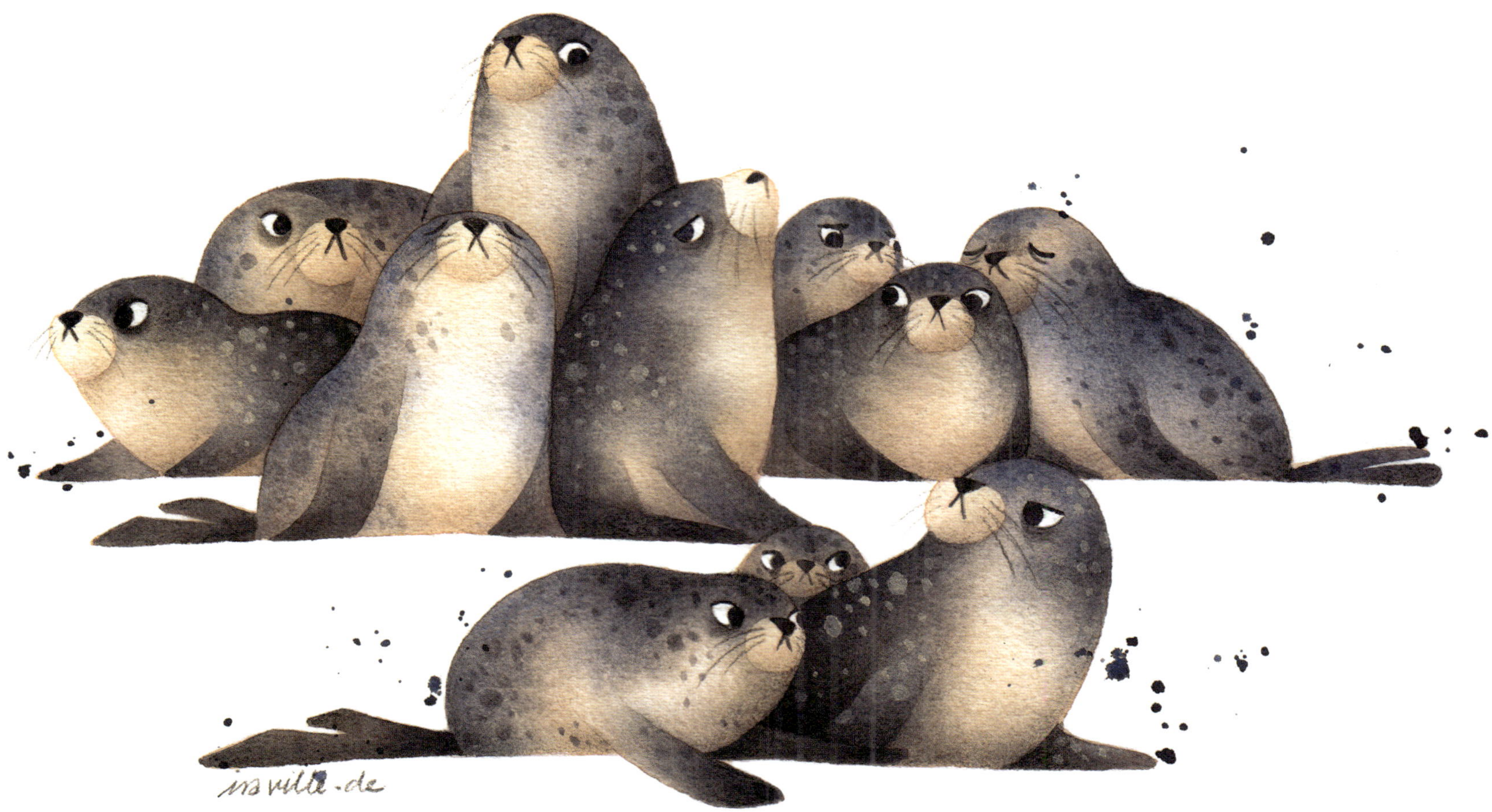

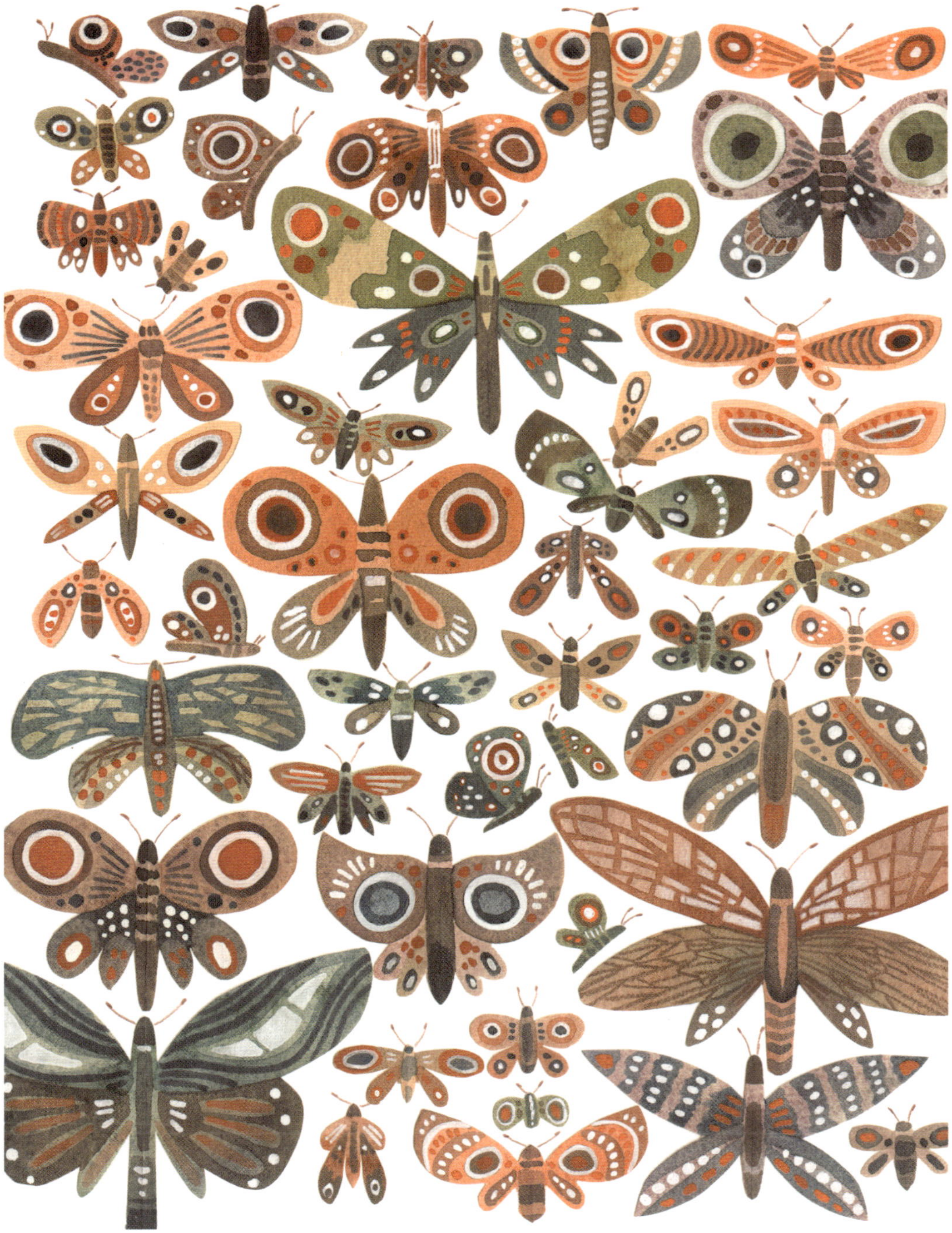

PATTERNS

Left:
Butterflies Collage, watercolour and gouache, 2020

Below:
Mushrooms 4, watercolour and coloured pencil, 2020

Opposite page (above left):
Fish Pattern Sketch, watercolour, 2018

Opposite page (above right):
Corals Pattern Sketch, watercolour, 2018

Opposite page (below):
Corals Sketch, watercolour and coloured pencil, 2021

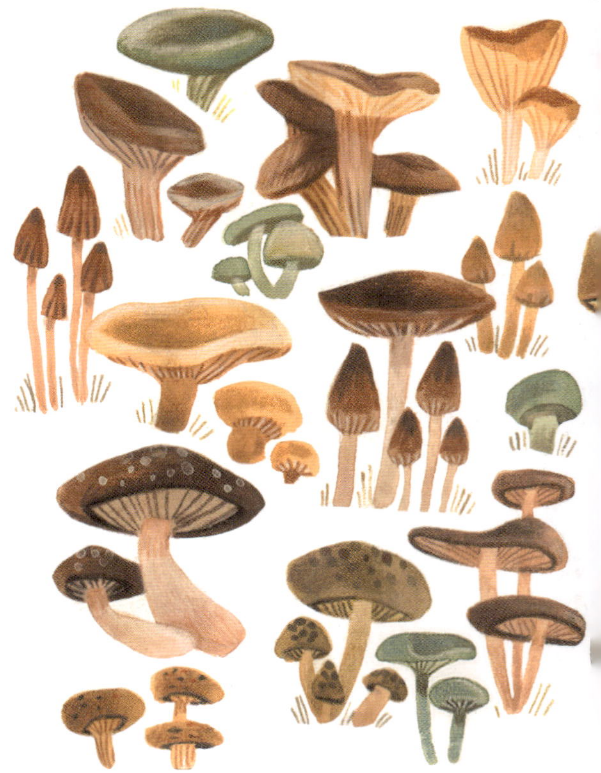

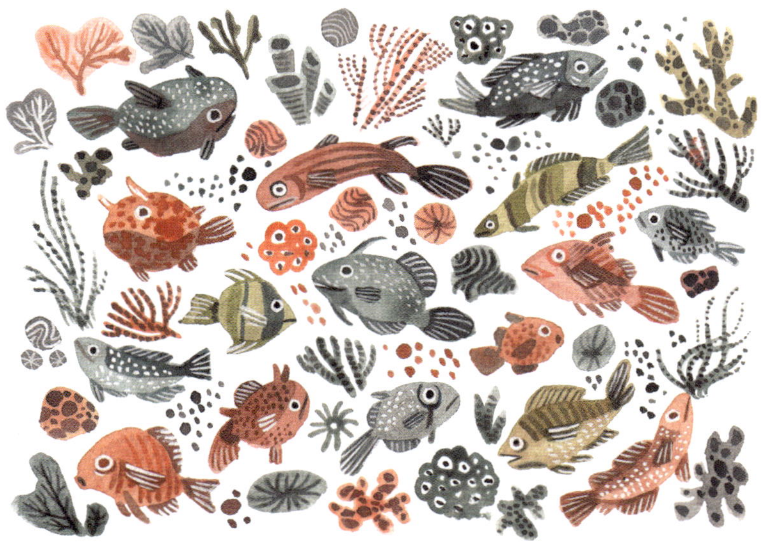

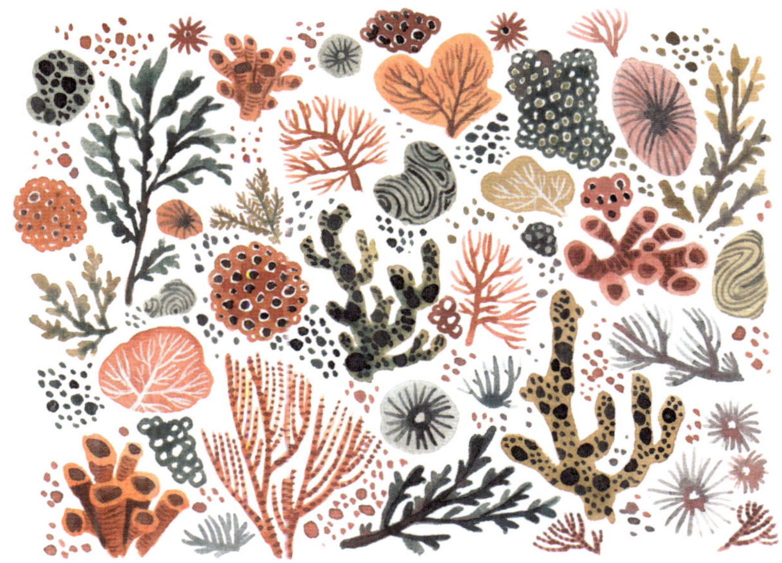

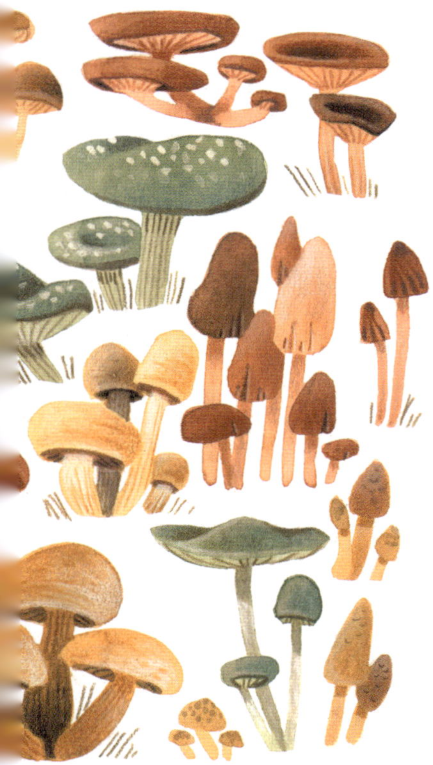

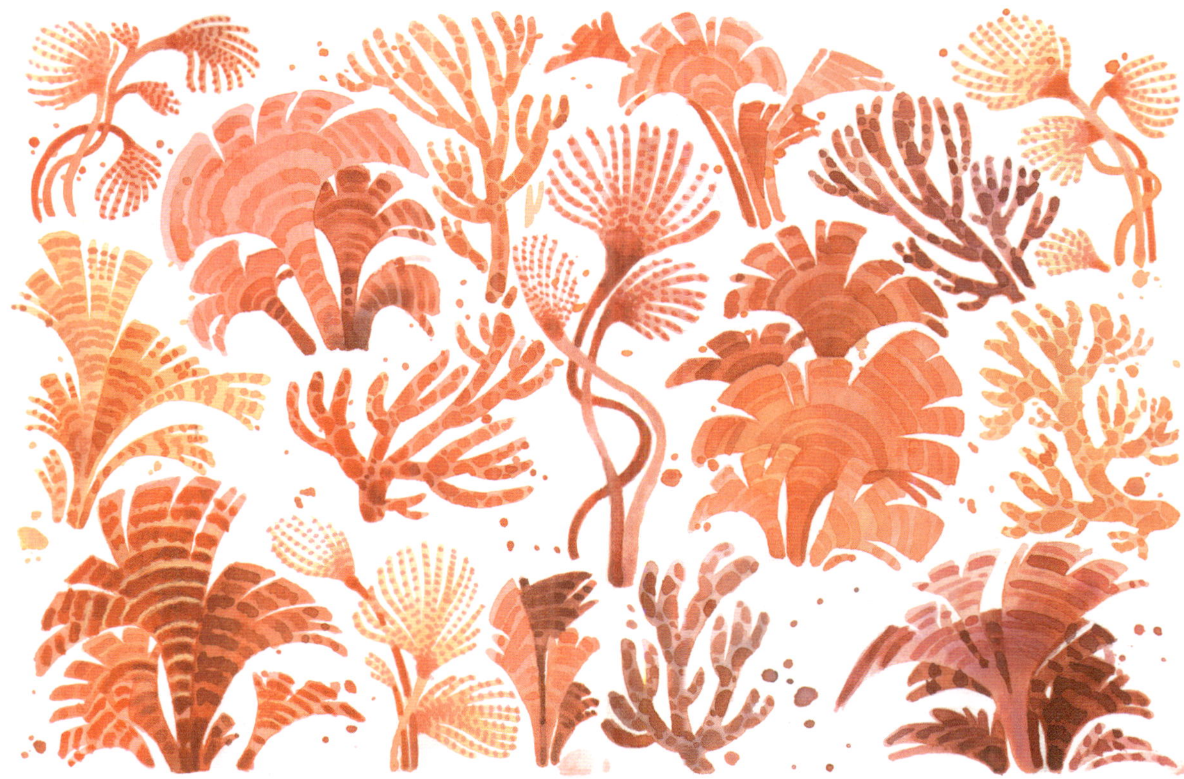

NEGATIVE PAINTING

Counter-clockwise from top:
Plant Study, watercolour and coloured pencil, 2019

Little Guy in the Thicket, watercolour and coloured pencil, 2020

Underwater, watercolour and coloured pencil, 2020

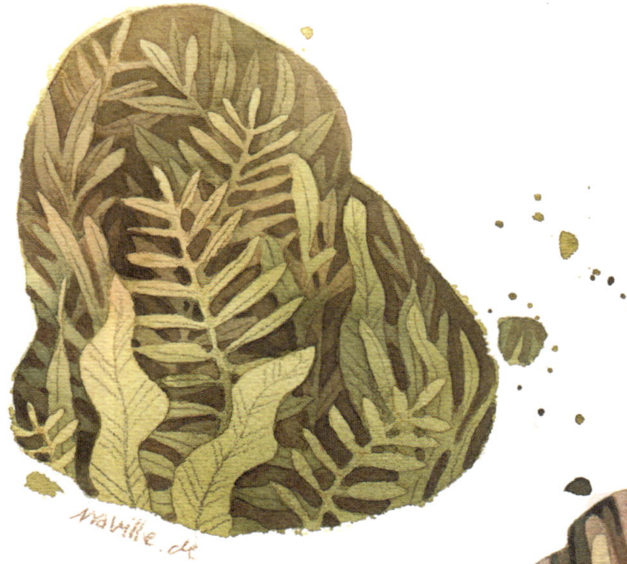

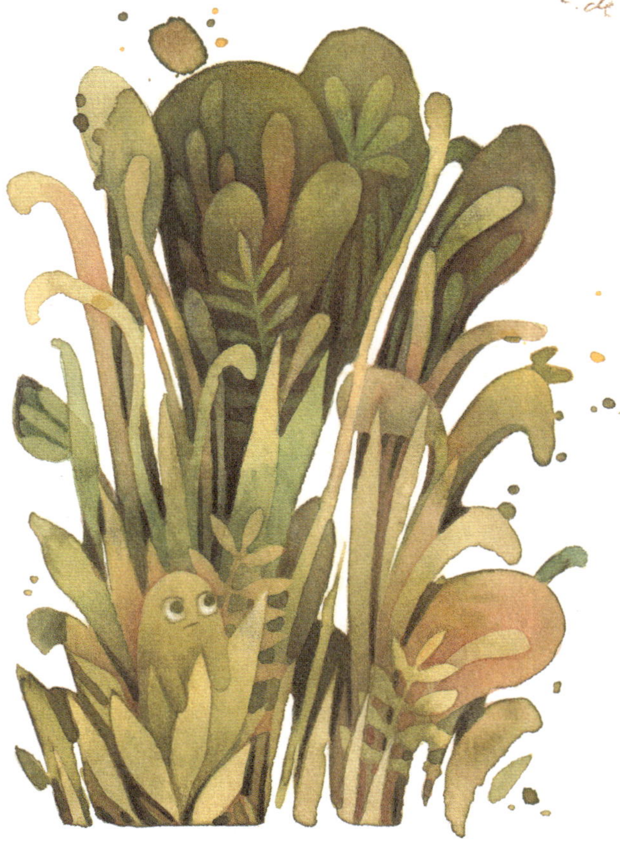

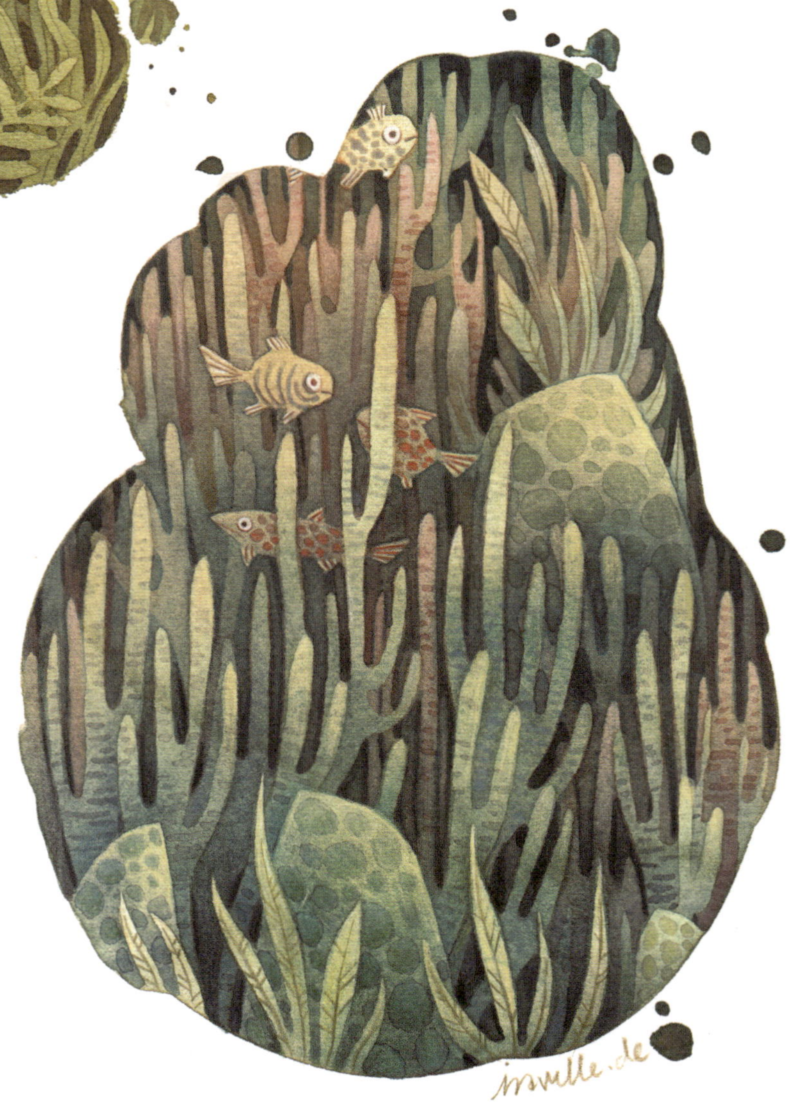

Right:

Bear in Cave, watercolour and coloured pencil, 2022

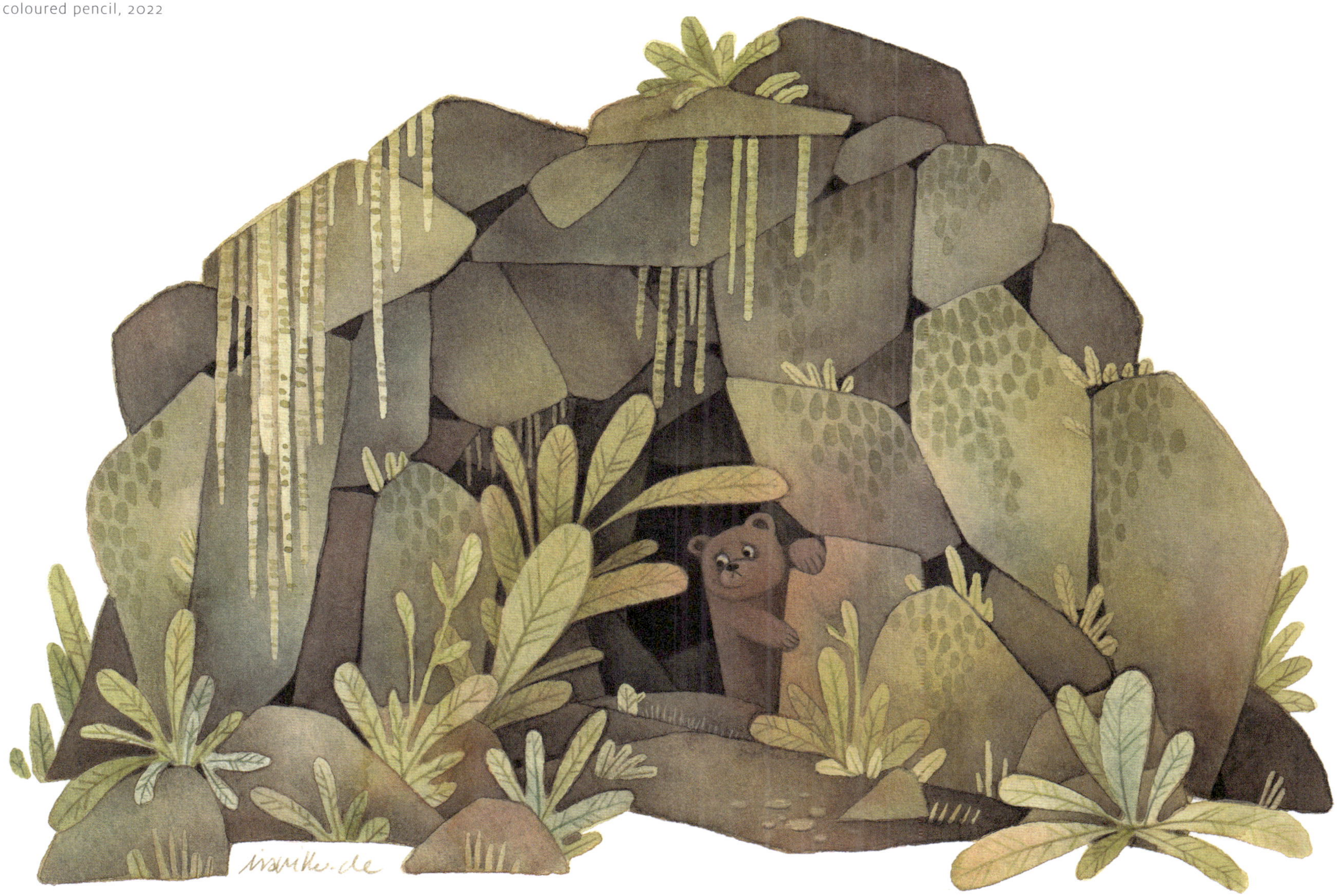

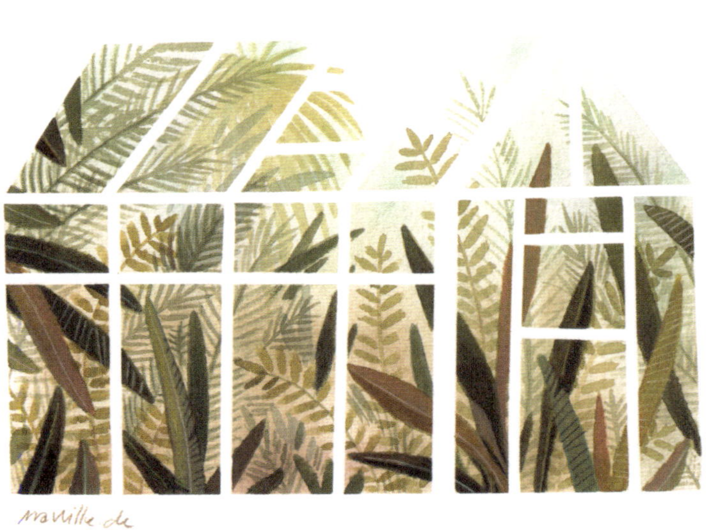

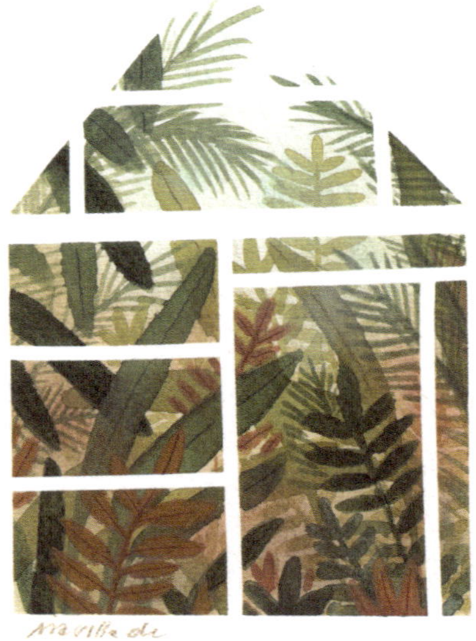

GREENHOUSES

This page:
Greenhouse, 1–5
watercolour, coloured pencil, soft pastel, 2019

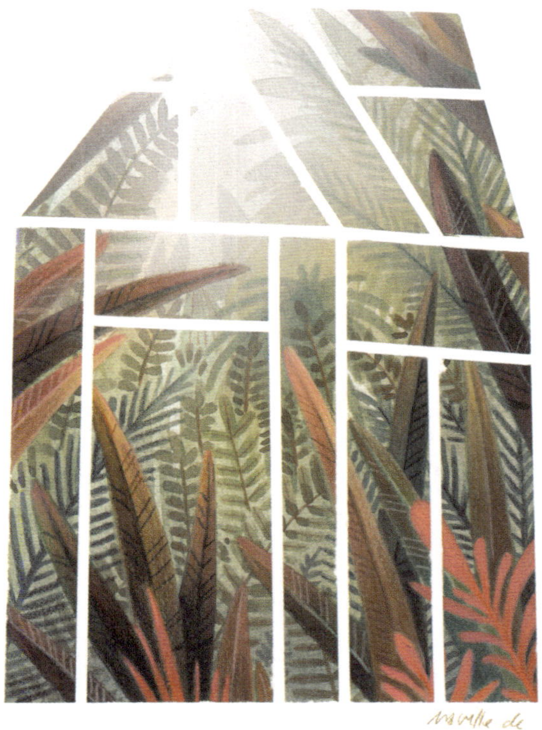

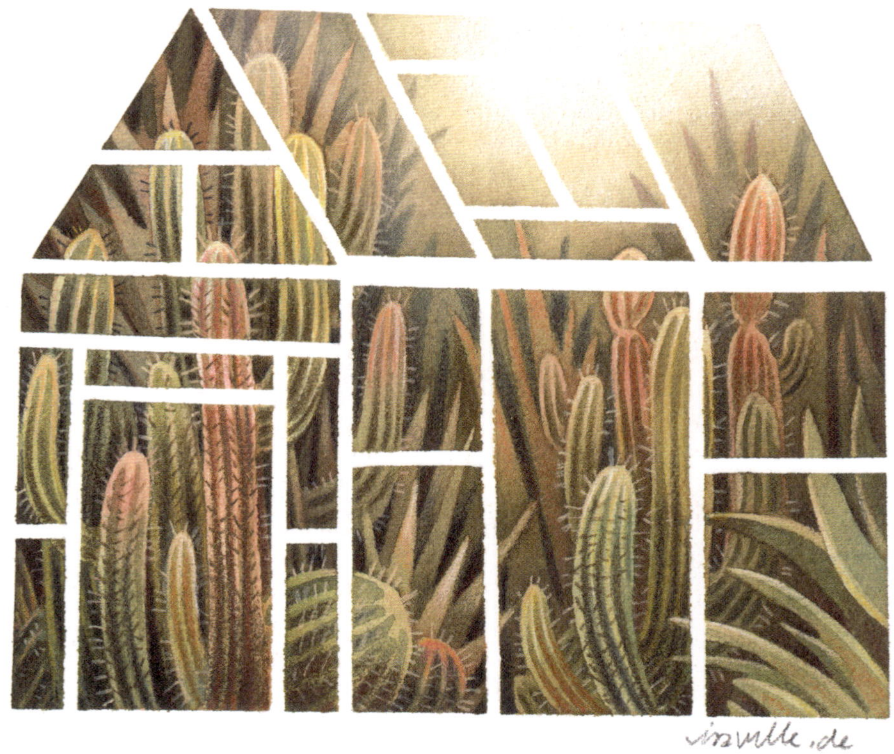

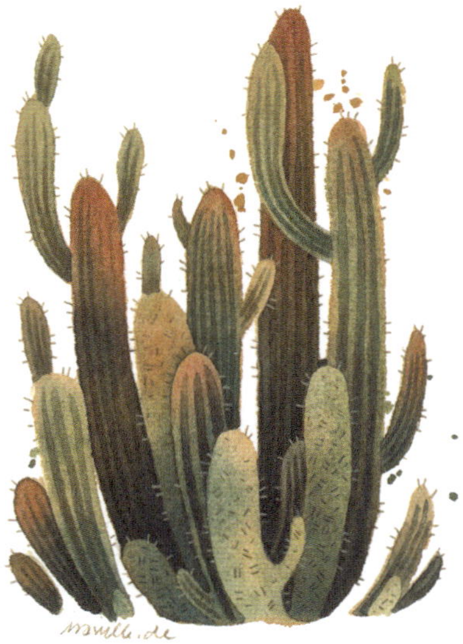

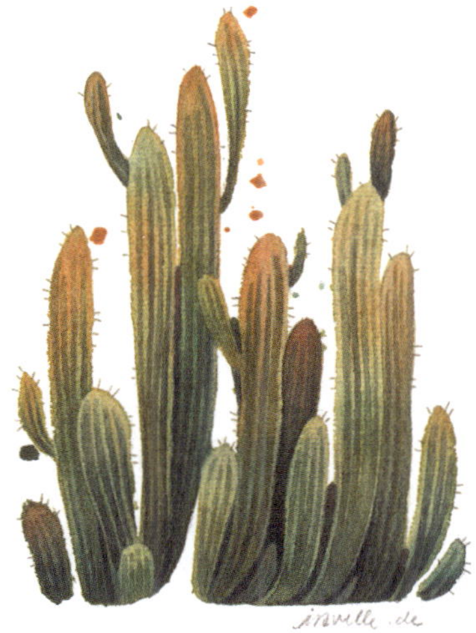

CACTI

Clockwise from top left:
Cacti 1–2, watercolour and coloured pencil, 2021

Cacti 3–5, watercolour and coloured pencil, 2019

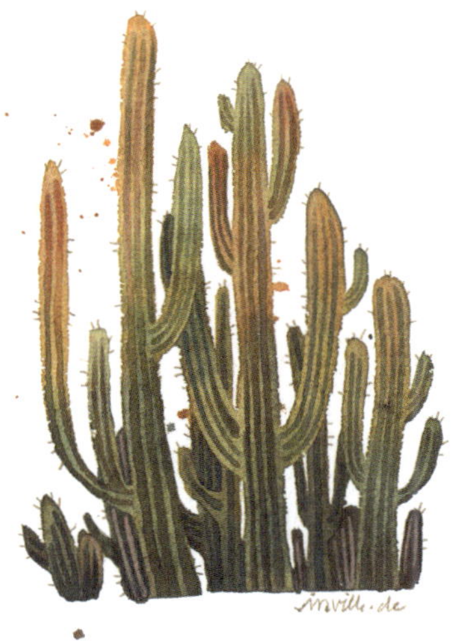

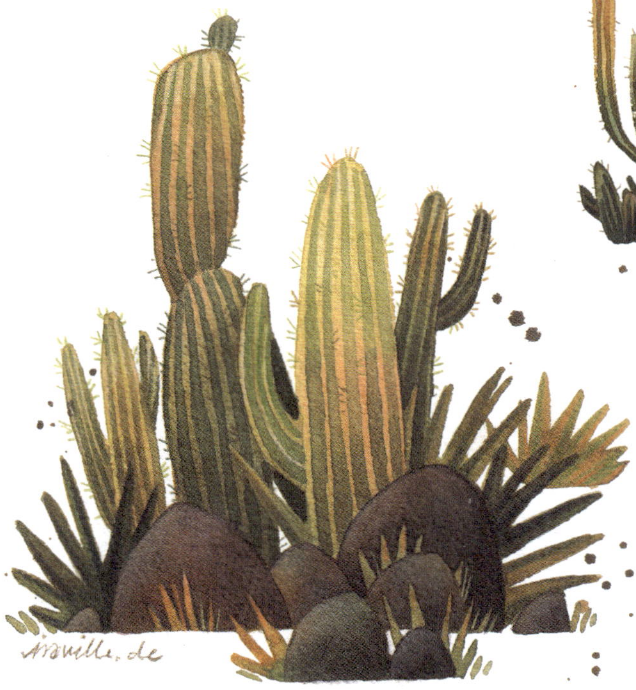

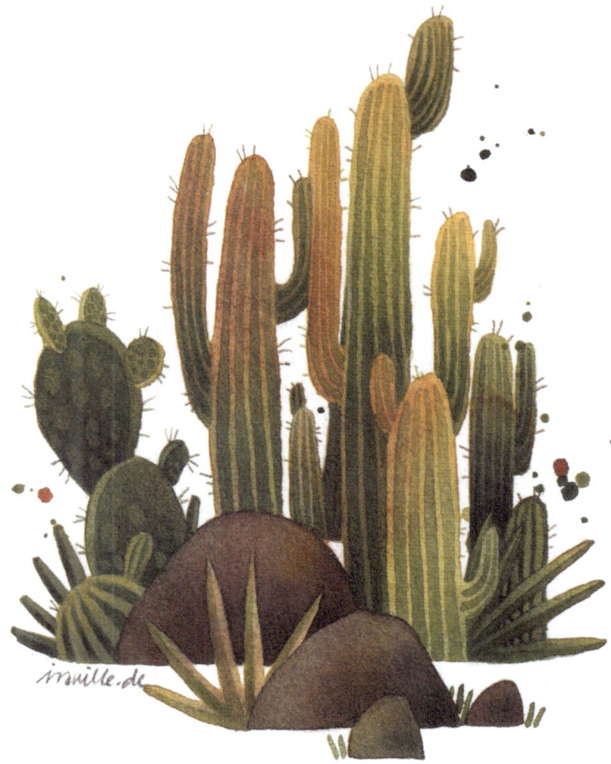

BOTANICALS

This page:
Botanical Illustration
1–5, watercolour and
coloured pencil, 2022

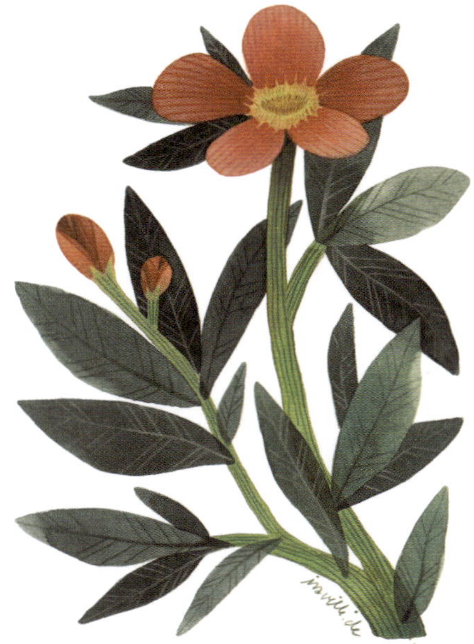

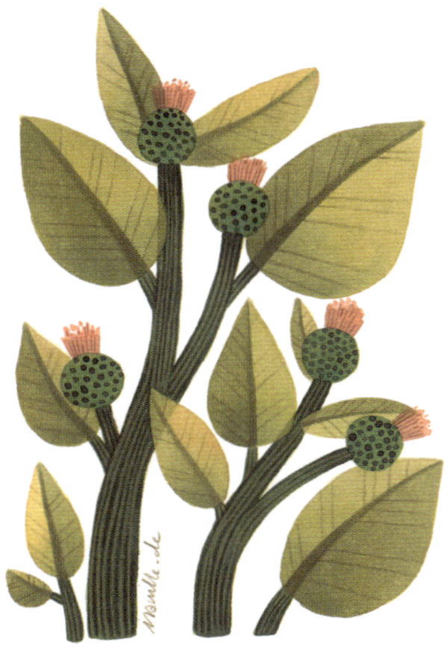

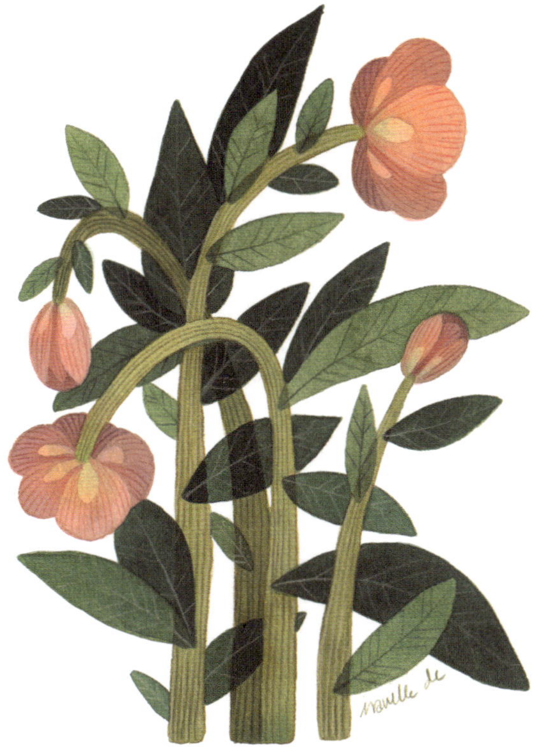

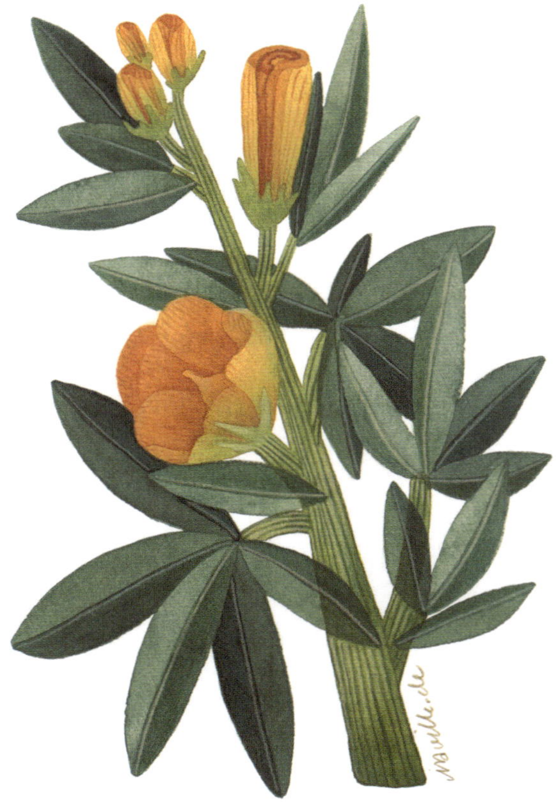

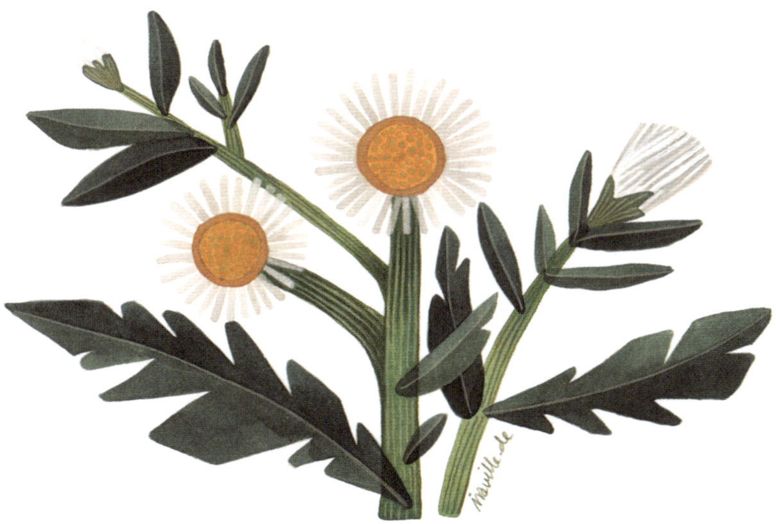

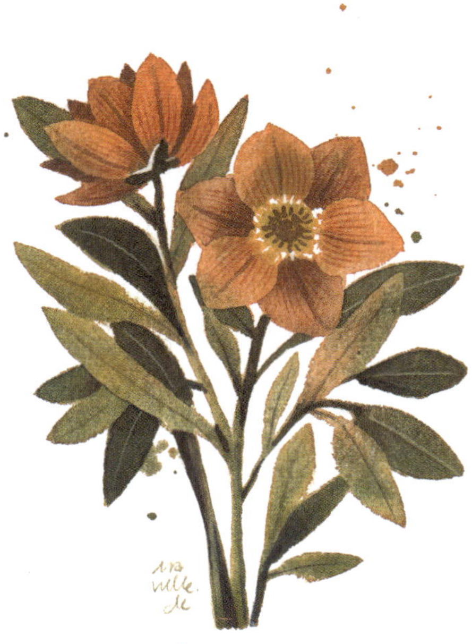

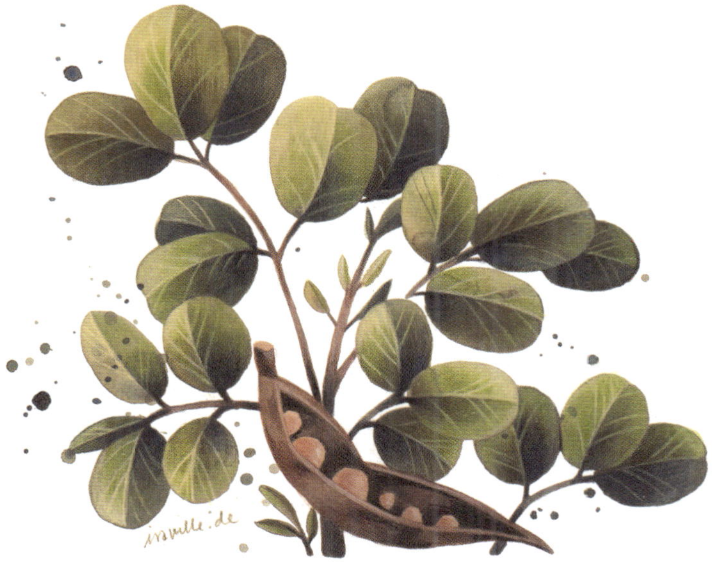

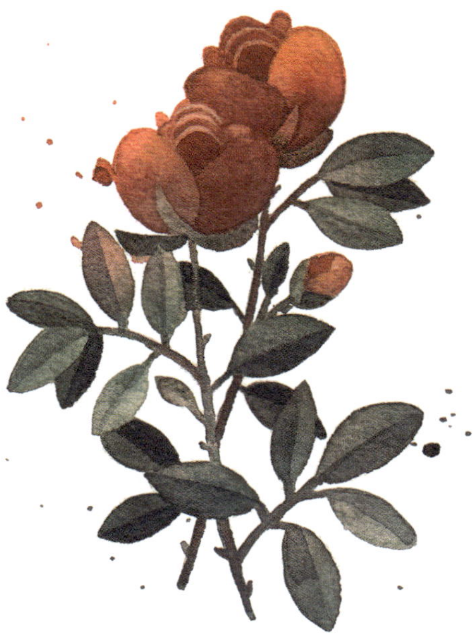

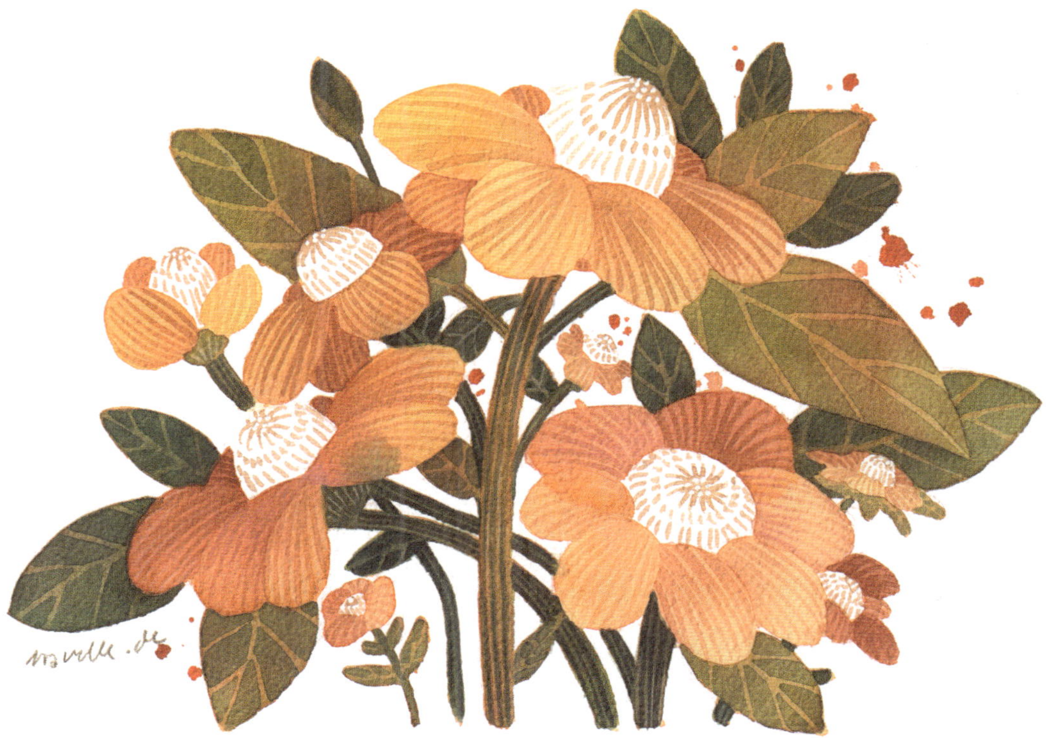

Clockwise from top left:

Flower, watercolour and coloured pencil, 2019

Branch and Fruit Pod of a Carob Tree, watercolour and coloured pencil, 2020

Freestyle Flowers, watercolour and coloured pencil, 2021

Roses 2, watercolour, 2018

MUSHROOMS

Right:
Mushrooms 3, watercolour and coloured pencil, 2019

Opposite page (above):
Mushrooms 2, watercolour and coloured pencil, 2019

Opposite page (below):
Mushrooms, watercolour and coloured pencil, 2019

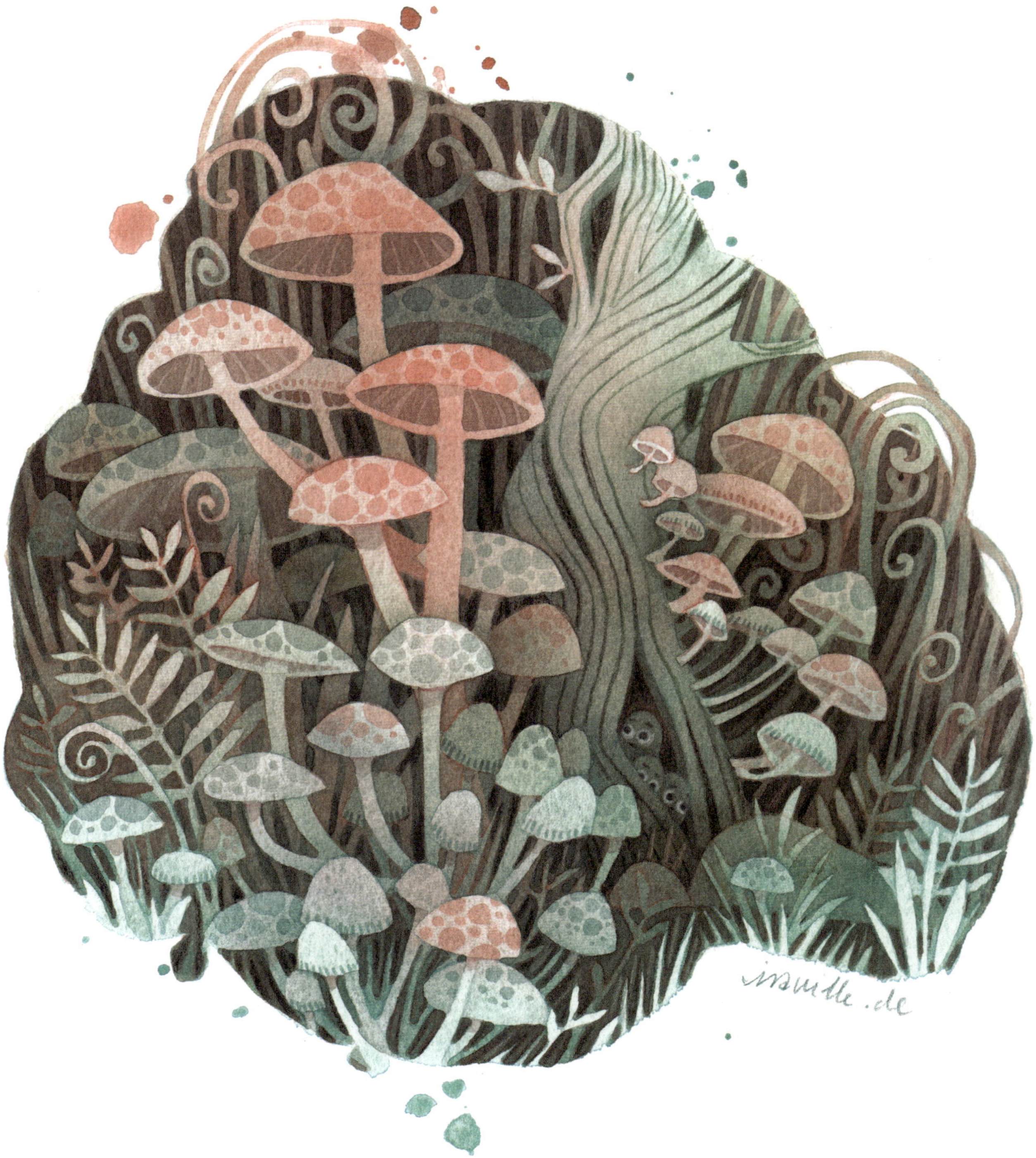

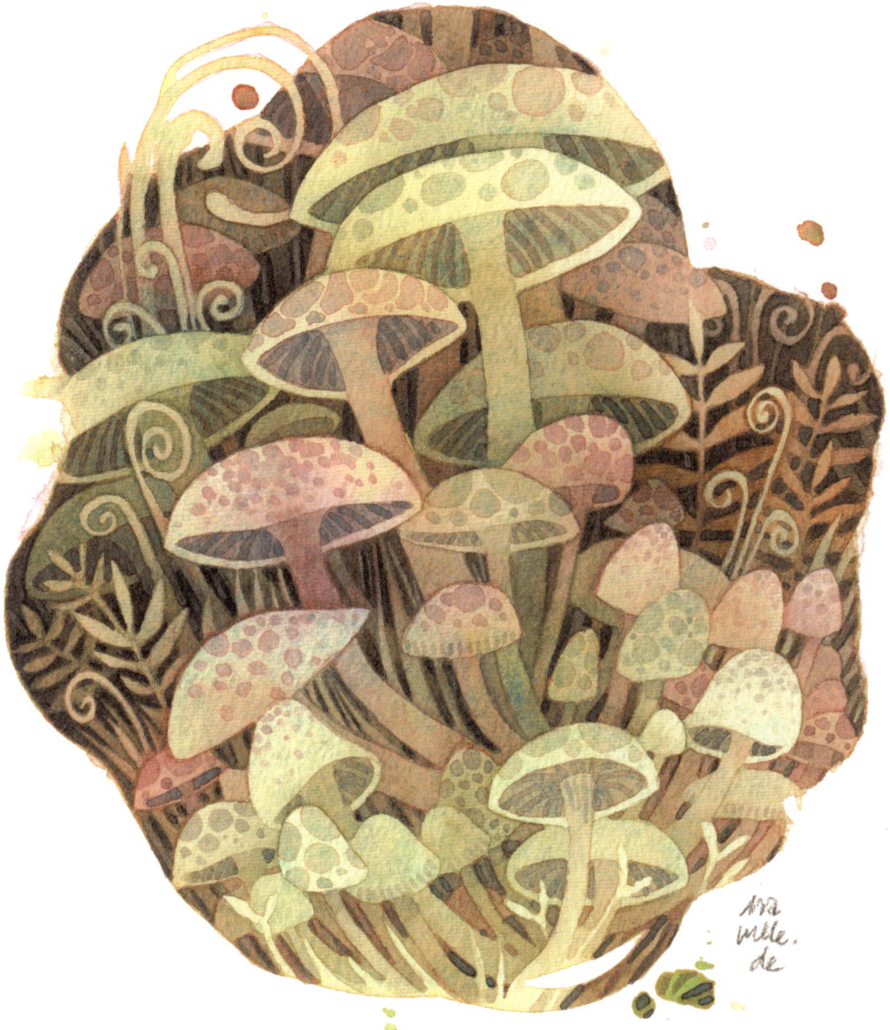

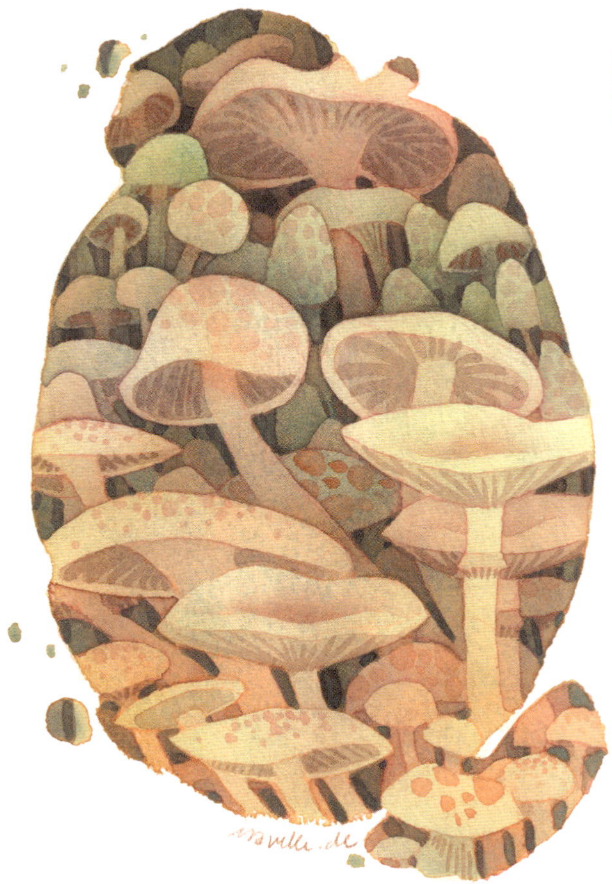

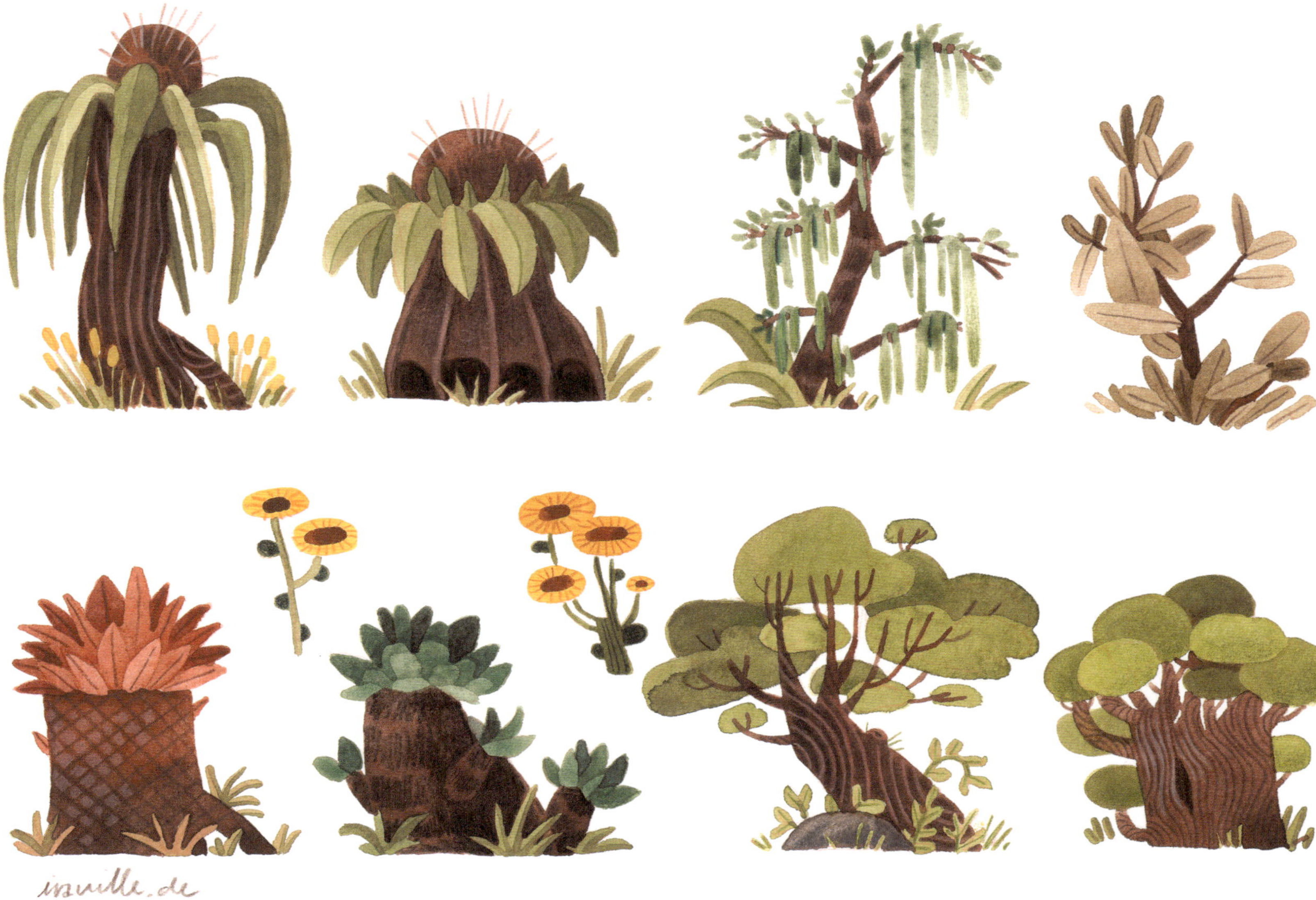

Tree Designs, watercolour and coloured pencil, 2022

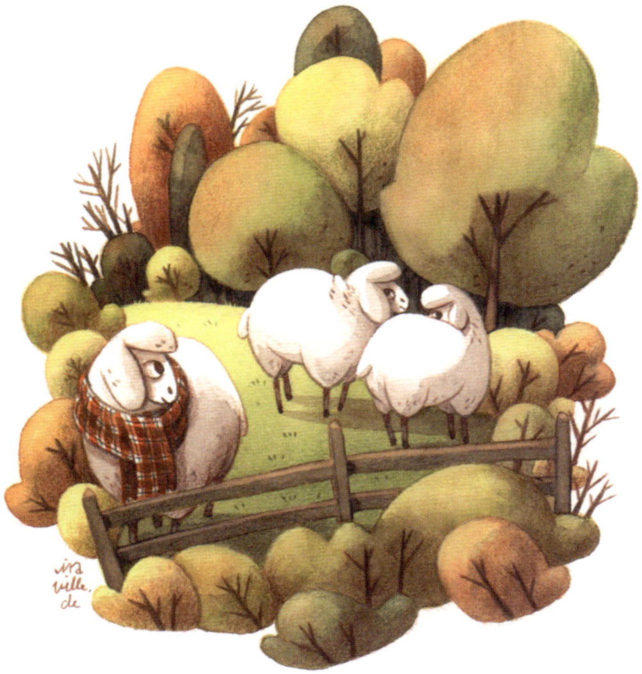

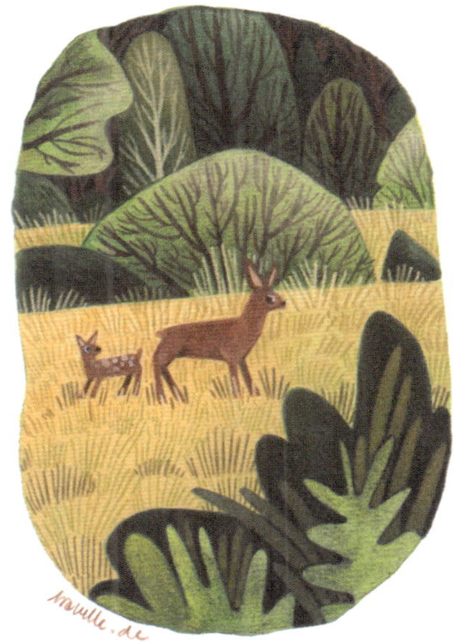

Far left:
Fluffy Sheep,
watercolour and
coloured pencil, 2015

Left:
Deer Collage,
gouache, coloured
pencil, wax pastel,
2022

Below:
Summer, gouache
and pastel, 2018

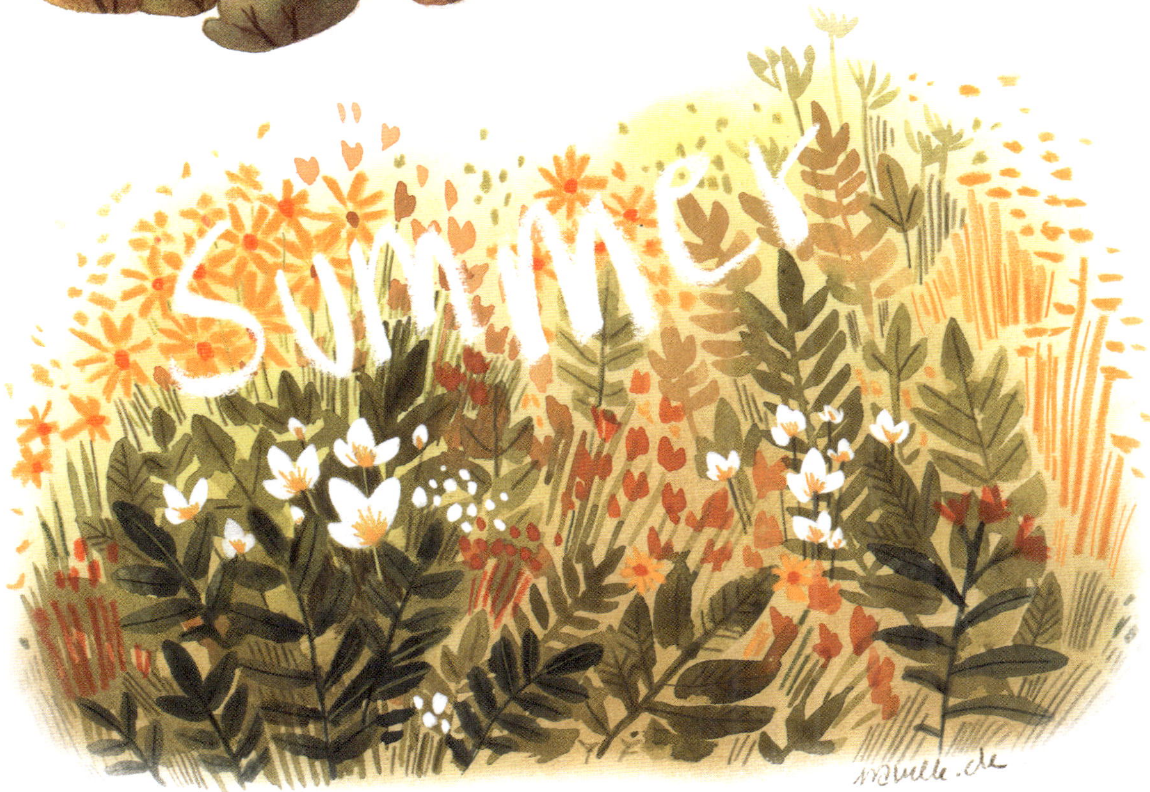

BEHIND THE SCENES

Make your own ink

From time to time, I like to work with ink.

The difference between ink and watercolours is not as big as you may think. Watercolours have a solid consistency and must be mixed with water, while ink is intensely coloured water and can therefore be applied directly to paper using a quill, pen, or brushes.

A distinction is made between dye ink and pigment-based ink. Dye ink is created directly from organic substances, so there is no need to create pigments from them. The disadvantage is that it is not lightfast, meaning the colours fade or discolour quickly.

Therefore, as an artist, I prefer pigment-based ink. Here, ink is created from pigments that are lightfast (or at least more lightfast, depending on the specific pigments used). When it comes to drawing ink, most people immediately think of black ink, which usually consists of carbon black and charcoal pigments. Of course, it is also available in other colours.

For me, it is important to understand the materials I work with. It helps if you get to know their characteristics because then you can use them in a targeted way. Years ago, when I first learned about the pigments that make up good paints, it helped me understand the differences between natural and synthetic pigments. It also helped me figure out why (in the case of natural pigments) inorganic ones (consisting of minerals, earth, or metals) behaved differently from the organic ones (plants or animals). This allowed me to use them more selectively for certain mixtures and effects on paper.

I also discovered that it is not difficult to make your own watercolours either, and even better, they are at least as good as what you would buy, but cheaper! You can find a tutorial about making watercolours in my first book.

To continue on from that tutorial, I will show you how to easily make your own professional-artist inks from the same pigments, using a slightly different process.

WARNING: Dust mask advised!

TOOLS

1. Towel
2. Cup of water
3. Brush
4. Spoons (I use different sizes, but you can also just use a teaspoon)
5. Labels and a pen
6. Pestle & mortar
7. Small funnel
8. Gum arabic
9. Essential oil (thyme)
10. Glycerine
11. Distilled water
12. Paper towels
13. Pencil
14. Airtight empty bottle with pipette made of brown glass
15. Pigments (I use alizarin red lake PR83 and indigo PB66)
16. Dust mask (FFP2)

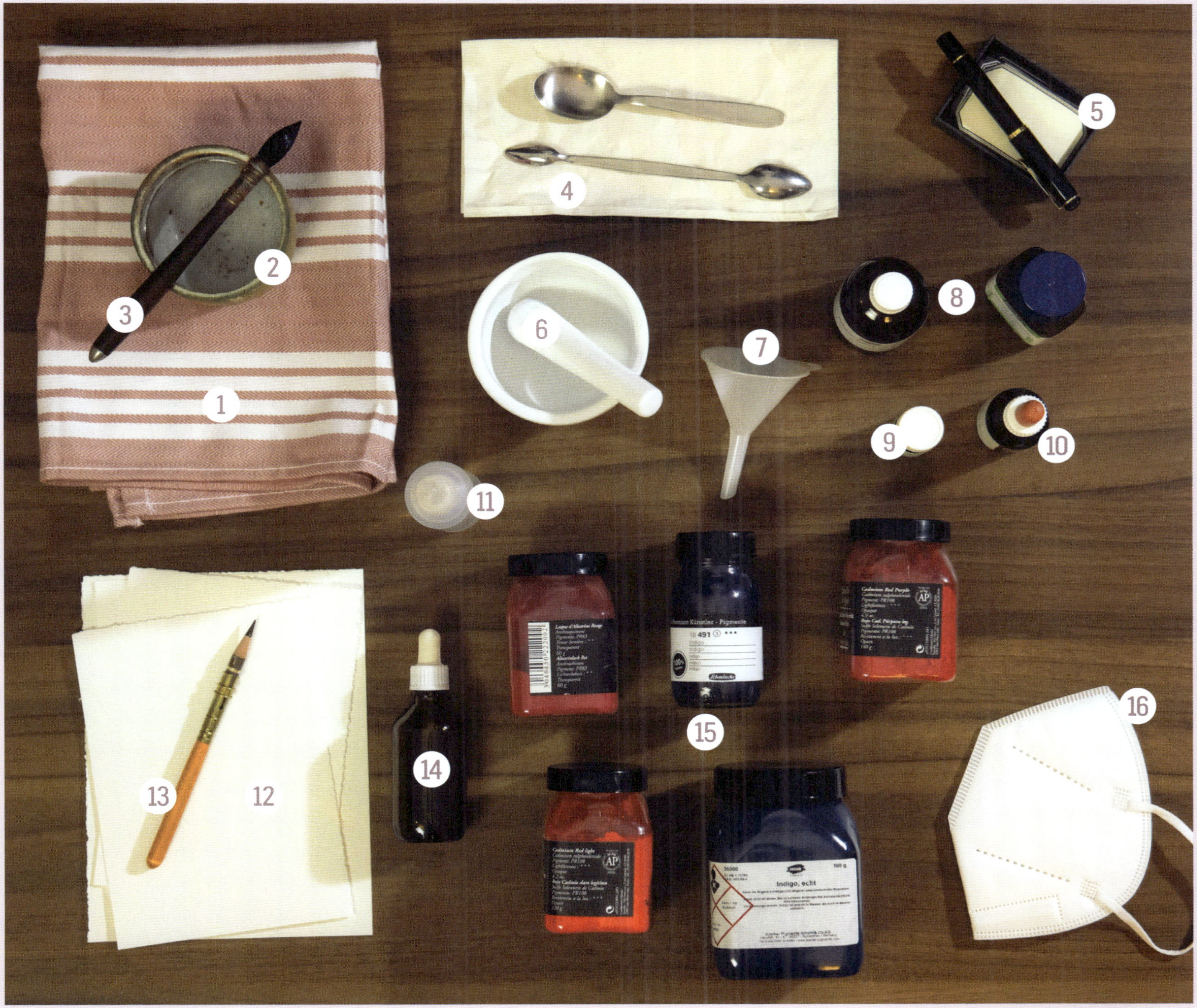
1
2
3
4
5
6
7
8
9
10
11
12
13
14
15
16
Indigo, echt

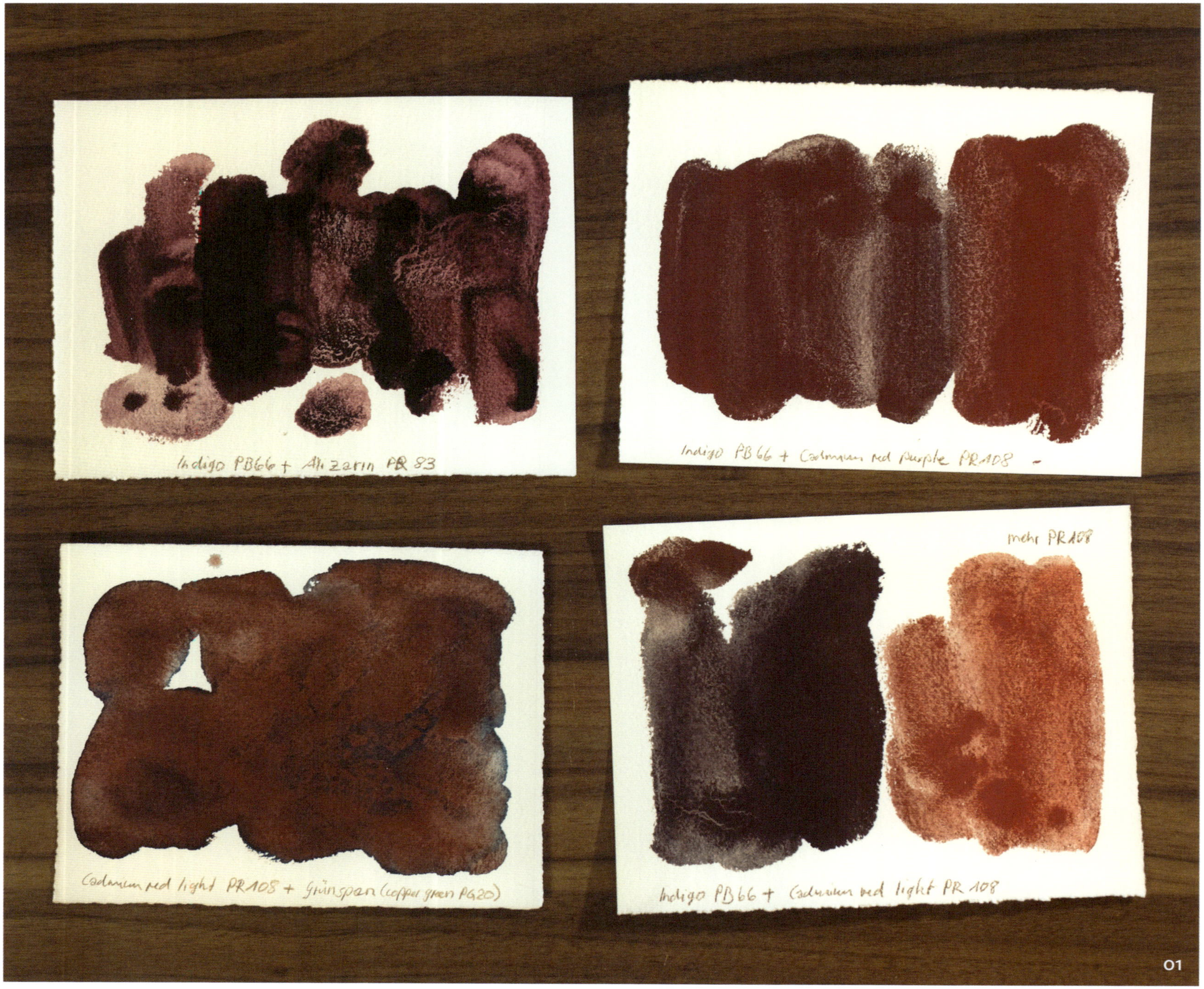
Indigo PB66 + Alizarin PR 83
Indigo PB66 + Cadmium red purple PR108
Cadmium red light PR108 + Grünspan (copper green PG20)
mehr PR108
Indigo PB66 + Cadmium red light PR 108

01

INSTRUCTIONS

01: The utensils should be cleaned well before use so that the finished inks do not grow mould.

Once the pigments are opened, I put on the mask and make sure to air the room out afterwards. Generally, you should not inhale pigments, eat them, pour them on the ground, or leave them on your skin.

If the pigment has high or extreme toxicity, it might be better not to use it at all. Please consider that before you buy them.

First, I make a few test mixes by simply mixing some pure pigments, which I bought ready-made, in a mortar with a little water. Using a brush, I then apply them to paper. You can find ready-made pigments in any good artist-supply store.

My goal is to create ink with a dark-purple hue.

I prefer mixing two organic pigments called alizarin red lake PR83 and indigo PB66 (top left). The first is a synthetic lake pigment that was developed as a replacement for madder lake, which was commonly used for many centuries. Indigo is another famous pigment and finds its origins in India and other areas around Asia. There is also a synthetic version of it.

I am aware that the mixture will not be very lightfast in parts because of the binding gum arabic. If you want to make it more lightfast, you could use shellac as a binder. That is the beauty of it: from the choice of pigments to the binder mixture to the desired density, you can pick and choose to achieve the result you want.

02: I put approximately one-and-a-half teaspoons of red in the mortar.

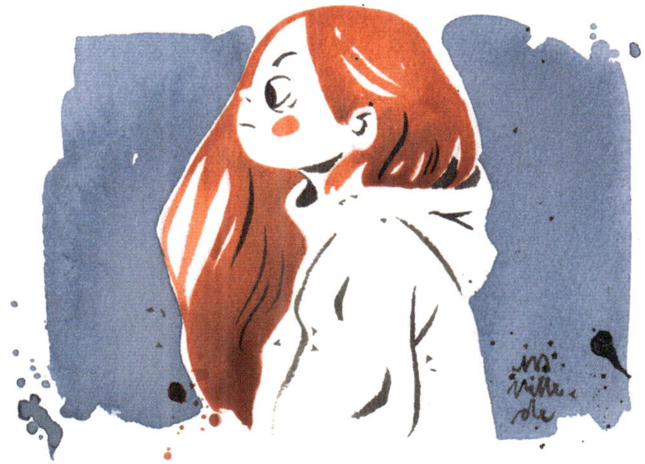

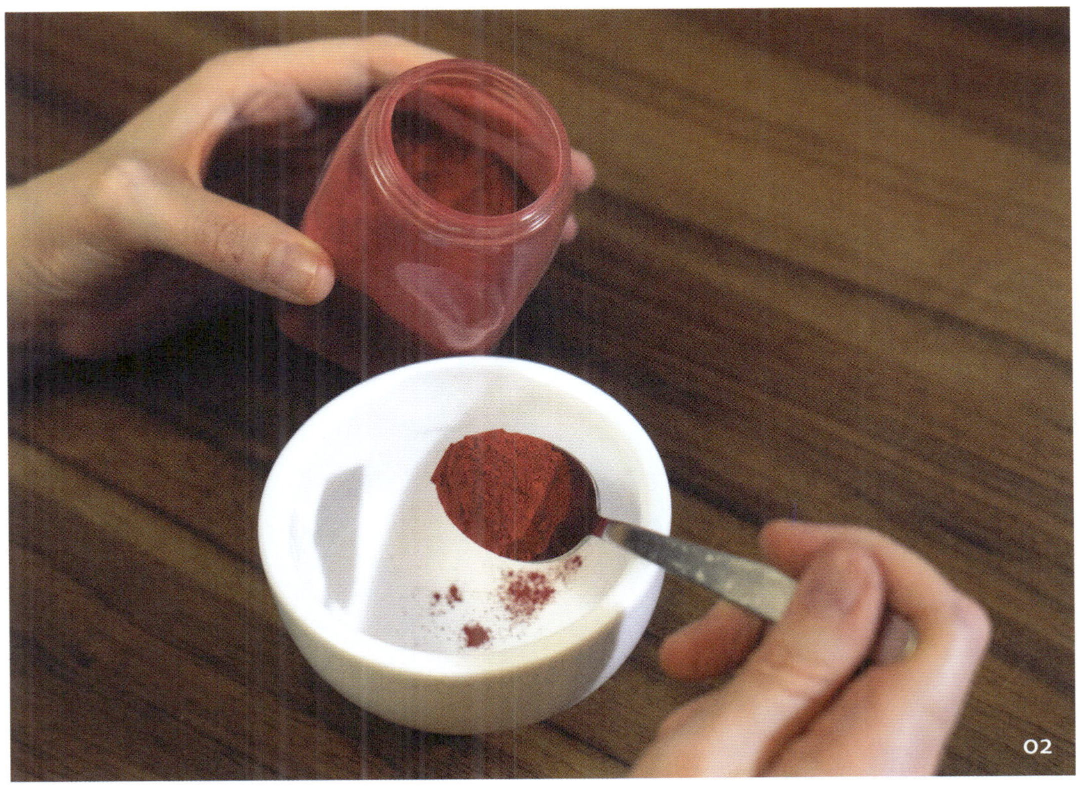

02

03: I add a very small spoonful of indigo.

04: I add three teaspoons of gum arabic. The binder serves as glue to make the pigments stick to the paper later.

If you use too little, the pigments will come off again. If that is the case, after testing, you can simply add a little more binder at the end. It is better to use a bit too much than too little. I also think the colour is nicer when gum arabic is added.

However, you must be careful if you plan on using the ink for a pen. Too much gum arabic could make it stick.

05: I add a little distilled water. I can always add more for desired colour density in later steps. The less water, the darker and more intense the colour will be.

06: Two or three drops of glycerine help to prevent the paint from drying too quickly. This can happen when the bottle is not completely airtight or it has been left open.

07: Now I mix everything with the pestle and mortar. It is interesting to observe how quickly the colour changes.

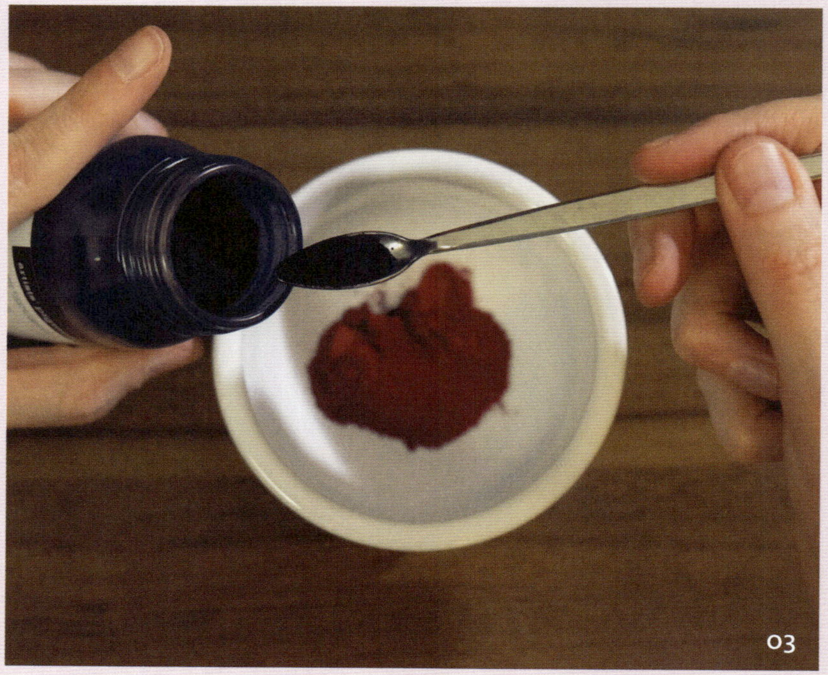

03

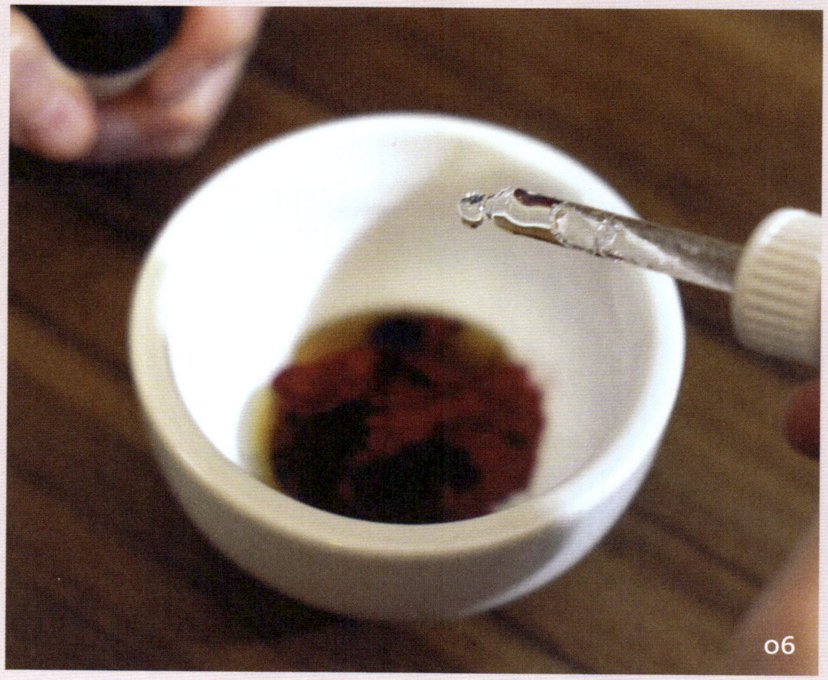

06

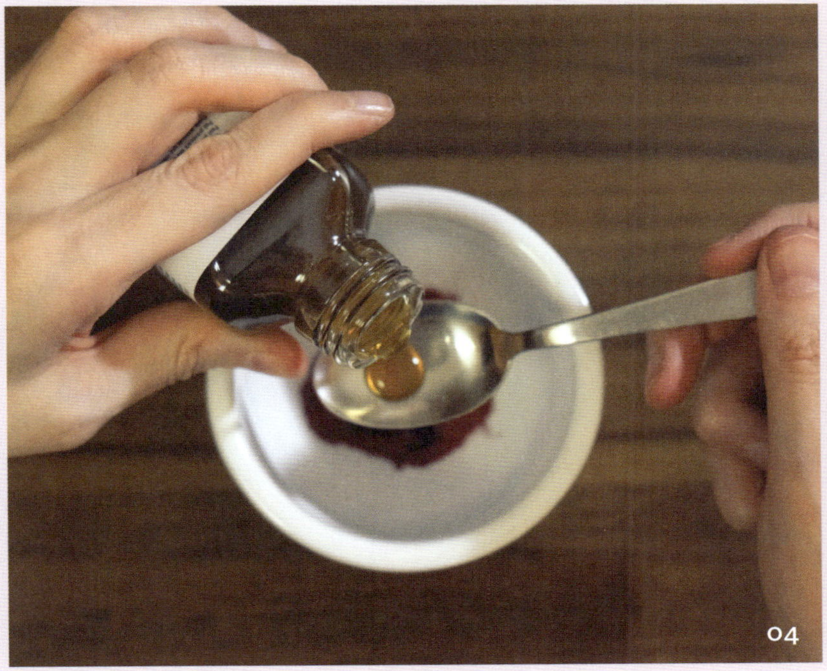

04

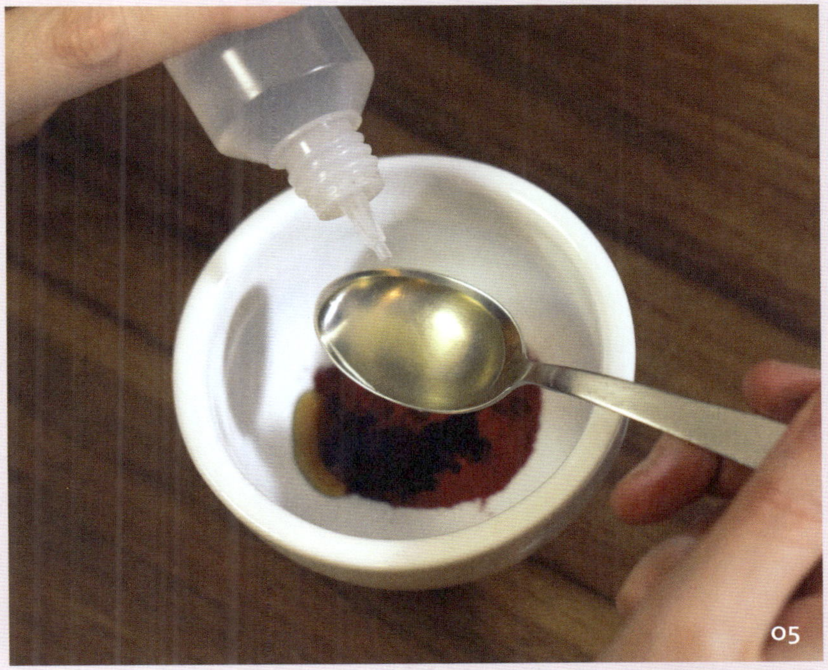

05

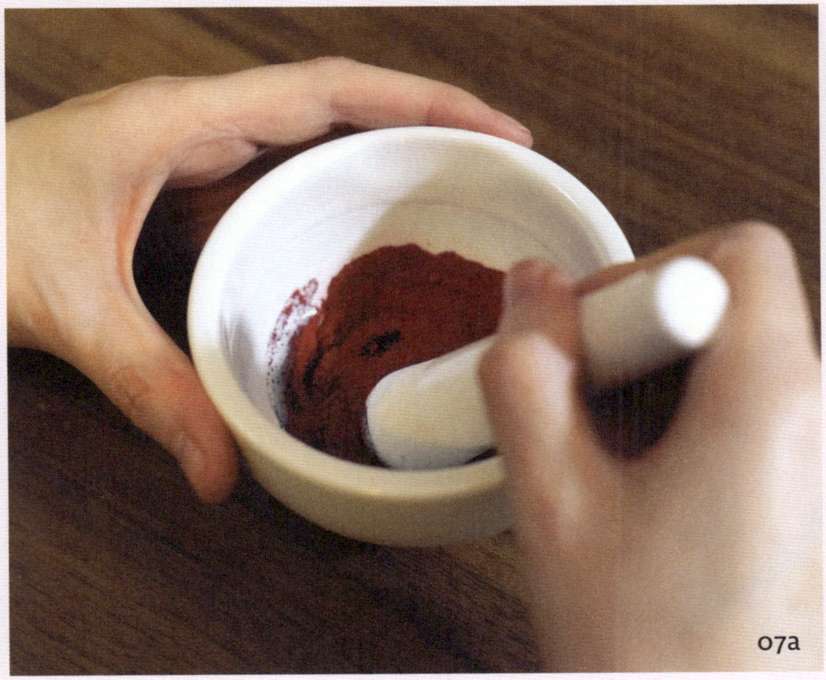

07a

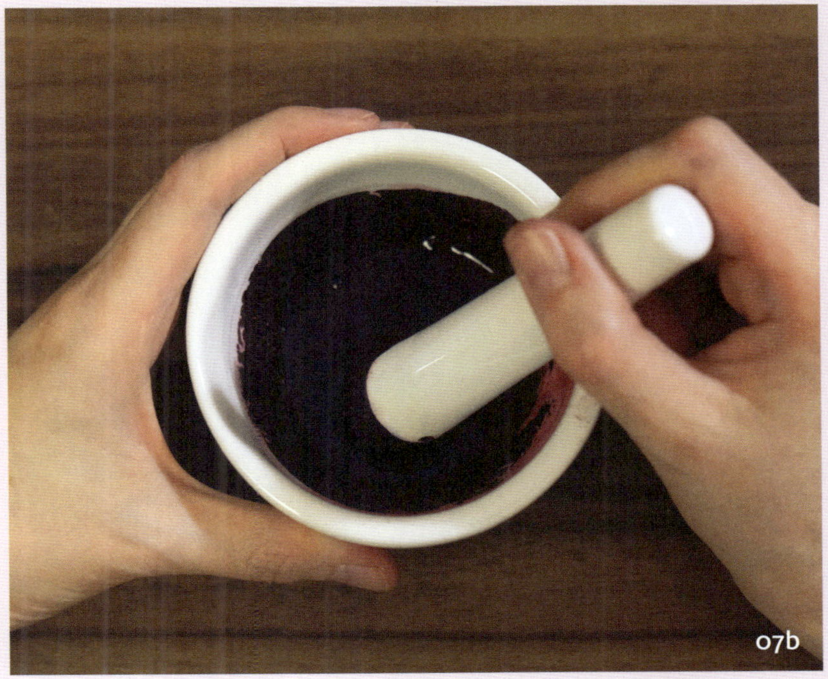

07b

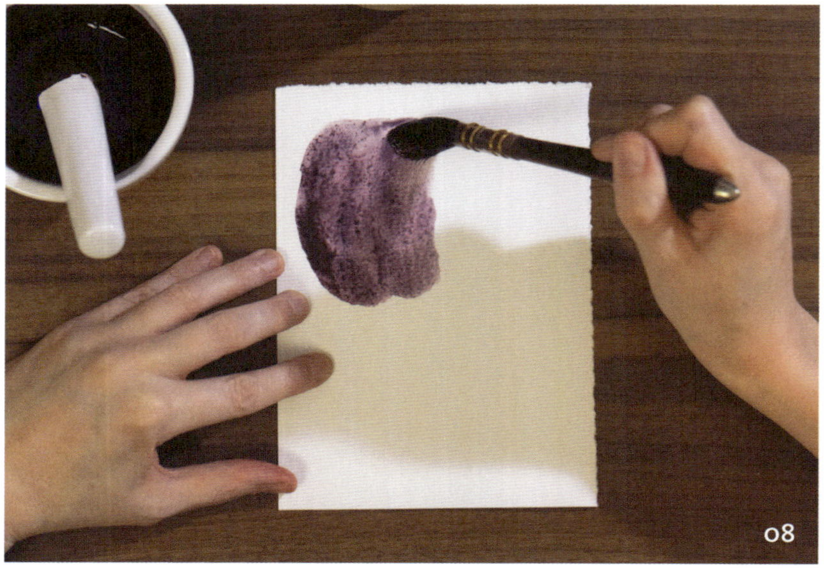

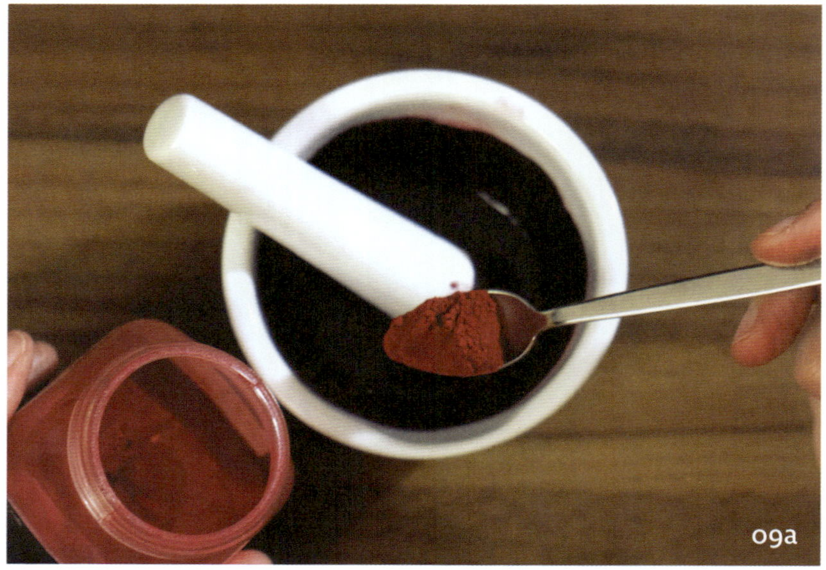

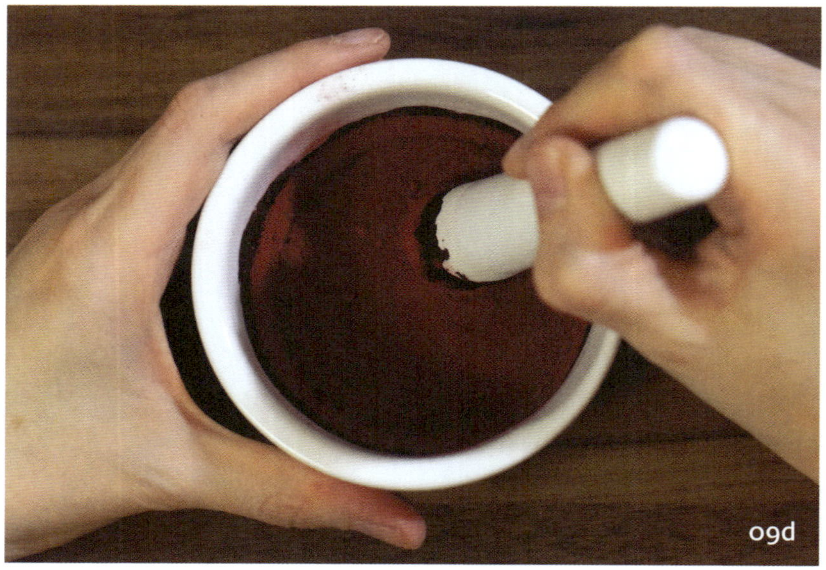

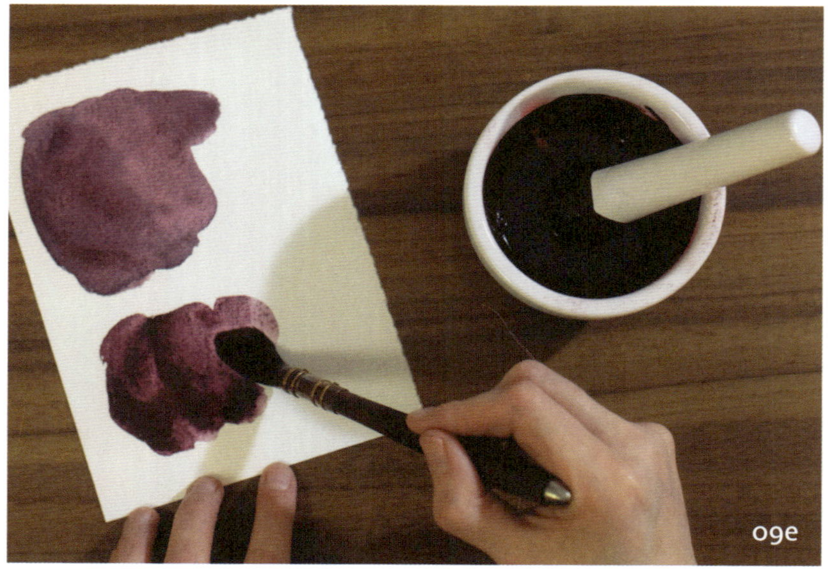

08: To check how the colour behaves, I simply brush it onto paper (ideally watercolour paper).

09: It is not quite purple enough for me, so I add a small spoonful of red. I also add more gum arabic, just to be on the safe side, as well as more water so that the mixture has enough liquid. I mix everything well. Afterwards, I do another colour test.

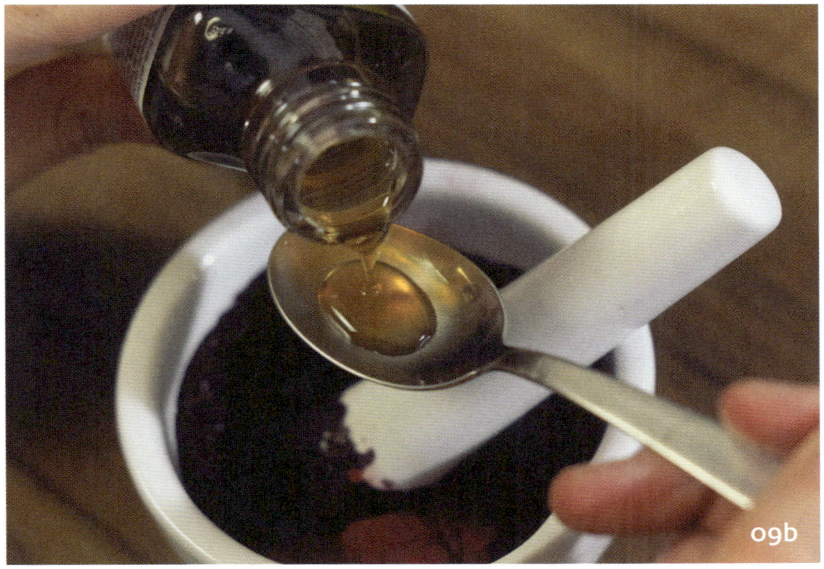

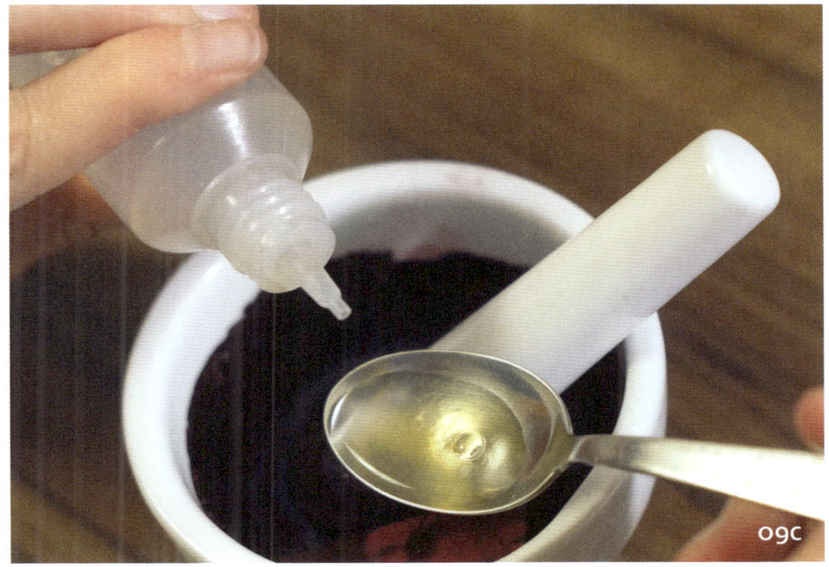

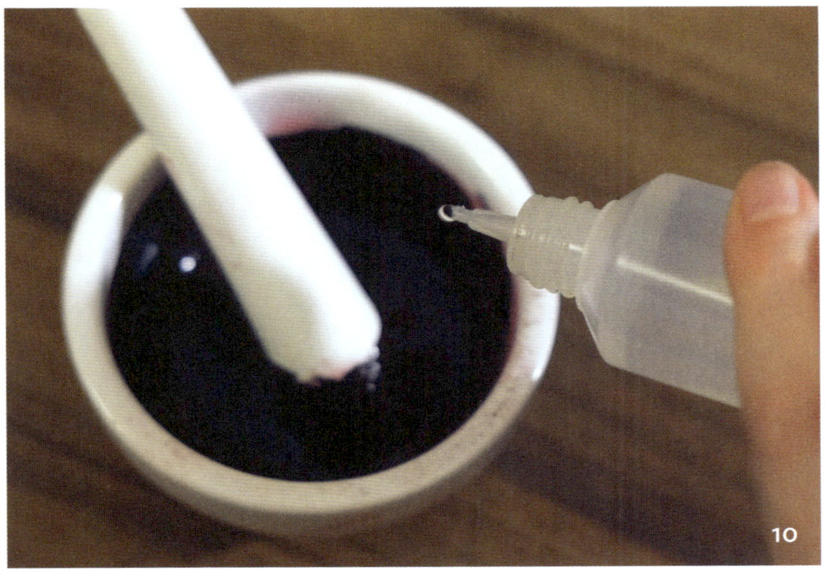

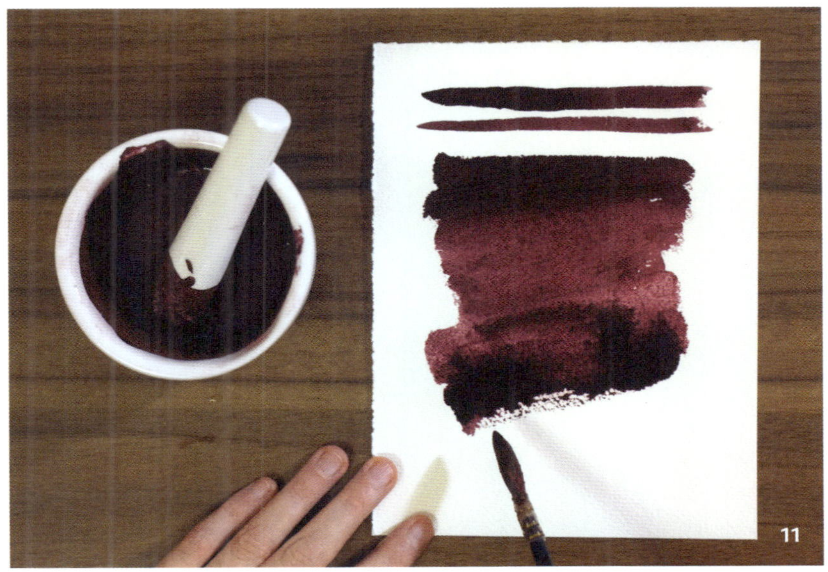

10: When I am satisfied with the colour, I adjust the final percentage of water.

11: One last colour test. I am happy with it!

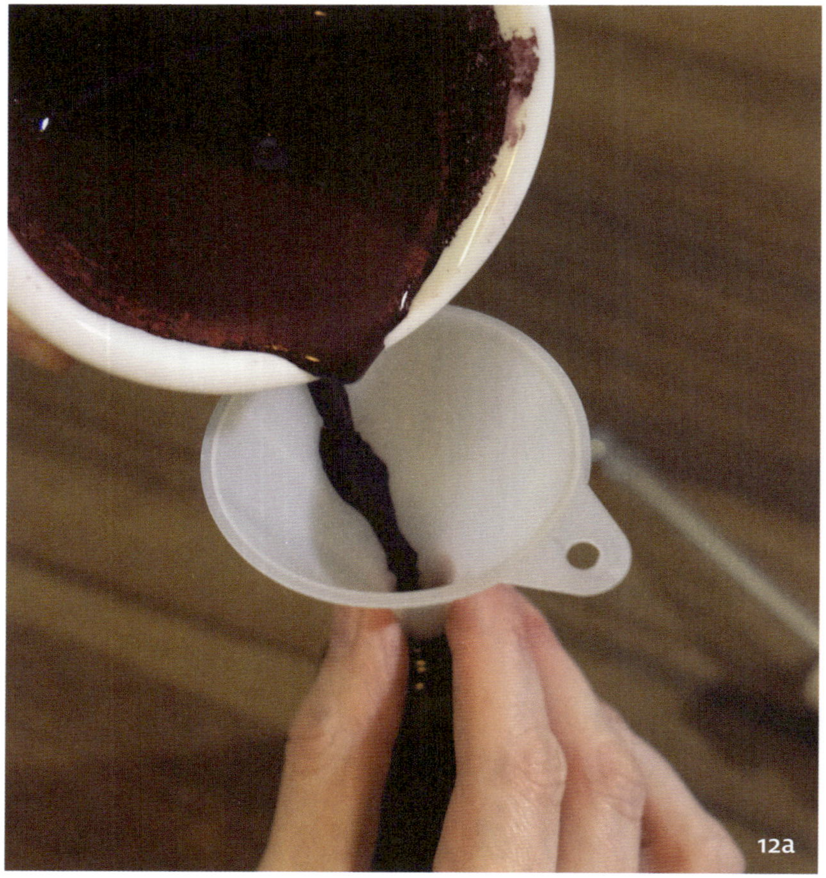

12a

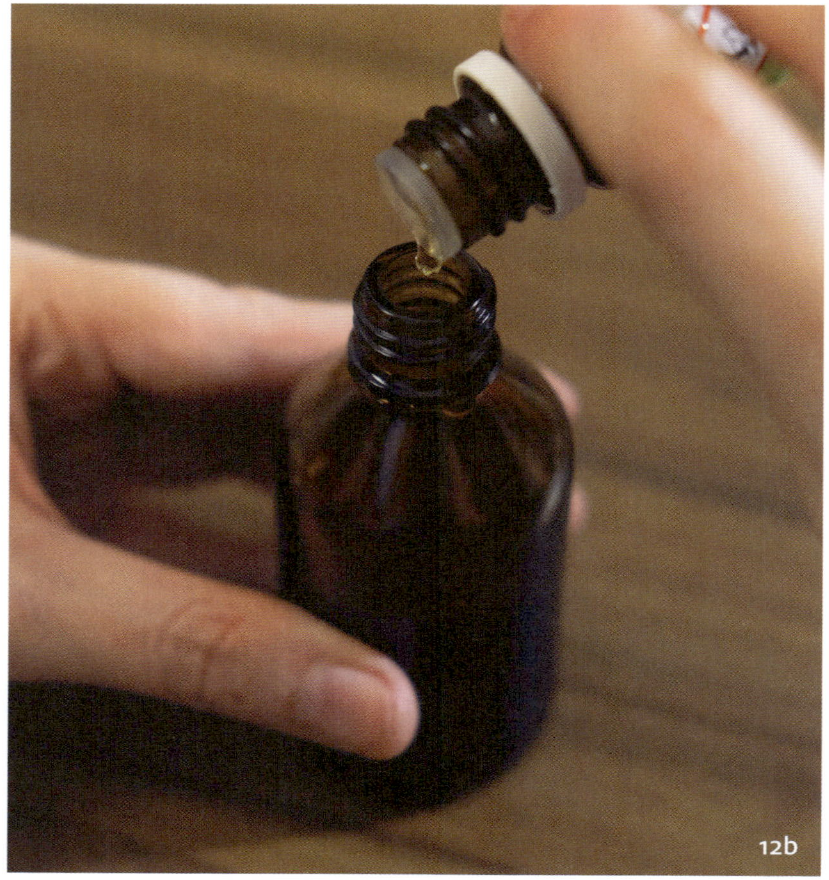

12b

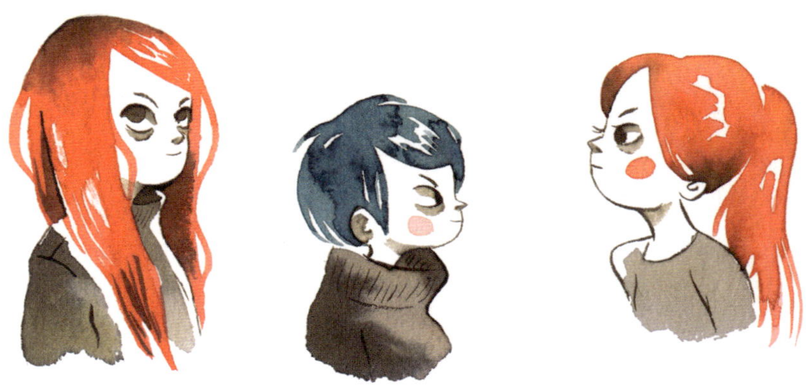

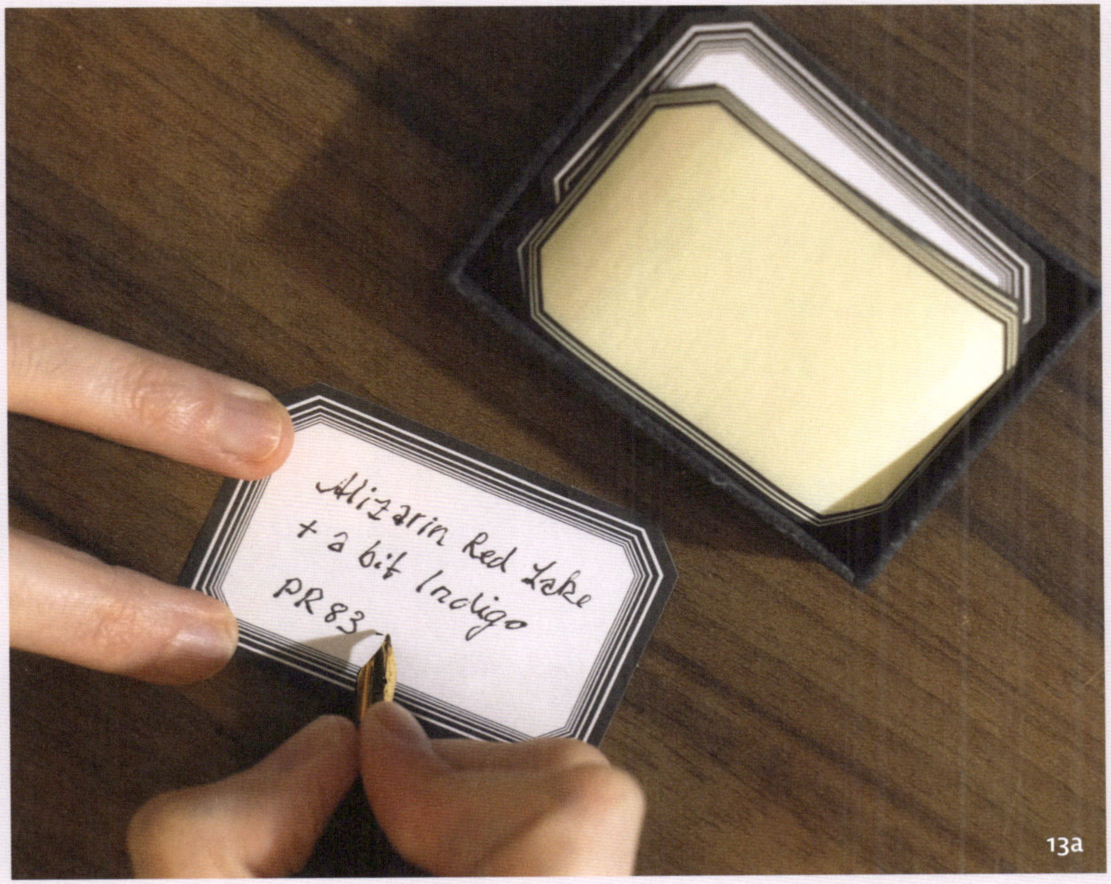

13a

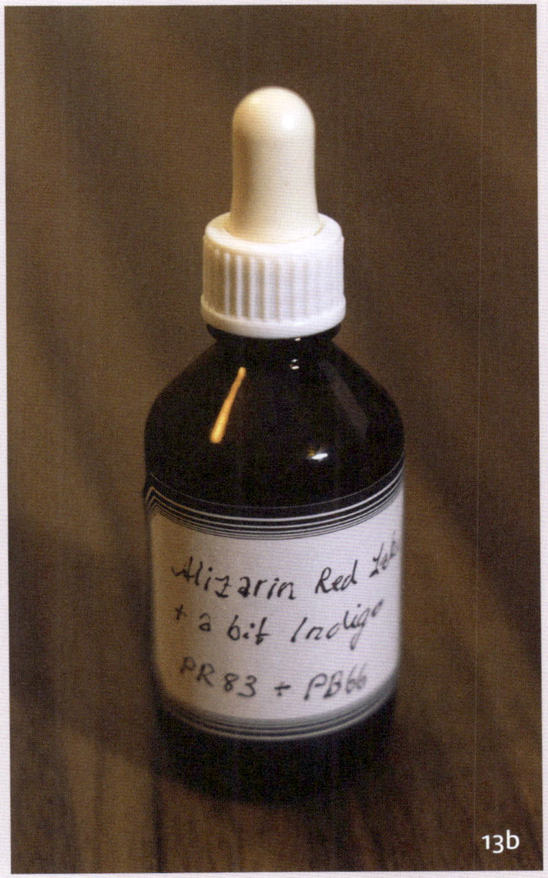

13b

12: I pour the paint into a storage jar with the help of a funnel.

Use any jar with a tight-fitting lid. It is best to sterilize it using boiled water beforehand so that the colour lasts for a long time. Brown glass protects the ink from sunlight.

A few drops of essential oil (I use thyme here) prevent the colour from moulding. Wintergreen oil is another option.

13: I label the bottle so that I know what is inside for later.

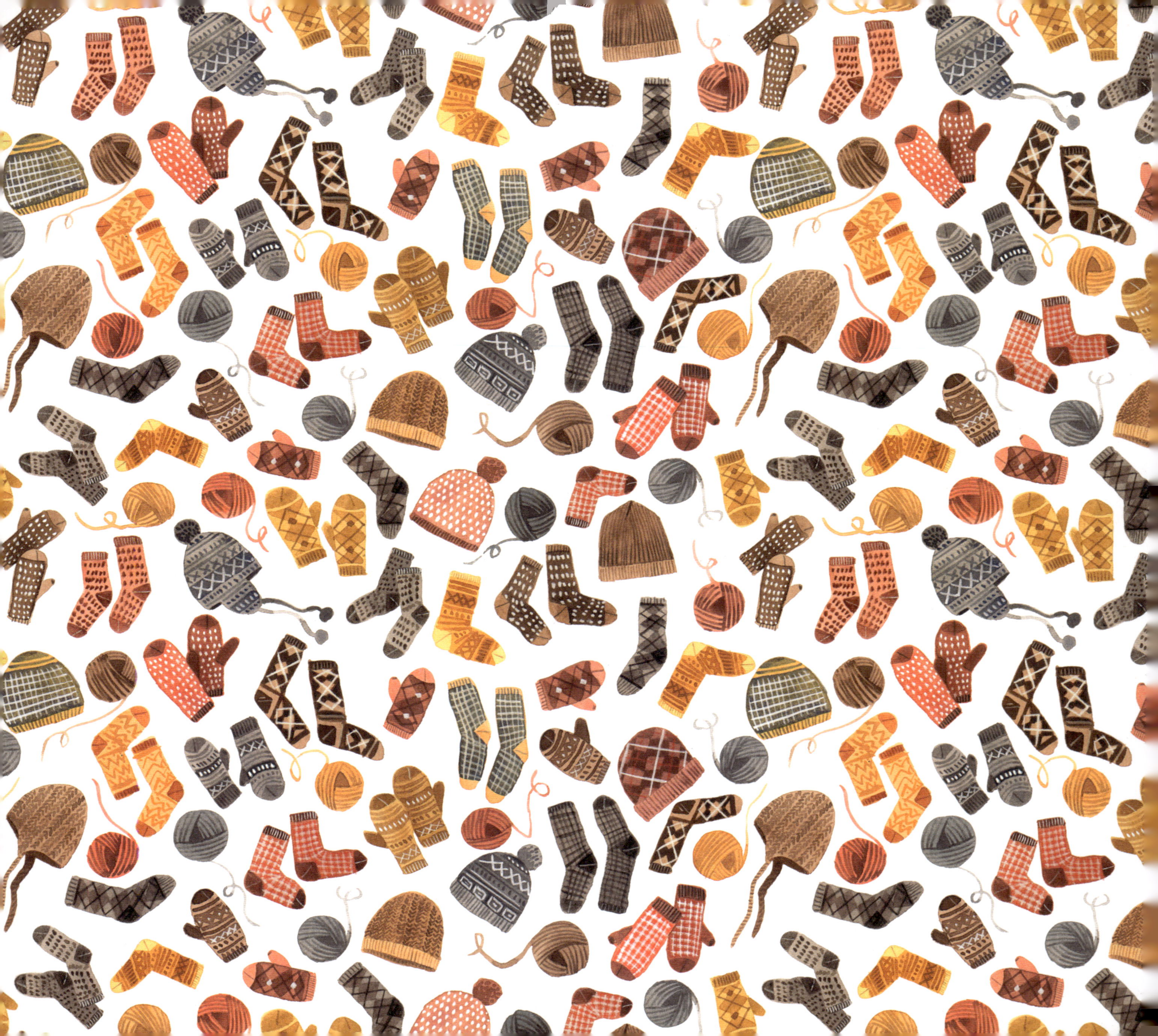

Thank you

This book would not be in your hands without the support of some very special people.

I would like to thank my parents, Mechthild and Wolfgang, for being the first to put a pen in my hand and for later reminding me not to worry too much about my career choices. Thank you to my husband Stefan for his support, beautiful photos, and helping me with the text, and to my editor Rhee for making it a pleasure to work on every aspect of this book. A big thank you to Lois for writing such nice things in the foreword (which means a lot to me!), to Simon for asking me to make a second book, and to everyone at 3dtotal who helped in its creation.

Last, but not least, to all the people who supported my work, and especially those who backed or bought my book ... thank you so much!

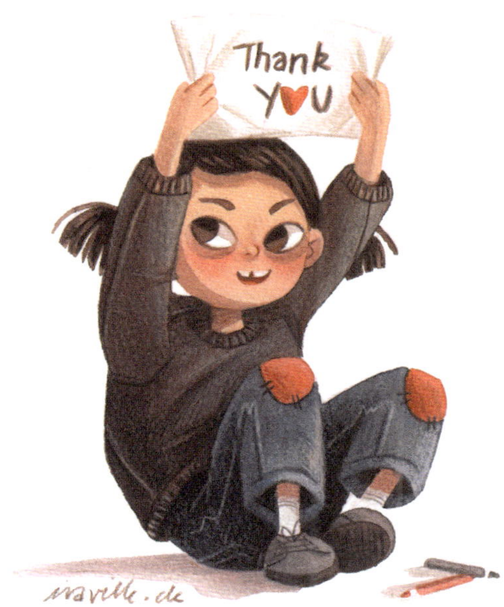

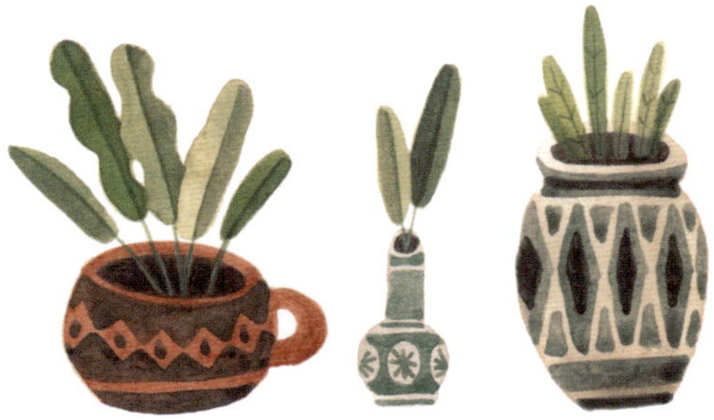

3dtotal Publishing is a trailblazing, creative publisher specializing in inspirational and educational resources for artists.

Our titles feature top industry professionals from around the globe who share their experience in skillfully written step-by-step tutorials and fascinating, detailed guides. Illustrated throughout with stunning artwork, these best-selling publications offer creative insight, expert advice, and essential motivation. Fans of digital art will enjoy our comprehensive volumes covering Adobe Photoshop, Procreate, and Blender, as well as our superb titles based around character design, including *Fundamentals of Character Design* and *Creating Characters for the Entertainment Industry*. The dedicated, high-quality blend of instruction and inspiration also extends to traditional art. Titles covering a range of techniques, genres, and abilities allow your creativity to flourish while building essential skills.

Well-established within the industry, we now offer over 100 titles and counting, many of which have been translated into multiple languages around the world. With something for every artist, we are proud to say that our books offer the 3dtotal package:

LEARN • CREATE • SHARE

Visit us at 3dtotalpublishing.com

3dtotal Publishing is part of 3dtotal.com, a leading website for CG artists founded by Tom Greenway in 1999

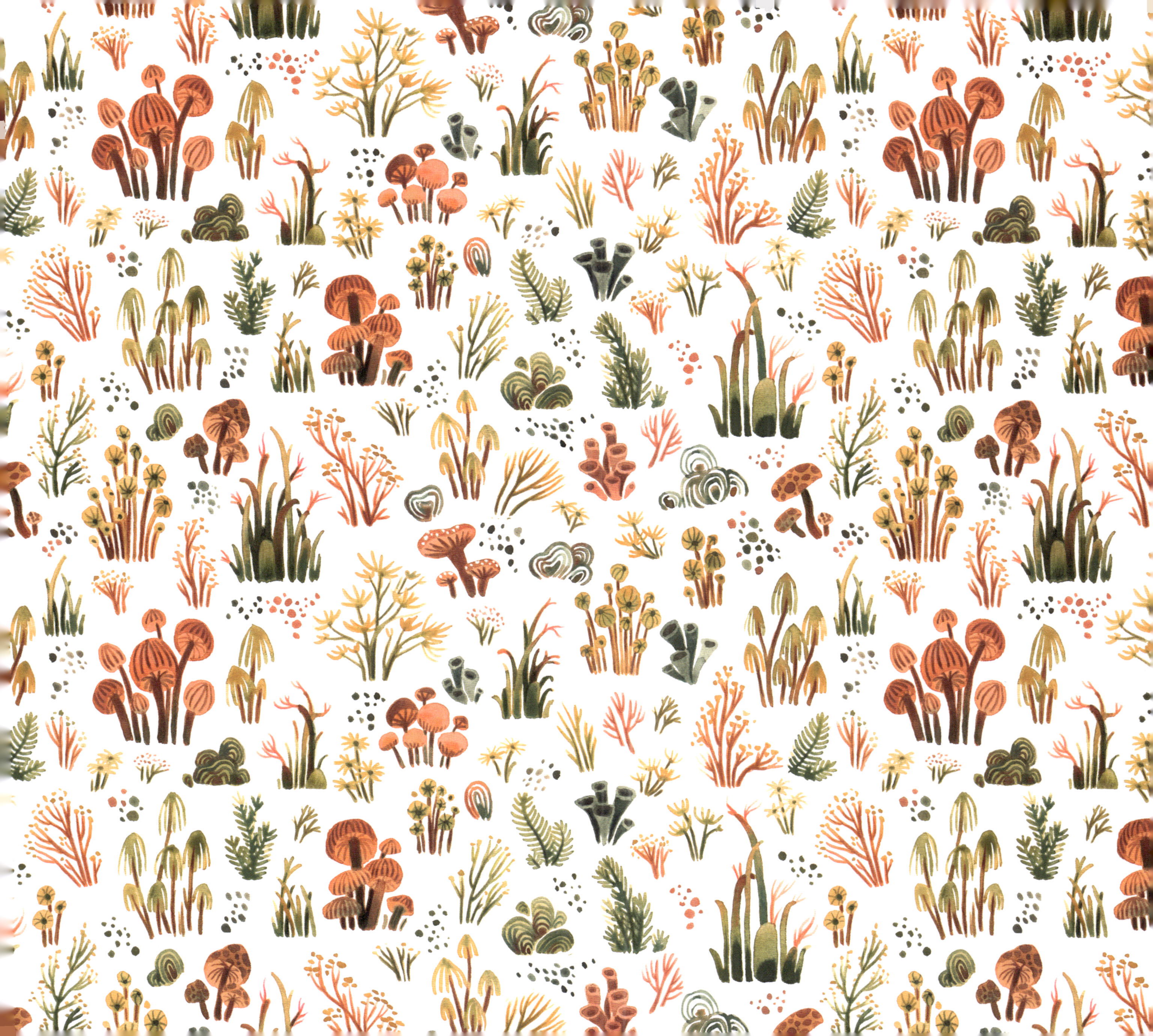

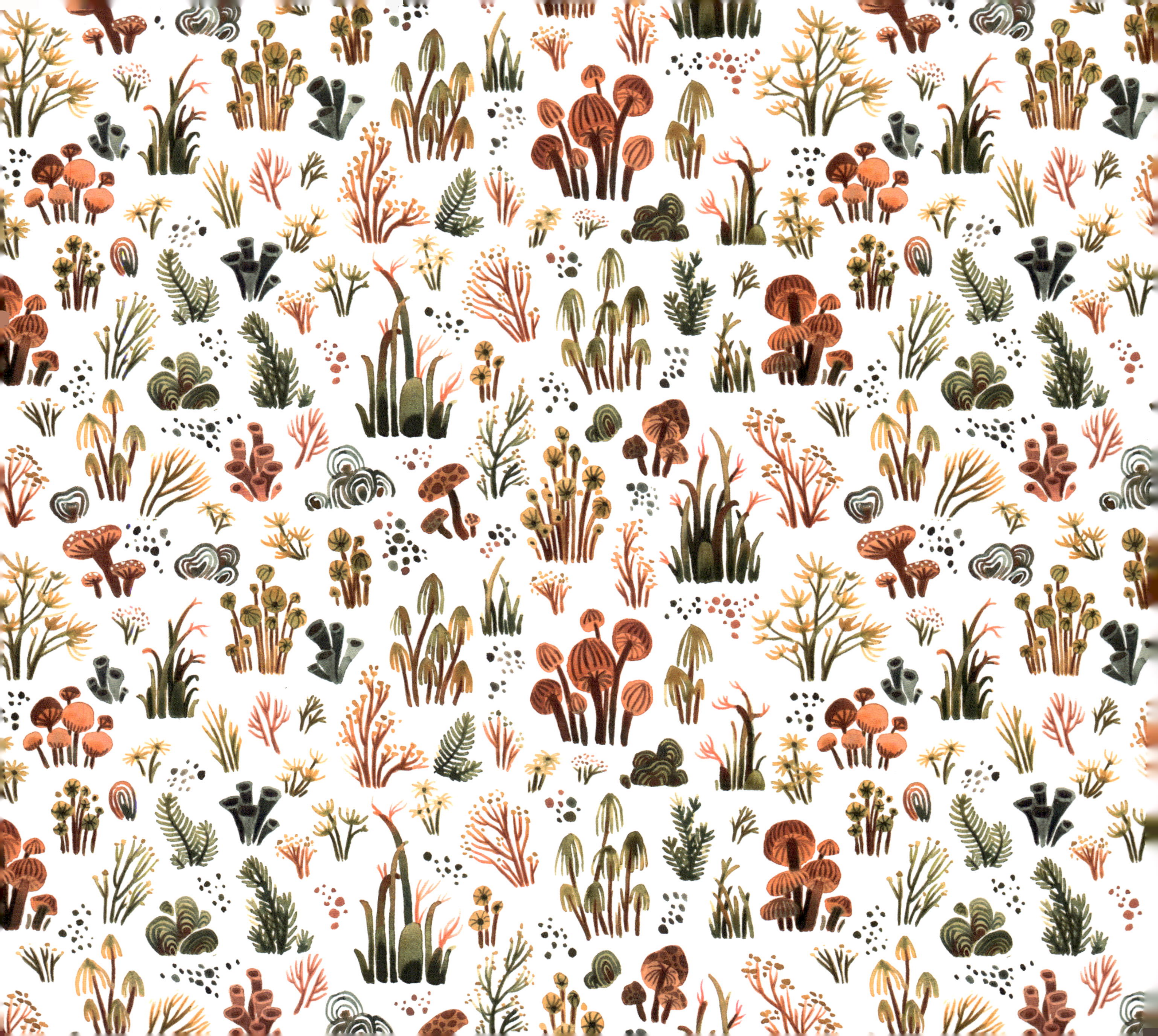